FIVE COMEDIES

PLAUTUS & TERENCE

FIVE COMEDIES

Translated, with Introductions, by
Deena Berg and Douglass Parker

Hackett Publishing Company, Inc.
Indianapolis/Cambridge

05   04   03   02   01   00   2   3   4   5   6   7   8   9

For further information, please address
  Hackett Publishing Company, Inc.
  P.O. Box 44937
  Indianapolis, IN 46244-0937

Cover design by Deena Berg.
Interior design by Meera Dash.

Library of Congress Cataloging-in-Publication Data

Five comedies / Plautus Terence ; translated by Deena Berg & Douglass
   Parker.
        p.   cm.
     Contents: Major Blowhard = Miles Gloriosus]. Double bind =
   Menaechmi]. The wild, wild women = Bacchides / [Plautus].—The
   mother-in-law = Hecyra. The brothers = Adelphoe / [Terence].
     ISBN 0-87220-362-X (paper).—ISBN 0-87220-363-8 (cloth)
     1. Latin drama (Comedy)—Translations into English.   I. Plautus,
   Titus Maccius.   II. Terence.   III. Berg, Deena, 1957–   .
   IV. Parker, Douglass.
   PA6165.F58   1999
   872'.0108—DC21   98-50732
                                                               CIP

Contents

General Introduction

It is rather like finding, long after, that the American national food at the end of the twentieth century A. D. was pizza. *And the analogy holds: Roman Comedy, cheese pies . . . both, at first blush, severely limited. No matter how you slice each, it keeps the same shape, it* is *the same thing. Hardly native. Frequently served cold. But assimilate a number of these, and marvel at the immense variation possible and attained . . .*

Roman Comedy

The trouble may start with its name: *Roman Comedy.* More than a tinge of oxymoron there. Consider a point of view still widely held:

Gravitas. Dignitas. Pietas. Officium.—Seriousness. Worthiness. Devotion. Duty. Our conceptual legacies from ancient Rome. Heavy stuff.

This heaviness is borne out in the Literary Monuments. Roman Oratory? The admirable weight of words assembled to annihilate an opponent. Roman History? The measured tread up the hill to greatness, followed by the long majestic slide. Roman Poetry? Lyrics can strike the desired note of high civic importance. Roman Satire? From philosophical roots, it aims at reform. But Roman *Comedy?* Almost an embarrassment. If it didn't exist, few would invent it, since this Comedy—so runs the litany—is trivial, primitive, and hardly Roman at all.

Laughter aside, Comedy should be where we can dissect a society, pick at its versions (*a-, ad-,* and *per-*) of itself, excavate its private antiquities. But the Comedies of Rome look like something else. We have been left with twenty-six[1] Roman Comedies, *Comœdiae Romanae: XXVI.* At first sight, they seem so *same.* Housefronts: two, or three, or one, facing on a till-now quiet street. Comfortably well-off families, featuring the externalization of family stresses and the ceaseless struggle with stock characters from the wrong side of the *cloaca.* In sum, the washing of mildly soiled linen in public.

But all of that linen is *Greek.* In fact, that's what they called these dramas: "The plays that go in Greek clothes"—*fabulae palliatae.* And that street? No Roman street, but one in Athens or environs.

Fabulae Palliatae

Rome notoriously borrowed from Greece, and its comedy was no exception. Prior to the mid–third century B.C., Roman public entertainment had been, if simple, at least relatively *local.* Officials had treated the populace on festival days to a variety of

---

[1] Twenty-six and a fraction, actually, if one includes the hundred lines of *Vidularia* [*The Gladstone*].

unscripted, unsophisticated amusements: *Atellanae,* slapstick improvisational farces borrowed from the Oscans to the south; and *saturae,* fusions of music and rustic lampoons on loan from the Etruscans to the north. But, in 240 B.C., Old Rome received new comic relief, when the first Latin version of Greek New Comedy was performed in celebration of the Roman triumph over Carthage. Both process and product stuck, somehow. The new plays exposed the fledgling audience at Rome to the subtleties of Hellenistic humor: intricate plots, ironic twists of fate, clever slaves, stern fathers, heartsick lovers, pompous soldiers, savvy courtesans. For the next hundred years, Latin poets joyously turned Greek comedies into Graeco-Roman ones, which have returned to the stage again and again for over two millennia.

Greek New Comedy

The Greek plays upon which the *fabulae palliatae* were based were written from approximately the mid–fourth to the mid–third century B.C. Unlike the plays of Athens's Old Comedy, which burst with political satire, wild social upheaval (for example, women boycotting sex to protest against war), and choruses of creatures (frogs, wasps, animate clouds), New Comedy plays are about relatively plausible characters trapped in implausible situations—implausible in real life, but the staples of the Comic World of Manners. A standard plot involves a pair of lovers, who, thwarted by a parent, a pimp, or some other blocking character, ultimately find happiness together thanks to the schemes of a cunning slave. There were a number of popular writers—Diphilus and Philemon, for example—whose works are quoted at length by later ancient authors, but whose full scripts, sadly enough, disappeared centuries ago. Still, we do have one entire play—the *Dyskolos*—and major portions of others by one of the most prolific and highly regarded of New Comedy playwrights: Menander of Athens (343–291 B.C.). The recovery of these and other comic leavings has brought general joy, not only to Greek, but to Latin scholars as well, since these texts tend to confirm what has long been suspected: Plautus, Terence, and the other Roman poets did not merely translate the Greek texts, but *adapted* them—at times, very freely—to suit their Roman audiences, recasting, renaming, salting all with local Italian reference and sensibility, and justifying the label for this hybrid: *Roman* Comedy.

Roman New Comedy

Livius Andronicus has traditionally been given the credit for introducing Greek theater to Rome at the Roman Games of 240 B.C. His writings, along with those of other noted comic poets, such as Gnaeus Naevius and Caecilius Statius, are mentioned by later Roman authors. But the complete works of only two comic playwrights have survived to be steadily copied and recopied over ensuing centuries: Plautus and Terence. What they left is what we know.

Titus Maccius Plautus is thought to have been born in a small town in Umbria in 254 B.C. He may have started out as an actor, judging from his nickname, "Maccius" (or "Maccus"—i.e., "fool, schlemiel"), which is the name of a stock character in Atellan farce. He certainly understood his audience, and developed a style that kept him at the top of his profession. His jokes are broader and bawdier than the Greek originals; he makes up new words with Seussian panache and Saussurean slyness. His philosophy on puns is "once is not enough": for those who missed the first time, he provides instant word replay. Though spare in plot, his comedies bulge and burgeon and burst their bounds with vaudevillelike shtick and sight gag, not to mention song (*canticum*) and dance. His love of downright silliness, music, and general cynicism may call the Marx Brothers to the minds of moderns; the stagecraft his lines demand is prodigious on its own. He was a compleat man of the theater who wrote prolifically to supply his acting companies. Of the more than a hundred titles attributed to him in later antiquity, he may have written fifty before his death, at a venerable age, in 184 B.C. We possess twenty and a fraction.

Publius Terentius Afer saw his first play produced in 166 B.C. According to his ancient biographer, he was born in Carthage and came to Rome as a slave. Purchased by Terentius Lucanus, he was given his name, his education, and later his freedom. He then acquired the patronage of two well-read, high-standing Roman aristocrats— Scipio Aemilianus and Gaius Laelius—who fostered his literary career, much to the annoyance of competing playwrights. Terence preferred Greek originals with higher moral content and remained true to their philosophical spirit; on the other hand, he borrowed bits from some plays to pep up others. This approach got him in trouble both with the lowbrows, for not being funny enough, and with the snobs, for not being pure enough. Nonetheless, his career in writing was highly successful, although cut short by his premature death on a visit to Greece in 159 B.C. Five out of his six plays are about families and explore the tension between father and son, husband and wife, brother and brother. His characters are complex and believable. At times he rivals Plautus's wordplay, but his plots are tighter and more finely mortised, his tone more polished. Terence's characters do not step out of character; by their depth and detail, they produce an acrid humor, akin to the pointed laughter that appeared and peaked a generation ago in the semiserious family situation comedies of Norman Lear and others.

In fact, resemblances noted between these two ancients and the flood of modern comedy that has inundated this country in this century on stage, screen, and television should surprise no one. Our shtick and sitcom are, to a great extent, their descendants.

The Roman Stage and Its Conventions

Republican Rome was a tough crowd to play, especially when Plautus and Terence were writing. Dramatic performances were merely one part, and hardly the central part, of religious festivals, which were open to all members of the public. The audience included male citizens of all ages, women, children, babies, slaves, as well as prostitutes seeking to expand their portfolios. The Roman officials responsible for organizing these festivals usually had further political ambitions on their minds; they would even dig into their own pockets to delight a populace that ran from keen to uncouth. And so dramatic performances *competed* for their attention, on the same ground with more visceral spectacles . . . boxing matches, horse races, tightrope walking, gladiatorial combats.

To make matters even more difficult, Rome had no permanent structure like the venerable stone theaters common in Greek cities. The *fabulae palliatae* were acted out upon temporary wooden stages set up in the city's large open areas—the Forum, the Circus Maximus, or the Campus Martius. Written sources, ancient paintings, and later Roman theaters give us a picture of the Republic's physical venue. The basic stage (*proscaenium*) in the third and second centuries B.C. was long and narrow, usually representing a city street (*platea* or *via*). Behind the stage was the scene building (*scaena*). The side that faced the audience had three doors, each of which represented the entry into a house (in cases in which only two house entries were required, the middle door might be changed to represent a shrine or a garden, or simply be covered by a blank panel). A porch (*vestibulum*) might be added in front of each entry, and would provide a good place for characters to hide, eavesdrop on one another, or give plausible asides. The "house" itself might be painted to look as if it stood on a foundation, so the actors would then descend a small flight of stairs to the stage. Roofs, balconies, and window openings, which could be accessed from inside the scene building, would have been constructed per the requirements of the particular play. The open sides of the stage constituted exits, indicating routes to the standard imaginary offstage locales—harbor, countryside, forum. Stage properties can be inferred from the plays themselves and also appear in vase paintings: shrines, altars, small columns surmounted by statues. At some point, trompe-l'oeil painting was introduced to enhance the stage building (and the front of the stage itself) and so further the architectural illusion.

Men acted all the parts in Roman New Comedy. The costumes (*ornamenta*) of all characters began with an undergarment (*tunica*), over which a long cloak (*pallium* for male characters, *palla* for female) was worn. Slaves wore short tunics, likely with padding to make them look pot-bellied. A cloak, if worn, was thrown over the shoulders to facilitate movement (*pallium collectum*). Cooks wore short tunics as well, and carried spoons and other tools of their trade. Thin sandals (*socci* or *soleae*) were standard footwear. A short cloak (*chlamys*) and hat (*petasus*) were essential for soldiers and other characters engaged in travel, whereas goatskin jackets helped to identify farmers and other country folk. Different-colored wigs established a character's age and role: white for old men and women, black for young people, and sometimes red for unusual characters, such as very cunning slaves.

Masks (*personae*) were used traditionally in Greek Comedy, but scholars are divided on whether masks were standard in the time of Plautus or even Terence.

A Word from the Translators

"Why," the reader might ask, "have you made these translations? Haven't these plays been translated already?" The point is well-taken. We could argue up-to-dateness. Popular comedy, Greek and Latin, was topical and timely in its diction, and our language changes rapidly these days. However, Plautus and Terence certainly don't lack for other versions into American English, especially in this decade. But we come at a particular concatenation of criticism and sensitivity, and share a particular conviction (or delusion, as you choose): the time is one when the standard categories in which these playwrights have been seen have been inverted; Plautus, the knockabout king of farce, is now admitted to have Said Something; Terence, the dour delineator of character, is allowed to have Been Funny. And our shared conviction/delusion is that we can accomplish, in broad American, something like a reproduction of the marvels that each attains in the use of language and the stagecraft it implies: Plautus's sophisticated skyrocketing and Terence's brocaded richness. The extravagant and the imperial.

"Well, then," the reader might persist, "why did you choose these five particular plays?" The first answer is simple: we like them, as others have liked them. The fact that neither Plautus nor Terence wrote much that we do not think is terrific made the choice difficult, but ultimately we thought it would be nice to gather together some of our favorites, which by happy coincidence, scan (though they scarcely exhaust) the range of preserved Roman New Comedy. The second answer goes into specifics: the staggering achievement of Terence's *Adelphoe,* which, even for the Aristophanist among us, may well be the greatest comedy of Graeco-Roman antiquity, and the thorny balance of his *Hecyra*—these circumscribe the achievement of the younger playwright, presenting him both at his best and at his most controversial. The huge central character of Plautus's *Miles Gloriosus,* the consummate stagecraft of his *Menaechmi,* the linguistic and conceptual extravagance of his *Bacchides*—these survey from different angles the workings of his unmatched theatrical vision.

"And how accurate," the dogged reader might further inquire, "are your translations?" To answer this, we must take a hard look at the original material. The Latin texts, as they have come down to us from numerous medieval manuscripts, do possess act and scene divisions, clearly added later to fit theory or to aid schoolboys; but they are hardly reader-friendly, and less audience-friendly than that. Of stage directions, for example, they possess effectively none. In fact, there is sometimes confusion about which lines belong to whom, and even where one *word* starts and another leaves off. Here we have gone beyond the received text, though we are quite aware that some translators, choosing a neutral path, allow the reader or director to fill in the gaps. For the experienced thespian, especially one with access to the Latin text, this practice can be a great amount of fun. But for the general readers—especially those not exactly clubby in Latin—we've taken the liberty of filling in the gaps—missing lines, missing speech-attributions, even missing *scenes,* and especially stage directions, in plenty— to keep the action rolling with some coherency.

Regarding the words of the translations themselves, we confess outright that our first loyalty is to our target language, English. For the purist, it may seem we stray at times somewhat far, but there it is. Our job is to capture the humor, the pace, and the *sound* of the ancient language. We have tried to make the dialogue seem as natural as possible, while still keeping the high-flying wordplay that crops up: a "colloquial rhetoric" that revels in the possibilities of High and Low American, and especially in their melding. As far as meter is concerned, we opt for loose five- or six-beat lines (five-beat for iambic *senarii,* six-beat for most other meters) and introduce strict rhythm (or rhyme, or even parody of American songs) when a character might reasonably burst into song or "poetry." Our second loyalty is to the audience. Some two thousand years have passed, during which time we have evolved into creatures imbued with comedy of sorts and extents unexperienced by Greeks and Romans alike. We have reaped the harvest of mirth sown by Shakespeare, Shaw, and even Seinfeld, and have used the crop to convey in our Romans, not the primitive and the gauche, but the sophistication that was always there. We can no more turn our backs to the comic sensibilities of our audience than could Plautus or Terence. While we have not dismembered the ancient plays and rebuilt them into new wholes (for example, "A Funny Thing Happened on the Way to the Forum"), we have taken the liberty to prod the characters into shape, substitute a joke here for a joke there, inflate the rhetoric to achieve the prodigal effect, and do whatever possible to bring forth the "Plautine" or "Terentian" spirit of the plays. We wish, then, to afford the reader some conception of what the stage experience must have been like, and to present the prospective producer with sufficient materials to revivify that experience by putting the plays on again.

One more thing.

We hope that you enjoy them as much as we did and do.

DEENA BERG
DOUGLASS PARKER

A Note on Staging

Our first aim is to show how these plays worked, and thus may work again. Consequently, these versions are studded with many more stage directions than are usually encountered in translations. Roman Comedies are not recitations, or "concert readings." The effect of what is said depends a great deal, not just on who says it, but on *to whom* it is said, where on stage, and how in delivery. And our directions imply a basic stage, as in the illustration. This diagram implies a much narrower and much deeper stage than the standard construction in Rome, which was both very wide and very shallow. This distortion is made for reasons of practicality. Such venues as this version may find in production are likely to be those with a standard proscenium setup, where "upstage" and "downstage" have meaning, rather than the squeezed strip of actable place (rather like doing an entire modern play "in four," in front of the curtain) that seems to have characterized the early Roman stage. Second, the aim of this diagram

House   Alley   House

To the harbor
(stage right)

To downtown
(stage left)

and its fellows is primarily to show blocking in relation to set, and, quite simply, the rendition of this takes more space. So: proportions are wrong, but the overall effect should approach the demonstration of what's happening.

Acknowledgments

This project was born in a translation seminar conducted by Douglass Parker over a decade ago at the University of Texas. Our gratitude and fond memories go out to all members of that class for their feedback and encouragement. Since that time, several of these plays have been tested at readings. For this we owe thanks to all our theatrical guinea pigs, especially Joan and Gareth Morgan, our frequent hosts and finest actors. Also among our list of patron saints are: William Levitan, wise reader and good friend; Stanley Lombardo, who steered us to Hackett Publishing; Brian Rak and Meera Dash, our eternally patient and persistent editors; Stott Parker, our beloved moral supporter; Haverly Parker, who endured with grace; Dossie, who held the fort; and all the other kin and friends who backed us up and tolerated our absence from general duty, especially Austin Parker. Gratitude is also due to those who constituted pickup casts in shakedown performances: Tim Moore, John Stillwell, Tom Palaima, Paula Perlman, Rich Pianka, Cynthia Shelmerdine, David Armstrong, Greta Ham, Lisa Kallet, Carol Esler, and a host of others. Our thanks also goes out to those who picked their ways through unpolished drafts, wrote kindly words in our behalf, and sought for fonts: Sander Goldberg, John Wright, Karl Galinsky, and Chris Williams.

We have since lost Gareth Morgan and Richard Berg, both of whom graced the English language with unparalleled style. We miss them dearly and dedicate this work to them.

Further Reading

Anderson, William. *Barbarian Play: Plautus' Roman Comedy* (Toronto: University of Toronto Press, 1993).

Arnott, W. Geoffrey. *Menander, Plautus, Terence.* "Greece & Rome. New Surveys in the Classics No. 9." (Oxford: Clarendon Press, 1975).

Beacham, Richard C. *The Roman Theater and Its Audience* (Cambridge, Mass.: Harvard University Press, 1991).

Beare, William. *The Roman Stage: A Short History of Latin Drama in the Time of the Republic,* 3rd ed., rev. (London: Methuen, 1964).

Csapo, E., and W. J. Slater. *The Context of Ancient Drama* (Ann Arbor: University of Michigan Press, 1995).

Duckworth, George E. *The Nature of Roman Comedy* (Princeton: Princeton University Press, 1952).

Goldberg, Sander M. *Understanding Terence* (Princeton: Princeton University Press, 1986).

Hunter, R. L. *The New Comedy of Greece and Rome* (Cambridge: Cambridge University Press, 1985).

Konstan, David. *Roman Comedy* (Ithaca: Cornell University Press, 1983).

Miola, Robert S. *Shakespeare and Classical Comedy: The Influence of Plautus and Terence* (Oxford: Clarendon Press, 1994).

Moore, Timothy. *The Theater of Plautus: Playing to the Audience* (Austin: University of Texas Press, 1998).

Sandbach, F. H. *The Comic Theatre of Greece and Rome* (New York: Norton, 1977).

Segal, Erich. *Roman Laughter: The Comedy of Plautus,* 2nd ed. (New York: Oxford University Press, 1987).

Slater, Niall W. *Plautus in Performance* (Princeton: Princeton University Press, 1985).

Wright, John. *Dancing in Chains: The Stylistic Unity of the Comoedia Palliata* (Rome: American Academy in Rome, 1974).

Zagagi, N. *Tradition and Originality in Plautus: Studies of the Amatory Motifs in Plautine Comedy "Hypomnemata 62."* (Göttingen: Vandenhoeck und Ruprecht, 1980).

MILES
Major Blowhard
GLORIOSUS

TITVS MACCIVS
Deena Berg
PLAVTVS

Introduction to *Major Blowhard*

Major Blowhard (*Miles Gloriosus*) was produced around 205 B.C., making it one of Plautus's early masterpieces. The stage is a battlefield: on one side stands the camp of Major Blowhard, a philandering mercenary; on the other, that of Hospitalides,[1] a bachelor patron of pleasure. Neither of these characters presents a model for ancient family values, but the Major is unquestionably the more repugnant of the two.[2] The balance of power tilts from one side of the stage to the other, as the two characters vie to seize each other's female. Victory falls to the side of True Love; the military man's sword-waving in Act I comes back to haunt him in Act V, when Hospitalides' cook wields a cleaver dangerously close to the Major's privates.

Directing the war effort is Dexter, cleverest of clever slaves, who advises both sides for the benefit of his young master and himself. Sophisticated and street-smart, he executes complicated troop movements with the know-how of an experienced general. The "business women" sustain their supporting roles with dazzling finesse, matching Dexter's wild improvisations move for move. Nautikles, the stereotypical young lover, has the charm and cunning of a sofa, and so must be maneuvered around the stage lest somebody stumble over him. The Major's minions are no match for Dexter. In fact, the sole member of the Major's entourage with even a whiff of élan is Ingestio, the parasite who shows up in Act I as a foil to the Major. Unfortunately, his appearance in this play is singular and short; but the character does light the way for later sponges and freeloaders of the stage.

The play has some minor chinks. To start with, it is *very* long—the longest work, in fact, of Plautus's known repertoire. At this point in his craft, Plautus had not yet added his trademark songs to vary the pace, and the action sometimes sinks under the weight of repetitious conversation and lengthy monologue. There is, for example, the seemingly endless exposition on bachelorhood by Hospitalides in the beginning of Act III that threatens to send the audience out for popcorn. Casts in antiquity undoubtedly kept

---

[1] It is likely that Plautus made up many of the names of his characters, which are sometimes Greek and sometimes Latin. I have approximated these puns in English by using quasi-Graeco-Roman-sounding names, so that the actors will not be unnecessarily tortured by ancient tongue twisters that the general audience would probably not understand anyway. *Pyrgopolynices,* whose name means "great tower-sacker," is here Major Topple d'Acropolis; *Periplectomenus* ("embracer") is Hospitalides; *Palaestrio,* the name of the clever slave derived from *palaestra,* meaning "wrestling area" or "adroitness," is Dexter; the parasite, *Artotrogus*—literally, "bread chewer"—is Ingestio. Likewise, *Philocomasium* ("party lover") is Convivia, *Acroteleutium* ("the tops") is Climax, *Sceledrus* ("cursed") is Haplus, and so on.

[2] Hospitalides holds a philosophy similar to the one later refined by Micio, in Terence's *Adelphoe:* he accepts the pleasures of unclehood but shirks the obligations of marriage and procreation. Such an attitude about parental and familial responsibility was frowned upon by the Romans—at least officially.

the action rolling with snappy choreography, shticks, sight gags, etc. I have attempted to interpolate some of these items from the dialogue, and in the Plautine spirit of "more is more," suggest that performers feel free to chip in.

Then there is the problem of the subplot. The duping of the Major's slaves, Haplus and Lurch, is an entertaining side story, but does not completely intersect the bilking of the Major. This gap arises partially from some confusion in the manuscript: Haplus disappears into the Major's house at the end of Act II, and the Latin text is unclear as to whether it is Haplus or an unnamed slave who comes back from the port at the end of Act V. Since there is no indication in the manuscript that Haplus ever leaves the house, the unnamed slave usually lands the part in Act V. Here, however, I have dispatched Haplus to the port as one of the baggage carriers at the end of Act IV (that he does not speak at this point seems reasonable, given his hangover). This exit solves the subsequent entrance problem and gives the ending a further shade of irony: Haplus realizes that he was right all along about the amorous scene he witnessed—the scene that set the play in motion—but in order not to incriminate himself in front of the Major, he must yet again stifle the truth.

Texts and Commentaries: I depended upon W. M. Lindsay's text, *T. Macci Plauti Comoediae.* 2 vols. (Oxford: Clarendon Press, 1903–5). For commentaries, I looked to Mason Hammond, Arthur M. Mack, Walter Moskalew, eds., *Plautus: Miles Gloriosus* (Cambridge: Harvard University Press, 1963), and Robert Yelverton Tyrrell, ed., *The Miles Gloriosus of T. Maccius Plautus* (London: Macmillan, 1899; repr. 1927).

DEENA BERG

Basic Set

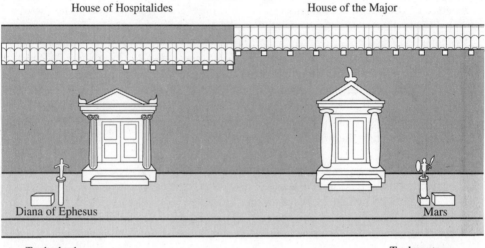

House of Hospitalides   House of the Major

Diana of Ephesus   Mars

To the harbor
(stage right)

To downtown
(stage left)

SCENE: *A well-to-do street in Ephesus, a well-to-do town in Asia Minor. Stage left, the house of Major Topple d'Acropolis, a soldier of fortune. Stage right, the mansion of Hospitalides, a wealthy bachelor. The two houses share a common wall and adjoining tile roofs. The entrance to the Major's house has a porch, which is approached by a short flight of stairs and is sheltered by a small but pretentious pediment, supported by overly muscular Doric columns. The entrance to Hospitalides' house also has a porch and low step; the style of the covering and columns is graceful Ionic. There are two altars. Downstage left is that of Mars, which includes a free-standing column (chin-height with a footstool-high base). Surmounting the column is a pudgy bronze statue of the god himself, who bears a sword and shield, the latter polished to mirror quality. Downstage right is the altar of Diana of Ephesus, with a statue of the same. The goddess has her arms outstretched in a welcoming fashion. Stage left leads downtown, stage right to the Harbor.*

While the stage is still dark, the audience hears the sounds of heavy feet stumbling over rooftiles, followed by muffled cursing, then silence.

Dramatis Personae

MAJOR TOPPLE D'ACROPOLIS (Pyrgopolynices)	a soldier of fortune
INGESTIO (Artotrogus)	his parasite
HAPLUS (Sceledrus)	his faithful old slave
LURCH (Lurcio)	his slave
TWO OTHER SLAVES	
A BAG-BOY	
NAUTIKLES (Pleusicles)	a young man
DEXTER (Palaestrio)	his faithful and cunning servant
HOSPITALIDES (Periplectomenus)	his host, an old friend of the family
CHEF (Cario)	Hospitalides' cook
TWO SLAVES	
CONVIVIA (Philocomasium)	a working girl
CLIMAX (Acroteleutium)	another working girl
MILLY (Milphidippa)	Climax's maid

Major Blowhard

Act I, Scene 1 [1–78]

(The Major enters from his house, carrying a short sword and shield. He has a head of luxuriant long hair, and his garb includes a breastplate, boots, a short cape, and a scabbard. Ingestio and two slaves follow.)

MAJOR: FALL IN!

(Ingestio and his slaves form a more or less straight line.)

> Objective:
>> implement shining of shield.

(He admires himself in his reflection, then hands the shield to one slave.)

> Make sure it outshimmers the merciless rays of summer.
> Thus, when its time is at hand,
>> when I'm toe to toe
> with battle line "A"

(He draws an imaginary line at toe level with the tip of his sword.)

>> the dazzling blaze of light
> will addle line "B"!—

(He raises his sword and pokes across the line, almost jabbing the slave in the eye.)

>> the enemy's line of sight.
> Second objective:
>> condolences to my sword.

(He admires his reflection in the sword; the second slave reaches for it; the Major recoils.)

> NO!
>> I want to do it myself. It's mine.
> "Sad sword, who hath ached so long at my sash,
> droop not, 'though you long to make foe into hash."

(He inserts sword in scabbard and begins to stride back and forth between the altars.)

> Now where the hell is Ingestio?

(Ingestio hastens to the Major's side. The slaves retire to the steps of the Major's house, sit down, and follow the Major's movements as if watching a ping-pong match.)

INGESTIO: Here and directly
adjacent, sir. Next to a hero so forceful,
so favored by fate,
                              flaunting so noble a profile
a warrior of such—
                              why, Mars himself would blanch
to mention his manliness, much less rank it with yours.

MAJOR: And did I not save Whatshisname on the Green
of Gallinippers, where Clamorus Hostilities,
the son of Egregius Mercenarius, grandson
of Neptune, was highest supreme commander-in-chief?

INGESTIO: I remember him well. You mean, of course, whatshisface—
with the priceless panoply. One touch of your breath
was all it took to blow his troops away,
as the wind snatches leaves—NAY! the thatch—from a rooftop!

MAJOR: Oh tush, that was nothing.

(The Major quickens his pace, while Ingestio struggles to keep up.)

INGESTIO: By gosh, it certainly was—
that is, compared to what I could say of the rest

(He stops to catch his breath.)

of your derring-do

(Aside.)

                              that you didn't.

(To the audience.)

                                      Ever heard
a bigger fibber? A breezier bag of wind?
If you have, you can haul me off in chains. I'll surrender
myself into legal bondage.
                              The only thing is—
the olive dip here in this joint is insanely delicious.

MAJOR: Where did you go?

(Ingestio falls in step.)

INGESTIO: Right here, sir. And what about
that elephant back in India? Remember how
you bashed your fist straight into his funny bone?

(The Major stops abruptly next to the statue.)

MAJOR: What do you mean, "his funny bone"?

INGESTIO: I meant
                   "his massive thigh."

MAJOR: Ah, merely a casual swat.

INGESTIO: With a little effort, you *would* have been up to your elbow
                   in elephant, fist poking through the guts and bone,
                   transpiercing the hide through the other side.

(The Major notices his reflection in the statue's shield and begins to preen.)

MAJOR: I don't want to
                   hear anymore. At least not here and now.

INGESTIO: By gosh, of course not. Why should you bother to sing
                   your praises to ME, the man who knows them all?

       (Aside.)

                   It's my stomach's idea to put up with this pain in the ass.
                   Unless my ears are willing to swallow a snootful,
                   my molars have nothing to mull. I salute whatever
                   he says.

MAJOR: Where was I?

(The Major resumes his striding; Ingestio falls in step again.)

INGESTIO: Let's see. Ah yes, of course—
                   I remember it well. Indeed, that you did.

MAJOR: Did what?

INGESTIO: Whatever it was that you did.

MAJOR: Do you happen to have—

(Ingestio stops to pull out a stylus and tablet from his tunic.)

INGESTIO: —your writing tools? Right here at your beck and call.

MAJOR: How clever of you! Two minds precisely in step.

(Ingestio hurries to catch up.)

INGESTIO: My duty, sir. To study the you-ness of you,
                   to inhale the aroma of every whim you exude.

MAJOR: And what do you recall?

INGESTIO: As I remember:
                   Cilicia, one hundred and fifty; Scythosnatchya,
                   another hundred; sixty Macedonians,
                   Sardonians—thirty. That's merely the number you slew
                   in one day.

MAJOR: And the bottom line? How many in total?

INGESTIO: Seven thousand even.

MAJOR: That sounds correct.
             Your addition is perfect. Very exact.

INGESTIO: No ledgers
             for me—I have it all here in my head.

MAJOR: A damn fine
             memory you've got there. First class.

INGESTIO: The modest morsel
             jogs it.

MAJOR: As long as you keep up this conduct—you have
             my permission to stuff yourself freely. My table is yours.

INGESTIO: And what about Cappadocia? Five hundred dead
             with a single thrust—had not your sword been blunt.

MAJOR: A smatter of measly peons. I spared their lives.

INGESTIO: Oh, why do I tell you what's known to all mortal men?
             That no one on earth can claim the fame of Major
             Topple d'Acropolis?
                               You, O sublimely unconquered
             zenith of manhood, deedhood, and beautyhood?
             All femininity squats at your feet—and who
             could sue them for loving a man so handsome—and winsome?
             In fact, it was only yesterday two ladies
             grabbed me by the sleeve.

         (The Major stops abruptly.)

MAJOR: And what did they say?

INGESTIO: They were very persistent. They asked me over and over,
             "Isn't that Achilles?"
                               "His brother," I answered,
             "to be precise."
                               And then, the other piped up,
             "My goodness gracious, THAT's the reason he's totally
             gorgeous—and so well-bred. Just look at that luscious
             mane! Such bliss if only to share his sheets!"

MAJOR: Really, now? Those were their very words?

INGESTIO: The both of them begged me to bring you by, did they not?
             Today, in fact. A private parade just for them.

MAJOR: To be as becoming as I—'tis a bitter burden.

INGESTIO: Precisely so, sir. Tedious creatures, these women.
              They throng, they badger, they importune—"Pretty please,
              just a glimpse!"
                              They drag me over, demand introductions;
              they even force me at times—

              (He pauses to hang his head.)

                                              to neglect my duties.

              (The Major resumes striding.)

MAJOR: Speaking of which, it's time we were pressing onward.
              Our target: downtown; our mission: distribute cash
              to fresh recruits appended to yesterday's payroll.
              King Seleucus—the major potentate
              of Asia Minor—has recently made an urgent
              appeal for soldiers of fortune. He begged my help
              in the rounding and signing up thereof.
                                                      And so
              I vow that today I do nothing but succor the king.

              (Ingestio falls in step.)

INGESTIO: Yes, come, let us succor.

              (The Major waves his arm at the slaves.)

MAJOR: Forward march, my minions!

              (The slaves fall into step behind the Major and Ingestio, all heading stage right. The
              Major, realizing that he is headed in the wrong direction, makes an abrupt about-
              face, which is executed poorly by the rest. All exit stage left.)

Act II, Scene 1 [79–155]

              (Dexter enters from the Major's house, looks around cautiously, then strides to
              center stage.)

DEXTER: Beloved fans of the stage:
                              I'll explain the plot as a favor—
              but *you* must promise to keep your ears on their best behavior.
              Those of you who can't sit still and listen, please rise
              and take a hike: an adult with an adequate span of attention
              will gladly take your seat.
                              And now, the reason you're sitting
              here in this lovely festive setting is, of course,
              this comic drama, which we are about to enact—
              but not before I unravel the title and story.
                                              Ahem.
              In Greek, this play is known as "The Blowhard";
                                              in Latin, we call it
              "Major Blowhard." The city of Ephesus stands before you;

that man in military garb who just went downtown
is my master—
             Major Blowhard himself.
                       A shameless bastard.
Full of perfidy,
       perjury,
             not to mention crap.
He claims all the ladies swoon at his heels whenever he passes;
it's true:
        the weight of his bullshit can't help but knock them down flat.
And the working girls in the streets?
                 They make the usual kissy
faces, but nine out of ten have their tongues in their cheeks.
                       Ahem.

But back to the subject of masters and slaves. The Major's house
is the latest step down in my servile progression. You ought to know
why I'm slaving away for him and not serving my former boss.
So WAKE UP and pay attention. I'm unveiling the plot.
                       Ahem.

I used to have an owner in Athens. The very best kind—
a kid. He's wildly in love with a working girl in Athens
—the very exact same city—who's equally wild about him.
Romantically speaking, things were going superbly.
                  But HE
gets sent on some urgent mission of state to Naupactus; meanwhile
the Major shows up in Athens, and slithers around the girl—
that is, my old boss's girl. Then he—the Major—smooth-talks
her mother, wooing the old bat with wine, while scattering doodads
and dainties left and right. So her madam—that is, her mother—
winds up in the Major's pocket.
              And the first chance the Major gets,
he pulls a fast one on her (by whom I mean the madam,
that is, the girl's mother;
             the girl is, of course, my master's sweetheart).
You see, the Major dragged the daughter off in a boat
without her mother's knowledge. Then he brought her to Ephesus—
here, in other words—against the young girl's will.
The minute I saw that my master's girl had been nabbed, I hopped
on board a ship as soon as I could and shoved right off
to Naupactus, in order to give him—my master, that is—the news.
But then, as we're plowing across the high seas, the gods butt in:
our boat is plundered by pirates, the urgent message squelched,
and all because brigands have bundled me off as a gift to the Major.
After HE gets me home, I take a look around
and whoa! I spy my master's girlfriend—the one from Athens.
She catches me staring, then gives me a wink: the code for "pretend

you don't know me, later we'll talk."
                        So as soon as we get a chance,
we chat: the woman breaks down in tears,
                                my heart goes to pieces.
"Athens!" she cries. "I want to go home and get out of this place!"
She swears she loves my master—her lover in Athens, remember?
—and never hated a man as much as that nasty Major.
Deeply moved by her tale of woe, I jot down a message,
sign it, and sneak it out on the sly to a trustworthy merchant:
the idea being for him to convey said note to my master
—the Athenian one, that is, the one who's in love with the girl—
and get him to come here.
                    My call for help did not go unheeded—
He's already here. Next door, in fact, as a guest of our neighbor,
who happens to be a friend of his father. A nice old man,
who's become his lovelorn houseguest's biggest ally, boosting
morale and supplying vital provisions.
                         I, myself,
have managed to engineer within our house the consummate
contrivance by which the lovers may . . . convene. Together.
With each other.
                  You see, the Major had cooped up his cupcake
in sort of an armored boudoir that she alone may enter.
I breached that bulwark—I made a hole in the wall—thus allowing
the girl to advance and retreat undercover between our two houses.
What does the old man know? Every bit. He helped me out.
And what of my fellow slave, the one the Major handpicked
to stand guard outside her quarters? Hardly top-notch material.
With a bit of expert shuffling and shrewd excogitation,
we'll fuddle his eyeballs and make him think he's seeing double.
But then, don't YOU get confused. The girl will create the *illusion*
she's two:

(He points to the Major's house.)

             first one girl here,

(He points to the house of Hospitalides.)

                    then one girl there—but in fact
she's all the same person, making herself just *seem* like another.
Her guard will look like a chump when she slips out under his nose.

(The door to Hospitalides' house begins to open, with sounds of cursing.)

            But say, what's that noise?
                        It sounds like it came from next door.

(Hospitalides appears in the doorway, brandishing a whip.)

                                             It did.

And here he comes himself, that nice old man I just mentioned.

(He retreats to the Major's porch.)

Act II, Scene 2 [156–271]

(Hospitalides enters from his house, still speaking to his servants inside.)

HOSPIT.:   DAMMIT ALL!
                      The next time you see some stranger
sneaking around on our rooftop,
                              BASH IN HIS SHINS!
If you don't, I promise to thrash your tushies to tatters.
All I need now is my neighbors gawking away
at whatever goes on in my house, from front-row seats
ABOVE MY PRIVATE PATIO![3]
                              NOW HEAR THIS!
Any servant from yonder Major's house found traipsing
across our roof—any servant, that is, excluding
Dexter—SHALL BE DASHED HEAD DOWN, FACE FIRST,
TO THE STREET BELOW.
                      And *if* he claims he's chasing
a chicken,
          a pigeon,
                  or even a runaway monkey,
it's your life or his! Understood?
                              WE SHOW NO MERCY!
I want him a pulsating mound of pulpaceous flesh.
You know gambling here is strictly taboo:
                              so make sure
he hasn't a knucklebone left to shake with his buddies.

DEXTER:

(Aside.)

Sounds to me like some nasty work on the part
of the Major. That would explain why our neighbor wants
all my colleagues next door deboned—
                              that is, all but me.
Well, I could care less about them. I think I'll go over
and greet the old boy.

(He emerges from the porch.)

---

[3] The translator has used the more familiar term "patio" for Plautus's *atrium*. The *atrium* was a central room with a skylight in an upper-class Roman house of the Republican era. Plautus adapted this detail for the Roman audience, since Greek houses were organized around open courts.

HOSPIT.:   Is that Dexter coming this way?

DEXTER: Hospitalides, sir, what seems to be the trouble?

HOSPIT.: You're just the man I wanted to see.

DEXTER: Why's that?
And why are you ranting at "yonder Major's house"?

HOSPIT.: The tide has turned against us.

DEXTER: What's the matter?

HOSPIT.: A security leak.

DEXTER: What leaked?

HOSPIT.:   The roof. This morning
a fellow servant of yours—I don't know who—
caught a bird's-eye view of my patio. Saw them kissing.
Convivia, that is, and my guest.

DEXTER: And who was this peeker?

HOSPIT.: One of your coslaves.

DEXTER: What's his name?

HOSPIT.:   Who knows?
One moment he's there, the next thing I know he's gone.

DEXTER: I deeply suspect this does not bode well.

HOSPIT.:   As the culprit
fled, I shouted,
     "HEY, YOU THERE! WHY ARE YOU POKING
AROUND ON MY ROOF?"
         He answered—still fleeing—"I'm trying
to catch a monkey!"

DEXTER: Alas, my poor life cut short.
Because of a worthless furball.
        But where's Convivia?
Still here?

(He nods in the direction of Hospitalides' house.)

HOSPIT.:   She was when I left.

DEXTER: I beg you, sir—
RUN! And tell the girl to return on the double.
Make sure the Major's staff can see that she's home;
unless she wants this affair to end with her faithful
servants tying the knot—with matching nooses.

HOSPIT.: I've already told her all that. Unless you have
something else to add—

DEXTER: I do. Relay this message:
RETREAT FROM PRIOR COURSE OF ACTION. FALL BACK
ON GIRL'S INTUITION. DEPLOY ALL FEMININE CHARM.

HOSPIT.: But why?

DEXTER: To seduce her spy into thinking he never
saw her. Although she's been seen a hundred times,
she must flat out deny it.

(He takes Hospitalides by the arm, and the two walk back and forth between the
altars.)

                    I have a two-phase plan.
First, a diversion.
                    But is she well-equipped?
Elegance—CHECK!
                    Eloquence—CHECK!
Impudence—CHECK!
                    Confidence—CHECK!
Audacity,
          mendacity,
                    and just a tad of pugnacity—
CHECK CHECK CHECK! Her shape's tip-top.
Next, a counterattack.
                    If cross-examined,
she double-crosses her heart and condemns her accuser.
How well is her arsenal geared for that? Let's see:
Fibs and perfidy—CHECK!
                    Fraud and perjury—CHECK!
Obfuscation,
          manipulation,
                    prevarication—
CHECK CHECK CHECK! It's all in order.
As a rule, the clever woman never depends
on the vegetable vendor; her garden and pantry are always
well stocked with the basic stuffs for cooking up trouble.

HOSPIT.: I'll give her the message—assuming she hasn't left yet.

(Dexter stops abruptly at the column of Mars. He smites his forehead and closes his
eyes.)

          And now what's whirling around in your head?

DEXTER: A moment
of silence. I must summon my wits to order, then ask
for their counsel regarding what type of cunning action

to launch against that servant who saw Convivia
smooching in here. The goal is to make him unsee
what he saw.

HOSPIT.:   Go search your brain, by all means. I'll step
to the side over here for a while and give you some room.

(He withdraws to center stage and addresses the audience.)

Just look at him standing there with furrowed brow,
completely frozen in thought.

(Dexter taps the side of his forehead three times and squints.)

His finger taps thrice
on his temple[4]—the call to arms goes out to his genius.

(Dexter props his left foot on the column base and rests his left hand on his left
thigh, while drumming up and down his right thigh with his right hand.)

Uh oh! He shifts his weight and strikes a new pose!
The left hand steadies itself upon the left thigh,
while right flitters down the opposing femur in feverish
calculation.

(Dexter slaps his right hand on his right thigh and frowns.)

Uh oh! A whack of disgust!
The plot won't hatch.

(Dexter puts his foot back down, snaps his fingers, and shifts from side to side.)

Now see how his fingers snap:
Positions change in rapid succession, contractions
begin to quicken!

(Dexter stops shifting. He shakes his head violently.)

Uh oh! He shakes his head,
rejects his own brainchild. Won't serve up some half-baked plan:
this scheme must be done to perfection.

(Dexter rests his chin and wrists upon the column.)

Uh oh! He's propped
his chin on the pillar—a monumental idea!
No, take it off! I don't like the composition.
It reminds me too much of that playwright—some Roman poet
I heard of—who got his noodle stuck in a pillory.

(Hospitalides waves his hands on either side of his own face.)

---

[4] In the Latin text, he drums on his chest (*pectus*) to summon forth his heart (*cor*), which was
considered in antiquity to be the seat of the intellect as well as the spirit.

Had two little watch guards flanking him day and night.[5]

(Dexter props one elbow on the column and leans sideways, feet crossed, eyes closed.[6])

By god, behold! How statuesque! The comic
slave in a classic pose.
                    He won't catch a wink
today 'til he finds—and refines—the consummate scam.

(Dexter opens his eyes, raises an index finger, then closes his eyes again and smiles.)

I think he's got it.

(Hospitalides walks over and taps Dexter on the shoulder.)

                    Hey! If you have an agenda,
then ACT! WAKE UP!
                    This is no time for taking a scholarly
interest in snoozing! Unless, of course, you'd like
to stay up all night lingering over the lines
I'm about to make on your heinie.

(He waves his whip menacingly.)

                              DEXTER! I'M TALKING
TO *YOU!* Did you hear what I said?

(He prods Dexter lightly with the whip.)

                              I SAID, WAKE UP!
I SAID, GET MOVING—IT'S MORNING! I SAID—

(Dexter yawns and stretches, without opening his eyes.)

DEXTER: I *hear* you.

HOSPIT.:   But don't you *see* that the enemy's breathing down
             your back? We're under siege!
                              Convene the council
             of war!
                    Signal for aid!
                              Send for reserves!
             This crisis calls for all deliberate speed—
             not sloth!
                    Strike a first blow!

---

[5] The foreign poet (*poeta barbarus*) is generally identified as Plautus's fellow Roman playwright, Gnaeus Naevius, who was thought to have been imprisoned sometime around 210–207 B.C. for lampooning aristocrats. The exact meaning of "columned face" (*os columnatum*) and "two guards" (*bini custodes*) isn't known. "Pillory" captures the pun, although Naevius may well have been chained to a post.

[6] The drunken *Leaning Satyr,* a well-known sculpture by the Greek artist Praxiteles, would be a good model.

                                                    Cut off his men
at some pass!
                            Erect a bastion!
                                            Beleaguer the bastards!
Strangle their lines of supply!
                                            Stake out an inroad!
Stick up an outpost!
                            Secure safe passage for soldiers
and sustenance!

(Dexter stretches and yawns some more, with eyes still closed.)

                        YOU MUST LEAP INTO ACTION NOW!
MAYDAY!
                MAYDAY!
                            Devise!
                                    Maneuver!
                                            Plot!
Dish up some hot ideas—and dammit, make it
snappy!
                        Undo what's been done! Erase what's been seen!

(Two servants emerge on the roof of the Major's house and begin to beat dust from
a carpet. Hospitalides shakes Dexter awake with both hands then points to the roof.)

THE MAJOR IS ON THE MOVE!
                                    HE'S MOUNTING A MASSIVE
OFFENSIVE!

(The servants, bewildered, disappear from the roof. Dexter opens his eyes, looks at
the roof, and then looks at Hospitalides with some confusion. Hospitalides drops to
his knees to plead, still holding on to Dexter's tunic.)

                        Promise you'll take on this mission. You
and you alone can rouse our troops and rout
the opposition.

(Dexter, caught off balance, struggles to free himself.)

DEXTER: I promise. The mission's all mine.

HOSPIT.:   I promise you'll get whatever it is that you want.

DEXTER: May Jupiter bless you.

(He helps Hospitalides to his feet.)

HOSPIT.:   But won't you share just a teensy
            bit with me?

(Dexter looks around and leads Hospitalides over to Diana's altar.)

DEXTER: Hush up, and I'll usher you through
the complex terrain of my mental convolutions.
That way you'll know my plans as if you were me.

HOSPIT.:   Of course. You may bank on my brain as if were yours.

DEXTER: My master—the Major—is hardly the sensitive sort:
his hide is, in fact, as thick as an elephant's.
Intelligence-wise, I believe he's no match for pumice.

HOSPIT.:   I've suspected as much.

DEXTER: I'm launching a scheme that's hinged
on the following premise:
                    I'll put out the word that Convivia
has a twin sister. Yes, an identical double.
She—the "sister"—has just arrived from Athens
along with some lover of hers. They can't be told
apart—the "sisters," that is—anymore than two drops
of milk.
                    I'll say that you're putting the lovebirds up
as your guests.

HOSPIT.:   Touché! Touché! A stroke of brilliance!
My compliments to your genius.

DEXTER: So, if that snitch
reports the girl to the Major and claims that he saw her
kissing another man in *here,*

(He pauses to indicate Hospitalides' house.)
                         I'll swear
that the girl he saw was her sibling. Yes, HER TWIN
was the one engaged in all that smooching and squeezing.

HOSPIT.:   A tour de force! If the Major asks me, I'll ditto.

DEXTER: Remember to stress that the sisters are highly identical.
Brief Convivia well in advance with all
essential details. Make sure she's completely prepared;
we can't have her slipping up in front of the Major.

HOSPIT.:   Your plan is an absolute coup! Too cunning for words!
But what if the Major wants to see them together,
side by side? Then what do we do?

DEXTER: That's easy;
we dream up lots of excuses. Hundreds of them:
"She's not in;
              she stepped out;
                         she had to go lie down;

she's sprucing up;
                    she's bathing;
                              she's wining;
                                        she's dining;
she's busy, overbooked, and can't be bothered."
Put him off all you want: we just have to start him
down the right path so he'll swallow the story as fact.

HOSPIT.:   I like the way you think.

DEXTER: So go and tell
the girl—assuming she's still inside—to hurry
back home. Then spell the whole thing out so she'll know
exactly how we fabricated her sister.

HOSPIT.:   I'll brief her at length. Is there anything else you want me
to tell her?

DEXTER: Nothing. Just go inside.

HOSPIT.:   Will do.

(He exits into his house.)

DEXTER: And as for me, it's time to go home and start
my investigation. With utmost discretion, of course.
Just who among my peers was chasing a monkey
this morning? He must have spilled the beans and blabbed
how he saw Convivia kissing a stranger next door.
I know the type:
                    "I'll just burst if I don't tell someone!"
When *I* find out WHO, it's out with my siege equipment,
up with the armored ladders,
                         and down with the walls!
I'll conquer that fort by force, and take him captive!
But what if I can't?
                    Then I'll have to sniff him out.
Like a hound on the trail, I'll pick up his scent and hunt him
down.

(The door to the Major's house opens.)

Uh oh. That sounds like the Major's door.

(He ducks behind Diana's altar as Haplus appears at the Major's door.)

It's one of my fellow servants: in fact, it's the guard
who keeps tabs on Convivia. I'd better lower my voice.

Act II, Scene 3 [272–353]

(Haplus descends the Major's steps, talking to himself.)

HAPLUS: Unless I was walking around on our roof in my sleep
this morning—
             No, by cracky! I'm positive
that I saw Convivia—the Major's very own girlfriend—
right next door here, getting herself in trouble.

DEXTER:

(Aside.)

     So THIS is the man who saw her kissing—I just heard him
say as much.

HAPLUS: Who's there?

DEXTER:

(Aside, as he comes out from behind the altar.)

                   Just one of the family.
     Hi, Haplus. What's up?

HAPLUS:

(He runs over and grabs Dexter's hand.)

               It's Dexter! Gee, am I glad
     to see you!

DEXTER:

(He pats Haplus's hand.)

           Why's that? Some trouble with business? Tell all.

HAPLUS: I'm scared—

DEXTER: Scared? Scared of what?

HAPLUS: We're all gonna take
     a leap.
         First into the pan—then into the fire.
     O suffering snakes!

DEXTER:

(He tries to free his hand, but Haplus clings.)

               Go take a leap by yourself.
     I'm not the leaping kind. Not in, not out.

HAPLUS: You mean that YOU don't know the horrible thing
that happened this morning?

DEXTER: What sort of horrible thing?

HAPLUS: A naughty sort.

DEXTER:

(He places Haplus's own hand over Haplus's mouth.)

                                        You must stifle that information!
               Don't tell me! I don't want to hear!

HAPLUS:

(He pulls his own hand down and releases Dexter's.)

                                                    I'll make you hear.
               I chased our little pet monkey across the neighbor's
               roof this morning.

DEXTER: Haplus! How awful! Imagine,
               one dumb animal leading another.

HAPLUS: Jove
               will strike you for that.

DEXTER: The same to you. Go on.
               As long as you've started, you may as well tell me the rest.

HAPLUS: Well, accidentally by chance I peeped in next door
               and saw Convivia kissing a stranger. A young one.
               And foreign.

DEXTER: What hoopla, Haplus! How could such libel
               spring forth from your lips?

HAPLUS: I'm sure I saw her.

DEXTER: You did, eh?

HAPLUS: I did indeed. With THESE—my own two eyes.

DEXTER: Get out! You're making this up—you didn't see her.

HAPLUS: You think I'm blind or something?

DEXTER: Go ask a doctor.
               But now, for heaven's sake, put a stop to this blather!
               He who makes heady charges usually winds up
               headless.
                              Unless you renounce this imbecilic
               locution, you'll end up yourself in double jeopardy.

HAPLUS: What do you mean by "double"?

DEXTER: I'll tell you. First,
               if your allegations are false regarding Convivia,
               that's grounds enough for capital punishment; then,

if the charges are true and you were the guard on duty,
that's equal grounds for a second execution.

HAPLUS: What happens to me, I don't know. But I'm sure I saw her.

DEXTER: Still you persist, you miserable misguided wretch?

HAPLUS: Well, what on earth do you want me to say except
that I didn't see her? She's still next door even now!

DEXTER: So, she isn't at home, you say?

HAPLUS: I don't expect
you to take it from me. Go in and see for yourself.

DEXTER: I think I'll just do that.

HAPLUS: And I'll wait out here. In the meantime,
I aim to corral that little heifer, as soon as
she moseys back to the shed from her romp in the hay.

(Dexter exits into the Major's house. Haplus paces between the altars.)

Now what do I do? The Major made ME her guard.
If I open my mouth, I'm dead. But I'm just as dead
if I seal my lips and the secret still slips out.
When it comes to being cheeky, there's no one worse
than a woman.
                    I bet while I was up on the roof,
she picked up her skirt and scooted outside. A dirty
thing to do. She's gutsy, by gosh.
                                        If the Major
finds out about this, THUNDERING HEAVENS! I'm sure
he'll hang the entire household—and me—by the thumbs.
Whatever she's doing, it's best if I don't breathe a word.
That's better than dying a horrible death. I can't
keep watch on a girl who's selling her stuff on the side.

(Dexter enters from the Major's house, shaking his head, and meets Haplus at center
stage.)

DEXTER: O Haplus, Haplus! You reckless fool! What creature
would dare what you've done? A foul and fiendish mood
struck the gods the day you were born!

HAPLUS: Is something wrong?

DEXTER: O Haplus! Why don't you beg them to poke out your eyeballs?
Those orbs that make you see what never was there?

HAPLUS: What do you mean, "never there"?

DEXTER: I wouldn't bet
a stale nut on your life.

HAPLUS: What's all this business?

DEXTER: "What business?"
you ask?

HAPLUS: I shouldn't?

DEXTER: O Haplus! Beg them to lop off
your tattling tongue!

HAPLUS: And why would I want to do that?

DEXTER: Go look! She's home! Convivia, the very same girl
you said you saw next door, the one who was smooching
and hugging away with some stranger!

HAPLUS: You know, it's a wonder
you nibble on poppies when wheat's such a bargain.[7]

DEXTER: And THAT
means WHAT?

HAPLUS: Hallucinations. Your eyes are fuzzy.

DEXTER: You dimwit! Your eyes don't even rate fuzzy! You're BLIND!
My vision is fine. The girl's at home—that's a fact.

HAPLUS: At home?

DEXTER: I swear by the gods. At home.

HAPLUS: Go on!
You're pulling my leg.

DEXTER: That explains this muck on my hands.

HAPLUS: And THAT means WHAT?

DEXTER: I'm pulling a leg that's ass-deep
in doo-doo.

HAPLUS: May Jupiter knock your fat head off!

DEXTER: O Haplus!
That noggin of yours will roll, I promise—unless
you rectify your vision—and version.

(The Major's door swings open. Convivia gives a thumbs-up from the doorway.)

                                                Hey look!
Our door has just come open!

(He points to the Major's house.)

---

[7] The plant in the Latin text is darnel (*lolium*), a ryegrasslike weed that infiltrates crops. Some varieties are toxic (or intoxicating), hence the notion that it would affect Dexter's vision.

HAPLUS:

(He turns and points to Hospitalides' house.)

Nope. I'm keeping
my eyes glued to THAT door. She can't get from there to here
without crossing THAT threshold.

DEXTER:

But look! She's home! O Haplus,
you hopeless half-wit, unhinged by this evil affliction!

HAPLUS:

I see what I see; I know what I know; I have every
reason to trust myself. And no one is going
to shoo me away from the fact that she's still in THAT house.

(He points emphatically.)

I'm blocking THAT door. She might try to catch me off guard
and sneak on back to her room.

DEXTER:

(Aside.)

I've got him cornered
atop the ramparts. And now, to shove him off.

(Aloud, rejoining Haplus; meanwhile, Convivia yawns and goes back inside.)

You want me to make you admit you have double vision?

HAPLUS: Sure. You do that.

DEXTER:

You want me to make you confess
that your mind is unsound and your eyeballs don't work?

HAPLUS:

I'd love it.

DEXTER: All right. Now YOU say the Major's girlfriend was THERE?

(He indicates Hospitalides' house.)

HAPLUS: I do. And I swear I saw her in there kissing
another man.

(Dexter leads Haplus to the midpoint between the entrances.)

DEXTER:

You know that no passage exists
between these two houses?

HAPLUS:

Right.

DEXTER:

No sun porch, no garden.
There's no way out at all—except for the little
space above his private patio?

HAPLUS: Right.

(Dexter leads Haplus to the Major's steps.)

DEXTER: And now, I ask you, what if, in fact, she IS
               at home? And what if, in fact, I have you watch
               the girl come out of THIS very house? Would you,
               in fact, deserve a solid flogging?

HAPLUS: I would.

(Dexter pushes Haplus toward the house of Hospitalides.)

DEXTER: Go guard that door. Make sure she can't squirm past you.

HAPLUS: That's what I'm planning to do.

DEXTER: One moment. I'll have her
               standing in front of you. Right here in the street.

(He exits into the Major's house, while Haplus stands in front of Hospitalides'
house.)

HAPLUS: You do that.
                            I want to know if I saw what I saw.
            Or will he really make me believe she's at home,
            like he said he would?
                                NAH! I've got eyes of my own.
            I don't need a second opinion from somebody else's.
            But he IS her pet. A big sucker-upper.
            She always calls him to dinner first,
                                              and she always
            lets him have first dibs on dessert.
                                          He's been here
            maybe three years; but every slave in this house
            is drooling to be in his shoes.
                                    But I've got to do
            what I've got to do. I'll block the door like this.

(He stands stretched out in Hospitalides' doorway, chest inward, looking to his
right.)

            By cracky, they'll never make an ass out of me!

Act II, Scene 4 [354–410]

(Dexter enters from the Major's house. Convivia, lavishly jeweled, follows.)

DEXTER:

(Aside, to Convivia.)

            Remember your orders.

CONVIVIA:

>(Aside, to Dexter.)

>>AGAIN you have to remind me?

DEXTER:

>(Aside, to Convivia.)

>>I fear you lack sufficient guile for the part.

CONVIVIA:

>(Aside, to Dexter.)

>>Sufficient guile? Oh please! I've got oodles to spare.
>>Give me ten unvarnished virgins: I'll teach them the slickest
>>tricks in the business with just what I've got in my pinkie.
>>Hang on—
>>>let me hold back while you start the ambush.

(She retreats to the Major's porch. Dexter approaches Haplus and taps him on his right shoulder.)

DEXTER:

>(Aloud.)

>>So Haplus, what's say?

HAPLUS:

>>>>>I'm minding my business. Talk all
>>you like, I still have ears.

DEXTER:

>>>>>And arms—keep them up.
>>Good practice for when you're drawn and quartered outside
>>the town gate.[8]

HAPLUS:

>>>>How's that?

(Dexter whistles, and Convivia emerges from the Major's house.)

DEXTER:

>>>>>>Look left. Who is that woman?

HAPLUS: GREAT GODS ABOVE! It's her! The Major's girlfriend!

DEXTER: My goodness! That does seem to be the case.

(He pulls Haplus away from the doorway and nudges him toward center stage.)

>>>>>>>Go on.

>>Whenever you're ready.

---

[8] The reference here is actually to the position he would assume on the crossbar (*patibulum*) for crucifixion. Plautus plays on the meaning of *extra portam*, which would mean "outside the door" and "outside the gate," the latter meaning the Esquiline gate at Rome where public executions took place.

HAPLUS: What do I do?

DEXTER: Hurry up
and go hang yourself.

CONVIVIA: AND WHERE is that "faithful servant"
of mine? That slave who made up the groundless charge
that I, an innocent maiden, was party to sin
in the first degree?

(Her gaze lands on Haplus.)

DEXTER: That's him all right. He's your man.
I told you whatever he told me.

CONVIVIA:

(She confronts Haplus eye to eye.)

                                          So YOU are the bonehead!
You say you saw me next door? And kissing no less?

DEXTER: In fact, what he said was, "kissing a strange young man."

HAPLUS: By Jove, it's true. I said it.

CONVIVIA: YOU saw ME?

HAPLUS: By Jove, indeed I did! With my very own eyeballs.

CONVIVIA: I do believe you'll be saying "bye-bye" to those eyeballs:
they see much more than there is to see.

HAPLUS: By Jove,
I'll never be scared out of seeing what I saw.

CONVIVIA: How stupid of me. Dear god, I'm a fool to stand here,
chatting away with this silly loon. Why not
just lop off his head?

HAPLUS: You can't threaten me. I know
I'm destined to die on the rack—it's a family tradition.
My father, grandfathers, great-grandfathers, even
not-so-great grandfathers—all of them went that way.[9]
None of your threats can budge my eyeballs an inch.

(He steps away from Convivia and grabs Dexter by the sleeve.)

Psst! Hey Dexter! Can I have a word with you?
Please tell me—where did she come from?

DEXTER: From home. Where else?

---

[9] Because slaves were property, they did not have biological fathers according to Roman law, merely owners. Thus, the irony of a "family tradition."

HAPLUS: From home?

DEXTER:

(He holds up two fingers in front of Haplus's face.)

How many fingers?

HAPLUS: I see you just fine.
It's just too amazing. The way she was able to get
from THERE—

(He turns and points from Hospitalides' house to the Major's house.)

to HERE.
                    No sunporch, no garden, the windows
have bars. I know that for sure.

(He looks back and forth between the houses, shakes his head, then returns to
Convivia.)

                              But I'm sure I saw you
in THERE.

(Dexter steps between Haplus and Convivia.)

DEXTER: Impenitent twit! You persist on denouncing
this woman?

CONVIVIA: Good heavens! This means the dream I dreamt
last night was true!

DEXTER: What dream?

CONVIVIA: The one I'm about
to reveal—but both of you please pay attention.

(She steps between Haplus and Dexter.)

                                    Last night—
in my dream—it seemed that my sister—we're twins, you know,
identical ones—had come with her boyfriend from Athens.
It seemed that our neighbor next door had put the two up
as his houseguests.

DEXTER:

(Aside.)

                HER dream, of course, as scripted by me.

(Aloud.)

But please, I beg you, forge right ahead.

CONVIVIA: I was happy,
it seemed, because she had come;

and yet, because
of *her,* a cloud of suspicion had settled on *me.*
Because one of the family slaves—in my dream—seemed
to charge—like you do now—that I was kissing
a strange young man,
                          when the kisser, in fact, was my sister—
the twin—and the kissee, her very own boyfriend.
                                                    And so
I dreamt I was wrongly accused on groundless grounds.

DEXTER: You're kidding! Whatever seemed to take place in your dreams
is happening now that you're wide awake? FANTASTIC!
Good grief! Your dream has come true!
                                      You must run inside
and appease the gods with prayer!

(He holds her arm as she turns to go.)

                                I think a report
to the Major regarding your dream would be in order.

CONVIVIA: I'll do that, of course. No man who sullies my image
without my permission gets off with impunity!

(She exits into the Major's house.)

HAPLUS: This scares me. Maybe I did something wrong after all.
My rump is getting goosebumps.

DEXTER: You know you're a dead man.

HAPLUS: At least I know she's home. And I know my job
is to guard THIS door, no matter wherever she is.

(He stands spread-eagled in the Major's doorway, facing outward.)

DEXTER: But I ask you, Hapless, that dream she dreamt—like a warning,
almost, it's so similar—
                          even the way you imagined
you saw her kissing!

HAPLUS: I have no idea of what
to believe in now. At this point, I reckon I didn't
see what I thought I saw.

DEXTER: My god, you're regaining
your senses. But too late, I guess. If word of this business
reaches the Major first—the execution
is bound to be exquisite.

HAPLUS:

(He steps down from the doorway and rubs his eyes.)

                                         Yes, I suddenly feel
that my eyes were completely fogged over.

DEXTER: My goodness,
         of course! It's been clear all along that the girl was at home.

HAPLUS: I can't say a thing for sure. I didn't see her—
         even if I did.

DEXTER: We ALL might have died,
         because of your silly behavior. There you were,
         so carried away with playing "the faithful slave"
         they almost carted you off.
                                    Hush! It's the door!

Act II, Scene 5 [411–480]

(Convivia enters from the house of Hospitalides, dressed modestly as her "twin."
Her head veiled, she carries a box of incense to the altar of Diana and pretends to
call to a servant within.)

CONVIVIA: You, boy—
                        be so kind as to kindle a flame on this altar:
         that I, with my bosom brimming with joy, may send up
         some smoke—the Arabian kind, that smells so sweet—
         in thanks to Ephesian Diana.

(She pauses to see whether Haplus has noticed her.)

                                    She saved my life,
         you see, from the turbulent nooks and crannies of Neptune,
         where I was cruelly bruised by the savage waves.

HAPLUS:

(Aside to Dexter.)

         Psst! Dexter! Dexter!

DEXTER:

(Aside to Haplus.)

                        Haplus! Haplus! What is it?

HAPLUS: This woman who just came out—she's Convivia, right?
         The master's girlfriend? Or is she not?

DEXTER: My goodness,
         I think so. She looks like her. But isn't it odd?
         The way she was able to get from HERE
                                    —to THERE—
         if indeed she's *her*—

HAPLUS: You have any doubt she's *her?*

DEXTER: She *looks* like *her.*

HAPLUS:

      (He pulls Dexter toward the altar.)

                    Let's go and greet her.

      (Aloud.)

                                HEY YOU,
CONVIVIA! What's THAT all about?

      (He points to Hospitalides' house.)

                        And what's THAT you're doing
THERE in THAT house? What sort of business is THAT?

      (Convivia fusses with her box of incense without looking up.)

      Well, cat got your tongue? I'm talking to you.

DEXTER:

      (Aside to Haplus.)

                                 Correction:
you're talking to *you,* because *she* has not said a word.

HAPLUS: Well, I'm talking AT YOU, then—you shameless, sinful
creature, cavorting among the neighbors.

CONVIVIA: To *whom*
are you speaking?

HAPLUS: To *whom* but you?

CONVIVIA: And you would be *who?*
And *what* is your business with me?

HAPLUS: Oh ho! You're asking
ME?

CONVIVIA: And why not ask what I do not know?

DEXTER: If you don't know him, then who am I?

CONVIVIA: You are both
a giant pain in the butt. Whoever you are.

HAPLUS: You don't know either one of us?

CONVIVIA: Neither one.

HAPLUS:

(Aside to Dexter, as he pulls him away from the altar.)

I'm afraid, I'm very afraid.

DEXTER:

(Aside to Haplus.)

Afraid? But why?

HAPLUS:

(Aside to Dexter.)

Afraid we're not us anymore. We've lost ourselves
somewhere. She doesn't know you, she doesn't know me.
Well, that's what she said.

DEXTER:

(Aside to Haplus.)

I'd like to follow that line
of logic, Haplus:
are we *we*—
or *not* we?
Could it be that while we weren't looking, somebody—
one of the neighbors, perhaps?—transformed our we-ness?

HAPLUS:

(Aside to Dexter, as he surveys himself.)

I'm very sure I'm we.

DEXTER:

(Aside to Haplus.)

Of course you are.
And the same goes for me.

(Aloud, as he pulls Haplus back to the altar.)

You're looking for trouble, woman!
Convivia! I'm talking to you!

CONVIVIA: Just what is this odd
obsession you have, that compels you to call me peculiar
names? It's quite perverse.

DEXTER: That so? Then what
are you *really* called?

CONVIVIA: Virginia. That's who I am.[10]

HAPLUS: A cheater, Convivia, that's who you are, pretending
               you have some phony name. Virginia? HAH!
               No virgin you. You're cheating on the Major.

CONVIVIA: ME?

HAPLUS: Yes, YOU.

CONVIVIA: But I arrived in Ephesus
               just last night. From Athens. Along with my boyfriend.
               He's still in his teens. An ATHENIAN.

DEXTER: So tell me, what business
               have you in Ephesus?

CONVIVIA: News that my sister is here.
               We're twins. Identical. I came to find her.

HAPLUS: YOU are a liar.

CONVIVIA: No. Just an utter fool,
               dear heaven, for trying to chat with the two of you.
               I'm going.

(She turns to go into the house of Hospitalides, but Haplus seizes her left wrist.)

HAPLUS: I won't let you go.

CONVIVIA: RELEASE ME!

HAPLUS: This hand
               is caught in the cookie jar now! I won't let you go.

CONVIVIA:

(She waves her right fist at Haplus.)

               And THIS hand will give you a great big smack on the nose
               unless you release me.

HAPLUS:

(To Dexter.)

                              Why are you standing there, darnit?
               Grab her other hand!

DEXTER: I'd rather keep
               my behind out of trouble. How should I know if she is
               or isn't Convivia? She could be someone else
               who just looks like Convivia.

---

[10] In the Latin text, she gives her name as the Greek word "Fair" (Dicea), which prompts the
response that she is "Unfair" (*adicea . . . non dicea*) to the Major.

CONVIVIA: Will you, or won't you release me?

HAPLUS: I won't. Unless you go home on your own free will,
               I'll drag you kicking and screaming. By force, if I have to.

CONVIVIA: My home is in Athens, and so is my patron's. We're guests
               in THIS house;

(She indicates Hospitalides' house with her free hand, and nods at that of the Major.)

                              of THAT house, I know and care nothing at all;
               and the same goes for you two.

HAPLUS: So sue me. I'll never let go.
               Unless you cross your heart and promise that if
               I do, you'll go inside—over there.

(He indicates the Major's house with his free hand.)

CONVIVIA: Whoever
               you are, you're twisting my arm.
                                        Oh, I promise I'll go
               inside, wherever you say. That's *if* you let go.

HAPLUS: All right. I'm letting go now.

(He releases her. She rubs her wrist.)

CONVIVIA: And I, now am free—
               to go.

(She dashes into Hospitalides' house.)

HAPLUS: She kept her promise—just like a woman.

DEXTER: You cornered your prey, and then let her slip through your fingers.
               How could she possibly look anymore like the Major's
               girlfriend?
                        Say, you want to show some gumption?

HAPLUS: How's that?

DEXTER: Go fetch me a sword from our house.

HAPLUS: What for?

DEXTER: I'm going to bust down THAT door.

(He indicates Hospitalides' house.)

                                        Whomever I see
               in Convivia's arms, I'll decapitate on the spot.

HAPLUS: She looked like her to you?

DEXTER: Good grief, it's as plain
               as day. Of course it's her.

HAPLUS: But the way she acted—

DEXTER: GO FETCH ME A SWORD!

HAPLUS: I'll have it here in a jiffy.

(He exits into the Major's house.)

DEXTER: From lowly private to lofty major,
                              no soldier
can muster the boldness,
                      the brashness,
                             the self-assured smugness
it takes to be a woman.
                    The perfect poise
with which she plays both parts;
                     the dainty detail
with which she dupes her guard;
                    the joy of watching
her pop back and forth through that wall—
                              it's almost too much.

(Haplus enters empty-handed and dazed from the Major's house.)

HAPLUS: Uh, Dexter. We don't need the sword.

DEXTER: What's that? Why not?

HAPLUS: Go look. The Major's girl is at home.

DEXTER: At home?
How so?

HAPLUS: In bed. Lying down.

DEXTER: O Merciful Heavens!
If what you say is true, you're in serious trouble.

HAPLUS: *Now* what for?

DEXTER: You dared to lay a finger
upon the lady who's staying next door.

HAPLUS: I'm afraid.
I'm afraid even more than ever.

DEXTER: There's no doubt about it:
that girl must be this girl's identical sister.
Good gosh! Then SHE's the one you saw kissing in there.

HAPLUS: Yup, she's the one. It's plain to see, like you said.
But what if I'd actually told the Major? I almost
got myself killed.

DEXTER: If you have any sense at all,
          you'll shut up.
                         "Know more, say less" is the good slave's motto.
          And now,
                    I'd like to remove myself from your presence,
          lest I get tangled up once more in your plans.
          I'll be right here at our next-door neighbor's house.
          This rumpus-rousing of yours is not my idea
          of fun.
                    If the Major returns and happens to ask
          where I am, I'll be in HERE. You know where to find me.

(He exits into the house of Hospitalides.)

Act II, Scene 6 [481–595]

(Haplus paces back and forth, flapping his arms in despair.)

HAPLUS: He walks away just like that?
                                   He couldn't care less
          about doing the Major's bidding. Doesn't he know
          he's a slave?

(He walks up to the Major's door.)

                         At least the girl is at home, and THAT
          I know for sure because I woke her up.
          Well, now to my post: I'll watch this door like a hawk.

(He spreads himself in the doorway, facing inward. Hospitalides emerges from his house.)

HOSPIT.:   HELL AND DOUBLE HELL! A DIRECT ASSAULT
          ON MY MANHOOD!
                              They're toying with me! The Major's boys
          must think I'm a maid instead of a man!
                                   My poor houseguest!
          She's hardly had time to breathe since she landed here
          last night from Athens
                              —along with her boyfriend, also
          my houseguest—
                              and now, this decent, freeborn lady
          finds herself mocked, even manhandled!

(He notices Haplus in the Major's doorway.)

HAPLUS:

          (Aside.)

                                   Mercy! I'm trapped!
          He's looking directly in this direction. From what
          I heard him just say, I'm afraid that things are not good.

HOSPIT.:   AH! I'll confront him.

    (He approaches Haplus.)

                    You there, Haplus! You worthless
worm brain! Did you just hassle my guest right here in front
of my house?

HAPLUS: I beg you, dear neighbor, sir, please listen—

HOSPIT.:   *I* SHOULD LISTEN TO *YOU?*

HAPLUS: I have an excuse.

HOSPIT.:   AN EXCUSE? How can there possibly be an excuse
for this level of shocking behavior? Just because
you people plunder and loot for a living, you think
you can do as you like? You should be flogged!

HAPLUS: But please—

HOSPIT.:   Yes, indeed! May the grace of heaven no longer
fall on my head if I don't take a switch to your fanny.
Long and hard. From dawn to dusk. And why?
Let's count the reasons:
                    One. You shattered the tiles
on my roof while chasing your mate, that stupid monkey.
Two. You peeked in my house while my guest was engaged
in hugging and kissing his sweetheart—HIS girl, mind you.
Three. You had the gall to charge the Major's
girlfriend—chastity herself—with indecent
behavior, and me with moral turpitude.
And four. You harried my houseguest in front of my door.
Unless I get to take a strap to your keister,
I'll swamp your boss with counts of misconduct enough
to outnumber the ocean's waves in the foulest of weather!

HAPLUS:

    (He abandons his position and descends the stairs to face Hospitalides.)

           I have to say, Hospitalides, sir, that it's fairer
for *me* to demand an apology from *you*—
but if *she*—

    (He points to Hospitalides' house.)

          isn't *her*—
             and *she*—

    (He points to the Major's house.)

                   isn't *her*—
                   then it's fairer

for *you* to demand a confession from *me.*
                                                That is,
I mean, that now I'm not sure what I saw, you see,
because the *she* in your house looks a lot like the *her*
in ours—that is, if indeedy, she isn't the same.

HOSPIT.:   Go in and see for yourself.

HAPLUS: May I?

HOSPIT.:   No,
I insist. And take your time.

HAPLUS: I certainly will.

(He exits into the house of Hospitalides, while Hospitalides ascends the Major's steps.)

HOSPIT.:

(To Convivia within.)

Psst! Convivia! Trouble ahead! Retreat
on the double! As soon as Haplus walks out the door,
you double back here as fast as you can.

(Aloud.)

                                            Oh god,
I'm scared to death she might muddle things up now. What
if he doesn't see her?
                          Ah! There goes the door!

HAPLUS:

(He enters from the house of Hospitalides and kneels at the altar of Diana.)

BY HOLY OLYMPUS!
                          A likeness more alike—
a sameness more the same—although she's not—
I didn't believe the immortal gods could do it!

HOSPIT.:   What now?

HAPLUS: I deserve to be punished.

HOSPIT.:   Why's that? She's there?

HAPLUS: If she is, she isn't her.

HOSPIT.:   You mean you saw—

(He points to the Major's house.)

                                        HER?

HAPLUS: I saw her hugging and smooching away with your guest.

HOSPIT.:   You mean—

(He points to his own house.)

SHE?

HAPLUS: I don't know.

HOSPIT.:   You want to know for sure?

HAPLUS: I'd love to.

HOSPIT.:   Then hurry home and look! Go see
if she's there—*your* she, that is.

HAPLUS: I certainly will.
That's nice advice. I'll be back with you both in a moment.

(He exits into the Major's house.)

HOSPIT.:   Gracious me! I've never seen a more charming
patsy! The number of ways to outwit him—why,
it boggles the mind.
                  But here he comes.

(Haplus enters from the Major's house, falls to his knees, and clutches Hospitalides.)

HAPLUS: Hospitalides,
sir, I beg you!
              In the name of mankind!
                        And the gods!
And my thick old skull!
                  I beg in the name of your knees—

HOSPIT.:   Why are you groveling?

HAPLUS: Forgive me my thoughtless and brainless
behavior. At last I see what a stupid lunkhead
I was. Convivia—lo and behold!—is at home.

HOSPIT.:   So what are you saying, you inexcusable lout?
You saw them both?

HAPLUS: I did.

HOSPIT.:   I want you to summon
the Major.

HAPLUS: I confess that torture's too good for me, sir.
And I do agree I insulted your guest. But I thought
that she was Convivia, the girl I was ordered to guard
—by the Major himself. Why, two drops of water drawn

from the very same well couldn't look more alike than her
and your guest!

                    Oh, I also admit I peeked in your patio.

HOSPIT.:   Big confession: THAT much I saw for myself.
And in there you spied my two guests kissing?

HAPLUS: I did.
Why deny what I saw? But I thought I saw Convivia.

HOSPIT.:   So THAT'S the piddling amount you reckon I'm worth
as a human being?
                    You think I'd let my neighbor
suffer a slap in the face like that? Right here
in my very own home?

HAPLUS: Well, now that I know the story,
I think I did something stupid. But not on purpose.

HOSPIT.:   But shameful nonetheless.
                        The good slave keeps
his eyes and hands on a leash, along with his tongue.

HAPLUS: If ever I mumble a word from this day forward—
even something I know for a fact—I'm yours
to punish. I'll personally hand myself over.
                             But this time,
please forgive me.

HOSPIT.:   I'll try to convince myself
you meant no harm. This once I forgive you.

HAPLUS: May all
the gods bless you, sir.

HOSPIT.:   If the gods give a fig for you,
you'll keep your lips sealed, by Jove. From here on out
you'll never know what you know or see what you see.

HAPLUS: That's good advice. Exactly what I'll do.
Have I begged enough for you, sir?

HOSPIT.:   Go on, get out.

HAPLUS:

   (He turns away, then pauses.)

     Anything else you'd like?

HOSPIT.:   Yes. Leave me alone.

   (He retreats to his porch, while Haplus walks to the Major's porch.)

HAPLUS:

(Aside.)

It's just a bunch of pretty words, all this niceness
without getting angry.
           I know he's up to something:
as soon as the Major gets back from downtown, I'll be snared.
The old man and Dexter, I bet they're planning to sell me
down the river. I knew it. The trap is baited—
but HAH! Today this fish won't bite,
                      because *I* am
swimming to safety.
           I'll find a hole for a day
or two, 'til the storm dies down and tempers cool off.
I've been struck with more bad luck than a village of heathens.
Come what may, there's no place to hide like home.

(He exits into the Major's house, while Hospitalides descends from his porch.)

HOSPIT.:   The foe has fled the field. I swear to god
I've known pork chops more quick on the uptake.
                       We've repossessed
what's been seen, so now he has no longer seen it. I think
his eyes and ears have in fact deserted to our side.
So far the action's gone smoothly:
                  the girl was superb
in executing her task. With Dexter at my house,
and Haplus back home, we can now convene our council
of war with all members present. I'd better go in,
in case they start to divide and conquer without me.

(He exits into his house.)

Act III, Scene 1 [596–812]

(Dexter enters from the house of Hospitalides, still addressing Nautikles and
Hospitalides within.)

DEXTER: Nautikles!
           You two hang back for a while inside.
Before we hold our top secret session, I must
survey our camp and search for signs of sabotage.
First rule of war:
           secure a tight perimeter.
Don't let your enemy cart your ideas off like booty.
When plans fall into the enemy's clutches, best laid
is worse than unmade. They'll use them against you, believe me.
As soon as the foe gets wise to your scheme, you've had it.
You're bound hand and foot, and they'll do unto you whatever

it was you wanted to do unto them. Yes, spare
an ounce of discretion, and victory's snatched from your jaws.
I'll cover the area left and right, in case
some hound is snooping around with his ears unfurled.

(He looks both ways.)

The place looks deserted down to the end of the street.
I'll give the all clear.
                              Hey! Hospitalides! Nautikles!
OUTSIDE MARCH!

(Hospitalides and Nautikles exit from Hospitalides' house, and line up.)

NAUTIKLES: All here! We await your orders.

DEXTER: Command comes easy with first-rate troops. But I need
your response: do we forge ahead with the plan we drew up
inside?

HOSPIT.:   We couldn't do any better.

DEXTER:

(To Nautikles, as he frowns at Hospitalides.)

                              Not you.
Nautikles, what do YOU think? Yay, or nay?

NAUTIKLES: ME disapprove of something that's met your approval?
When YOU more than anyone else hold my interests at heart?

DEXTER: Ah, neatly put. And nicely, too.

HOSPIT.:   By god,
that's just the sort of thing you'd expect from this boy.

NAUTIKLES:

(To Hospitalides.)

But something about this plan is gnawing away
at my heart and soul.

HOSPIT.:   It is? What's eating you, then?
Come now, my boy.

NAUTIKLES: Well, here I am, imposing
my troubled romance upon a man of your age,
a thing improper for you as you wind down your life.
I'm sapping your waning vigor all for my own selfish
sake, enlisting your help in the name of love

with demands that would make most elderly folk hobble off
in the other direction.
                              I've burdened your golden years.
I'm ashamed of myself.

DEXTER: A boy in love feel shame?
What kind of weirdo passion is that? You call
yourself a lover? HAH! You're not even a wisp
of a lover.

NAUTIKLES: But bother a man his age with my heartache?

HOSPIT.:   Just WHAT do you mean?
                              You think it's high time I was shuffling
off to Hades? That it's time to turn in my toga?
Shop for a shroud? Do I look like such an antique?
Dear god, I'm hardly FIFTY-FOUR! My vision
is flawless; I'm fleet of foot, and nimble of finger.

DEXTER: Silver crested, but nothing crusty about him.
Innate disposition still even.

NAUTIKLES: Oh. I agree!
By golly, it's just like you told me, Dexter: the heart
and mind of a man even half his age.

HOSPIT.:   Or less.
Just test me, my boy. The more you do, the more
you'll see what an asset I am in the sphere of romance.

NAUTIKLES: But why? I know that already.

HOSPIT.:

(He takes Nautikles by the arm, and they stroll between the altars, while Dexter tries
to keep up.)

                              Learn from an expert,
by firsthand example. Don't pick up things in the street!
A man can but poorly fathom the soul of a lover—
unless he's known love himself.
                              There's plenty of use
—as well as juice—still left in this body of mine.
I'm not so shriveled and dry that I can't have some fun.
As dinner guests go, I play the sparkling wit
or sensitive listener with equal aplomb; I never
contradict my host; I always remember
to bypass boorish behavior; I hold up my share
of the conversation, and shut up when others are talking.
I never spit or drool;

I don't hack up phlegm;
and I don't blow my nose in my napkin.
                                        After all,
I'm a full-blood Ephesian, not some mule from Apulia.[11]

DEXTER:

(As he squeezes between Nautikles and Hospitalides.)

You lovely . . . um . . . middle-aged man! From the charms you list,
you were obviously nursed at the very bosom of Venus.

HOSPIT.:

(As he brushes Dexter aside and continues to stroll with Nautikles.)

My charms are even more venerable seen than heard:
I don't fondle or paw another man's girl at a party;
I don't horde the hors d'oeuvres or beat a path to the punch bowl.
Wine never makes me surly in social settings.
Some wise mouth shoots off? I go home—end of discussion.
At table I wield the charm and cheer of a goddess.

DEXTER:

(As he squeezes between Hospitalides and Nautikles.)

You're a garden of elegance mulched by the Graces. Show me
three men of such mettle—I'll pay their weight in gold!

NAUTIKLES: But you won't find another man that old who's nicer
in every way. Or a better friend to his friends.

HOSPIT.:

(As he brushes Dexter aside again and continues to stroll with Nautikles.)

I'll ply you every which way with so many favors,
you'll have to admit I'm really a child at heart.
Need legal help? The voice of indignant outrage?
Ta-dah! I'm your man.
                                Or someone to smooth things over?
You'll swear I'm more soothing still than the silent sea,
more placidly flaccid than any fair-weather zephyr.
You need some life for your party? The consummate sidekick?
The king of the catered buffet?
                                All here in one package.
What's more, the lithest show boy can't match my fandango.

---

[11] In the Latin original, Plautus has his character state that he is not from the small town of "Animula" in Apulia. "Animula" may have been a notorious cultural backwater, as well as a pun on *animal,* a beast or brute.

DEXTER:

> (To Nautikles, as he pulls him away.)

> Such talent! What more could you choose
> > —if given a choice?

NAUTIKLES:

> (To Dexter, as Hospitalides pulls him away from the same.)

> To give this man the amount of thanks he deserves.
> And the same goes for you.

> (To Hospitalides.)

> > As for me, I've been such a nuisance!
> I'm very upset that you've gone to so much expense.

HOSPIT.:

> (As he resumes strolling with Nautikles, with Dexter following.)

> That's foolish.
> > Income is only outgo when spent
> on nagging wives and foes; but money spent
> on guests and good friends is bound to pay back with interest;
> *and*
> > —as wise investors know—
> > > what's spent
> on the Holy Portfolio yields the highest return.
> By the grace of god, I can put you up in comfort.
> So eat! And drink! Indulge yourself with me,
> and pile up some cheer. My house is fraught with freedom,
> and so am I. My life is mine to live.
> By the grace of god, I've amassed enough wealth to acquire
> a wife—the highbrow type, complete with dowry—
> but why invite all that yapping and yowling in?

DEXTER:

> (He pulls Hospitalides away from Nautikles and tries to lead him home.)

> But why don't you want to? It's nice to be a father.

HOSPIT.:

> (As he pushes Dexter away.)

> Ho! But nicer still to be unfettered.

DEXTER:　　So wise! You advise unto others as unto yourself.

HOSPIT.:

> (As he takes Nautikles and resumes strolling.)

> My boy, it's a pleasure to have a good wife—assuming

one lives on the face of the earth.
                              But bring home a woman
whose lips will never beg me,
                              "Buy some wool,
my dear husband. I want to make you a warm, fuzzy robe
and winter tunics to keep you from catching a chill
this season."—
                    you think you'd hear that from a married woman?
Hah!
        Before the cock had a chance to crow,
she'd poke me awake saying,
                              "Gimme, ol' hubby wubby,
to buy a present for Mommsy on Mothers' Day";
then, "Gimme, to make some jam";
                              and "Gimme, to tip
the girls at Minerva's Annual Hoodoo Convention:
the gal who casts spells, the gal who reads dreams, the gal
who reads palms, the gal who reads livers—oh yes! And what
a shame it would be to leave out the gal who reads eyebrows."[12]
Then, "We must give a generous gift to the lady
who folds the laundry;
                              the pantry maid is put out
because she got no tip;
                              the midwife is all
in a snit—she says she's been grossly shortchanged;"
                                          "what's that?
No bonus this year for the nanny who raised the family
slaves?"
        Yes, fear of bankruptcy keeps me single.
Women know many roads to ruin: a wife
would sow my ears with similar seeds of disaster.

DEXTER:

(To Hospitalides, as he pulls Nautikles away once again.)

        The gods have truly blessed you. Once you let go
of that freedom, it's no easy job to get back where you started.

NAUTIKLES:

(To Dexter, as Dexter pulls him to center stage.)

        But having kids is a virtue, isn't it?
I mean, for a terribly wealthy upper-class man.
It's a tribute to him as well as the family name.

---

[12] The Romans believed in many forms of fortune-telling, in addition to reading palms and interpreting dreams. *Haruspicium* was the Etruscan form of divination from inner organs. "Eyebrow-reading," however, may be a joke.

HOSPIT.:

(As he brushes Dexter aside, repossessing Nautikles.)

> With so many relatives, why in the world have children?
> Right now I live well, I'm happy, I do what I please.
> When I die, I'll distribute my physical wealth to my kinfolk.
> They'll swarm my house and coddle me, paying
> attention to all that I want and do. Before dawn
> they're over here asking "How did you sleep last night?"
> Instead of kids, I'll have nephews who send me surprises!
> When roasting a holiday pig, they invite me to feast—
> and always make sure my plate is piled higher than theirs.
> For lunch and dinner, it's "Come on over!" Whoever
> sends me the smallest gift is smitten with grief.
> One nephew rivals the other;
>   they ply me with presents;
> I say to myself, "They're hungering after my earthly
> goods, yet fighting to see who gets to feed me."

DEXTER:

(As he steps between the two and tries to pull them both toward Hospitalides' house.)

> Your view of life is exceedingly keen and logical.
> Play things just right, and you've got yourself twins—even triplets!

HOSPIT.:

(As he brushes Dexter aside once more and resumes strolling with Nautikles.)

> My god, with sons of my own, I'd only be getting
> a big pile of trouble. Kids are a nonstop heartache.
> If one came down with a fever, I'd think he was dying.
> What if he fell down drunk or slid off a horse?
> I'd worry he'd broken both legs or even his neck.

NAUTIKLES:

(To Dexter, as he stops at center stage and stands back to admire Hospitalides.)

> This man deserves to be rich and live long. He saves
> his money, does things right, and helps out his pals.

DEXTER:

(As he seizes Hospitalides by the arm and begins to stroll between the altars.)

> Indeed, such an awfully nice man! So help me heaven,
> if only the gods had seen fit to set up some standards—
> that way we wouldn't all live out the end of our lives.
> You see, in the market, an honest inspector prices

the goods. If the goods are good, he raises the price
so they sell according to worth; if the goods are not good,
their worthlessness dictates the vendor's capital loss.

(He steers Hospitalides toward his porch.)

The gods should have likewise doled out the human life span.
He who's inherently nice? The gods should grant him
a long and lengthy life. But he who's immoral
and selfish should have his soul repossessed on the spot.
If the gods had seen fit, then naughty men would be fewer
and far less daring in doing their nasty deeds.
And then, for the men who are upright, the market price
of corn and wheat would drop by a hefty percentage.

HOSPIT.:   He who nitpicks the master plans of the gods
and impugns the immortals themselves—is an ignorant ass.

(He pushes Dexter aside and returns to join Nautikles at center stage.)

But enough of this blather already.
                                        I want to go shopping.
I intend to entertain you at home, my dear guest,
in a manner suiting two gentlemen such as ourselves;
which is to say, we'll have a nice little dinner,
with all the niceties for that extra touch.

(He turns to leave stage left.)

NAUTIKLES:

(To Hospitalides, as he holds on to his sleeve; Dexter throws his hands up in
disgust.)

I feel I've put you through plenty of trouble already.
No guest can impose on a welcome like this for more
than three days and not turn into a pest; but ten
whole days in a row? It's like hosting the Trojan War.
And though the host might not mind, the servants will grumble.

HOSPIT.:

(To Nautikles, as he places his arm around him.)

My servants maintain severely high standards of service.
The rule is: they don't give orders; I don't take them.
They find it a bore to suit my pleasure? They'll do it
as long as I'm at the helm. No matter how loathesomely
painful they find it, they'll do it. Like it or not.
And now, like I said, to shop.

(He heads stage left.)

NAUTIKLES: Okay—if your mind
              is made up. But buy just a little, and don't spend too much.
              I'll be fine with whatever you get.

HOSPIT.:

              (He returns to center stage.)

                                          Oh, ditch that tired
              old line. You sound, my dear guest, like a common dullard.
              You know, the type who says when dinner is served,
              "You went to all this expense for little old me?
              My god, you're insane! There's more than enough for ten!"
              He bitches he's too well catered, then eats every bite.

DEXTER:

              (As he attempts to nudge Hospitalides offstage.)

              Good grief! That's exactly what happens. You're so perceptive!

HOSPIT.:

              (As he forces his way back to center stage.)

              However high you heap the buffet, you don't hear:
              "Have *that* thing taken away; Remove this platter;
              Get rid of the ham, who needs it? Return that pork loin;
              This eel should go in cold storage—remove it, return it,
              take it away!"
                            No such emphatic assertions.
              Rather, they pitch themselves forward, hoisting their midriffs
              halfway across the table, and assault the pâté.

DEXTER:

              (As he nudges Hospitalides away again.)

              Exceedingly ugly manners. A lovely description.

HOSPIT.:

              (As he fights back yet again to center stage.)

              A fraction of what I could tell you, had we the time.

DEXTER: **BUT WE DON'T!**
                                          So why don't we first pay attention to what's
              going on right here.
                            Now both of you listen up.
              Hospitalides, sir, your assistance is of the essence.
              I've thought of a nice little ruse whereby we can fleece
              our wool-headed Major, thereby giving this lover
              the chance to kidnap his girlfriend and carry her off.

HOSPIT.:   I'd like that plan.

DEXTER:

    (To Hospitalides, as he points to one of Hospitalides' fingers.)

                And I'd like that ring.

HOSPIT.:   What for?

DEXTER: As soon as I have it, I'll give you the plan.

HOSPIT.:

    (He hands over the ring.)

                           Here, take it.

DEXTER: And now, the two of you kindly embrace the plan
             I've devised.

HOSPIT.:   Our ears are yours and as clean as a whistle.

DEXTER: The Major—my boss—is a lecher of epic proportion.
             No man has ever out-leched him—nor, do I
             believe, ever will.

HOSPIT.:   I strongly share that belief.

DEXTER: He's mentioned he's much better looking than Paris—you know,
             the stud that legends are made of. Thus, he claims
             the Ephesian wives have made unsolicited passes.

HOSPIT.:   And many Ephesian husbands wish that were so.
             But I'm well aware of all that you've said. If possible,
             Dexter, try and skip to the bottom line.

DEXTER: Can you locate a nicely shaped woman? Cunning of mind,
             clever of heart?

HOSPIT.:   Born a lady, or recently freed?

DEXTER: It doesn't matter, as long as you get me a girl skilled
             at commerce. One who uses her body to meet
             her bodily needs.
                     But make that a clever bosom:
           she can't have a clever heart. They never have hearts.

HOSPIT.:   An unscrubbed recruit? Or someone who's been through the wash?

DEXTER: Just juicy. Impossibly pretty and *very* young.

HOSPIT.:   I have a protégée. She's young, she's employed—
             but what do you need her for?

DEXTER: For you to bring home.
           You get her all decked out like a married lady—

hair piled up, the standard topknot with ribbons—
and have her pretend she's your wife. You'll have to coach her.

HOSPIT.: I don't see where this is going.

DEXTER: You'll see in a moment.
And does this girl have a maid?

HOSPIT.:   A very shrewd one.

DEXTER: We'll need her too. Now, rehearse with the girl and her maid
the following story.
      The GIRL pretends she's your WIFE,
but also pretends SHE'S MADLY IN LOVE with THE MAJOR.
SHE gives this ring to HER—that is, HER MAID—
who gives it to ME, so I can give it to HIM,
as if I were their GO-BETWEEN.

HOSPIT.:   I hear you.
My ears work fine. Don't hammer away 'til I'm deaf.

DEXTER: So I give the ring to the Major. I say it was sent
by your wife, then given to me, so I could—"unite"
the two.
      He's just the type to take the bait:
he's pitifully hot to trot. The hard-up lug
can't focus on anything else but chasing skirts.

HOSPIT.: The sun could scour the earth and find no nicer
girls for the job than these. You may rest assured.

DEXTER: Then get them. And hurry.

  (Hospitalides exits stage left.)

         Nautikles, pay attention.

NAUTIKLES: I'm at your service.

DEXTER: Get this: when the Major comes home,
remember not to use Convivia's name.

NAUTIKLES: So what do I call her instead?

DEXTER: You call her—"Virginia."

NAUTIKLES: Right. That's the name we just gave her a while ago.

DEXTER: That's enough! Get going.

NAUTIKLES: I won't forget. But still,
I'd like to ask what the point is in not forgetting?

DEXTER: I'll let you know when the need arises. Meanwhile,
shut up, so the old boy can do his job. You'll get
to play your part soon enough.

NAUTIKLES: In that case, I'll go
            inside.

DEXTER: Be sure to follow instructions. Don't panic.

    (Nautikles exits into the house of Hospitalides.)

Act III, Scene 2 [813–873]

    (Dexter struts back and forth at center stage.)

DEXTER: Such a marvelous ruckus I'm raising! March on, my machines
              of war! Today's the day I snatch the Major's
              mistress—
                           assuming my troops can fall into proper
              formation.
                        But now to check on *him*.

    (He approaches the Major's house and knocks on the door.)

                                                  Hey, Haplus!
              Come out, if you're not too busy. It's me. You know, Dexter.

    (Lurch enters from the Major's house, tottering, and sits down on the steps.)

LURCH: Haplus is not . . . available.

DEXTER:

    (As he descends the stairs.)

                                              What's he doing?

LURCH: He's sleeping. Having himself a little snort.

DEXTER: And what do you mean by "a little snort"?

LURCH: What I mean
              by that, is, uh, "having a little snore." You know, snoring,
              snorting—it's pretty much the same sort of thing.

DEXTER: Aha! So Haplus is in there, down for the count?

LURCH: His nose excluded. That much is up and roaring.

DEXTER: He snuck a cup from the Major's private reserve?

LURCH: As maître d', he had to decant the vintage.[13]
              Needed a hint of fennel for better bouquet.

DEXTER: Aha! And YOU, as assistant butler, you rat—

LURCH: —So what's the matter?

---

[13] The *cellarius* oversaw the storage room where the wine was kept. The Romans flavored their
wines with herbs. "Fennel" has been substituted for the more obscure "nard."

DEXTER: Indulging himself in sleep!

(He strides to center stage and paces.)

Oh, how could he do it?

LURCH: I think he just closed his eyes.

DEXTER: That's not what I asked, you smart-ass. Get over here.
Your life isn't worth a lead pot if I don't get the truth.

(Lurch totters over to Dexter.)

Did YOU unseal the wine?

LURCH: UNSEAL? I did not.

DEXTER: You deny it, then?

LURCH: Upon my solemn oath.
He's forbidden me to confess. I did not pour
or mull it in any carafe. And he did not sip it
warm for lunch.

DEXTER: And you yourself had no sip?

LURCH: May lightning strike if I took a sip—or could have.

DEXTER: Why's that?

LURCH: It was way too spicy. Scorched my throat
when I choked it down.

DEXTER: So, the two of you get soused,
while the rest of us vie to chug down vinegar water![14]
Gallant butlers, indeed, protecting our storeroom!

LURCH: Heck, you'd do the very same if you had this job.
And now you're just jealous because you can't do likewise.

DEXTER: Aha! So he's tapped the supply before this, has he?
Answer, you swine. And just so you know, if you lie,
dear Lurch, I'll have you skewered.

LURCH: Is that a fact?
So you can blab every word I've said? So you
can get yourself another assistant butler
when YOU distribute the goodies, after I'm stripped
of my feedbag and chucked from the storeroom?

DEXTER: I promise I won't.
Now show some spunk and tell me.

---

[14] *Posca* was a humble mixture of vinegar and water, imbibed by slaves and other have-nots.

LURCH: I swear, I never
          saw him unstop a jug. That's a fact. I didn't
          unseal the lids until after he gave me the order.

DEXTER: That's why those jugs keep tumbling onto their heads.

LURCH: No, that's NOT why they tumble over. I swear
          by the gods. There's this little bit of a slippery place
          in the storeroom, next to those jugs, where the dregs gets stewed
          in a two-gallon kettle. I've seen that pot filled and emptied,
          oh, maybe ten times. When it works itself to a frenzied
          boil, the jugs can't help but do the shimmy.[15]

DEXTER: Go on! Inside! A shrine for orgies, THAT's
          what you've made of our storeroom. By god, I'm going downtown
          to fetch the Major at once.

          (He turns to leave stage left.)

LURCH:

          (Aside to the audience.)

                                        My tail is toast.
          The Major will order some very distasteful torture
          as soon as he gets here and finds out I didn't report
          what was going on.
                                        To the hills! I'll stuff myself
          in a hideout somewhere, and leave that hideous fate
          for another day.
                                        I beg you, don't snitch on me, please.

          (He turns to sneak off stage right. Dexter tiptoes up behind him.)

DEXTER: And what are you doing?

LURCH: I'm off on a mission. To somewhere.
          But I'll be home soon.

DEXTER: Who sent you?

LURCH: Uh, Convivia did.

DEXTER: Go on. And hurry back.

LURCH: While I'm gone, would you do me
          a favor, please? If the Major decides to dole out
          some lashes,
                              feel free to help yourself to my share.

          (He exits stage right. Dexter retires to Hospitalides' porch and sits down on the
          steps.)

---

[15] The Romans habitually boiled the lees (grape skins and pits) to produce another weak
beverage for the household workers.

DEXTER: Ah, now I see what Convivia's doing. With Haplus
             asleep, she's sending this subslave of his on some goose chase.
             That way she's able to sneak from here to there.
             I like it.
                        But here's Hospitalides now, and leading
             the sweet young thing I requested.

(Hospitalides enters stage left, followed by Climax, who is dressed as a matron. She
in turn is followed by Milly. They pause at center stage, where Climax twirls around
to show off her garb to Hospitalides.)

                                    She's nice to look at.
             Outstandingly nice. The gods have given our plan
             their stamp of approval. She looks so darn—well, proper.
             Such grace in that walk: you could hardly tell she's a pro.
             In my expert hands, this project is shaping up nicely.

Act III, Scene 3 [874–946]

(Hospitalides clears his throat and salutes. Climax stops twirling. She and Milly
stand at attention and return the salute.)

HOSPIT.:

(To Climax and Milly.)

             I've briefed you both on our plans for battle, Climax.
             You and Milly heard all from start to finish,
             before we left your house. If you have any doubts
             regarding the general fabric or finer threads
             of this fraud, start over again and get it down pat.
             If it's perfectly clear, then on to a subsequent subject.

CLIMAX: Dear sir, I'd be a fool and a dope to commit
             to a job and promise my help if I had no grasp
             of the tissue of lies required to bring home the bacon.

HOSPIT.:   I thought I'd better remind you.

CLIMAX: A prostitute never
             forgets—most everyone knows that. Besides, as soon as
             my ears drank in your opening line, I suggested
             a way we could cut our Major down to size.

HOSPIT.:   But one head is never enough. There's many a man
             who's fled the field of good counsel before he set foot there.

CLIMAX: If something spiteful and nasty is on a woman's
             agenda, her long-term memory always stays fresh
             and unfaded. But gestures of goodness and kindness induce
             almost instant amnesia—"Gee, I just can't remember!"

HOSPIT.:   I'm afraid of exactly that, since you'll have the chance
                to do both: what's harm to the Major, is help to me.

CLIMAX: As long as we're not aware we're doing good,
                don't sweat it.

HOSPIT.:   You deserve a thousand spankings!

(He gives her a playful pat on the rear.)

CLIMAX: Oh, stop!

(She gives him a pat on the cheek.)

                And don't worry: the whips come out when we're REALLY
                naughty.

HOSPIT.:   That's it—keep up those standards. And march right behind me.

DEXTER:

(Aside, as he rises.)

                What am I waiting for? I'd best go greet them.

(Aloud, as he approaches Hospitalides.)

                I'm delighted to see you're already back safe and sound—

(He steps between Hospitalides and Climax.)

                And good gracious! So nicely decked out!

HOSPIT.:   What lucky timing,
                Dexter. Observe—the girls you requisitioned.
                Equipped as ordered.

DEXTER: Well done, sir. You're one of us.

(He bows and offers his hand to Climax.)

                I, Dexter, salute you, Climax.

CLIMAX: And who is this man,
                if you please, who thinks he's on a first-name basis?

HOSPIT.:   This is our chief engineer.

(Climax extends her hand to be kissed.)

CLIMAX: Hello, Engineer.

DEXTER:

(He kisses her hand and then holds on to it.)

                Hello, to you too. So tell me, have you both
                been saddled with ample instructions?

Hospit.:   They're thoroughly drilled.

Dexter: I want it exactly.

(To Hospitalides.)

I worry you muddle things up.

Hospit.:

(Grossly offended.)

I conveyed your orders with nary a word of my own.

Climax:

(She frees her hand from Dexter and pats Hospitalides' cheek again.)

Of course.

(To Dexter.)

You want the Major bamboozled, correct?

Dexter: You said it.

Climax: The plan's all set: it's neat, it's smart,
it's tailored, it's sassy.

Dexter:

(He takes Climax's hand again.)

I want you playing the part
of his wife—

Climax: Done it.

Dexter: —as if you're madly in love
with the Major—

Climax: So it shall be.

Dexter: —with your maid and myself
conducting the romance as go-betweens—

Climax: You know things
before they happen—you could have had a future
in prophecy.

Dexter: —acting as if you told your maid
to give me this ring to give to the Major as pledge
of your passion.

Climax: Truer words have never been spoken.

HOSPIT.:

(Taking Climax's hand away from Dexter.)

        Why do you keep rehashing what's already hashed?

CLIMAX: It's more efficient. Think of it, sir, like a ship.
An engineer—if he's good—will lay his keel straight
from the start. As soon as he has it shored and plumbed,
the rest of the ship is a snap.
                        Our keel is set
to perfection and squarely shimmed. No lack of experienced
foremen and boatwrights; as long as our lumber supplier
delivers and doesn't throw us off schedule, I'm sure
with our multiple talents we'll have this ship sailing in no time.

DEXTER:

(Taking Climax's hand again.)

        You do know the Major, of course.

CLIMAX: I'm amazed that you ask!
That overinflated, overcoiffured, over-
perfumed, oversexed threat to the public at large?
Pray, how could I not?

DEXTER: But does he know you?

CLIMAX: The man's never
seen me, so how could he know me?

DEXTER: So nice the way
you chitchat. With YOU things will turn out nicer still.

CLIMAX:

(As she repossesses her hand.)

        Then can't you just leave the Major to me and relax
about everything else? If I don't make a "nice" enough stooge
of the man, you can blame the whole thing on me.

DEXTER: Proceed.
The two of you go inside and get ready for action.
Use all the smarts you can muster.

CLIMAX: Not to worry.

DEXTER:

(As he takes a step back and gestures to Hospitalides.)

        Come, Hospitalides. Take these ladies inside.

(He speaks very slowly, grabbing Hospitalides aside as he attempts to steer the ladies into Hospitalides' house.)

I'm going DOWNTOWN to find the MAJOR and give him
this RING. I'll say it was given to me by your WIFE,
and tell him she's DYING to MEET HIM. As soon as we're BACK
from DOWNTOWN, send over the MAID. And make it look like
she's COME ON THE SLY to the MAJOR.

HOSPIT.:

(Releasing himself from Dexter's grasp.)

Will do. Don't worry.

DEXTER: While you see to that, I'll fatten him up for the kill.

(He exits stage left.)

HOSPIT.:   You have a good walk! And good luck!

(To Climax.)

If I pull off this stunt
and my guest runs away with the Major's girlfriend to Athens—
that is, if we manage to swing this bait and switch,
I'll give you a present so big—

CLIMAX: Is the girl in on this?

HOSPIT.:   She's playing her part very nicely. And tastefully, too.

CLIMAX: In that case, I'm sure things will turn out just fine in the end.
Once we combine our wicked little minds,
I'm afraid we're invincible. No one can match the lot
of us, scam for sham, or flim for flam.

HOSPIT.:   In that case,
let's go inside. We need to review our plans
with absolute care. Our job is precise execution,
with utter exactness. Once the Major arrives,
we don't want to trip.

CLIMAX: Well, you're the one holding us up.

(Hospitalides leads the two women into his house.)

Act IV, Scene 1 [947–990]

(Dexter and the Major enter stage left.)

MAJOR: What a pleasure it is when things go so nicely—as well as
on schedule. Today I sent Ingestio—you know,
my top subordinate—off to King Seleucus.
He's taking a shipment of freshly recruited hacks.
While THEY guard his kingdom, *I* get a little vacation.

DEXTER: Enough royal business, sir; you must tend to your own.
            A new proposition arrived—and she's highly attractive.

MAJOR: Indeed? Let other affairs fall back!
                                          Speak freely.
            You have my attention. My ears are at your service.

DEXTER: Secure the area. We don't want some little birdie
            listening in on our conversation. I'm instructed
            to keep this deal hush-hush.

MAJOR:

     (As he looks around.)

                                     There's no one here.

DEXTER: Begin by accepting this ring—

     (He hands over the ring.)

                                     —the earnest money
            of passion.

MAJOR: What's this? Who sent it?

DEXTER: A female. Frisky,
            attractive, in love. And hot to have that bodacious
            body of yours. She just sent her maid with this ring,
            with orders for me to give it to you at once.

MAJOR: So tell me about her. A lady? Or just an ex-slave,
            merely freed by the wave of a wand?[16]

DEXTER: As if
            I would dare set you up with a former servant! You,
            without even the time to sate the upper crust's lust?

MAJOR: Ah, married, she is? Or manless?

DEXTER: Married. Yet manless.

MAJOR: How can she be both?

DEXTER: A tender bride
            who's hitched to a geezer.

MAJOR: Delicious!

DEXTER: Nicely brought up
            and filled out.

---

[16] In manumission, the slave was freed by a ritual touch with a rod.

MAJOR: You'd better be sure you're not pulling my leg.

DEXTER: No other woman can rival your beauty.

MAJOR: That stunning,
you say? Good god, who is this girl?

DEXTER: The wife
of old Hospitalides: he who lives right next door.
But it's you she burns for; she hates the old guy and is itching
to leave him. On her behalf, I beg you to do
whatever you can to improve her availability.

MAJOR: Hell's bells, I'll burn for her too, if that's what she'd like.

DEXTER: What she'd like? The woman is smoldering!

MAJOR: What do we do
about whatsherface, back in the house?

DEXTER: You tell her to scram.
Wherever she wants. In fact, her twin sister's in town,
along with her mother. They want to take her home.

MAJOR: Damnation! You say her *mother* is here in Ephesus?

DEXTER: So says the news from the grapevine.

MAJOR: By Jove, the timing
couldn't be nicer to give her the boot.

DEXTER: Even better—
you yourself could come out looking darn nice.

MAJOR: Surrender your thoughts and speak.

DEXTER: You want her gone,
but still grateful?

MAJOR: I'd love that.

DEXTER: Then this is what you do.
You've got pot-loads of money. Tell her to keep for herself
all the baubles and gold you gave her. Say they're a gift.
Then tell her to take them wherever she wants, so long as
it's far from you.

MAJOR: I like the way you talk.
But I'd hate to see one of them getting away while the other one
changes her mind.

DEXTER: Don't be skittish.

(He nods at the house of Hospitalides.)

                                        SHE loves YOU!
          With a passion that's—blind.

MAJOR: Yes, Venus feels the same way.

DEXTER: Hush and keep still. There's somebody coming out.
          Get down and hide.

(They crouch behind the altar to Mars. Milly appears on Hospitalides' porch.)

                              A signal ship is departing
          from port and heading our way.

MAJOR: I don't understand.
          What ship?

DEXTER: I mean that her maid's coming out. She's the one
          who transported the ring that I gave you.

MAJOR: WOW! What a fox!

DEXTER: Hah! Next to her boss, she's an ape. Or a bat. Just check out
          those eyes and ears: she looks like she's hunting for prey.

Act IV, Scene 2 [991–1093]

          (Milly descends Hospitalides' steps.)

MILLY:

          (Aside.)

                    Well, here's the arena, so let the games begin.
                    I'll pretend I don't see them. I'll act like I don't know they're here.

MAJOR:

          (To Dexter.)

                    Be quiet and eavesdrop. Has she made any mention of me?

MILLY:

          (Aloud.)

                    Is somebody poking his nose into business that isn't
                    his own? Is somebody on my trail? Some selfserving
                    loafer with time on his hands?
                                        I'm afraid of those types
                    who might step out, then stand in the way and stop things
                    while SHE is on route:
                                        my lady whose body boils
                    breathlessly for HIM;
                                        my lady whose heart beats a pitiful
                    patter for HIM;
                              my lady who loves a man too

ruggedly handsome—and nice—for words; that soldier
of fortune, Major Topple d'Acropolis!

MAJOR:

(Aside to Dexter.)

This maid
has the sweats for me too. You hear how she praised my splendor?
Damn! Her words couldn't stand more spit.

DEXTER:

(Aside to the Major.)

How's that?

MAJOR: They're already highly polished. No smidge of vulgarity.

DEXTER: Not when the subject at hand is unsmudged.

MAJOR: The maid
herself has a pretty nice sheen on her too, eh Dexter?
My god, already I feel a twinge of arousal.

DEXTER: Before you've even laid eyes on her mistress?

MAJOR: Need I
inspect what you've led me to trust? Although the lady
is absent, this slip of a ship inspires my passion.

DEXTER: For god's sake, don't woo this one! This one's been promised
to me. You marry her mistress today and VOILÀ—
this one becomes my wife.

MAJOR: So why are you waiting?

DEXTER: Good point. You follow my lead.

MAJOR: I'm right at your heels.

MILLY:

(Aloud.)

IF ONLY I had the chance to meet up with that MAN,
that HE on whose account I have ventured forth.

DEXTER:

(Aloud.)

And so shall it be that your hankering comes to an end.
Buck up and fear not: there's a special someone who knows
whereof what you seek.

MILLY: Oh, whose is that voice I just heard?

DEXTER: Your colleague in council, your counsel in cahoots.

MILLY: Oh mercy! I haven't kept my secret a secret!

DEXTER: Au contraire! You have, and you haven't.

MILLY: How's that?

DEXTER: Secrets you keep from traitors. With me you have utter
             trust.

MILLY: If you're part of our Secret and Sacred Order
             of Orgies, what's the password?[17]

DEXTER: "Someone loves someone."

MILLY: That goes for a lot of people.

DEXTER: Not many would send
             a present slipped off a finger.

MILLY: Ah, now I get it.
             Indeed, you have leveled our field of play.
                                            But someone
             else is here?

DEXTER: Uh, maybe, maybe not.

MILLY: I want to see you ALONE.

DEXTER: A short chat or long?

MILLY: Three words at most.

DEXTER:

             (Aside to the Major, as he stands up to leave.)

                                 I'll be back with you in a minute.

MAJOR: But what about me? I should wait around in the meantime,
             wasting these looks?
                                 Squandering this legend called "Me"?

DEXTER: Stand by and be patient. I'm working your end of the business.

MAJOR: Well, hurry. The waiting is—painful.

---

[17] The reference here is to the secret worship of Bacchus, which was suppressed by Roman law
in 186 B.C.

DEXTER: One step at a time—
that's how we're expected to manage these types of transactions.
You know that.

MAJOR: Go on, then. Take measures as you see fit.

DEXTER:

(Aside to Milly, as he joins her.)

The Major is denser than marble.
                                         I'm back. So what
did you want me for?

MILLY: Instructions for setting up
the siege of Troy. So what did you have in mind?

DEXTER: For starters, pretend she's consumed with desire.

MILLY: Got it.

DEXTER: Praise his features as well as physique, then mention
his manly qualities.

MILLY: Hogwash loaded and locked
on target, the way I showed you in training.

DEXTER: Keep
your eyes fixed on whatever else happens, and listen for cues.

MAJOR:

(Aside to Dexter.)

Are you planning to get to MY needs at all today?

(Dexter returns to the Major.)

Ah, back at last, you straggler.

DEXTER:

(Aside to the Major.)

Here at your orders.

MAJOR: What did she say to you?

DEXTER: She reports her mistress
is smitten with grief. The poor thing's beside herself,
bewailing the fact that she craves you but doesn't possess you.
That's why she's here. The maid, that is.

MAJOR:

(As he stands up and dusts himself off.)

Bid her come.

DEXTER: But say—you know what you ought to do? Look picky
                 and full of pride. Pretend the whole thing disgusts you.
                 Berate me for letting the public access your assets.

MAJOR: I'll keep that in mind. In fact, I'll take your advice.

DEXTER:

       (Aloud.)

       Shall I summon this woman who seeks you?

MAJOR:

       (Aloud.)

                                        She may come forth,
           if there's something she wishes.

DEXTER: Hey woman! Come forth, if there's
           something you wish.

MILLY:

       (She approaches them, steps between Dexter and the Major, and curtsies.)

                      Glad greetings, Beautiferous One.

MAJOR:

       (Aside to Dexter.)

           She knows my title.

       (To Milly.)

                      May heaven fulfill all your wishes.

MILLY: A lifetime filled with your love—

MAJOR: That's asking too much.

MILLY: Not for me. I mean for my mistress. She hovers near death,
                 so overheated is she with ardor for you.

MAJOR: Like so many others. There's just not enough to go 'round.

MILLY: My word, it's hardly surprising you set such a price
                 on your stock. An attractive man like you, endowed
                 with such perfect physique and unparalleled prowess in battle.
                 What man could more pass for a god?

DEXTER:

       (Aside.)

                                        He sure can't pass
           for human. Dear god, a buzzard is more humane.

MAJOR:

> (Aside to Dexter.)

>> And now, to display myself in fullest grandeur—
>> as long as she's on the subject of praise.

> (He puffs out his chest and parades between the altars.)

DEXTER:

> (Aside to Milly.)

>> Would you look
>> at how that feeble cluck struts around?

> (Aloud, to the Major.)

>> Sir, won't
>> you answer this woman? She's sent from her of whom
>> I spoke a while back.

MAJOR: From which of whom? So many
> tug at my sleeve—I can hardly remember them all.

MILLY: From she who has looted her finger in order to render
> your own more lovely. I brought this ring from my lady,
> who's consumed with desire. I handed it over to HIM

> (She indicates Dexter, as the Major passes by.)

>> to give to you right away.

MAJOR:

> (He stops to fondle the statue of Mars.)

>> And now, woman, what
>> do you want? Speak up.

MILLY: Spurn not the lady who needs you.
> She lives to be part of your life. If she takes her next breath—
> or doesn't—all depends on you.

MAJOR: What is it
> she wants right now?

MILLY: To tease you,
>> and squeeze you,
>>> and please you.
> Unless you save her, she'll give up the ghost.

> (She drops to her knees and clutches his scabbard.)

>> Achilles,
>> my hero! I beg you! You must rescue that pretty young thing—

and pretty soon. Will you not whip out your generous
gift, O slayer of cities and sacker of kings!

MAJOR:

(He turns to Milly and pulls away his scabbard.)

Well said, but frankly I'm bored by this business.

(To Dexter.)

                                                    Such blatant
defiance of orders! Have I or have I not
forbidden you time after time to proffer my service
in such a promiscuous manner?

DEXTER: You hear what he said there,
woman? I told you before, and I'll say it again:
this boar always takes in a stud fee; he doesn't put out
for any sweet sow who trots by.

MILLY:

(As she stands up.)

                                        Let the man name his price.
We'll pay it.

DEXTER: The going rate is sixty minae.[18]
In gold, and official issue. Nobody gets
a discount.

MILLY: That's fine—but gracious, it's awfully cheap!

MAJOR: The urge to hoard is simply not in my nature.
I'm modestly wealthy: more than a thousand quarter-
bushels of minae. In mint condition, of course.

DEXTER: That's not including his treasury. We're not talking molehill,
but mountain of silver. It makes Mount Aetna look puny.

(The Major turns back to the statue of Mars and preens in the shield.)

MILLY:

(Aside to Dexter.)

Well done! My word, you're a big fat liar!

---

[18] The price is given as a weight—one talent, equal to sixty minae—to be delivered in gold
coins minted by Philip II of Macedon, which were known for their purity and uniformity.

DEXTER:

    (Aside to Milly.)

                                     You like
how I play this?

MILLY:

    (Aside to Dexter.)

                And me? Pretty quick on the uptake, no?

DEXTER:

    (Aside to Milly.)

    Expert handling.

MILLY:

    (Aloud to the Major, as she tugs on his cloak.)

               Oh, please send me back right away!

DEXTER: Sir! Won't you give this woman your answer? Either
"I will" or "I won't"?

MILLY: Why jab holes in the poor dear's heart?
What harm has she done to you?

MAJOR:

    (To Milly, pulling away his cloak.)

                    Command your lady
to march herself out and meet us in person. Tell her
I'm ready for action on any front she desires.

    (He turns to inspect his teeth in the shield.)

MILLY: That's exactly the sort of action that justice demands:
the craver—that's her—craves you; ipso facto, then you—
the craveé—crave her back. And—

DEXTER:

    (Aside.)

              This girl is god's gift to comedy.

MILLY: —since you allowed my entreaty, it's only fair
to treat me—the entreater—nicely.

    (Aside to Dexter, who is bent over double.)

                  Is something wrong
with my acting?

DEXTER:

>   (Aside to Milly.)

>>>>   God no. I just can't—hee hee—stop laughing.

MILLY:

>   (Aside to Dexter.)

>>   That's why I'm facing the other way.

MAJOR:

>   (As he cleans out his ears with his pinky fingers.)

>>>>   Colossal
>>   heavens, woman. You haven't the vaguest idea
>>   of the honor I'm paying your mistress.

MILLY: I do, and I'll tell her.

DEXTER: Other women would pay his weight in gold
>>   for this service.

MILLY: Mercy, I trust you on that one!

DEXTER: Full-pedigreed
>>   fighters spring forth from the wombs he makes fecund! His sons
>>   live eight hundred years. Apiece.

MILLY:

>   (Aside to Dexter.)

>>>   Oh stop, you big ham!

MAJOR:

>   (Without a pause in his preening.)

>>   That's not quite correct. They live for thousands of years
>>   on end. Forever and ever.

DEXTER:

>   (To the Major.)

>>>   I lowered the figure
>>   a bit just in case the girl might think I was stretching.

MILLY:

>   (Aside.)

>>   I can't go on!

(Aloud.)

> How old will he get himself,
> if his sons live that long?

MAJOR:

(As he sniffs his armpits.)

> I was born the day after Jove
> sprang forth from Mother Earth.

DEXTER:

> If the Major'd been born
> the day before, *he'd* be the one running heaven.

MILLY:

(Aside to Dexter.)

> All right! That's enough. Allow me to leave the both
> of you while I still can breathe!

DEXTER:

(Aloud and sternly.)

> Well, why aren't you leaving?
> You have your answer.

MILLY:

(Aloud.)

> I'll go and lead forth the lady
> on whose behalf I act. Do you want something else?

MAJOR: That I never be lovelier more than I am at this moment.
There's not a second of peace for the hopelessly handsome.

(He repeatedly bends over, fluffs his hair, stands up, throws it back, and then shakes it out; Milly stares.)

DEXTER: What are you standing around for? Why don't you leave?

MILLY: I'm going.

(She turns to leave, still staring at the Major's activities.)

DEXTER: And don't forget—are you listening?—be especially
sensitive breaking the news. Don't spit out the words.
Her spirits should soar.

(To Milly, as he pulls her aside by the hand.)

> And tell Convivia—in case
> she's still there—to go back home. Himself is here.

MILLY:

>(Aside.)

>>She's there, along with Climax. The two have been eavesdropping.

DEXTER: Nicely done. If they've caught the conversation,
they'll have much smoother sailing.

MILLY: Stop clutching me.
>I need to go.

DEXTER:

>(As he drops her hand.)

>>>I'm not clutching you. I'm not even
>>clinging.
>>>I'm not even—

>(The Major stops fussing with his hair and approaches.)

>>>>Or maybe I'll just shut up.

MAJOR:

>(To Milly.)

>>Instruct your lady to exit posthaste. The time
is nigh this pressing matter was given due precedence.

>(Milly exits into Hospitalides' house.)

Act IV, Scene 3 [1094–1136]

>(The Major begins to pace back and forth; he signals for Dexter to follow.)

MAJOR: Dexter, what's your sage opinion regarding
how I should handle Convivia? Clearly I can't
bring in the new one before I've cleared out the old.

DEXTER: Why are you asking *me* what to do? I already
told you the gentlest possible way to get rid of her.
SHE keeps all the outfits and solid gold jewelry—
whatever you dressed her up in. SHE picks out her skirts,
pockets the baubles, and presto!—YOU send her packing.
And tell her the timing is perfect to go home to Athens:
there's news that her sister—the twin—is here with her mother,
chaperones suited to make the voyage look proper.

MAJOR: How do you know they're in town?

DEXTER: I saw the sister
>here. With my very own eyes.

MAJOR: Did they meet?

DEXTER: They met.

MAJOR: And what of this sister? Young? Single? Attractive?

DEXTER: You *do* want to have it all.

MAJOR: Did this sister happen
to mention where the mother might be?

DEXTER: She's in bed,
on board the ship. Her eyes are swollen shut—
conjunctivitis. That's what the skipper who brought them
told me. He's staying next door as a guest of our neighbor.

MAJOR: And what of this skipper? Young? Single? Attractive?

(Dexter stops pacing and throws up his arms.)

DEXTER: I've had it!
                     Get out!
                         That's fine behavior indeed
for a stud, to go sniffing the stallions as well as the mares!

(Dexter starts to pace and signals for the Major to follow.)

          Now, back to business.

MAJOR: Speaking of which, that advice
you're suggesting—I think that YOU should give her the word.
The two of you seem to agree with each other quite well.

DEXTER: Why me instead of you? Why not be bold
and tell her yourself? You say that you have to get married:
your friends all insist; your mother can't wait.

MAJOR: You think so?

DEXTER: Of course I think so. Why else would I say it?

(They stop pacing. The Major blinks in thought for a moment.)

MAJOR: I'll proceed
directly inside, in that case.
                              And meanwhile, you stay
out here in front of the house. Advise me at once
of the lady's advance.

DEXTER: Just tend to your own end of business.

MAJOR: I fully intend to. But if she's unwilling to vacate,
I'll force her out.
                     By force, if I have to.

DEXTER: I'd caution
against that, sir. Far better to part on good terms.
And give her those things I mentioned. Make sure she leaves
with all that gold and jewelry you snazzed her up with.

MAJOR:　　　Yes, certainly. Of course.

DEXTER: I'm sure you'll surmount her resistance
with ease. Now go and stop wasting time.

MAJOR: Yessir.

(He exits into his house. Dexter moves to center stage to address the audience.)

DEXTER:　　　So what do you think of our Major? Does not this philandering
phalanx of one match every description I gave you?
And now what I need is for Climax to show.
                                        Or Milly,
her maid. Or Nautikles.

(Climax, Milly, and Nautikles enter from the house of Hospitalides.)

                        What amazing good luck!
The goddess of Flawless Timing keeps popping out everywhere.
Right next door comes the crowd I wanted to see.

Act IV, Scene 4 [1137–1199]

(Milly enters from Hospitalides' house, with Climax and Nautikles peeking out
behind her.)

CLIMAX:　　　Come on, but watch out. Make sure that nobody spots us.

MILLY:　　　There's no one in sight except Dexter. And him we want.

DEXTER:

(As he takes Milly's hand and kisses it.)

                        And I want you too.

MILLY: O Chief Engineer, how's it going?

DEXTER:　　　ME CHIEF? You've got to be kidding!

MILLY: Why's that?

DEXTER: Next to you
I'm a clod, unworthy to pound in a peg.

MILLY: Be honest,
you tease!

DEXTER: You lie with exquisite precision,
                                        deceive

                        in such fine detail.
                                        She leveled the Major quite nicely.

MILLY: He still has rough edges.

DEXTER: No reason to pout. This project
                is right on schedule; you just pitch in a helping
                hand, just like you've been doing.

(He pats her hand, and pulls her to his left, as he turns to address Climax and
Nautikles.)

                                        In brief: the Major
                himself has gone to Convivia's room, to beg her
                to leave with her sister and mother for Athens.

NAUTIKLES: Hooray!
                Terrific!

DEXTER: And that's not all: to get her to leave,
                he's making her keep all the gold and jewelry he gave her.
                At my suggestion, of course.

NAUTIKLES: That seems simple enough,
                if SHE wants to do it, and HE can't wait 'til she does.

DEXTER: Ah, but beware the light at the top of the cistern!
                The danger of falling back in is always greatest
                when scaling the rim.
                                    This business is presently poised
                on the brink: should the Major catch on, we won't get away
                with a thing. The pivotal moment of bluff is upon us.
                Have we amassed here the number we need for attack?
                Three women;

(He points to Nautikles.)

                            with you, that's four;
                                        then I make five;
                and our senior citizen brings the total to six.
                With half a dozen of us, I'm sure, there's a stock
                of gimmicks ready to take any stronghold by scam.
                Now pay attention.

CLIMAX: That's why we're here. We came
                to see what you want.

DEXTER: You do that so nicely. And now,
                to you I delegate the following duty.

CLIMAX:

> (As she salutes Dexter.)

> And I shall deliver, O Delegator-in-Chief,
> as best as I can whatever you ask.

DEXTER: Go bilk
> the Major. Make it nice. And classy. And clean.

CLIMAX: I delight in your every demand.

DEXTER: But do you know how?

CLIMAX: Why, of course. I pretend to be ripped apart by desire—

DEXTER: Check.

CLIMAX: —and that's why I've dumped my husband. Because
> I long for a night of connubial bliss with the Major.

DEXTER: Check. Operation in order, except one last thing:
> You tell him this house—

> (He indicates the house of Hospitalides.)

>   belongs to you, that it's part
> of your dowry. Tell him the old boy left when you filed
> for divorce. We don't want the Major thinking the place
> belongs to another man: he might get cold feet
> later on.

CLIMAX: Good point.

DEXTER: And one more thing: when the Major
> comes out, you keep your distance. Pretend your beauty's
> no match for his. Pretend to be in awe
> of his opulence. Praise it all: his body, his charm,
> his face, his radiant skin.
>   Enough explanations?

CLIMAX: Check. Would it do to provide a performance so thoroughly
> polished you can't find a flaw?

DEXTER: I'll settle for that.

> (He pulls Climax to his left and turns to address Nautikles.)

> Your turn. First memorize these instructions. As soon
> as Climax has finished—as soon as she's gone inside—
> you hightail it back to us, disguised as a skipper.

> (He pushes Nautikles back a step and eyes him.)

> Get a hat—
>   a big Macedonian number,

white with a floppy brim. And rub it with rust.
An eye patch, too—make it wool—

(He drops his eyes.)

and a little cloak.
Rub rust on that too—corrosion gives it that nautical
look.
Um, drape the cloak around your left shoulder,
yes, leave your arm poking out.

(He drops his eyes further.)

Find something to cover
your middle. Remember to try and think like a helmsman.
The old man should have this stuff at the docks, since his boys
do some fishing.

NAUTIKLES: Then where do I go in this getup? And what
do I do?

DEXTER: You come here to fetch Convivia, bearing
this message sent by her mother:
                                        if she wants to go home
to Athens, she must hasten at once to the harbor—
with you—and have her belongings carried on board.
You say unless she comes soon, you plan to cast off
without her. The wind is rising.

NAUTIKLES: I like this picture.
Go on.

DEXTER: The Major will urge her to leave right away.
In fact, he'll want her to hurry and not strand her mother.

NAUTIKLES: Gee, you're smart. And in so many ways.

DEXTER: I'll tell her
to ask the Major to make me one of the bag-boys
who'll carry her luggage down to the dock. He'll command me
to go to the harbor with her. So don't be surprised
when lickety split!—I'm off to Athens beside you!

NAUTIKLES: And when we arrive, I won't let you slave one more day.
Two days from now you'll be absolutely free.

DEXTER: Then hurry and go get dressed.

NAUTIKLES: Is there anything else?

DEXTER: Just keep in mind what I told you.

NAUTIKLES: I'm off.

(He exits stage right.)

DEXTER:

(As he turns to the women.)

> You both
> get back inside. I have no doubt the Major
> is coming out shortly.

CLIMAX: No need to repeat your orders.

DEXTER: Then report to your battle stations at once!

(Climax and Milly exit into Hospitalides' house, just as the Major emerges onto his porch.)

> What timing!
> There goes the door. He's out, he's smiling, he's won.
> The poor dope is gloating over a hollow triumph.

Act IV, Scene 5 [1200–1215]

(The Major strides to join Dexter at center stage.)

MAJOR: I've exacted my wishes exactly as wished from Convivia.
Thanks to my charm, we're still on good terms.

DEXTER: And what,
may I ask, delayed you so long?

MAJOR: I never knew
before this how much that girl adored me.

DEXTER: How's that?

MAJOR: A barrage of words was needed—like hacking through rock.
But finally I got what I wanted: I gave her presents,
granted her every demand; I also threw in
yourself as a gift.

DEXTER: Even me!
                     But how can I live
without you?

MAJOR: Come, come! Now pick up that chin! I'll free you
all the same. I exerted my effort in searching
for ways to get her to leave without you; but fact is,
she caught me off guard.

DEXTER: I must put all my faith in heaven—
and you. It's a baneful blow, to be forcibly freed
from the finest of masters; at least I console myself
in knowing the lady next door was overcome

by your physical charm;
                              and that I made my small contribution
by joining you both in conjugal consummation.

MAJOR: What time is this for words? I'll give you freedom
                and booty—just get me the lady.

DEXTER: I'll return with her gotten.

MAJOR: I'm very—
                              excited.

DEXTER: Restraint. Repress those urges.
                And try not to drool.
                                        Look there! She's coming outside!

(He pushes the Major over to the altar of Mars, and the two crouch down.)

Act IV, Scene 6 [1216–1283]

(Milly and Climax emerge onto Hospitalides' porch.)

MILLY:

                (Aside to Climax.)

                              Psst! There's the Major.

CLIMAX:

                (Aside to Milly.)

                                        Where?

MILLY: To the left.

CLIMAX: I see him.

MILLY: Glance at him sideways. Don't let him know we're watching.

CLIMAX: Okay, I still see him.
                              Enough being naughty—it's time
                to get really nasty.

MILLY: You first.

CLIMAX:

                (Aloud.)

                                        Do tell! You met him
                in person?

                (Aside.)

                              Don't stint on the volume—we want him to hear.

MILLY: I SWEAR TO GOD, I SPOKE WITH HIS VERY SELF.
                No rush, took my time, stayed just as long as I liked.

MAJOR:

(Aside to Dexter.)

You heard what she said?

DEXTER: I heard her. She's thrilled to death
to have stood in your presence.

CLIMAX: O, you lucky girl!

MAJOR:

(Aside to Dexter.)

They do seem to love me!

DEXTER:

(Aside to the Major.)

Who better than you?

CLIMAX: Will wonders
never cease? You say you walked right up to the man?
You asked in the flesh? They say he can only be reached
by mail or messenger—just like a king!

MILLY: I swear! To get in and plead my case wasn't easy!

DEXTER:

(Aside to the Major.)

Such a reputation you have with the women!

MAJOR:

(Aside to Dexter.)

But put up I must—for such is the will of Venus.

CLIMAX:

(Climax descends the steps and drops to her knees.)

Yes!
To VENUS, I give my thanks!
And what's more,
I hope and pray she'll open my pathway to him,
the man I desire,
the man I love.
Oh, may he
be gentle with me,
may he not find my ardor a burden.

MILLY:

> (As she joins Climax on her knees.)

> So it will come to pass, though many's the female
> who wants him all to herself. Most girls he snubs,
> the rest he shoves aside. The exception is YOU.

CLIMAX: Except he maintains such exceptional standards. I'm worried
          sick he'll change his mind when he sees me. His delicate
          sense of refinement might make him reject me offhand.

MILLY: He'll never do that. Now, perk yourself up.

> (She rises and assists Climax to her feet.)

MAJOR:

> (Aside to Dexter.)

>   Such aspersions
> she casts on herself!

CLIMAX: I'm afraid the description you gave
          of my looks overstates my actual beauty.

MILLY: I made sure
          you'd meet and surpass all of his expectations.

CLIMAX: Dear god, if he turns up his nose at my marriage proposal,
          I'll fall on his knees and beg him; otherwise—
          if I can't persuade him that way—

> (She pretends to stab herself.)

>   it's "Hello, Death."
> I know I can't live without him.

MAJOR:

> (Aside to Dexter.)

>   I see it's up
> to me to save this woman from dying.

> (He stands up.)

>   Shall I go?

DEXTER: And cheapen yourself by volunteering? For free?

> (He pulls the Major back down.)

> I think not. Let her come on her own. Let her pine, and yearn,
> and wait for hours and hours. You want to lose
> that reputation of yours? For god's sake, don't do it!
> I know for a fact no mortals save two—that's you,

and Phaon, the man for whom Lesbian Sappho[19] switched teams—
have been graced by such love from a woman.

CLIMAX: I'm going inside—
unless, dear Milly, you call him forth.

MILLY: Instead
why not wait until someone comes out?

CLIMAX: I cannot hold on.
I must go in.

MILLY: But the door is shut tight.

CLIMAX: I'll smash it!

(She rushes up to the Major's door.)

MILLY: The woman's gone mad!

(She dashes to catch up with Climax.)

CLIMAX: If he's ever been in love—
if his brain is a match for his beauty, he'll pardon whatever
I do out of love. Yes, surely he'll show me his mercy.

DEXTER:

(Aside to the Major.)

Pitiful, no? The way she flounders around
in love?

MAJOR:

(Aloud as he stands up.)

THE FEELING IS MUTUAL!

DEXTER:

(Aside to the Major, as he tries to pull the Major down.)

Quiet! She'll hear you!

MILLY: Why are you standing there dazed? Go knock, why don't you?

CLIMAX: The man I want is not home.

MILLY: But how do you know?

CLIMAX: I know him by scent. My nose would sniff him out,
were he in fact inside.

---

[19] Sappho was a famous Greek poetess born on the island of Lesbos in the seventh century B.C.
Many of her poems refer to love between women or girls, but comic writers and others linked her
to a list of male lovers, including Phaon, for whose love she allegedly committed suicide.

MAJOR:

    (Aside to Dexter.)

                       Her love is such
she can sense my presence! Venus has given her foresmell!

CLIMAX:

    (As she sniffs around.)

        The love I desperately seek is somewhere nearby—
There's a definite odor.

MAJOR:

    (Aside to Dexter.)

                     Damn! That one little nose
sees more than both eyes!

DEXTER:

    (Aside to the Major.)

                     It has to. She's blinded by passion.

CLIMAX:

    (She sniffs and suddenly sees the Major.)

    Oh, catch me, please!

    (She pretends to faint.)

MILLY: Why's that?

CLIMAX: So I don't hit the ground.

MILLY: Oh! What's wrong?

CLIMAX: I can't stand up. My mind is failing—
Oh, blame it all on my eyes!

MILLY: Good grief! You saw
the Major?

CLIMAX: I did.

MILLY: I don't. Where is he?

CLIMAX: You'd see him,
dear god—
        if YOU were in LOVE.

MILLY: You'll never match
my passion for him—that is, if you gave me permission.

DEXTER:

> (Aside to the Major.)

>> No doubt about it: women fall in love
>> the moment they see you.

MAJOR:

> (Aside to Dexter.)

>>>> I can't recall—did I ever
>> happen to mention the fact I'm the grandson of Venus?

CLIMAX: Milly, dear heart, I beg you! Go meet with him.

MAJOR:

> (Aside to Dexter.)

>> She's in awe of me. Have you noticed?

DEXTER: Here comes the maid.

MILLY:

> (To the Major, as she approaches with head bowed.)

>> I need you.

MAJOR: And we need you too.

MILLY: I've summoned my lady,
just as you ordered.

MAJOR: I see.

MILLY: So invite her over.

MAJOR: I've made up my mind not to snub her like all the others—
because you begged.

MILLY: Oh, I promise she won't be able
to utter a word if she comes any closer. Setting
her eyes upon you cut off all use of her tongue.

MAJOR: I see. Such affliction demands an immediate cure.

MILLY: You see the way she shivers? She went into shock
as soon as she saw you.

MAJOR: Men in full armor do likewise.
The woman's reaction is hardly any wonder.
But what exactly is it she wants me to do?

MILLY: Come over;
          move in;
               live as one 'til the end of time.

MAJOR: Come over? Me? But she's married! Her husband would catch me.

MILLY: On the contrary. She kicked him out just for you.

MAJOR: But how could she do that?

MILLY: The house was part of her dowry.

MAJOR: Really?

MILLY: Really! Honest to god.

MAJOR: In that case,
          send her back home. I'll be there posthaste.

MILLY: Don't torment
          her mind any further. Make sure you don't keep her waiting.

MAJOR: Of course I won't. Now go.

MILLY: All right. We're going.

(She returns to Climax, whom she leads by the hand back to Hospitalides' porch.
Climax stumbles blindly on the stairs, but with Milly's help, the two exit into
Hospitalides' house.)

MAJOR:

(As he pulls Dexter to his feet, the Major spots something offstage right.)

          But what's this I see?

DEXTER: What is it?

MAJOR: Look! There's somebody
          coming. He's dressed like a sailor.

DEXTER: And heading for us.
          No doubt he's looking for you.
                              It's the skipper! He's here!

MAJOR: To fetch the girl! But of course!

DEXTER: I do believe.

Act IV, Scene 7 [1284–1310]

(Nautikles enters stage right in disguise, wearing an eye patch over his left eye.)

NAUTIKLES:

(Aside to himself.)

          If I didn't know the course of true love was already
          paved with the sneakiest tricks in the book, I'd sure be
          a lot more anxious, running around in this get-up
          to get back my girlfriend.
                          They say that many's the man

who's done a bad thing—and other deeds less than noble—
all in the name of true love. Not to mention Achilles,
who sulked about whatsherface, while his buddies got skewered.
Hey, it's Dexter, standing right there with the Major!
I'd better disguise my voice.

(Aloud, in a gruff but somewhat stiff and halting manner.)

>   Aye, women! I tell you,
> Lateness herself gave birth to the lot of 'em. Uh,
> no matter how late, it always seems later whenever
> a woman's concerned. Uh, BAH! I swear they practice
> slowin' us down.
>   And now to fetch this Convivia.
> I'll knock on the door.

(He pounds on the Major's door.)

>   AHOY! IS THERE ANYONE HOME?

DEXTER: What is it, young man? What do you want? And why
do you knock?

NAUTIKLES:

(As he joins the Major and Dexter.)

>   I'm here to fetch one Convivia. I come
> on behalf of her mother. She'd better come on, if she's coming.
> She's holding the lot of us up. We want to shove off.

MAJOR: She's ready and waiting for loading.

(Giving Dexter a shove.)

>   Hop on it, Dexter!
> The gold, the jewelry, the clothes, the expensive baubles—
> get bag-boys to help you tote it all down to the ship.
> The entire trousseau I bestowed—let her take it away!

DEXTER: I'm going.

(He exits into the Major's house.)

NAUTIKLES: Aye! And please shake a leg, if you would.

MAJOR: He won't waste time.
>   And what, may I ask, is THAT?

(He begins to inspect the eye patch.)

      Your eye—what happened?

NAUTIKLES: Me eye? Uh, AYE! I GOT ONE!

(He points to his right eye and winks.)

MAJOR: I mean the left.

NAUTIKLES: I'll tell you.

    (He points to the eye patch.)

                              I use this eye less,
      by Neptune, because—it's my wont;
                                    had I wanted her less
      I'd use it as much as the other.
                          AYE! But avast
      this delay! I won't be kept waiting!

    (He turns to go. The Major tugs him back.)

MAJOR: Look! They're here!

Act IV, Scene 8 [1311–1377]

    (Dexter emerges from the Major's house, pulling Convivia by the arm.)

DEXTER: Please, WHEN will this weeping and wailing all come to an end?

CONVIVIA: Oh, how can I help but weep? Right here's where I spent
           the happiest days of my life—
                          and now, I'm LEAVING.

DEXTER: Look! The man who was sent by your mother and sister!

CONVIVIA: I see him.

MAJOR:

    (To Dexter, as he pushes him back to the house.)

              My orders, Dexter! Didn't you hear me?
        Why aren't they hauling away all that stuff that I gave her?

    (Dexter exits into the Major's house. The Major goes to the door to supervise, with
his back turned to the audience.)

NAUTIKLES: Ahoy, Convivia.

CONVIVIA:

    (She advances and embraces Nautikles.)

                 "Ahoy" to you.

NAUTIKLES: Your mother
      and sister insisted I bring you greetings.

    (He kisses her wildly.)

CONVIVIA: My greetings
            to them.

(She kisses him back wildly.)

NAUTIKLES:

(Still holding Convivia, with whom he exchanges kisses between sentences.)

                    They beg you to come: they want to unfurl
            the sails while the wind is still fair.
                                    If your mother's eyes
            weren't all bleary, they would have come too. The both of them.

CONVIVIA: I'll go, but against my will. My duty belongs to—

NAUTIKLES: —I know. You're a reasonable girl.

(Convivia and Nautikles break their embrace, just before the Major turns around.)

MAJOR:

(He descends the stairs and strides over to Convivia to give her a hearty pat on the
back.)

                                    All thanks to me.
            Without my help, she'd still be a fool today.

CONVIVIA:

(She turns to the Major and falls to her knees.)

            And that's what I find so excruciating, to be
            deprived of such a man! A man with the power
            to make whomever he wishes awash with wit.
            At your side, my spirit grew bolder; but now I see
            I must forcibly forfeit that lofty feeling.

(She begins to weep into her hands.)

MAJOR: Don't cry.

CONVIVIA: I can't help it, whenever I see you—

(Dexter emerges onto the Major's porch and gives a thumbs-up.)

MAJOR: Keep up your spirits.

CONVIVIA: No one can know the depth of my heartache but me.

DEXTER:

(As he descends the steps of the Major's house.)

            Well, I'M not surprised at how much you loved this place,
            Convivia, dear. His beauty, his conduct, his masculine
            charm—
                    they hold your heart in a death grip. When I,

a mere slave, gaze upon him, I burst into tears at our parting.

(He falls to his knees, between Convivia and Nautikles, and weeps into his hands.)

CONVIVIA: Please sir, permission to hug you before my departure.

MAJOR: Permission granted.

CONVIVIA:

(She stands up, extending her arms toward the Major.)

O light of my life! My soul!

(She suddenly goes limp and falls backwards on Dexter.)

DEXTER:

(To Nautikles, as he struggles to rise under Convivia's weight.)

For god's sake, catch the woman BEFORE she crashes!

(Nautikles carries Convivia a few steps away. She lies down with her upper body in his lap, and they kiss. Dexter blocks the Major's view of the couple.)

MAJOR: And what, may I ask, was all that?

DEXTER: The thought of leaving
you made the poor thing pass out.

MAJOR: Fetch water within!

DEXTER: Oh, why waste time with water? Much better she rests.
And don't interrupt—I beg you—until she comes
to her senses.

MAJOR:

(As he peers around Dexter.)

Their heads are far too close. I don't
approve.

(He pushes Dexter out of the way and addresses Nautikles.)

HEY, SAILOR BOY! Get your big fat lips
off her mouth! You're looking for trouble!

NAUTIKLES: Just checking to see
if she's breathing or not.

MAJOR: Your ear would have done just as well.

NAUTIKLES: If you want, I'll give her back.

MAJOR: No, no. I don't want.
Resume your position.

(Convivia and Nautikles again kiss. Dexter draws the Major's attention away by rushing onto the Major's porch and embracing one of the columns.)

DEXTER: A homeless wretch I've become!

(The Major pushes past Dexter and addresses the slaves within.)

MAJOR: Come out at once! Carry forth from inside all goods
                I've rendered unto this woman!

DEXTER: Once more, before parting,
                I pay my respects to you, Ye Gods of Hearth
                and Home.

(To the slaves inside.)

                        Coslaves and coslavesses all—good-bye.
                And have a good life. I beg you, speak well of me,
                although I'm long gone.

(He falls upon the Major's chest and weeps, while turning the Major away from
Convivia and Nautikles.)

MAJOR: Buck up now, Dexter!

DEXTER: Alas!
                How can I help but cry when I'm leaving YOU?

MAJOR: You must look on the bright side.

DEXTER: I know just how much this hurts me.

CONVIVIA: Hey, what's going on? What happened? What's this I see?
                Is it light?

(Aside to Nautikles.)

                        Hello there, sunshine!

NAUTIKLES: Hello yourself,
                my moonbeam!

(Aloud.)

                        All shipshape again?

CONVIVIA:

(Aloud.)

                                        I beg your pardon!
                Who is this man I'm hugging? My reputation
                is ruined! Am I out of my mind?

(She faints again.)

NAUTIKLES: Fear not, my snuggums!

(He kisses her again. The Major untangles himself from Dexter and descends the
stairs, with Dexter following.)

MAJOR: Now what's all this?

DEXTER: The girl has just lost her senses.
              I'm worried. I'm afraid this is getting far too public.

MAJOR: What is?

(Baskets roll out from the Major's door. Haplus, looking very hungover, and a bag-
boy emerge. They stumble under the weight of clothes and jewelry and try to cram it
all in the baskets.)

DEXTER:

(Turning the Major towards the baggage.)

                    Uh, going through town with all of this trailing
              behind—why, people might think it a failing on your part.

MAJOR: I gave her what's mine, not theirs. I don't give a damn
              what they think.

(To the bag-boy and Haplus.)

                        Now march! Forge on, with heaven's blessing.

(Bag-boy and Haplus exit stage right.)

DEXTER: I say this only for your sake.

MAJOR: I'm know.

DEXTER: Well, good-bye.

(He takes a few steps stage right.)

MAJOR: And a big good-bye to you too.

DEXTER:

(He prods Nautikles.)

                                Get moving and hurry!
              I'll be with you shortly. I want a few words with the Major.

(Convivia and Nautikles exit stage right. Dexter addresses the Major.)

              Although you have always considered your other servants
              more trusty, I still forgive you—and gratefully so—
              for all that has passed. And if you so wished, I'd rather
              slave for you than find freedom with somebody else.

MAJOR: You must keep up morale.

DEXTER: Alas, as soon as the thought
              comes to mind of how I must change my lifestyle! To sip
              with ladylike manners!
                                To spit out the glory of war!

MAJOR: Well, try to be useful.

DEXTER: That I can do no longer.
               I've lost my will to live.

MAJOR: Go forward! Don't dawdle!
               Catch up with them now!

DEXTER: Good-bye.

MAJOR: And good-bye to you.

DEXTER: If by chance I become a free man—I'll keep in touch—
               remember not to forsake me.

MAJOR: That's not my style.

DEXTER: Recall my devotion to you, again and again.
               If you do, then you'll finally see who's been nice to you—
               and naughty.

MAJOR: I know. I've often been on the lookout.

DEXTER: But that was before. Today is especially important.
               Today you'll say I REALLY outdid myself.

MAJOR: I can hardly refrain from calling you back into service.

DEXTER: A bad decision. People might say you're deceitful—
               and not very honest. "No sense of duty," they'll say,
               "and likewise the servants. Except for Dutiful Dexter."
               If I thought you'd save face, I'd do some fast talking;
               fact is, you can't. I advise against it.

MAJOR: Then go.

DEXTER: I'll suffer what may.

MAJOR: In that case, I bid you good-bye.

DEXTER: I guess I'd better hurry.

          (He exits stage right.)

MAJOR: And good-bye yet again.
               Before this happened, I always thought him the dregs
               of my slave pool. But now I see he's as loyal as a puppy.
               The more I think it over, how stupid I was
               to give him away.
                              Oh well. To my passion fruit,
               who awaits me inside.
                              What's that?
                              Her door just opened.

Act IV, Scene 9 [1378–1393]

(A slave enters from the house of Hospitalides, still speaking to someone inside.)

SLAVE: You don't have to nag. I fully remember my orders.
I'll find him somehow, wherever on earth he may be.
I'll hunt him down 'til the pain makes me drop in my tracks.

MAJOR:

(Aside.)

He's looking for me. I'll advance and display myself.

SLAVE: OH HO! I was searching all over for you! All hail
the sum of perfect proportions! The consummate wit!
That he who's preferred by the ultimate duo of deities!

MAJOR:

(Aloud.)

What duo would that be?

SLAVE: Why, Venus and Mars!

MAJOR: Clever boy.

SLAVE: My lady begs you to enter. She wants you, she needs you,
her anticipation has ants in its pants. Why wait?
Why not stanch her longing and rush in right now?

MAJOR: I'm off!

(He strides quickly into Hospitalides' house.)

SLAVE: And now the Major has snagged himself in our snare.
The trap is sprung: inside, the old man's at his post,
preparing to pounce on that flesh-hound, whose bravery is only
skin deep;
                that swine who thinks women swoon in their sandals
the moment they see him.
                      The truth is that no one—that's men
and women alike—can stand the sight of him!

(Screaming and noise are heard from within.)

Why, I think I hear screaming! It's time to join the fray!

(He exits into Hospitalides' house. More screaming is heard.)

Act V [1394–1437]

(Hospitalides enters, still speaking to his slaves inside.)

HOSPIT.:   Escort him out here! And if he won't come, then grab
his ankles and let him soar between heaven and earth.

After that, you can carve him in two.

(Two slaves enter, holding the Major, who is wearing only his underwear. Chef follows, wielding a large butcher knife in his hand and two mallets in his apron.)

MAJOR: Hospitalides!
In the name of Mars, I beg you!

HOSPIT.:   You grovel in vain.
Don't pester the gods.
                              Say, Chef: make sure that cleaver
of yours has a nice sharp edge.

CHEF: Oooo! Zis blade'z been aching
to trim zoze libidinouz tidbitz and dangle zem 'round
hiz neck like zee baby'z rattle!

MAJOR: I'M DEAD! IT'S ALL OVER!

HOSPIT.:   Not quite. You're one step ahead.

CHEF:

(To Hospitalides, as he raises his cleaver.)

                              Zo now I zlice?

HOSPIT.:   Not yet. We must tenderize him first with the mallets.

(Chef pokes the Major in the belly with one of the mallets.)

CHEF: Zere iz a muchnezz of meat on him.

(He hands the slaves the mallets and gives them a nod. They pound the Major, who screams, until Hospitalides holds up his hand to stop.)

HOSPIT.:   So tell me:
how could you dare move in on another man's wife?
For shame!

MAJOR: But SHE was the one who made the first move!

HOSPIT.:   He's lying. Whack him.

MAJOR: STOP! I'll explain!

HOSPIT.:   Don't stop.

MAJOR: But won't you grant me permission to speak?

(Hospitalides holds up his hand and signals his slaves to wait.)

HOSPIT.:   Oh, speak.

MAJOR: I was begged to seduce her.

HOSPIT.:   And you dared follow through? Take that!

(He grabs a mallet from one of the servants and gives the Major a good whack.)

MAJOR: OW! I've had enough whacking!

CHEF: Zo when do I zlice, eh?

HOSPIT.:   Whenever you're ready. Divvy him up and drag
            the wretch apart.

    (The slaves stretch the Major out.)

MAJOR: I'M BEGGING YOU, DAMMIT! Please,
            won't you hear me out before he "zlicez"?

HOSPIT.:   Oh, speak.

MAJOR: It's not that I had no good reason. I swear I thought
            she was . . . unattached. Her maid, the one who set
            us up, kept telling me so.

HOSPIT.:   Then will you swear
            you won't hurt a soul for what happened here today?
            For the whackings received, or whackings still due, providing
            we free you—the "wee widdle grandson of Venus"—intact?

MAJOR: I swear by Jove and Mars, the holy gods
            of manhood, I won't harm a soul for the whackings received
            here today. I believe that justice was served. And if
            I'm allowed to go without dying—
                                            —intestate, then all's
            the more I owe for my crime.

HOSPIT.:   And if you renege?

MAJOR: Let all my future deeds go—
                                            —unattested.

CHEF: Whack him zome more, zen let him go. Zat'z my vote.

MAJOR: God bless your heart, for speaking on my behalf.

CHEF: Zen hand us a couple of minae. In gold.

MAJOR: What for?

CHEF: For letting ze "wee widdle grandzon of Venuz" ezcape
            wiz hiz two testimoniculz.

    (He lifts his cleaver.)

                                    If not, NO GO.
            And no fooling.

MAJOR: Payment approved.

CHEF: Zmart man. Don't wait
            for ze breaztplate, ze cape, or ze zword. Zey don't go wiz you.

SLAVE: More whacking, Boss? Or now you want him loose?

MAJOR: I'm loose enough, no thanks to your mallet. I beg you!

HOSPIT.:   Untie him.

MAJOR: You have my deepest gratitude, sir.

HOSPIT.:   If ever I catch you again in my house, those pals
              of yours—

(He points to the Major's underwear.)

                         —will be making their final testimony.

MAJOR: I cannot object.

HOSPIT.:   Let's go inside now, Chef.

(He exits into his house, followed by Chef and slaves. Haplus and the bag-boy enter stage right.)

MAJOR: Oh good! My slaves! Convivia hasn't left yet,
              has she? Well, answer!

HAPLUS: She's long since gone.

MAJOR: .   I'm damned!

HAPLUS: You'd say that twice if you happened to know what I know.
              That man with the woolen eye patch? THAT was no sailor.

MAJOR: Who was he?

HAPLUS: Convivia's lover.

MAJOR: How do you know?

HAPLUS:

(He pauses uncomfortably.)

              Uh, I know because, uh as soon as they got outside
              the city gate, they didn't stop hugging and kissing.

MAJOR: HELL! I've been ambushed!
                                Dexter, that treasonous weasel!
              He egged me on,
                         he made me break the law!
              And now here I stand brought to justice,
                                     a lesson to would-be
              lechers, whose numbers throughout this land would lessen
              if only they found that fulfillment were always this awful.

(He signals to his slaves.)

Homeward march, my minions!

(The three parade stage left, make an about-face. The Major salutes the audience.)

Permission to clap.

(All exit into the Major's house.)

Finis

Double
MENAECHMI
Bind

TITVS MACCIVS
Douglass Parker
PLAVTVS

Introduction to *Double Bind*

The Play

Menaechmi—Double Bind—may well be Plautus's best-known[1] play in these parts these days, but its reception and retention suffer from what might be termed *originity*— the condition of being a source.

First, it is the oldest surviving twin play in the Western tradition. Twins afford the perfect beginning for a theory of comedy. They engender mistakes, in actors or audience or both, and thus produce the Error that is comedy's endemic virus. And they do this effortlessly, *naturally.* If rare, they are *there,* nature's datum, able to produce both Error Simple (unplanned mistake) and Error Complex (deliberate deception), according to taste and necessity. As Smug (Messenio) remarks to the Syracusan Clueless (Menaechmus B) at line 1087,

> *You see that man right there?*
> *He's either the acme of con men, or else your long-lost twin.*
> *I have never beheld a man so much a* match *for another.*
> *No bead of liquid is liker—you're two drops of milk in a pod.*

For some present critical inclinations, twinnage is the unadorned zero case of *The Other,* whose contemplation gives us a rationale for turning, however briefly, from the approval of Tragedy to the toleration of Comedy. The honor accruing to the play-as-icon is considerable, but it veers from the play's own peculiar excellences.

Second, literary history dotes on *Menaechmi.* It serves as a stalking-horse for Shakespeare's early *Comedy of Errors,* and so it often appears as the *cartoon* on which the Bard stippled his arabesques, doubling twins and pyramiding misapprehensions. There is nothing wrong with this approach except for its incidental result: willy-nilly, the first-time reader of the Plautine play will regard it as something failed or at least incomplete, a *source* whose fulfilled product did not appear until 1595 A.D.

Plays have their own particular destinies, of course, and it is something to be remembered and read after two millennia, even as a forerunner, but *Menaechmi* deserves better. Its liveliness and bite do owe a great deal to its employment of twins, but twins hardly exhaust what the play is *about.* Let me offer two themes for consideration:

Mental Deficiency

The word *insanus* has a field day in *Menaechmi.* We are treated to two "Mad Scenes," one feigned, one real. The common reaction of any character who apprehends Error is

---

[1] Admittedly, the success, continuing in video, of the film of the Sondheim/Shevelove/Gelbart *A Funny Thing Happened on the Way to the Forum* may well have raised *its* source, Plautus's *Pseudolus,* to first place—but as object of dramatolatry.

the supposition that the others involved are out of their minds. But this observed "insanity" is only symptomatic, the *n*-case of *stupidity*. What we really have here is "dumb-and-dumber" comedy, the free play of ineptitude throughout the *Dramatis Personae*. The only competent character is the slave Smug, and he is kept offstage for half the play, while the feckless twins gripe and grope their way through life. Clueless One, the resident Epidamnian, has built his sand castle of existence on his own inadequacy, choosing a mistress for propinquity and putting up with the sorriest of parasites. Clueless Two may be minimally the brighter, but the triumph of such low cunning as he has is a pretended madness that culminates in playing dead; indeed, the mad complications of the play as it stands are presented as the result of his staggering thickness. Hear him on his first entrance, at line 232:

We're on a search for my longtime-lost twin brother.

And again at 245:

> *. . . while I'm alive, I search.*
> *Only a brother can fathom brotherly love.*

Yet, furnished thirty lines later with a striking clue that the search is over and the lost brother found, he might as well be unconscious. One wonders whether the Greek forerunner of *Menaechmi* might not have been prefaced by cautions from *Aporia,* the Goddess of Utter Funk.[2] Certainly her speech might well have contained the announcement of some meddling, such her intention of depriving the out-of-town brother of all remembrance of the engulfing obsession that has driven him around the Western Mediterranean for seven long years.

But in Plautus's play the only viable cause is *stupidity*. Not for the first time, our playwright has performed a variation on a theme by restricting its application. In *Persa,* the fixed power structure that normally structures society from top to bottom is confined to a truncated polis, the lower half of the Way Things Are. In *Menaechmi,* a hypertrophied error-plot is confined to the mentally challenged: like Shakespeare's Agamemnon in *Troilus and Cressida,* the beset twin brothers have not so much brains as earwax: total strangers not only to themselves but also to deductive reasoning. And the play is the working-out of their brainlessness.

Community

To cite a general rule: ancient drama, especially New Comedy, tends toward assimilation, integration. Even old men can be dragged back into society's womb. The collective must finally be seen to profit from all the foregoing frenzy.

But the rule is not always observed—or, as in this play, thrown down and danced upon. *Double Bind* may bring the separated twins back together, but hardly as mem-

---

[2] It should be emphasized that this is a *druther,* a desire on the part of the writer to posit an utterly unprovable state of affairs. If this sounds an impossible deity, it should be recalled that surviving from Menander's *Maiden in Dis-Tress* (*Perikeiromenê*) is a good part of that play's delayed prologue, spoken by Agnoia, the improbably hypostasized Goddess of Ignorance.

bers of a larger community, for the community in this play is not the usual, approved, warm-and-fuzzy Athens of New Comedy, the city to which one would always prefer to belong, but is instead the baneful and baleful *Epidamnus*. And Epidamnus is Somewhere Else.

Like the Brecht/Weill "Mahagonny," Plautus's Epidamnus is a *Netzestadt* —a Nettown, a Snare-ville. Messenio [Smug] points out this identity early:

> *This is Epidamnus the Damned.*
> *The stamping grounds of swingers, and lechers, and drunks,*
> *all state-of-the-art. The natural abode of grifter,*
> *flimflam man, con artist, of shyster and shill.*
> *The home sweet home of flocks of foxy doxies,*
> *hookers to hook the suckers with tongues of honey.*
> *A town of ill repute—Epidamnus, dammit! That's why*
> *they call this seaside town the Last Resort!*   (258–264)

And in spite of his unbearable self-righteousness and the air of ad hoc improvisation that lurks behind his overly frequent Universal Truths, one must agree. Epidamnus might well be called *Entrapmentum*—or, given that everyone has a con, an inveiglement, Dodge City. But Smug has the details wrong. What lies in wait at Epidamnus for the Syracusan Clueless is not the enticements of the flesh (though he gets a minor dose), but the knotty skein of mutual obligations that goes to make up Life in Cities: family, friends, associates, the sheer business of living. Clueless Two's voyage of discovery has been free of all that citizen existence imposes, the insistent *musts* that every citizen of Epidamnus struggles with, as we see from Diddley's first speech. But the money is running out. (Smug is quite correct.) Clueless Two must tie into the network again, and quite soon.

The network? Recall Dr. Johnson's definition: *Anything decussated or reticulated, with interstices between the intersections.* Here, the intertwining of society, the communal system. And as the resident Clueless says, the communal system is what's wrong:

> *ut hoc utimur maxume more moro*
> *molestoque multum, atque uti quique sunt*
> *optumi, maxume morem habent hunc.*

> **The System** is The Trouble . . .
> **The System** is a pest,
> **The System**'s the addiction
> Of the brightest and the best.   (571–573)

The Stupid System (*more moro*) is the public life of the citizen, the devoirs of being Political Man. Add to this the inevitable inadequacies of his home life, and Clueless One is in the net, *nimis sollicitus,* victim of terminal overbother, decussated and reticulated out of what mind he has. To make this bearable, he has jury-rigged an accommodation, a retreat—wine and woman. Being true to himself, he has located this snug retreat in the worst possible place: the house next door.

The goal of the play is of course the reuniting of brothers, but to an end: to effect Liberation from Community. Clueless Two arrives in "Snareville," usurps the pleasant portion of his brother's life, and confines One to unabated suffering; but the reunion of the twain will set them loose, free, *elsewhere*. A finely seditious conclusion. Except . . .

The Stage

Menaechmi employs one of the standard variants of the New Comedy set. We are in the outskirts of the City, or at least not at its center. The meaning of the locale is determined by the side exits: stage right, to the harbor, outside, *away;* stage left, deeper into the City, down to its center, the confining forum/agora. Before us here there are two houses, each allied with its nearer exit: stage right, Clueless One's retreat—Loveykin's *maison de joie,* as near liberation as a citizen of this town may know; stage left, One's own house, container of his wife and other obligations. Little does One know, when he leaves his house this ill-starred morning, that he will not be allowed inside *anywhere* until he has suffered through an Odyssey of pain. And then, at play's end, with the new old brother, he cuts all ties. Courtesan and parasite disposed of, he will sell house and wife, and the pair will fare off to the West, to a New Frontier where one can breathe free. Except . . .

The staging is all wrong for liberation. And so is the time: breaking up housekeeping and wife-keeping will take a week. And so the brothers enter, not Loveykins's place, the house of liberation, stage right, at worst a liminal transition to freedom, but Clueless One's own house, stage left, where this all began. A lot can happen in a week; look at today.

One wonders whether the Brothers Clueless ever *will* get out of Dodge.

Texts

The translator of *Menaechmi* is fortunate in the standard editions of the Latin text: W. M. Lindsay's *OCT,* Alfred Ernout's *Budé,* the Hammond/Mack/Moskalew classroom edition. The most happy encounter has been with the very recent edition with notes by A. S. Gratwick (Cambridge University Press, 1993), which addresses the right questions and employs unfailingly rigorous analysis in answering them. It is even a pleasure to disagree with.

Names

Supplied in the *Dramatis Personae* are not only the names of the characters in the translation but also the names in the Latin original and their definitions. It will be noted that they are not the same.

Characters not named *in the text of the play* usually possess only Latin generic names, describing the stock character. Menaechmus One's wife is thus in the *Dramatis Personae* as *Matrona,* "matron"; Matrona's father is down as a *Senex,* "old man"; the doctor is simply *Medicus,* "doctor." I have given them names ("Dovey," "Antiquides," "Dr. Klyster") purely out of whim, simply to endow each with some individuality.

Named characters in a Plautine play, which is to say the characters that *are* referred to by name in the text of the play, possess Greek names, for the most part. This is not to say that they are the same names that they carried in the Greek play that Plautus adapted. He adopts for his names Greek words that either confirm the character (*euonymy*) or undercut him or her ironically (*dysonymy*), and sometimes lead to, or depend on, wordplay in the text.

For example, the parasite. In Plautus, his name *Peniculus* ("brush; small penis") is elaborately set up by the character himself, with an obsessive insistence on its gustatory sense: "Brush the table" = "Lick the platter clean"; a parasite is basically an alimentary canal. I have tried to combine the gustatory and sexual areas analogously in English, calling him *Diddley*.

The Clever Slave is another problem. In Latin, his name is *Messenio*, indicating that he comes from the very south of Italy and is hence, in a Greek context, a slave. But were Messenians traditionally clever by nature, or self-satisfied, or what? We don't know. So, since Messenio is extremely happy with himself, even for a *servus callidus*, I have picked on that euonymically and called him *Smug*. Greek, it doesn't sound . . . but it does fit.

. *Menaechmi*, the name of the play and its twin principals, offers another problem. The Greek name in the Latin play may be nothing more than a ridiculously highfalutin appellation (= "Spearthreat") for a middle-class drudge. But it was also the name of an illustrious astronomer from the century before and would thus be even more dysonymic; I toyed, for the teeniest of moments, with calling this play about twin ninnies "The Einsteins." Finally, since *Menaechmus* would be incomprehensible to a modern audience, and *Einstein* would open up more cans of worms than I cared to, I split the difference. The dullard brothers were presented with a popular adjective that sounds Greek or Latin and that describes them succinctly: *Clueless*. But the play itself bears a term that became, a few decades back, the emblem of a dysfunctional family: *Double Bind*. Thanks are due to the British psychiatrist R. D. Laing for this.

Other names should be self-explanatory. But one word, at least, needs comment. The principal prop in this play is a woman's garment, referred to in Latin by the Greek word *palla*. *Dress* or *gown* hardly seemed vivid enough, and so I resorted to the Franco-English *pelisse*, translating by the Humpty-Dumpty Rule: it means what I want it to mean. *Pelisse* refers to a garment, at one time upscale . . . but the one in this play avoids its etymology: it has no fur. And it sounds odd enough.

DOUGLASS PARKER

Basic Set

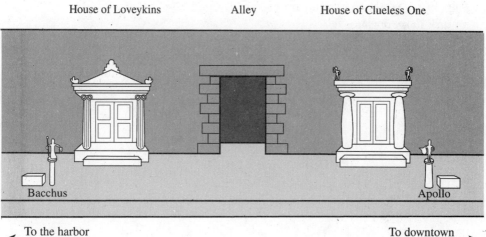

Bacchus   Apollo

To the harbor   To downtown
(stage right)   *(stage left)*

SCENE: *A quite comfortable middle-class street in the seaside town of Epidamnus—
a town innocent of zoning requirements, but little else. Stage left, the house of
Clueless One, a well-off middle-class burgher of the town. Stage right, the
establishment of Loveykins, a well-off daughter of joy. The distance between these
houses is negotiable for the designer, but it should be sufficient to indicate that they
are not connected in any way. Both houses have practical double doors opening
directly onto the stage.*

 *Due effort should be taken to differentiate the houses: Clueless's residence is
solid and dull, the place of Constriction; Loveykins's is gaudy and entrancing, the
place of Release. It is conceivable that on every opening of Loveykins's front doors,
wild music should blare upon the stage. In any case, make it clear that no adult
male would enter Clueless's house except by necessity, not even Clueless himself
. . . but every Anyman would pay a visit to Loveykins, or at least seriously
entertain such a desire.*

 *The symbolism is emphasized by two shrines to antitypical gods. Downstage
from Lovey's establishment is a sculptured representation of the god Bacchus;
downstage from Clueless's house is a like statue of Apollo. These are by no means
elaborate, but the gods so honored should be recognizable. They will serve as foci
for the wild figure-eights of the "mad scene" in Act V, Scene 2, and may well find
other employment.*

 *The stage possesses two side entrances, down toward what might be called its
apron. Stage left leads to downtown, the forum/agora, the place of business and
law, the turf of Epidamnian male citizens. It is remarkably structured, this offstage*

spot: the place of Transaction, where Spatula the cook will buy food, and Clueless One will find himself unwillingly involved in a lawsuit. Stage right leads to the harbor, the entrance by which strangers, complications, and new ideas enter this well-appointed society: the place of Arrival, Departure, and general Chaos, the way by which Clueless Two and Smug will enter to turn this section of town topsy-turvy. And offstage residences will confirm this pattern: Clueless Two's sailors will find lodging somewhere off stage right; the Doctor's surgery (or whatever) is towards town, off stage left.

The stage is empty at start. Enter the Prologue, uncertainly moving across the set. He moves center front and addresses the audience.

Dramatis Personae

The Starter
    PROLOGUE (Prologus)   an inept metatheatrical

The Brothers
    CLUELESS MAXIMUS ONE (Menaechmus A)   a bourgeois of Epidamnus
    CLUELESS MAXIMUS TWO (Menaechmus B)   a tourist from Syracuse

The Dames
    DOVEY (Matrona)   the spouse in the house
    LOVEYKINS (Erotium)   the whore next door

The Gofers
    DIDDLEY (Peniculus)   parasite to Clueless One
    SMUG (Messenio)   slave to Clueless Two
    SPATULA (Cylindrus)   cook to Loveykins
    SKIVVEE (Ancilla)   maid to Loveykins
    TIDEE (Deceo [?])   maid to Dovey

The Fogy
    ANTIQUIDES (Senex)   father to Dovey

The GP
    DR. KLYSTER (Medicus)

The Muscle
    ASSORTED PORTERS (Pompa)
    ASSORTED SAILORS (Nautae)
    FOUR ORDERLIES (Lorarii)

Double Bind

Prologue [1–76]   •

(Enter Prologue, the man. Prologuing is not what he does; in fact, speaking to
groups of people is not what he does. He is, to come down to it, the world's worst
Prologue, pathologically afraid of Leaving Anything Out. This fear is compounded
by his one excellence: he is one of the world's Great Digressors. Worse, he is in love
with what he says and fancies himself quite a wit. He scans the audience.)

PROLOGUE: I have an announcement:
Greetings!
        —that's my announcement, to start off right
at the very beginning—
               And salutations.
                    —to me—
And—not to forget the audience—to *you*.
To you I make delivery of PLAUTUS—
not really, not in the flesh, but on the tongue—
with the standard humble request that you take possession
with most indulgent ears.
               The time is ripe
for the PLOT. Please—uh—take possession with intent attention.
I shall supply it as briefly as is consonant
with . . .
    Oh.
           A word on standard comedic practice:
Playwrights would have us believe that everything happens
at ATHENS. Evidently on the theory that states
the Greeker, the better.
              For my part, I refuse
to report any action as taking place anywhere
but where it in fact . . . took place. Which is the reason
that my synopsis, though very Greece-y, or rather
Greekish, is hardly Attish, or rather Attic,
but rather Si*cil*ic. Make that Sicilian.
                  Well.
So much for the *prelude* to the plot synopsis.
I now dole out, as it were, the synopsis itself—
not by the quart,
          not by the bushel,
               but by

the barnful. When I recount a plot synopsis,
I make it a principle never to stint in the slightest.
There was once a businessman in Syracuse.
He was getting on, when he became the father
of twins. Twin sons. Which is to say, he had two.
They resembled each other to the point that even
the wet nurse wasn't sure which one of the two
she was giving the teat to.
                    In point of fact, their *mother*—
the woman who *physically* brought them into being—
she couldn't tell them apart.
                    From each other.
                              —Don't take
my word for this. I wasn't there. But I have it
on the best authority, an eyewitness account from someone
who *was* there, and saw it all. With his very own eyes.—

Well, when the boys—both boys—were seven years old,
the father packed a large ship rather full
of salable items, took one of the two twin boys
on board that ship, and sailed away to Tarentum.
On business. He left the other boy at home.
With his mother.
                    Well, when they got to Tarentum, it was
—as luck would have it—a holiday there, and crowds
of people had crowded into Tarentum.
                              The way
they do on holidays.
                    Anyway, in all those crowds,
the little boy managed to wander away from his father.
There was a businessman there from Epidamnus who
picked the little boy up and took him off home.
His home. Epidamnus.
                    Now, losing a son like that
was quite traumatic to the father. It broke his heart . . .
and from that very affliction he, well, he died
a day or two later.
                    When he died, he was still at Tarentum.

Finally, the news got back to Syracuse:
the boy abducted, his father dead at Tarentum.
The twin boys' grandfather changed the other boy's name,
the remaining boy's name, to the first, kidnapped, boy's name.
Because he loved the lost one so very much
that he gave *his* name to the boy still at home, the name
CLUELESS—which had belonged to the *other* boy,
and was, in fact, the name of the grandfather, *too*.

—I'll never forget it, because I heard it so often,
when the town crier was running him down for a bill.—

I don't want you to get at all confused,
so let me establish this right at the very beginning:
There are *two* twin brothers; both have *one* name—the same.
To reason this out for you perfectly, step by step,
it's back to Epidamnus for me. Right now. On foot.
Pursuant to which, I herewith solicit commissions:
does anyone here need business attended to at
Epidamnus? Don't be shy. Speak up! Your wish
is my command.
                        Provided you underwrite
your undertaking, of course. No money up front,
you don't get squat. But give me the money up front,
well, that makes all the difference:
                                        you *do* get squat.
But look! I'm back at the place I left. And all
without a single step from this selfsame spot.

—Oh. That man from Epidamnus—remember him?
The one I told you about a while ago,
the one who kidnapped the first little boy—the twin?
Well, he adopted the kidnappee for his own son,
and supplied that son a wife with a hefty dowry,
and made him his heir, and quite conveniently died
—on a trip to the country. There'd been lots of rain.
He waded into a stream, swollen with rain—
not really much more than a little distance from town—
and the coursing current swept him off his feet,
and ducked that abductor, conducting him off to hell!
His money—lots of money—devolved on the boy.

(He points to the house of Clueless One, stage left.)

And here we have the home of the kidnapped twin.
Today the other twin, the one who lives
in Syracuse, is going to come to Epidamnus.
He'll bring a slave along. He'll be on a Quest
to find his twin—*this* twin—his long-lost brother.

(He waves sweepingly at the set, stage left to stage right.)

And *here* is the city of Epidamnus . . .
                                        while this play
is running, of course.
                        When they do another, it changes:
a different play, it becomes a different town.
—Just like families. They move from house to house.

(Indicating one of the two houses.)

> Sometimes a pimp lives here, sometimes a respectable
> senior citizen, then a nice young man,
> sometimes a bankrupt wastrel, perhaps a king,
> or else a beggar, a gofer, a fortune-teller . . .

(Somehow, mercy is taken on the audience, and Prologue's exit is effected—
preferably by mild violence of someone offstage.)

Act I, Scene 1 [77–109]

(Diddley enters from town [stage left]. He is a nasty piece of work, really. His anger
at his occupation forestalls any excellence at it.)

DIDDLEY: Hi, there.   .
                    I'm the parasite in this play.
              Just call me DIDDLEY. Short John DIDDLEY. The name
              my buddies gave me. When I get up from the dinner
              table, what I leave is
                                diddly.

(He shifts to an official mode of presentation.)

                                —TEN-*SHUN!*
              A personal disquisition Of Human Bondage.
              I submit:
                    Most people shackle POWs
              with chains.
                          Most people restrain recovered slaves
              with irons and gyves.
                                Most people are klutzes.
                                            You cannot
              hobble a loser by doubling his load of trouble;
              it only increases his craving for breakout and crime.
              No matter how fast his fetters, the fetteree finds
              some way to effect an exit. He files the weakest
              link, or hammers the grommet flat with a rock.
              Mechanical gimmicks, *pah!*
                                No. Bend your efforts
              to keep your potential escapee from flying the coop
              the *natural* way—with Food & Drink. It's a cinch:
              Attach your man by the gullet to a table heaped up
              every day with an endless supply of the items,
              edible and potable, that suit his particular taste,
              and he is hog-tied: even a sentence of death
              won't make that man miss dinner. He's never out of
              sight or control; no trouble at all.
                                Now, *that's*
              The Tie That Binds.
                          Humane, too; yessirree:

Victuals are such *agreeable* shackles; the looser
they stretch, the tighter they catch.
                                        Take me, for example.
I've been drafted. Called up for service right *there*—
the house of Clueless. Do I object to this toothsome
indenture? No, indeedy; I'm ready, I'm *fit* to be tied.
Clueless, you see, is no mere feeder of men;
he's a *stuffer* of men, a positive makeover artist.
No doctor does better with drugs than Clueless with food.
A lusty young man and consummate consumer himself,
his idea of everyday lunch is Festival Blowout,
course upon course upon course, with towering piles
of saucer and dish and bowl and platter and plate.
To get a bite from the top, you need a ladder.
But . . .
                        for more days than I care to count
I've been on leave at home, serving myself
with delicacies rare enough to begin with, but now
that breakfast's broken loose and dessert's deserted,
so rare that they don't exist at all.
                                        And so
I'm making my way to my patron.
                                        —An opening door!
And look! Here comes CLUELESS now!

(He nips into the alley between the houses, where he is invisible.)

Act I, Scene 2 [110–181]

(Enter Clueless One from his house, singing back to the open door, behind which
[presumably] is his wife.)

CLUELESS I: IN-*COM*-PAT-*IBLE*,
                     That's what we're not.
                     AN-*I*-MOS-*ITY*,
                     That's what you've got.
                     Change your ways, give up your virulence,
                     Hate, dementia, dumbness, violence,
                     And we'll soon be quite COM-PATIBLE, yup.

                     IN-*COR*-RIG-*IBLE*,
                     Don't be that way.
                     Be SUS-CEPT-IBLE
                     To what I say:
                     One more sample of this nastiness,
                     Home to Daddy go in hastiness,
                     And we're really IN-COM-PAT-IBLE then.

                       I can't go out of our happy home

Without a full inquisition:
Where'm I going?
What'm I doing?
What'm I up to?
What've I got?
What'd I do when I was out?
I didn't marry a wife; I married a customs agent.
Full declaration required of actions past and present.
I spoil you, sweetie, but that's all through:
NOW HEAR THIS:
What'm I gonna DO?

WHEREAS
I duly supply you the standard and current
Items as per the marriage agreement:
The wool, the woolies, the wardrobe,
The household expenses in solid gold,
The millions of maids, the upscale provender,
And enough dye to make everything lavender . . .
THEREAS
Be smart, and save yourself a good deal of woe,
Let your husband go unwatched wherever he wants to go.

(The door slams shut. Clueless One preens himself and strikes a macho attitude.)

And another thing: So all your spying
Should have something to be about,
I'll take the handy hooker to lunch,
And book a couch: we're dining OUT!

DIDDLEY: *He's faking. That's not wife-abuse—*
            It's ME-abuse instead;
       If he goes out to dinner, I'm
           The one that won't get fed.

(Clueless One, still not noticing Diddley, turns to the audience and advances down center. He addresses the audience.)

CLUELESS I: Three cheers! Employing the standard invective, I have repulsed my wife from the door.

(No acclaim is forthcoming.)

              —I sense a certain reticence. Where's the applause? the awards?
              No cheating husbands in the crowd?
Look: I have strained mightily in the breach, and every man here owes me congratulations.

(Pulling up his cloak, he displays a somewhat soiled Pelisse that he is wearing underneath.)

My trophy! An intimate garment:
It's all my doing: this Pelisse has given my wife the slip.
This job's a model: Slick husband outfoxes sly jailer.
What dazzling daring!
                              What a dandy deed!
                                              What a cunning stunt!
(Not that I profit at all for my peril. This costly item
goes in the debit column—straight to the neighborhood harlot.)

It's booty time, boys, without the loss of a single man!

(At "booty," Diddley advances unseen to Clueless One and claps his hands over his patron's eyes.)

DIDDLEY: Please, sir, is any bit of that booty bespoken for me?

(Clueless One jumps in terror but does not dare take the hands off.)

CLUELESS I: A trap! Cut down in my prime!

DIDDLEY: No, sir: Propped up this time.

CLUELESS I: Who's there?

(Diddley removes his hands from Clueless One's eyes and moves into view.)

DIDDLEY: It's only me.

CLUELESS I: My Luck! My Advantage! My Edge!
Hel*lo!*

DIDDLEY: Hello to you.

CLUELESS I: What're you doing?

DIDDLEY: I'm shaking the hand
that watches over me, sir—that Special Someone's hand.

CLUELESS I: You couldn't have come at a better time.

DIDDLEY: My little way, sir.
Right time, right place: I know all the nooks and crannies of Luck.

CLUELESS I: Would you like a peek at something really superb?

DIDDLEY: Who cooked it?
One lick of those leftovers, sir, and I'll know if he slipped up.

CLUELESS I: You've seen those friezes that fill a wall, of course, where an eagle
is inveigling Catamite, or Venus is snatching Adonis?

DIDDLEY: Ah. Frequently, sir . . . but how do these friezes relate to *me?*

CLUELESS I: Shut up and *behold.*

(He opens his cloak, displaying the Pelisse in all its glory.)

                    Do I remind you of those friezes?

DIDDLEY:

   (Aside.)

     I'm chilled.
            —You're striking an attitude, sir?
                         What *is* that outfit?

CLUELESS I: That outfit is very *in,* and very *elite.* So'm I.
     So pronounce these words: "You're very IN and very ELITE."

DIDDLEY: I'll eat? But when?

CLUELESS I: I gave you an order, I think; speak out!

DIDDLEY: Okay: "You're very in and very elite."

CLUELESS I: That all?
     No little *lagniappe* of your own that you might throw in?

DIDDLEY: Sorry.
        You're *genial.*
             Actually jolly, by golly.

CLUELESS I: Pray continue.

DIDDLEY: I will *not* continue until I know what good this does me.
     I have to be careful with you; domestic disputes bring danger.
     I have reservations, for self-preservation: I never meddle
     in family rancor.

CLUELESS I: But this will be On the Sly. A spot
     that she knows nothing about. Oh, what a luscious experience!
     We'll burn the day to ashes.

DIDDLEY: Just what I wanted to hear.
     So sign me up, and put me down to light the pyre.
     The day's half-dead already. It's charcoal down to the navel.
     Right next to the *stomach.* In case you've forgotten.

CLUELESS I: I wish you'd stop
     interrupting like that. You're only keeping yourself from dinner.

DIDDLEY: You can hammer my eye till it rattles inside my skull if I utter
     one word unless I'm ordered.

   (Clueless One backs away.)

CLUELESS I: Uh—*fine.*
                Now move over here.
     Let's get away from that door.

   (They move downstage right, away from Clueless One's door.)

DIDDLEY: Your word is my command.

   (He follows.)

CLUELESS I: And just a little farther . . .

(The same process ensues.)

DIDDLEY: No problem.

CLUELESS I: And now, one last
    heroic dash away from the cave of the Lion Queen.

(And again.)

DIDDLEY: What a charioteer you'd make!

CLUELESS I: What do you mean by that?

DIDDLEY: Your rearview instinct. Those constant backward looks to see
    if your wife's tailgating.

CLUELESS I: What are you saying?

DIDDLEY: Whatever you want.
    My little way. I yea your yeas and nay your nays.

CLUELESS I: How are you at deciphering smells?

DIDDLEY: I beg your pardon?

CLUELESS I: Can you tell from a smell what the hell befell, or will befall?

DIDDLEY: I'm no soothsayer. If you want an odor decoded, convene
    the College of Augurs.

CLUELESS I: You've noticed this Pelisse?

(He lifts his cloak again.)

DIDDLEY: God, yes.

(Clueless One faces away from Diddley and hikes up his cloak in back, exposing his
Pelisse-clad rear, to which he points.)

CLUELESS I: Now apply your nose right here, and *sniff,* and kindly inform me
    about the aroma's inner meaning.

DIDDLEY: Yuck.

CLUELESS I: Do I sense reluctance?

DIDDLEY: If you have to go around smelling clothing, start at the top.
    The whiff of a wife in this location . . . no, that won't wash.

CLUELESS I: Won't wash?

DIDDLEY: No matter how hard you scrub, the stench remains.

CLUELESS I: PLACE NOSE AND SMELL—*RIGHT HERE!* Picky, picky, picky!

(Gingerly and briefly, Diddley complies, after one final statement:)

DIDDLEY: In this spot, picky is peachy.

CLUELESS I: Was that so bad?

(Diddly is recovering his breath.)

                                         Your diagnosis?
                 Deliver!

DIDDLEY: I'd say the stench says: PINCH, WENCH, LUNCH.

CLUELESS I: Precisely.
           This intimate garment is on its way to the Girl Next Door—
           Loveykins, there. I'm on my way to order a lunch,
           for me, for her, for YOU.

(They make their way to Loveykins's front door.)

DIDDLEY: I *do* like your taste in pronouns.

CLUELESS I: And then we drink till the stars come out . . . and *go* out, too.

DIDDLEY: Excellent schedule. You do have a way of putting things.

(They are at Loveykins's door.)

           Do I do the honors and knock?

CLUELESS I: You *batter.*

(He thinks this over and restrains Diddley.)

                                         —No, better not.
                 Not yet.

DIDDLEY: Oh, damn. My meal recedes, at topmost speed.

CLUELESS I: Proceed.
                 Knock *nicely,* please.

DIDDLEY: Your girl has pottery doors?
           Now, that shows class but makes for a pretty brittle portal.

(He raises a tentative hand but is stopped by Clueless One, who has seen the door
move slightly.)

CLUELESS I: Not yet! For god's sake, don't knock yet!

(The door opens suddenly. Clueless One and Diddley spring stage left, considerably
out of the way of Loveykins's entrance. Clueless One strikes the attitude of a heroic
herald.)

                                         Behold, she comes!
           And casts the sun in shade before her gorgeous glow!

Act I, Scene 3 [182–218]

(Loveykins bursts from the house and twines herself around Clueless One.)

LOVEYKINS: Sweetie!
                      My darling Clueless!

CLUELESS I: Er . . . hi, there.

DIDDLEY: No greetings for me?

LOVEYKINS: Sorry. You're not on my roster.

DIDDLEY: The army all over again.
             Backup reserves—we never quite make the muster.

CLUELESS I: Ten-SHUN!
             Order of the Day: lay on a battle for me at your place.

LOVEYKINS: A *battle?*

(He nods. She shrugs.)

                      Of course: one battle, coming up.

CLUELESS I: And from this battle
             the two of us will drink to settle who's better battler.
             Decide which one's your fighting machine, your flying column.
             And spend the night with the happy winner.
                                              Oh, You Kid.
             The more I look at you, the more I hate my wife.

(In spite of his gustatory predilections, Diddley is miffed.)

DIDDLEY: And that's why you're wearing her clothes, of course.

(He flips up Clueless One's cloak, exposing the stolen Pelisse. She tentatively
touches the Pelisse.)

LOVEYKINS: And what might this be?

CLUELESS I: Once, the dragon's slough. But now, your Golden Fleece.

LOVEYKINS: You win, hands down. The lover who triumphs with me is not
             the boor who keeps giving orders, but the sensitive gent like you.

(She becomes more affectionate. Diddley, disgusted, indulges in an aside.)

DIDDLEY: Typical bimbo bombast. It lasts as long as there's bait.
             But Love? *True* Love would have chewed his face off, even
                 swallowed
             his nose by now.

(Clueless One starts to take his cloak off.)

CLUELESS I: Hold this.
                              I'm about to slough my fleece.

(In his eagerness, he has trouble divesting himself.)

          I made a vow.

DIDDLEY: I'm ready.
                           And waiting.

(Clueless One has finally removed the cloak. He slings it at Diddley and starts to remove the Pelisse.)

                          No, no! I want
to remember you just like this: Could we have a dance?

CLUELESS I: Me dance? You're out of your mind.

DIDDLEY: I know; it's the company I keep.
Dance or take it off.

(Clueless One skins out of the Pelisse and holds it up.)

CLUELESS I: This abduction was only accomplished . . .
at very great personal . . . danger.
                        In relative ranking of risk,
Hercules' grab of Hippolyta's girdle . . .
                          to voice my opinion . . .
rates as no more than petty theft.

(Lovingly, he presents the Pelisse to Loveykins.)

                        Take it; it's yours.
You deserve it, you really do. The only person alive
who actually understands me.

(She accepts the garment gracefully.)

LOVEYKINS: The proper attitude
for genuine lovers. Lovers of taste.

DIDDLEY: And lovers in haste
to be genuine bankrupts.

CLUELESS I: Bought it last year for my wife. It ran me four hundred drachmas.

DIDDLEY: The bottom line? Four hundred drachs straight down the drain.

CLUELESS I: Now, I want something.

LOVEYKINS: I know.

CLUELESS I: Do you know *what?*

LOVEYKINS: I do,
I *do!* I'm getting it ready.

CLUELESS I: Be sure it's piping hot.

LOVEYKINS: It is, it *is!*

CLUELESS I: And make enough for three.

LOVEYKINS: For *THREE?*

(Clueless One spreads his arms, including Diddley in the group.)

CLUELESS I: The three of *us,* of course.
                                        A delectable lunch inside, here.
               Have somebody go to the forum and purchase toothsome goodies,
               the sweetest of pedigreed sweetbreads, bacon of noble birth,
               hog's half-heads on the hoof, sorts of stuff like that there,
               juicy delights whose very sight on the table rouses
               . a hunger in me that rivals a buzzard's.
                                                And right away!

LOVEYKINS: Oh yes indeed.

CLUELESS I: We're on our way to the City Center.
               Be back in a jiffy and have some drinks till the cooking's done.

LOVEYKINS: Come back whenever you want. It's always ready for you.

CLUELESS I: That's fine. Just *hurry!*
                                    So follow me, fellow.

(He starts off stage left, for the Forum.)

DIDDLEY: I follow you close,
               to keep you in view. I swear I won't lose you today, not even
               if I have to give up my claim to all the wealth of the gods.

(He skitters after Clueless One. All exit stage left.)

LOVEYKINS: Now where's the cook?
                              Call SPATULA out here on the double!

Act I, Scene 4 [219–225]

(Spatula enters from Loveykins's house. A sly menial, he speaks in something
resembling a stage Brooklyn accent.)

LOVEYKINS: Now here's the basket, and here's the cash. Check it: six drachmas.

SPATULA: Gotcha.

LOVEYKINS: On your way to buy groceries. Enough for three,
               that's *three* precisely, no more, no less.

SPATULA: What sort of t'ree?

LOVEYKINS: There's me, and Clueless, and Clueless's toady.

SPATULA: Dat's ten
               an' countin'. Dat sponge can eat for any eight,
               an' easy, too.

LOVEYKINS: I've filled you in on the guests; the rest
is up to you.

SPATULA: Gotcha.
                            Dinner's all ready already.
Hustle 'em in to duh table.

LOVEYKINS: Now hurry!

SPATULA: Back in a shot.

(With basket and purse, he exits to the Forum, stage left. Loveykins returns inside her house.)

Act II, Scene 1 [226–272]

(Enter, stage right [from the harbor], a train of laden sailors and porters, shooed along by Clueless Two [of Syracuse] and Smug, his slave in command, who also totes a heavy seabag.)

CLUELESS II: Smug! A pithy proverb. And all my own work.

(Smug dutifully stops the procession—right in front of Loveykins's house, as it happens—and waits at weary attention. He does not put the seabag down.)

> *For sailors, no bliss surpasses the distant view*
> *of far-off land from the deep.*

SMUG: *Except the view—*
I'll tell it like it is—*of distant* homeland
to returning *sailors.*
                          And now we've come ashore
at Epidamnus. Why?
                          Are we playing a game   ·
of *Ocean*—lapping every island there is?

CLUELESS II: We're on a search for my longtime-lost twin brother.

SMUG: And when, oh *when,* will that search conceivably end?
The search for your twin has stretched out into six years.
In the course of this chore, we've completely sailed the circuit:
Istria, Spain, Marseilles, Illyria now,
the Adriatic, and outer Greece, and Italy . . .
Our specialty—*shores.* If it's bounded by water, we land there.
Try seeking a needle: more speed, provided there *was* one:
you'd be back home, with your finger bandaged, long since.
We endlessly paw through the living to find a *dead* man.
If he were alive, we'd have struck on him years ago.

CLUELESS II: Okay, then, I'm searching for *confirmation*:
a witness to say he's dead. When I hear *that,*

chore over, task done, with no more effort expended.
But until that happens, and while I'm alive, I search.
Only a brother can fathom brotherly love.

SMUG: Needle? You're seeking a *noodle*. In a hassock. Give up!
Or are we writing a *Guide to the Scuzzier Ports
of the Adriatic?*

CLUELESS II: Enough of this endless grousing:
what I say—*do* it.
                    What I serve—*eat* it.
                                   What's trouble—*avoid* it.
Don't irk me. This has nothing to do with you.

SMUG: Gotcha. Message received:
                    I AM A SLAVE.
Plainly put in my place by the prince of pith.

(He shrinks back, beaten. But after a short pause, he brightens and steps up again.)

But what do I care?
                    I have to say my piece.
—A word, Clueless?
                    What word?

(He produces a smallish money-bag.)

                    The word is WALLET.
The WALLET wanes; the WALLET wants its wampum.
The wasp-waist WALLET's wasted, won't last the winter
unless you stop stalking this nonexistent twin
and go back home before they freeze our assets.
The reason?
                    This town is Epidamnus the Damned.
The stamping grounds of swingers, and lechers, and drunks,
all state-of-the-art. The natural abode of grifter,
flimflam man, con artist, of shyster and shill.
The home sweet home of flocks of foxy doxies,
hookers to hook the suckers with tongues of honey.
A town of ill repute—Epidamnus, dammit! That's why
they call this seaside town the Last Resort!

CLUELESS II: So I'll be careful.
                    Better give me the Wallet.

(Smug shoves the Wallet back into the seabag.)

SMUG: Fat chance.

CLUELESS II: You've got to face it, Smug:
you're a compulsive chaser, you womanize madly.
And I'm a tad cantankerous, short fuse, hothead.

So: if I hold the money, two roads to ruin are shut:
you won't screw it away and consequently
I won't explode in anger and shout it away.
You follow?

(Surprisingly, Smug is convinced. He reaches in the seabag, secures the Wallet again, and hands it over.)

SMUG: You keep it. Safe and sound. With my
enthusiastic approval. Your job, now: DO IT.

Act II, Scene 2 [273–350]

(Enter Spatula laden from the Forum, stage left. He is not perceived by those already onstage.)

SPATULA: Am I a slick shoppuh, or what?
                                   My ansuh: YEAH!
An' such a marvelous meal I'll serve my clients!
An' . . . uh-oh, here's Clueless.
                              I wince at the welts
awready.
                  Duh guests are takin' duh air out front,
and I'm not back with the groceries yet.
                                        Now what?
Go up, say hi.

(He moves to Clueless Two, still in front of Loveykins's house.)

                     —Clueless! To you a large *Hello!*

CLUELESS II: To you *Good-bye,* strange person I never met.

SPATULA: Strange person? You joker.
                              It's me—duh chef.
                                        You know me.

CLUELESS II: Damned if I do.

SPATULA: But where's duh rest of duh guests?

CLUELESS II: The rest of *what* guests?

SPATULA: You know 'em: *him.* Your pa-ra-site.

CLUELESS II: I'm parasite-free.

     (To Smug.)
                     —A completely obvious loony.

SMUG: Con men in gobs. Remember, you heard it here.

CLUELESS II: All right, young person. *Which* of my parasites
might you be meaning?

SPATULA: Which one?
                                    Diddley, of course.

SMUG:

  (Fumbling in the seabag, which he does not put down.)

                    Plenty of diddly in here. Look, see for yourself.
                    Or check the Wallet.

  (He points to the Wallet, which Clueless Two is holding.)

                                Diddly, that's what we've got.

SPATULA: You're way too early for lunch, Mr. Clueless, Sir.
                I'm just gettin' home wit' the groceries.

CLUELESS II: *Strange* young man,
                please answer me this question:
                                        What's the current
                quotation on pigs?

SPATULA: On *pigs?*

CLUELESS II: Yes, *pigs.* The pigs
                they sacrifice to mitigate sudden madness.

SPATULA: Two drachs per pig.

CLUELESS II: Two drachmas?

  (He fumbles in the Wallet, finds a coin, and holds it up for Spatula to view.)

                                    For you. My gift.
                Have someone take this money and *make you sane!*
                I'm sure of two items: first, you're deeply disturbed,
                and second, mad person, you are disturbing ME—
                whom YOU have never *ever* met!

SPATULA: You *know* me!
                Spatula, duh chef? You *gotta* remembuh my name!

CLUELESS II: Spatula, Shortbread, Sweetbread—*so?* Get stuffed!
                I DO NOT KNOW YOU.
                            I DO NOT *WANT* TO KNOW YOU.

SPATULA: But I know you, Clueless . . .

  (A shocked silence, as Clueless Two belatedly takes this in.)

                                Uh, dat's your name.

CLUELESS II: And it's the only sane word I've heard out of you.
                Okay, then: where did the two of us meet?

SPATULA: Us? Meet?
Right here. Your mistress's house.

(A beat of total incomprehension from Clueless Two and Smug.)

                                    In *Loveykins's* house!

CLUELESS II: I do not have a mistress. I do not have the slightest idea
of who the hell you are.

SPATULA: Duh hell you say!
Every time—and dat's a lot, believe me—
dat you've been soppin' up wine in dat very house,
who soived as youah *sommelier?* I did, dat's who!
Look, regular drinkuh, I'm your regulah waituh.

(Smug fumbles in the seabag.)

SMUG: Oh, damn. Why didn't I pack something heavy and hard
to knock this blockhead's block off?

CLUELESS II: Regular waiter?
Today is the very first time I've caught a glimpse
of this unspeakable town!

SPATULA: I nevvuh soived you?

CLUELESS II: Never in this world.

SPATULA: And, I suppose, you don't
live in dis house over heah?

CLUELESS II: I call down utter
perdition on any and all who reside in that house!

SPATULA:

(Aside. Impressed.)

Dat's really low self-esteem. An obvious loony.

(To Clueless Two.)

—Clueless, a woid.

CLUELESS II: What now?

SPATULA: A meah suggestion:
Remembuh doze drachmas, Clueless? Duh ones you promised
to give me? Keep 'em.
                          For you.
                                A guy what calls
down on his self, dat guy is *really*
over the edge, dat guy could stand some help.
Send out, an' have them deliver one quick pig.

CLUELESS II: He's a mob in himself—a babble of rabble—a pest!

(Spatula turns to the audience.)

SPATULA: Dat's our little way. Solid relationship. Joke
                after joke. Wit'out his wife, dis guy's a riot.

(He displays the groceries to Clueless Two.)

                Wojjuh say to *dat?*

CLUELESS II: What say? Well, WHAT?

SPATULA: Is dis sufficient provenduh for t'ree of youse,
                for you, for duh dame, and duh sponge, or should I buy more?

CLUELESS II: What dames? What sponges?
                                    What are you talking about?

SMUG: You're deranged: what drives you to hassle my master?

SPATULA: Excuse me—do we know each udduh? I'm engagin'
                In conversation wit' dis guy; *him* I know.

SMUG: I know enough to know that you're a nutcase.

SPATULA:

(Pointedly ignoring Smug, to Clueless Two.)

                Duh meal will be juicy an' tenduh, toot soot.
                No Waitin' Inside.
                                    Or, at duh very least,
                don't wanduh away from duh building. Stick around close.
                Will dat be all, sir?

CLUELESS II: Your head on a platter, perhaps?

SPATULA:

(Flashing into anger for just a moment.)

                Bettuh your head on a . . . *pillow* beside duh table.
                Duh poifect spot to relax while it cooks, while my
                trained hand applies dese classy ingredients
                to duh furious frenzy of Vulcan.

(Clueless Two doesn't move. Spatula shrugs.)

                                    So I'm duh one
                who goes in, an' lets Loveykins know you're waitin' here.
                She'll conduct youse to youah table. Won't let you loituh.

(Assembling his groceries, he moves into Loveykins's house with considerable
dignity.)

CLUELESS II: Is he really gone?
       —Based on that encounter,
    every word in your spiel was absolutely true.

SMUG: Just be on the lookout. Beware this house right here.
    It's my opinion that these are the haunts
    of a person of ill repute. You heard what he said—
    that madman who just entered that very door?

CLUELESS II: But how did he know my name? I'm really perplexed.

SMUG: What's to perplex? Another type of tricks
    these hookers turn. Standard procedure: they send
    their best-looking slaves and maids right down to the harbor
    to solicit news of the latest foreign arrival.
    Home port? they ask. The owner's name? they ask.
    Adhesive harlots: once appliqué'd to the owner,
    they can't be *pried* off. Tempted and vamped, the cast-off
    tourist casts off for home: no salvage value.

    A pirate frigate's lurking at anchor in *this* port:
    in my opinion, we'd better look out for her,
    or we'll be very unjolly and extremely rogered.

CLUELESS II: Gracious. That's sound advice you give me.

SMUG: The proof
    of the warning is in the turning. Out.
               Advice
    is only sound if it's taken. So take precautions!

(Loveykins's door begins to open.)

CLUELESS II: Shut up for a minute, will you? I heard that door
    go *creak*. We'd better watch and see who it is.

(At long last, Smug lowers the seabag.)

SMUG: A chance to put this down.

(He moves to the line of baggage handlers.)

          A humble request
    to the seagoing infantry?
          Keep an eye on this.

(He deposits the seabag in the middle of the line and takes up a position by Clueless Two.)

Act II, Scene 3 [351–445]

(Enter Loveykins from her house. Not immediately seeing the duo, she moves downstage, singing to a corps of housemaids who are presumed to have accompanied her to the door.)

LOVEYKINS:

> *The outside doors*   *are spread and wide.*
> *Leave 'em open!*   *Back inside!*
> *Get your broom*   *and start your biz—*
> *Inside's where*   *the action is!*
> *Insider, sweet*   *and neat spell CLASS—*
> *Whisk and dust*   *and bust your ass!*
> *CHARM gives johns*   *the panting hots,*
> *CHARM brings money*   *in, in pots.*
> *TASTE wastes lovers,*   *makes 'em whine;*
> *TASTE puffs up*   *our bottom line.*
> *Rub-a-dub-dub*   *will never lose—*
> *Mama needs a*   *new pair of shoes!*

(Puzzled, she looks around but does not see Clueless Two.)

—But where can he be? The cook swore he was out front.

(She sees him.)

—Oh.

> *There he is,*   *my mainest man,*
> *God's gift to*   *the courtesán,*
> *Heaven's gate*   *for any hooker,*
> *A ding-dong-daddy*   *whose name is Sugar!*
> *Open-handed,*   *flush, and stupid*
> *My own, my private*   *personal Cupid.*
> *That's why, though*   *he's not much fun,*
> *In my house,*   *he's Number One!*

(She moves to Clueless Two.)

—Now the approach, and then the confrontation:

> *Baby, why stand*   *here outside,*
> *When the door is*   *open wide?*
> *You're the one it's*   *open for,*
> *Opener than your*   *own front door.*
> *Everything is*   *fixed precisely*
> *Per directions,*   *neat and nicely.*
> *Don't be strange;*   *be satisfied:*
> *Ain't no waitin' . . .*   *COME INSIDE!*

The meal's on the table. Go in when you want; it's up to you.

CLUELESS II:

(To Smug.)

Who is this woman conversing with?

LOVEYKINS: No one but *you.*

CLUELESS II: —Excuse me?
                              Have we now or ever had business together?

(An awkward pause . . . until Loveykins decides it's a New Game.)

LOVEYKINS: Oooh, have we ever!
                              I am . . . *conversing* . . . with you because
                Venus, the goddess of Love, has seen fit to raise you aloft,
                to the topmost spot, above all others, in my affection . . .
                a place you richly deserve, since you and you alone
                have fertilized me with your generous gifts
                                        and made me *bloom*.

CLUELESS II:

(Totally flummoxed, he turns to Smug.)

                Smug, I'm sure this woman is either crazy or smashed.
                Such warmth—to a total stranger—what sort of welcome is *that?*

SMUG: I told you: Standard Procedure.
                              You ain't seen nothin' yet.
                These are but leaves, adrift on the gentle breeze. Just wait
                two days, when the gale's in force: whole trees will totter
                    and crash . . .
                and right on *you,* as it happens. Custom of the country: these are
                magnetic whores, as it happens, exerting their force on silver.
                —Just let me set some welcome a-waggin':
                                        Hey, you there—female!
                I'm talking to you!

LOVEYKINS: About what?

SMUG: When did you meet this man?

LOVEYKINS: Same place where he met me. In Epidamnus, of course.

SMUG: In Epidamnus he never set foot until today.

LOVEYKINS:

(Concluding the exchange with an absolutely flat reading.)

                Oh, how cute. I do believe you're pulling my leg.

(She turns back to Clueless Two.)

                This way, dear *sweet* Clueless. The atmosphere's nicer inside.

CLUELESS II: Oh damn. My name again! The woman got it *right!*
                What's up? I sense an enigma.

SMUG: None needed; she smelled your Wallet.
                The one in your hand.

CLUELESS II: Well, talk about your good advice!

(He forces the wallet on Smug.)

   —Here, you take it. And I'll find out who's the Loved One here: my wallet or me?

(He advances to Loveykins. Smug waits.)

LOVEYKINS: Now let's go in and have our lunch.

CLUELESS II: A very gracious invitation, but thank you, *No.*

LOVEYKINS: A *No?* Then why did you just tell me to cook you lunch?

CLUELESS II: I told you to cook me lunch?

LOVEYKINS: You certainly did. And lunch for your parasite, too.

CLUELESS II: WHAT PARASITE, damn it to hell?

(Aside.)

   —One thing's for sure. This woman's seriously addled.

LOVEYKINS: You know— your Parasite Diddley. No one gets Diddley out of his mind.

CLUELESS II: What possible diddly is that?
         The diddly you wipe off your shoes?

LOVEYKINS: The Diddley right on your tail when you gave me that Pelisse. The Pelisse you burgled away from your wife.

CLUELESS II: Oh god, not *again!*
I made you a gift of the Pelisse I burgled away from my wife?
 —She's flipped; she thinks she's a horse; she has dreams standing up.

LOVEYKINS: Does it turn you on somehow to make me the butt of your jokes? Why must you insist on denying that something that happened, happened?

CLUELESS II: Then what *did* happen? Just what did I do that I say I didn't?

LOVEYKINS: Today. You gave me. The Pelisse. Of your wife.

CLUELESS II: Again I deny it!
I have. No wife. I have never. *Had.* A wife. At all.
I never. Pushed foot. Or anything else. Inside. The portals.
Of this tawdry. Town. From the time. I was born until. *Today!*
Lunch I had on the boat.
     Then came here.
       Then met you.

LOVEYKINS: We're off again. Another variable—I can't stand it.
              Your story now has a boat . . . What boat?

CLUELESS II: Your basic boat
            of wood—of worn-out, punctured, sprung-asunder *planks*—
            resembling the boards too often trod by some hack actor.
            It's mainly *pegs* to hold the rest of the wreck together.

LOVEYKINS: All right, sweetie, put paid to your little joke, and let's
              go in to lunch together.

CLUELESS II: Look, ma'am, let's get this straight.
            The man you're hunting down's *not me*. It's someone else.

LOVEYKINS: I'm sorry. I'm seeking

> *a gentleman, Clueless,*
> *the scion of Copeless,*
> *product of Syracuse*
> *over in Sicily*
> > *ruled by Agáthocleez*
> > *sire of Epítomeez*
> > *sire of Anátomeez*
> > *third from the top who be-*
> > *gat Hippopotamus,*
> > *currently tyrant and .*
> > *emperor, too?*
>
> *That's not you?*

(Clueless Two, thunderstruck, moves back towards Smug.)

CLUELESS II: It's all true!

SMUG: I swear there's a simple solution: this dame is a Syracusan.
        How else could she possibly know your name by the numbers?

CLUELESS II: There comes a point where you simply have to *accept*.

SMUG: No, STOP!
        Step over that stoop, and you will be shut down!

CLUELESS II: I've got this firmly in hand.   Shut up.
                         I agree to whatever she says
        for a chance at some R and R.

(He moves to Loveykins.)

                    —Ma'am, please excuse
        my constant denials just now; all part of my little plan.

(He points to Smug.)

        It's *him*. I had to keep him in the dark, or else

he'd tell my wife about the Pelisse. And the Supper, too.
But that's all past.
                              Now let's go into the party.
                                                  Whenever.

LOVEYKINS: Aren't you expecting your parasite?

CLUELESS II: Not if I can help it.
The man is a nix, a nebbish, a nit.
                              In fact, if he comes . . .
please, ma'am, refuse him entrance.

LOVEYKINS: I *like* commissions like that.
Here's one for you, if you don't mind . . .

CLUELESS II: Your wish, my command.

LOVEYKINS: You know my present—the Pelisse?
                              I'd like it taken down
to the Doodad Shoppe. It needs repair, and I'd really like
to add some appliqués, and maybe furbelows, too.

CLUELESS II: Cleh-ver, by god, that's cleh-ver!
                              A completely different effect:
my wife won't know it at all if she meets it on the street.

LOVEYKINS: You'll take it along when you leave?

CLUELESS II: Oh yes; that's what I do best.

LOVEYKINS: So let's go in.

CLUELESS II: I'll be right with you. Just one last word
with my menial there.

(Loveykins enters her house. Clueless Two hangs back and turns to Smug.)

                              —Hey, Smug! You get over here!

(Smug hurries up.)

SMUG: And what's up now?

CLUELESS II: Reconnaissance in progress.

SMUG: We need
Reconnaissance?

CLUELESS II: We always require Reconnaissance.

SMUG: We do?
            Don't tell me, I know: You're sounding out the grounds
for personal bankruptcy. Down you go.

CLUELESS II: It's in the bag!

SMUG:

> (For a moment, he worries about the seabag, still by the sailors.)

> What's in the bag?

CLUELESS II: The booty.

SMUG: Your booty's on the line.

CLUELESS II: I've all but bagged the booty—that's what this battle's about!
You hurry and get this crew booked into an inn somewhere.
Then come back here and get me, before the sun goes down.

SMUG: But master, these are *whores*.
                              Their tricks you can't conceive!

CLUELESS II: SILENCE! If I screw up through lack of sophistication,
who suffers?
                 Me, not you.
                      But lack of sophistication
is what SHE has, not me. She is, in fact, a rube.
From my Reconnaissance,
                 this beauty's me booty!
                                        ARRR!

> (He stalks into Loveykins's house. Smug looks after him.)

SMUG: And so our simple sloop slips slowly into the scuppers
of the dreadnought woman-of-war, to sink without trace.
                                        But no:
only a hick like me would expect to pilot his master.
When he plunked down money for me, he was buying a yes-man
    vassal,
not a commander in chief.

> (He moves to the seabag, hoists it onto his shoulder, and addresses the sailors and porters.)

                 All right, men! Follow me!
        Quick-march!
                 Your captain has to return for a stint as private.

> (Smug and sailors and porters march off stage right.)

Act III, Scene 1 [446–465]

> (Diddley, rumpled, disheveled, and furious, staggers on stage left, from the Forum.)

DIDDLEY: In thirty—count 'em, thirty—ugly years of life
not one atrocity did I perpetrate rivaling this one:
I attended a PUBLIC MEETING!
                              Got trapped,
                                   went down with all hands—

except for Clueless: *I'm* gasping—but *he* bails out and bolts.
Slips back to his popsy, no doubt.
　　　　　　　　　　　　All disencumbered from *me.*

May heaven without exception blast and damn
the man who first conceived the mandatory meeting—
the compulsory convocation to hobble the already hassled!
They ought to require attendance by loafers and slackers and no-
　　　goods,
with instant incarceration for those who miss the shape-up—
that's the way to do it!
　　　　　　　　　　　And we have slackers in scads,
drones who never met a menu, one-snack-a-day types
who neither go out to dinner nor ever have anyone in.
That is the workforce to muster for public rallies and meetings.
With a law like that, I wouldn't be diddled out of dinner.
My dinner!
　　　　　　A dinner, I'm sure, that wanted me to eat it.

—But onward, still.
　　　　　　　　Hope springs eternal:
　　　　　　　　　　　　　　it's Leftover Time!

(As Diddley starts for Loveykins's house, Clueless Two, tiddly and satiated, party
garland on head and Pelisse in hand, totters from the door. Diddley pulls up and
hides behind the statue of Apollo.)

Oops. Clueless departs, still wearing his party garland.
The repast is way past,
　　　　　　　　lunch is history,
　　　　　　　　　　　　　even the table's
a snackless waste.
　　　　　　I'm just in time
　　　　　　　　　　to walk him home.

Standard plan: keen observation, sharp confrontation.

Act III, Scene 2 [466–523]

(Clueless Two addresses the unseen Loveykins from immediately outside her door.)

CLUELESS II:　Don't fuss—I'll bring it back in a flash, repaired,
　　　　　　remade, reaccessorized. I swear you'll swear
　　　　　　it's a different garment.
　　　　　　　　　　　My personal guarantee:
　　　　　　you won't see this again.

(Diddley watches from behind Apollo and seethes, unnoticed by Clueless Two.)

DIDDLEY:　　　　　　　　　*Errands?* Of course!
　　　　　　He's taking the Pelisse to the detail shop *himself!*

> The lunch is gorged, the wine is ravaged, the sponge,
> the faithful sponge, is purged, shut out, rejected.
> And now must I to mine own self be true:
> > REVENGE, I CRY, REVENGE!
> Terrible, swift, and *elegant*.
> > > Just watch me work.

CLUELESS II:

> (Moving center, he turns towards the audience and addresses the skies.)

> Almighty gods! I'm Number One! You've never
> bestowed more bounties and boons in a single day
> on a single man who expected less!
> > > Consider:
> food and sauce, and sex, and . . .

> (He holds up the Pelisse.)

> > > > look! A surprise—
> a legacy soon to be liquidated for good.

DIDDLEY: The trouble with ambush: I can't hear a thing from here.
  He got *his*; is he boasting how he got *mine?*

CLUELESS II: My gift to her, she claims; my theft from my wife.
  Perceiving her error, I instantly shout agreement.
  I play along as though this twaddle were truth,
  that some relationship obtained between us.
  Any fantastic assertion she voices, I echo.
  To cut to the bottom line: I've never ever
  taken in greater receipts for lesser outlay.

DIDDLEY: Now the attack: I'm spoiling to start a spat.

> (He springs from behind the statue and advances on the startled Clueless Two.)

CLUELESS II: Now what? Another encounter? Who can this be?

DIDDLEY: AHA! you featherweight phony, than whom
  no wickeder, nastier, *vicious-er* clown exists!
  You're not a man, you're a scandal! Shyster! Cheat!
  You absolute moral zero! What did I ever
  do to you, to deserve annihilation?
  Just minutes ago, you left me in the lurch downtown!
  While I was away, you lowered lunch in its grave
  and shut me out of the will!
> > > HOW COULD YOU DO IT!

> (The vigorous assault initially wearies rather than upsets Clueless Two.)

CLUELESS II: Excuse me, sir, but do we have business together?
  I don't know you, you don't know me—so why

this flood of scurrilous invective?

                                        Or would you prefer
impairment, perhaps, in return for vilification?

DIDDLEY: As god is my witness, you already gave me that!

CLUELESS II: Excuse me, sir, but might you tell me your name?

DIDDLEY: As if you didn't know it!

                                    I detest being dissed!

CLUELESS II: As god is *my* witness, I DO NOT KNOW YOU. Never
before today have I experienced you
in any shape or form.

                            But still, whoever
you are, let's keep this meeting on an equable level.
One simple rule. No hassle. No hassle of *me*.

DIDDLEY: Clueless! Wake up!

CLUELESS II: My oath: I AM AWAKE—
as far as I know.

DIDDLEY: And yet you do not know me?

CLUELESS II: Correct. If I knew you, I wouldn't say that I didn't.

DIDDLEY: You do not know your personal parasite—*me?*

CLUELESS II: This I do know:

                            you don't have a brain; you have headcheese.

DIDDLEY: One question: you purloined that Pelisse from your wife today
and presented it to Loveykins, did you not?

CLUELESS II: On oath: I have no wife. I neither presented
this Pelisse to Loveykins, nor, in fact, purloined it.

DIDDLEY:

     (A brief aside.)

               Lost it: there goes the Grand Plan.

                                        —Let's try again:
did I, or did I not; observe you emerging
from that door there, wearing—nay, *clad*—in that Pelisse?

CLUELESS II: Oooh, I despise your kind!

                                    Just because you're a pervert,
is that supposed to mean that I'm one, too?
You swear, or affirm, that I was clad in a *Pelisse?*

DIDDLEY: My oath: I swear you were.

CLUELESS II: Skedaddle! Git!
To any appropriate doom for scum like you!

　　　　　　　　　　Or try a course of moral purification
　　　　　　　　　　to turn your mind around!

DIDDLEY:　　　　　　　　　　　　　　　Then hear *my* oath:
　　　　　　　　　　I shall divulge this affair to your wife in detail!
　　　　　　　　　　Plaintive appeals are useless; I won't be deterred
　　　　　　　　　　till all your nasty language redounds on you!
　　　　　　　　　　No one eats my lunch and goes unavenged!

(He stomps into Clueless One's house without knocking.)

CLUELESS II:　So what the hell's going on? Am I a target,
　　　　　　　　　　a butt for derision from everybody I meet?
　　　　　　　　　　A laughingstock to everybody I look at?

(He suddenly turns back towards Loveykins's house.)

　　　　　　　　—But hark. The door over there. I heard a creak.

Act III, Scene 3 [524–558]

(Skivvee, Loveykins's maid, enters from Loveykins's house. She carries a golden
bracelet.)

SKIVVEE:　　　Clueless? A request from Loveykins, pretty please?
　　　　　　　　　　The goldsmith's is on your way downtown; could you drop
　　　　　　　　　　this bracelet off and have it *augmented* a little?
　　　　　　　　　　An ounce of gold . . .
　　　　　　　　　　　　　　　　　　and a full makeover, too.

CLUELESS II:　Nullo problemo.

　　(He takes the bracelet from Skivvee.)
　　　　　　　　　　　　　　　Any more errands? Tell her
　　　　　　　　　　The take-charge guy is here; no commission refused.

SKIVVEE:　　　You *do* recognize the bracelet?

(Clueless Two squints at it carelessly.)

CLUELESS II:　　　　　　　　　　　　　　　I can tell it's gold.

SKIVVEE:　　　But this is the very bracelet you claimed you burgled
　　　　　　　　　　out of your wife's chest, in secret. Some time back.

CLUELESS II:　I swear it never happened!

SKIVVEE:　　　　　　　　　　　　　You don't remember?
　　　　　　　　Oh, goodness me!
　　　　　　　　　　　　　　Well, if you don't remember,
　　　　　　　　then give the bracelet back.

(She reaches for it. He draws his hand back and affects close inspection.)

CLUELESS II: Now, wait. Let's see . . .
              Who could forget my wife's chest?
                                             Well, look at that!
              The very bracelet I gave her.

SKIVVEE: The very one.

CLUELESS II: Ahem. What about the expensive armbands I gave her?

SKIVVEE: You didn't. Ever.

CLUELESS II: You're right. I didn't. Just this.

SKIVVEE: Do I tell her you'll take it in charge?

CLUELESS II: Precisely. You tell her
              Charge Will Be Taken.
                             I'll make all the arrangements:
              Same-day delivery: Pelisse and bracelet together.

SKIVVEE: Now, could you do something for ME, nice Mr. Clueless?
              Have the goldsmith make me a pair of earrings?
              Four drachs worth of gold? Pendants with globular ends?
              That way, I'll be ever so . . . *nice* when you come to call.

CLUELESS II: Consider it done.
                             Just gimme the gold.
                                             I'll pay
              for the labor myself.

SKIVVEE: Oh. Couldn't you please
              supply the gold? I really sincerely promise
              to pay you back. Afterwards.

CLUELESS II: On the whole, *no.*
              Couldn't *you* please supply the gold? I promise
              I'll pay you back afterwards. Double. At least.

SKIVVEE: I haven't got it.

CLUELESS II: Then give it to me when you get it.

SKIVVEE:

              (Frostily turning to go into Loveykins's house.)

                   Will that be all?

CLUELESS II: You tell her that I am In Charge . . .

              (Skivvee flounces back into Loveykins's house.)

                   . . . of Quick Liquidation. How much can I get for this lot?
              —Is she inside yet?
                             No trace; the door is *shut.*

              (He moves center, then holds Pelisse *and* bracelet up to the sky.)

Ye gods! I am the pantheon's proper pet!
I'm on their list for patronage, increase, and love.

Better not dawdle, now opportunity
and chance conspire. It's time to blow this bordello.

Attention, Clueless! Forward, march! On the double!
—But wait! A stratagem, of course:

(He moves quickly to the stage left exit, removes the garland, and puts it on the
ground.)

                                        I sling
this garland slyly over here, to my left:
the road downtown.
                        Whoever spots my spoor
will think that I went thataway.
                                Not me, thanks. I go
*this*away, to meet my slave—I certainly hope
that he turns up—and fill him in on the goods
and chattels the gods have showered on me today!

(Joyous, he exits stage right, towards the harbor.)

Act IV, Scene 1 [559–570]

(Enter, from Clueless One's house, Dovey and Diddley. She strides; he creeps.)

DOVEY: HOW LONG DO I SUFFER IN SILENCE?
                                        My husband loots
        the house and drags the swag to his popsy next door . . .
        That isn't marriage, it's pillage!

DIDDLEY: Please—no more noise!
        The game is afoot, about to be caught red-handed.
        Stay close behind me.

                        Let's see. The subject was making
        his way to the detail shop with Pelisse in hand.
        Yours, in fact, that he burgled from home sweet home.
        Quite drunk . . .
                        and wearing a garland . . .

(He spies Clueless Two's cast-off garland on the way to town and pounces on it.)

                                        Got it in one!
        The garland itself!

(He points off stage left.)

                        He went thataway! Don't take
        my word for it; track him, and check me out,
        because you'll find . . . no, check that: here he comes.

Right on the dot of doom . . .
                              That's odd:
                                        No Pelisse.

DOVEY: But what approach do I take with him now?

DIDDLEY: The standard.
              Don't change. Just make his life hell.
                                        It works for me.
              Let's watch from here. A handy spot for an ambush.

(They secrete themselves in the alley between the two houses as Clueless One
enters.)

Act IV, Scene 2 [571–674]

(Enter from the Forum, stage left, Clueless One. He is bedraggled and disheveled
and distinctly annoyed. He sings "The Song of Annoying Obligation.")

CLUELESS I:

> *The System is The Trouble,*
> *The System is a dud,*
> *The System's gonna get you*
> *And make your morals mud.*
>
> *The System has no reason,*
> *The System is a pest,*
> *The System's the addiction*
> *Of the brightest and the best.*
>
> *The System is a custom*
> *That tries to be a science*
> *Where Patrons pick out others*
> *And make them into Clients.*
>
> *They don't pick out the Clients*
> *Who know their ought or should.*
> *The System isn't based on*
> *Who's awful or who's good.*
>
> *The saint who has no money*
> *Is, to The System, bad.*
> *The lowlife with high income's*
> *The man who must be had.*
>
> *The System maps our culture*
> *With notch and nook and niche;*
> *There's room for any bastard*
> *If the sonofabitch is rich.*

Which explains the staggering number of Clients
with absolutely no regard

For law or ethics, which renders the existence
                      of their Patrons quite hassled and hard.
Defaulters and dodgers, these human vultures
                      are forever entangled in lawsuits—
No great surprise, since extortion and lies
                      are the usual source of their assets.

> When Client has his day in court,
> It's Patron's day in court, too . . .
> For perjury, the very way
> **The System** says he ought to
> Defend his Client's dodge or grudge
> To jury, magistrate, or judge.

My Client's entanglements tripped me and trapped me the whole
    afternoon
With no chance of getting back here to the party anytime soon.
I presented his case at the hearing, a tissue of lies and omissions
That put the best face on his hideous tally of tacky transgressions,
And changed his brutalities into mere peccadillos—in short,
I hacked out a cunning compact to settle his case out of court.
Oh, what a deal I was cutting, a tailored brief that had style,
Contorted and twisted and studded with loopholes . . .
                                    until my vile
Client decided, the hell with agreements, he'd take it to trial—
Where hostile witnesses clustered to sink him, three in a row,
Where his guilt stood up in court and shouted out, "HelLO!"

> Damn that litigating clown,
> The man who shot my party down.
> Damn me, too, for going to court:
> My Ideal Day is cut off short.

> Still:
> The day's not over; there's a thought:
> I ordered lunch; is it still hot?
> Is my mistress waiting, too?
> Check it out—that's what I'll do.

> If Loveykins is really miffed;
>   What device to sue for peace?
> Loveykins must have a gift . . .
>   And that's the answer:
>   The Pelisse!

(His voice rises to a shout.)

The Pelisse I pinched from my wife and plumped in Loveykins's lap!
Oh, Bless that Dress!

DIDDLEY: Any comment?

DOVEY: My marriage in ruins! My spouse a roué!

DIDDLEY: I wouldn't want you to miss a word.

DOVEY: I hear quite well, thanks.

(Still not seeing the two watchers, Clueless One makes for Loveykins's house.)

CLUELESS I: If I have any sense, I'll go over here and improve my lot.
              The wiser path leads to Loveykins's house: pleasure at last.

DIDDLEY:

(Flanking Clueless One on his right as he passes.)

              But misery first.

(Dovey zooms in on Clueless One's left. Flanked, he stops, at first more surprised
than fearful.)

DOVEY: By all that's holy,
              you'll pay interest on that heist!

DIDDLEY: Good move.

DOVEY: Did you really think
              that you could commit these heinous atrocities under wraps?

CLUELESS I:

(Genuinely puzzled.)

              Oh, hello, darling. Did something happen?

DOVEY: You're asking *me?*

CLUELESS I: Well, I'll ask *him,* if that's what you want.

(He puts a placating hand on her arm. She shoves it violently away.)

DOVEY: Hands off! No foreplay!

DIDDLEY:

(Coaching her.)

              Now follow through.

CLUELESS I: You seem annoyed. Something I did?

DOVEY: You ought to know.

(Diddley continues coaching her.)

DIDDLEY: He knows, he knows. The bastard's faking.

CLUELESS I:

(Beginning to realize that not all is well.)

Something I did?

DOVEY: The Pelisse.

CLUELESS I: *The Pelisse?*

DOVEY: Someplace, the Pelisse . . .

DIDDLEY:

(To Clueless.)

You're panicked.

CLUELESS I: I am *not* panicked.

DIDDLEY: You are. At least, you're pale.
The Pelisse produces pallor, at least.
                             Gulping the feast
while I was away—you shouldn't have done that.

(To Dovey.)

                                    —Go on the attack!

CLUELESS I:

(With a minimal head-shake to Diddley.)

Please be quiet.

DIDDLEY: No, dammit, no quiet from me.

(To Dovey.)

                                    —See that?

A head-shake to shut me up.

CLUELESS I: No, not in the goddam least.
I am not shaking the head,

(He shakes his head at Diddley.)

                         nor am I slipping the wink.

(He winks violently at Diddley.)

DIDDLEY:

(To Dovey.)

There's chutzpah. What you see with your very own eyes, he denies.

CLUELESS I: By Jupiter *and* the other eleven—is that sufficient?—
              I shook no head!

(He shakes his head violently again.)

DIDDLEY: *That* point we grant. Get back to business.

CLUELESS I: What business is that?

DIDDLEY: Standard small business: the detail shop.
              Get back down there: we sue for return of one Pelisse.

CLUELESS I: Pelisse? Please, what Pelisse might that be?

DIDDLEY: I say no more.
              I leave the rest to my client, who does not appear to recall
              the particulars of her case.

DOVEY: I remember this: I'm RUINED!

CLUELESS I: Ruined? But how? But why? Come on, now, you can tell *me*.
              I know: it's a personnel problem.
                                   Have you been smart-alecked, sweetkins?
              Perhaps the maids, or maybe the males indulged in backchat?
              Just give me names and times and places. They'll pay!

DOVEY:

    (Demurely.)

                                               That's blahblah.

CLUELESS I: I understand. You're upset. And that upsets me.

DOVEY: That's blahblah.

CLUELESS I: You're obviously miffed at a member of the household staff.

DOVEY: Still blahblah.

CLUELESS I: But, dear, you couldn't be miffed with *me?*

DOVEY: Now, *that's* not blahblah.

CLUELESS I: Whatever for? My hands are clean.

DOVEY: And back to blahblah.

CLUELESS I: Sweet, spotless spouse, what can have caused such discomposure?

DIDDLEY: And Mr. Niceguy turns on the suave.

CLUELESS I: —Excuse me? Did I
              solicit your observations? Stop butting in!

(He strokes Dovey's shoulder.)

DOVEY: HANDS OFF!

(She hauls off and pastes her husband one, sending him reeling.)

DIDDLEY: By george, she's got it.

(As Clueless One regroups.)

                        —So dashaway, dammit, you oh-so-rapid
        to wolf down lunch in my absence, you all-too-rabidly-ready
        to flaunt your garland later and pan me with pie-eyed put-down
        out here in front of this house.

CLUELESS I: Hold on just a goddamned minute!
        I swear that I today have neither (A) had lunch,
        nor even (B) set a single foot inside this house!

DIDDLEY: You deny it?

CLUELESS II: I do deny it.

DIDDLEY: Effrontery, blatant and brazen!
        Did I not see you myself a moment ago right here,
        before this house, sporting a wreath all bloomy and budded?
        Did you, or did you not, declare me sick in the head,
        and deny you knew me, and claim you came from overseas?

CLUELESS I: Well, no.
                        It's quite a while since I lost you in the crowd;
        I just got back.

DIDDLEY: Don't try that; I know you inside out.
        Little did you think that Diddley'd devise a device for Revenge!
        I told your wife Everything. All. The Lot.

CLUELESS I: Which comes to *what?*

DIDDLEY:

(Suddenly coy.)

        Afraid I'm not really sure.
                        Perhaps you'd better ask *her.*

(He gloats as Clueless One turns to Dovey.)

CLUELESS I: —Well now, what's all this?
                        What story has he been telling?
        What's up?
                    What's with the silence?
                        What's up, *please?*

DOVEY: As if you didn't know. But why are you asking *me?*

CLUELESS I: I'm asking you because I don't know.
                        If I did, I wouldn't.

DIDDLEY: Typical culprit behavior: Avoidance, Denial, Concealment.
               —It's useless. You can't keep it hidden.
                                             —She knows it all. In *detail*.
               I laid it all out to her, dammit!

CLUELESS I: And what the hell does *that* mean?

DOVEY: It means that, inasmuch as you appear to have lost
               all sense of shame and all desire to give your (hah!) side
               of the story, you'd better come quite close and listen up.
               Now learn from me: what he told me—the reason I'm angry—is
                 this:
               My Pelisse was purloined from the house!

CLUELESS I: What's that? My Pelisse *purloined?*

DIDDLEY:

      (To Dovey.)

      Look out—a standard slick subterfuge.

      (To Clueless One.)

                                             Purloined from *her,*
               not you! If *you'd* been fleeced, we'd *never* find the Pelisse.

CLUELESS I:

      (To Diddley.)

      I have nothing to say to you.

      (To Dovey.)

                                             —Now, what's all this you're saying?

DOVEY: My Pelisse was fleeced from the house.

CLUELESS I: Aha. Who, please, was the fleecer?

DOVEY: The roach who poached it should know.

CLUELESS I: Does said roach have a name?

DOVEY: The name, I believe, is Clueless.

CLUELESS I: That was a *very* low blow.
               Which Clueless might this be?

DOVEY: For the record: you, to wit.

CLUELESS I: Me, you mean?

DOVEY: Yes: you, to wit.

CLUELESS I: Who's bringing the charge?

DOVEY: Me, to wit.

DIDDLEY: Me, too. You feloniously conveyed it
              into that dwelling to your mistress—one *Loveykins* by name.

CLUELESS I: It was *me* who gave it away?

DOVEY: For the record: you, to wit,
              You, to wit, YOU!

DIDDLEY: If you like this barrage of "to wits,"
              you'd better hire an owl. It's very tiring work.

CLUELESS I: By Jupiter *and* the other eleven—is that sufficient?—
              I did NOT give it away!

DIDDLEY: Okay.
                                  By Hercules, then,
              WE are NOT telling lies!

CLUELESS I: I did NOT give it away—
              not free and clear, that is. I, well, I *leased* the Pelisse.

DOVEY: Goodness gracious. I don't go renting your coats to people,
              or leasing your underwear out. There's a proper way to handle
              spare apparel: Women give *women's* clothes away,
              and men give *men's;* it's simple.

(Savagely. She is in command and knows it.)

                                  Now get that Pelisse back home!

CLUELESS I: I'll make sure it gets back.

DOVEY: It's to your advantage to do so.
              That frock is your ticket to homelife. Display it on entrance,
              or never pass through those doors.

(Smiling as she turns away.)

                                  I think I'll be going . . . *Home.*

DIDDLEY: What's to be my reward for all the assistance I gave you?

DOVEY: The same assistance, of course, when something's burgled from *your*
              house.

(Mistress of all she surveys, she returns inside what we shall still call the house of
Clueless One. Diddley sadly watches her go. He is utterly deflated.)

DIDDLEY: And that works out to Never; nothing to burgle at *my* house.
              Heartfelt damnation descend on the both of you, husband and wife!

              I see I've managed to alienate the whole damned family.

Time for a quick trot down to the center of town, now.

'Bye!

(And off he scoots for good, stage left, leaving Clueless One as frequently, alone.)

CLUELESS I: My wife may think she's put me out by putting me out,
              but hey, no problem. There's a place for me, a haven—
              a place where they Let Me In, and a *better* place, to boot.

(He yells at the closed door of his house.)

              I don't meet your high standards? I can live with that,
              because I meet my Loveykins's standards over there.
              She won't exclude me from *her* house, and oh, how that baby
                  *in*cludes!

(Shouting over, he ponders.)

              So what's the plan? I arrive and go down on my knees: will she .
                  please
              release the Pelisse I brought her? I'll buy her a sweeter and neater
              Pelisse. Perhaps cerise. That should easily keep the peace.

(Moving to Loveykins's house, he bangs lustily on the door.)

              Who's on the door today?
                              Hey there! Anyone home?
              You in there—open the door and call my Loveykins out!

Act IV, Scene 3 [675–700]

(Loveykins's door opens just a bit, and her voice is heard.)

LOVEYKINS: Someone asking for me? Now, who can it possibly be?

CLUELESS I: One far more foe to himself than to your sweet inner child.

(That this is a fairly inept compliment escapes him, as it does Loveykins, who is
doubtless used to his ineptness. In any case, she opens the door and emerges
affectionately.)

LOVEYKINS: Why, Clueless! Standing around in front? Come in—*this* way.

CLUELESS I: Hang on. Guess why I came.

LOVEYKINS:

(Willing to play along. It's like a game, and she likes games.)

                              I know: to play more house?

CLUELESS I: Not that, dammit! I came about the Pelisse.

(A silence. She is apprehensive.)

                              You know,
              the Pelisse I gave you today.

(Still silence.)

             Anyway, give me it back.

(The silence, still confused, turns frosty at the edges.)

    My wife's found out. The way it happened. By the numbers.
    I'll buy you a nicer Pelisse.
          Worth twice as much.
               Your choice.

LOVEYKINS: But I just *gave* it to you, to take to the detail shop.
    And that bracelet, too, to go to the goldsmith's, to be made over.

CLUELESS I: *I* took the Pelisse and the bracelet? Think hard; it never happened.
    Retrace it: early today, I gave the Pelisse to you.
    I then departed, left, *went away* downtown. And now
    I'm back for the very first time.
          I haven't seen you since.

LOVEYKINS: I see your little game. I entrust my goodies to you,
    and so you're finagling a way to keep them and diddle me out
    of what is rightfully mine.

CLUELESS I: Oh, damn! I am not trying
    to diddle you! *Of course* they're yours. What I am saying
    is this: MY WIFE'S FOUND OUT.
         THE WAY . . .

LOVEYKINS: It's not as if
    I *asked* for the item, you know. You brought it here on your own.
    You gave it to me, a *present,* of your own free will. And now
    you *demand* it back.
        All right, it's yours; I can handle that.
    Keep the Pelisse. Take it for walks. Wear it in health—
    you? your wife? who cares? Seal it up in your strongbox.
    But do not make the mistake of thinking that you will ever
    be welcome in this house again!
        I deserve better than this.
    But now that you deem me a creature worth only contempt and
      rebuff,
    you'd better bring buckets of cash, or else you won't have me
    to hook and hoax any more!
        In fact, from this day forward,
    find some other gullible goose to victimize!

(She stalks back to her doors. Clueless One turns to the audience.)

CLUELESS I: Notice that anger? She's overreacting.

(He turns to see Loveykins vanish between the doors of her house.)

            Hey, wait! Stick around!

Come back here, please!
                    Just do it for *me!*

(SLAM! go the doors.)

                                        She's gone inside.
And shut the door.
                    Than me there is no castouter outcast:
Both at home and in haven, my word's worth nothing at all.
So. Off to lay this maddening mess in front of my friends.
They're sure to have an opinion—what in the world should I do?

(Slowly he shambles off to downtown, stage left.)

Act V, Scene 1 [701–752]

(Enter, stage right, Clueless Two, with Pelisse and bracelet.)

CLUELESS II: Plumb the pits of idiocy—that's what I did.
              Put my wallet and money in Smug's tender care,
              and weighed him down to the bottom of some low dive.

(He stops and looks back off stage right. Dovey enters from Clueless One's house. She scans the street, first to the left . . .)

DOVEY: How soon will my husband return?
                                        How . . .

(. . . then to the right. She sees Clueless Two.)

                                        oooh!
              I'm safe! I'm whole! He's brought the Pelisse back.

(Clueless Two, center, does not yet see or hear her.)

CLUELESS II: Smug's gone out cruising, doubtless . . . Where would he go?

DOVEY: I shall advance and meet my mate in the words,
              hallowed by culture, that he so richly deserves:

(She nears the unsuspecting Clueless Two and screams into his ear.)

              LOUSY NO-GOOD EXCUSE FOR A MAN!
                                        For shame!
              Traipsing before me with that frippery, yet!

(Clueless Two is startled but hardly terrified. He recovers.)

CLUELESS II: Does something bother you, lady?

DOVEY: The very nerve!
              To utter the merest word in my direction,
              even in an undertone!

CLUELESS II: I committed some sin?
              So noxious I'm not allowed to speak?

DOVEY: Me?
Shameless audacity prompts you to question ME?

CLUELESS II: An inquiring mind, lady: you know, of course,
why Greek employs the proper name *Hecuba*
as a synonym for BITCH?

DOVEY: I would NOT know.

CLUELESS II: That's odd; there's such a similarity: she
performed precisely as you do now, unloading
floods of assorted abuse on all and sundry.
And so in time she won her formulaic
epithet, which, in case you missed it, was
                                     BITCH.

DOVEY: I do not have to endure these heinous habits!
I'd sooner drag out my existence single and alone,
without a trace of a husband, before I'd endure
this constant humiliation and utter disgrace!

CLUELESS II: It's nothing to do with me. Stick out your marriage,
or go back home.
                    Is this in your culture pattern—
compulsive tale-telling to new arrivals?
Or do all of you make up fairy tales to relay
to unwary tourists?

DOVEY: *Fairy tales!*
                              I repeat:
I'd sooner get divorced and stay that way
than try to cope with your heinous atrocities!

CLUELESS II: I couldn't care less . . . so get your divorce, and stay
divorced till heaven's under new management.

DOVEY: Just look at that Pelisse! Only a bit ago
you swore you hadn't stolen it, and now
you flaunt before my eyes the very Pelisse
you feloniously filched. Have you no shame?

CLUELESS II: Godalmighty, you are some brazen woman,
no shame at all! You really insist this Pelisse
was ripped away from your wardrobe, the very garment
another female gave me to be refurbished?

DOVEY: You dare to say . . . ?
                         Words fail me. Time to send
for Daddy. I'll give him chapter and verse on all
the disgrace I have to stand from your heinous habits!

Tidee!
    Oh, Tidee!

(The spruce young maid Tidee appears at the door.)

        Go find my Daddy *now,*
and bring him straight back here!
            Say I HAVE NEEDS.

(Tidee sprints off stage left, towards town.)

I shall proceed to expose your heinous habits!

CLUELESS II: You're crazy.
            Which heinous habits might you be
referring to?

DOVEY: Your theft, for starters: you burgle
my jewelery, my Pelisse—property of Your Wife—
and fence them off to your mistress.
               That *Fairy Tale*
strike a chord of truth?

CLUELESS II: Could you prescribe a potion
that I might take by mouth to build up resistance
against this galloping utter lack of restraint?
I haven't the slightest idea who you think I am,
but I do know this:
           Hercules was the husband
of Deianeira, who was the daughter of Oeneus,
who was the son of Porthâon . . . and him I met
on the very same afternoon that I met *you.*

DOVEY: Make fun of me if you will, but you can't deride
my Daddy . . . and here comes Daddy now!

(She points off left.)

               Look there!
You *do* know Daddy, of course?

CLUELESS II: I certainly do.
We shared a tent in the Trojan War. I turned
to him and said, "Look there—a horse!"
             And there
you were.

DOVEY: You mean to say you don't know ME?
You don't know Daddy?

CLUELESS II: Throw in your Grandaddy, too.
          I am intimately unacquainted with the whole damned family.

(He stalks away, stage right, and sets his face away from her.)

DOVEY: Abandon me—that's your answer to everything!

Act V, Scene 2 [753–875]

(Enter, stage left, Antiquides, Dovey's aged parent, supporting himself with a cane. He is very old and remarkably slow—the second slowest man in the world. He is also very determined.)

ANTIQUIDES: *And now for the*
                    Hotfooted,
                         Hightailed,
                              Breakneck CHARGE!
                                        Up, up, and away!

(He stumbles and nearly falls.)

                         Subject,
                              Of course,
                                   To the inroads
                                        Of Age

(Plod.)

                         And hamstrung
                              By that
                                   Outrageous
                                        Stage.
                                        Up, up, and awry!

(Splat. He rises, facing the wrong way.)

                    I don't mislead myself.

(He turns around.)

                                        Easy, it's not.
                    My get-up-and-go is long gone and got.

(Plod.)

                    My speed is sped,
                         My bod's a load.
                    I'm squeezed by years.
                                   I'm bowed and bôwed.
                         Old.
                              Age.
                                   Is heavy.
                                        Cargo.
                    Wherever.
                         You go.

You get there.
Largo.

(One final plod. Dance finished, he moves gradually on to the stage.)

In Age, afflictions come to call . . .
But an unabridged list with nothing missed
Would cut down my speed, which would mean that I'd
Never finish this hike at all.

Do let me discuss today's disorder,
Headache and heartburn:
Why would my daughter
Demand my immediate presence without
Giving a reason? What's this about?

And yet, it's really simple stuff;
I know the answer, near enough.
My darling daughter's got her spouse
In the dock inside the house:
And now proceeds to prosecute
A most uncivil domestic suit.
That's the way that women do—
Vicious vixens through and through:
Women's dowries go away
If their menfolk don't obey.
Not to say that men are perfect;
Every husband has his defect,
And wife should only have to stand
So much from hubby's heavy hand.

AND SO:

When Daddy's sent for on the run.
Something wrong's been said or done:
A conjugal catastrophe,
Or all-out quarrel.
Q.E.D.

Whatever the facts may be, I'll find out shortly.

(He sees Dovey and reacts with complete unenthusiasm.)

Well, look at this. She's out in front of the house.
And there's her husband, looking properly gloomy.
Hypothesis confirmed.
I begin the hearing with her.

(He moves toward his daughter but has not reached her. At best, he looks very dour.)

. . . —Hey there! Daughter!

DOVEY: Daddy?
Aren't you glad to see me?

ANTIQUIDES: *Of course* I'm Glad to see you.
                        Glad to be dragged across town,
                                            Glad to fetch up in Gloom . . .
                        But *Glad* is hardly the word—
                                            I'm positively *Glowing.*
                        My Daughter The Wife is all frown,
                                            my son-in-law's fuming aloof.
                        I've arrived on a field of battle during a temporary lull.
                        So answer the standard question:
                                            Whose fault? Who started this?
                        No orations, please: all that's needed's a simple "ME."

DOVEY: Let me unburden your mind on this point, Daddy Dear:
                        I'm not guilty of a single thing but losing my patience.
                        I simply can*not* exist in this house a moment longer.
                        TAKE ME BACK HOME TO LIVE WITH YOU AGAIN!

        (Antiquides recoils.)

DOVEY: Your darling daughter's been dissed!

ANTIQUIDES: Been dissed?

DOVEY: *Dis*paraged, *dis*dained . . .
                        and dumped on, too!

ANTIQUIDES: But what were the grounds?

DOVEY: The front yard here—
                        but mostly, inside.

ANTIQUIDES: Who did it?

DOVEY: That no-good you married me off to.

ANTIQUIDES:

        (A relieved aside.)

                        Oh, *that's* it. Merely a Typical Wedded Tiff.

        (To Dovey.)

                                            NOW HEAR THIS:
                        How many times do I have to make this completely clear?
                        I do not do domestic disputes!
                                            Neither of you
                        applies to me to referee tiffs!

DOVEY: But Daddy, where else
                        can I apply?

ANTIQUIDES: *I'm* asking the questions.

DOVEY:

> (A turn of the screw.)

> Please, Daddy, *please.*

ANTIQUIDES: How many times have I had to read you the simple rules?
Humor your Husband!
> *Pamper your Man!*
>> *And Play Along!*
No Checking Up on his actions, intentions, or destinations.

DOVEY: So what's to check? My husband cheats within earshot: He's having
a torrid affair with the whore whose lair is the house next door!

ANTIQUIDES:

> (Struck with admiration in spite of himself.)

> Now, *that* shows serious planning . . .

> (Recovering.)

>> *I mean,* the more you keep
on your husband's case, the more said affair will flourish and bloom.

DOVEY: And while he's there, he *drinks.*

ANTIQUIDES: And if you drive him to tippling
somewhere downtown, you think he'll turn teetotally dry?
You're a disaster.
> Can't you act like a wedded woman?
Start with these premises, what can we expect from you next?

> (He simpers in a high voice.)

> *I'm sorry, dear; no dining out for you!* or else it's
Having those loafers over to dinner? Not in this *house!*
You don't want marriage, but *Domination:*
>> Follow your logic
out to its end: Give your husband little jobs
to do around the house. Oh, I can hear you now:

> (High voice again.)

> Just pull up a stool over there with the maids, and card your wool!

DOVEY: Just my luck—I've retained my husband's counsel, not mine.
Get to the other side of the court; don't stand by me, and plead for
> *him!*

ANTIQUIDES: The slightest delinquency on *his* part, and I press charges
on *him* that make the ones I pressed on you resemble
extenuating circumstances! The Facts are these:
your husband keeps you chic and jingling, dressed to the nines,

ringed beyond the elbows, covered with allover gilt,
provided with maids in profusion, provision in positive scads.
Your only sensible recourse to a flood of goodies like that
is common sense, or Putting Up With.

DOVEY: He's stolen my gold,
and robbed my garb direct from my chests at home, and delivered
the loot to prostitutes on the sly!

(Antiquides is deeply shocked.)

ANTIQUIDES: But those are worth *money!*
Felony! Theft! He's committed a CRIME!

(He recovers himself.)

                              —provided, of course,
that he has actually done . . . well, what you said.
                                If not,
then *you,* of course, have committed the crime—defaming the name
of an innocent man.

DOVEY: *He's* committing it *now,* this very moment!
A pilfered Pelisse on his person, *plus* the bracelet from home,
the one he took next door to *her*—but now he's bringing
it back to me. Because, you see, I Checked It Out.

ANTIQUIDES: Just leave this mess to me. I'll grill him; he'll spill the facts
in no time at all.

(An advocate prepares.)

                    Now, first the approach, and then the address.

(He starts plodding towards Clueless Two, who, still located near Loveykins's door,
has been watching and disapproving; but a look from Clueless Two cows Antiquides,
and he winds up making his pitch from a position more or less behind Dovey.)

Clueless, an answer, if you please. Precisely what
is the subject under, let's say, *discussion* between you two?
Why are you frowning?
                    Why is my daughter fuming aloof?

CLUELESS II: Look, Mr. Whoever-the-hell-you-are, or Who-shall-be-nameless,
or, let's say, *Old Guy,*
                    I plead the pantheon in toto . . .

ANTIQUIDES: You're making *avowals,* yet? But what in the world *about?*

CLUELESS II: . . . to witness that I have committed no crime against that rancid
female obsessive there, who insists that I did extract
from the house before us

(He indicates the house of Clueless One.)

                              and, further, from her filch this garment!

(He holds up the Pelisse for all to see.)

DOVEY: He's committing a lie under oath!

CLUELESS II: I further affirm as follows:
                I have never. Pushed foot. Or anything else. Inside. This house . . .
                And if I have, I plead upon the powers that be
                to plunge me deep to the utter nadir of human agony,
                anguish, woe, and degradation!

ANTIQUIDES: You *want* to be wretched?
                You never pushed foot inside this house—your legal dwelling?
                You raving lunatic—don't talk crazy!

CLUELESS II: Look here, Old Guy:
                do you affirm that this house here's my legal dwelling?

ANTIQUIDES: Do you deny it?

CLUELESS II: On oath, I truly *do* deny it.

ANTIQUIDES: You truly deny it *falsely!*
                              Unless you moved last night.

(An incredulous gape from Clueless Two. Antiquides turns to Dovey.)

        —Honey, come over here.

(She complies.)

                              You answer the question:
                did you move out of here last night?

DOVEY: Of all the questions . . .
                Move out to where? And why?

ANTIQUIDES: I haven't the slightest idea.

DOVEY: He's making fun of you—what else?

ANTIQUIDES: Enough of the jokes,
                Clueless. Stick to business!

CLUELESS II: What business? We're partners, perhaps,
                with mutual obligations? I don't even know who you are.
                Just give me your name and address, and add the amount that's
                    owing.
                To you, I suppose.
                              Or come to think of it, *her.*

(He fuels his annoyance with a glance at Dovey.)

                                                        She *sticks!*

          A virtuoso *artiste* in unremitting Bother!

(He is now beside himself.)

DOVEY: Daddy! His eyes are positively *green!*
                                        He's turning all *pale!*
           It starts at his temples, goes to his brows, his eyes are aglimmer
           with that washed-out greenish glow . . .

CLUELESS II:

     (Aside, gloomily.)

                                        I know. The standard symptoms:
           they think I'm crazy.
                                   Well, why not? I do a good Crazy.
           I'll pretend I'm around the bend, and frighten these cretins away.

(He takes several deep breaths to prepare himself, looking around for inspiration.)

DOVEY: The hideous faces, the awful grimaces—what do I *do?*

ANTIQUIDES: You get over this way, daughter. As far from that loon as you can.

(But Clueless Two's gaze has landed on the statue of Bacchus, who, among other
things, is the mad god of the rural riot. The mortal takes his cue and goes wildly
mad.)

CLUELESS II: Bacchus of the Blast and Boom!
                                   Yoicks!
                                        Tantivy!
                                             WAHOOOO!
           You call me a-field to hunt? I hear thy harrying halloo,
           and would a-hunting go,

(He moves to the pair in a savage stalk.)

                                   but I am hampered and hindered,
           hemmed on my left by the slavering, rabid Bitchgoddess *there* . . .

(He charges at Dovey, who breaks for the statue of Apollo. Antiquides, alarmed,
breaks to stage right and cowers behind the statue of Bacchus.)

           not to neglect this dithering Dwarf behind you *here,*
           vapid veteran, throughout his career, of perjured witness
           in plenty to plunge the innocent low!

ANTIQUIDES: You're a dead man!

(Clueless Two shrugs him off and cups an ear at the statue of Apollo.)

CLUELESS II: What's this, Apollo? A sudden oracle doth bid me now
           to cauterize this bitch's eyes with burning brands?

(He mimes torches in either hand and advances on Dovey.)

DOVEY: Daddy—my final words! He says he'll burn my eyes out!

(Clueless Two stops and delivers an aside to the audience.)

CLUELESS II: Oboy. Both round the twist, and they call *me* insane.

ANTIQUIDES: Hey, daughter!

DOVEY: Hey, *what?*

ANTIQUIDES: Got a plan?

DOVEY: Why don't I get some slaves
to carry him off and tie him up inside the house?
I'd only be gone a moment . . .

(She gathers herself for the short dash to her door.)

CLUELESS II:

(Aside.)

Which way can I possibly turn?
If I don't get some overall plan, then I'm all over—
delivered in chains to their happy home.

(Back into the madness.)

—What say, Apollo?
A full-force fusillade of fists on this female's face
lest she slip slyly from sight on her way to total damnation?
Good thinking, Apollo.

(The torch-bit forgotten, he advances on Dovey with fists clenched and raised.)

ANTIQUIDES: Home, girl, home! As fast as you can,
or you're pulverized! Flee!

DOVEY: I'm fleeing, I'm fleeing!

(She is—but, arrived at her door, she stops in another sort of concern.)

Just one thing, Daddy:
Don't let him get away!
But oh! the distress, the disgrace!
No decent woman should have to hear such dreadful language!

(She goes inside. Clueless Two pats the statue of Apollo and drops the rhetoric for the moment.)

CLUELESS II: One down, Apollo. Pretty good job, if I say so myself.

(Back into the madness again.)

—And now I turn to this towering Titan of total abasement,
white-haired and trembling, the bearded Bitchdad!

(He cups his ear at Apollo's statue.)

                                     —Another order?
Crush and commingle his arms and his legs and his bones and his
    joints
in a bloody puree? And create this mess with the coward's own
    cane?

(He advances on Antiquides, who backs away, brandishing the cane in question.)

ANTIQUIDES: Look, sonny. If you lay a single finger on me, or come
             just one step nearer, you'll get into serious trouble, hear?

CLUELESS II: Good suggestion, Apollo. First, let me get mine *axe,*
           both edges agleam, and trim his innards from their bony cage,
           gobbet by greasy gobbet!

(He mimes a raised axe and continues the advance. Antiquides addresses the
audience.)

ANTIQUIDES: —I *think* we've reached the point
           where I'd better look after myself, and take a precaution or two.
           Am I right to worry that he intends me some serious harm?

CLUELESS II:

(Affecting to cope with a flood of commands, using invisible props.)

           Apollo! Not all at once!
                        Yoke two unbroken braces
of stampeding stallions?
                 Check.
                       Mount to my insolent chariot's
battle station?
             Check.
              Then grind to diminutive flinders
this stinking, feckless, toothless excuse for a senile lion?
Check and Double-check!

(He mimes mounting for epic attack.)

                      —I mount to my place in the car.
—I firmly grasp the reins.
                   —I cuddle the quirt in my fist.
—Onward, my steeds, to Attack!
                  —Now sound the boom of your hooves!

(He beats his chest with cupped palms, then grabs up "reins and quirt" again.)

    —Let savage spring impel the relentless speed of your feet!

(He poises to charge, then slumps.)

ANTIQUIDES: You're running me down in a four-horse rig?
                            That's what you're doing?

CLUELESS II: Yet one more order, Apollo?

                          One final rush on this loon
who blocks my way, to lay him low and wipe him out?

(He raises himself for action . . . but Antiquides raises his very real cane, deflating the younger man's ardor. Clueless Two stops and jerks his head backwards.)

        But hold! Who hangs his hand in my hair, and rips me forth
from my chariot's floor?

(He stumbles back and poises precariously for an instant.)

                    I know you won't like this one bit, Apollo.
Your power's revoked.

             You'll have to revise your edict.

(He spins around, falls on his back, and is still. After a slight interval, Antiquides inspects the body.)

ANTIQUIDES: Mercy me—this must be a swift and dreadful disease.
        Cut off in the full flush of madness—and only a moment ago,
how fresh and vital he was.

                What a quick and deadly attack!
I'd better go get the doctor. And quickly.

                  No speed spared.

(He shambles off, stage left, at his usual painful plod.)

Act V, Scene 3 [876–888]

(Clueless Two raises his head cautiously.)

CLUELESS II: So did they leave?
                Off to warp another sane man
into a loony?

(He scans the stage as well as he can from his back.)

        Nowhere to be seen.

              They're gone.

(He rises and looks around again.)

        Looks safe. Then now's the time to make for the ship.

(He rises and starts off stage right, stops, comes downstage and addresses the audience.)

        Hi, you out there. A simple request:
                If Old Guy
makes another appearance, please don't tell him
the route I took to make my escape.

                Goodbye.

(He sprints off stage right. As Clueless Two disappears, Antiquides makes his entrance stage left. Slowly, as on his previous entrance. He stops and addresses the audience.)

ANTIQUIDES: Don't doctors make you *well?* Just sitting and watching
for this one to meet his appointments has made me a victim
of vicious lower-back pain and a hideous squint.
He finally made it back from his patients, but just.
Mending a broken leg for Aesculapius,
or so he said, and setting an arm for Apollo.
I wanted a doctor . . . instead, I got a sculptor.

(He looks back, off stage left.)

Oh, look: he approaches.
Speed! An ant walks faster!

Act V, Scene 4 [889–898]

(Enter, stage left, the Man of Medicine, Dr. Klyster. Very aged and slower than
Antiquides, whom he joins, down left.)

DR. KLYSTER: Now, bring me up to date on the ailment's nature:
Schizophrenia—that what you said? Or good,
old-fashioned Possession?
Let me have the facts:
Narcolepsy? Shingles? Possibly Gout?

ANTIQUIDES: You've got it backwards. *You* tell *me* what's wrong,
and then you make him well.

DR. KLYSTER: The technical term
is *cure.* That's easy. I stake my reputation:
he shall be well. I assure you, the cure's secure.

ANTIQUIDES: But can you ensure me a cure that endures?

DR. KLYSTER: Why, sure.
My basic bedside mode, guaranteed to contain
no less than six hundred racking sighs per day—
concerned sighs—over the patient. Now, *that's* pure cure.
It's cure that's *mature.*

ANTIQUIDES:

(He looks off stage left again.)

Here comes your patient now.

DR. KLYSTER: We engage in close observation of subject's behavior.

(They move to down stage right and watch.)

Act V, Scene 5 [899–965]

(Enter, stage left, back from the Forum, Clueless One. He is frazzled, mussed, and
completely worn out.)

CLUELESS I: God, what a day! Been fingered by fortune every which way.
All my dirty little secrets exposed, and me
hung out to dry.
                         And who, pray, *who* is the cause of all this?
Who crammed me full to the brim with dread and utter disgrace?
My parasite! My half-price epic diddler, Diddley!
He's boiled his liege lord down and left him in the soup!
May I live to effect that reprobate's termination!

(He tries to calm himself.)

—But no. I'm being dense. It isn't his fault; it's mine.
It's nurture, not nature. That man is the product of *food* and *expense*
And every last bit of that food and expense came straight from *me*.
I'll choke off his life at the source!

(Another calming.)

                         Moving right along,
my hooker's behavior was perfectly proper, given the habits
of whoredom. I make my request: "Please, return the Pelisse,
for further return to my wife." Her answer, in Old High Bimbo,
"I already *give* it back!"
                         The result of which is the me you see,
true to my standard, the wretchedest sonofabitch on earth.

(He stomps around, upstage center, in a perfect mixture of anger and chagrin.)

ANTIQUIDES: Hear what he says?

DR. KLYSTER: He states he's unhappy.

ANTIQUIDES: Why not get nearer?

(The Doctor moves from Antiquides, down right, to Clueless One, up center.)

DR. KLYSTER: Clueless! I trust you're . . . *well.*

(Clueless One aims a blow at the Doctor, who skillfully avoids it.)

                         No sudden movements, please.
Undue strain exacerbates your tender condition.

CLUELESS I: Exacerbate yourself!

(He raises his arm for another blow, but the Doctor nips in deftly and pinches him
on the arm.)

DR. KLYSTER: Feel anything?

CLUELESS I: Oh, I do!

(He completes the blow, but the Doctor moves out of the way again and scuttles
back to report to Antiquides.)

DR. KLYSTER: A serious case.
                              Immediate tranquilization required—
            mountains of medication. Hellebore in heaps.

(He returns to Clueless One.)

            —Clueless, a word?

CLUELESS I: What word?

DR. KLYSTER: Just answer these simple questions.
            Your Potation of Choice—white wine or red?

CLUELESS I: YOU GO TO HELL!

DR. KLYSTER:

      (To Antiquides.)

            There, now, we have the first shy hint of encroaching madness.

CLUELESS I: Why not ask me about my taste in *Bread?* Blue bread?
              Vermilion bread? Or Canary bread with polka dots?

(The Doctor retreats to Antiquides.)

            Do I eat roast chicken with the scales left on, or do I prefer
            baked trout with every feather still in place?

ANTIQUIDES: Now, *that's* true madness, ravings, the real stuff! So would it
              be too much to *give* him something for it, Doctor—
              one of your potent potions, perhaps—before the affliction
              invades and takes over completely?

DR. KLYSTER: Patience yet a while.
            Some *deeper* questions.

(He moves back to Clueless One.)

ANTIQUIDES: More talk—the deadliest tongue in town.

(The Doctor renews his inspection of Clueless One.)

DR. KLYSTER: And now the next question: have you ever suffered from *Hard Eyes?*

CLUELESS I: Hard *what?*

DR. KLYSTER: Hard Eyes: the eyeball sheathed with transparent glaze.

CLUELESS I: It may have escaped your notice, Doc, but I'm no lobster.

DR. KLYSTER: I'll be the judge of that.
                              Now, do your bowels—as far
            as you can observe—ever exhibit a resonant rumble?

CLUELESS I: After I've eaten, no rumble; before, we have *serious* rumble.

(The Doctor returns to Antiquides.)

Dr. Klyster: No insanity there. His answer was fundamentally sound.

(Going back to Clueless One, who is, in spite of himself, caught up in the process.)

—Sleeping Habits: Sound sleep, through till the break of day?
Does sleep come easily? Off and snoring when you hit the bed?

Clueless I: I sleep right through . . . provided I've paid my creditors . . .

(Struck by annoyance at both the invasion of privacy and his collaboration with it.)

WHAT?
May the gods reduce you to rubble, you morbid, prurient *snoop!*

(He poises for a really mighty blow, but the Doctor scuttles back to Antiquides.)

Dr. Klyster: Now *there* we have the onset of *real* insanity . . . *and,*
to judge from what he's saying, you'd better protect yourself.

Antiquides: Well, what he's saying sounds like *Nestor's Rules of Order,*
compared with what he *was* saying just a little while back.
Slavering, rabid Bitchgoddess —that's what he called his wife.

Clueless I: *I* said that? *Me?*

Antiquides: You did. You were mad, of course.

(It's his turn now. Mighty in his wrath, he advances on Clueless One.)

Clueless I: I was?

Antiquides:

(Furious, waving a finger.)

You were. What's more, you threatened *me.* To flatten *me!*
Under the wheels of your four-horse chariot. That's what you said.
I was your witness . . . and I'm your accuser, here and now.

(Clueless One has had enough, and he advances to meet Antiquides.)

Clueless I: And *I* am witness that *you* purloined the holy wreath
from the head of Jove! Am witness that you were sealed away
in jail for such a crime! Am witness that on release
you found yourself stuck in the stocks and flailed with rods!
Am witness—sorry, I almost forgot—that you did dispatch
your father from life and sold your mother for what she'd fetch
in a life of shame!
It's tit for tat, and I can do
a pretty good Sane—or don't you agree?

(There may be a kernel of truth or more in the accusations—certainly Antiquides is *very* upset. In any case, he speeds back to the Doctor.)

Antiquides: Oh, Doctor, *help!*
And Doctor, *quick!* Whatever cure you're thinking of, *do* it!
Completely lost touch with reality—out of his mind!

DR. KLYSTER: An idea.

(He huddles with Antiquides. Clueless One moves nearer to the two.)

ANTIQUIDES: Yes, yes?

DR. KLYSTER: Your most effective course of action is this:
          Consign this man to my clinic.

ANTIQUIDES: That's your advice?

DR. KLYSTER: It is.
          There, I can cure this patient to my heart's content.

ANTIQUIDES: Whatever.

(Clueless One is very near the ancient duo. The Doctor looks up at him.)

DR. KLYSTER: You'll live on a liquid diet—straight hellebore, twenty days.

CLUELESS I: You'll serve me for target practice—straight arrows, thirty days.

(The Doctor begins to shuffle imperceptibly towards the exit stage left. He addresses
Antiquides.)

DR. KLYSTER: Go hire a corps of porters to bring him to my place.

ANTIQUIDES: How many?

DR. KLYSTER: Insanity, very advanced . . . a four-porter case. At least.

(His shuffling becomes more pronounced.)

ANTIQUIDES: I'll have them here in a moment.
                              And you keep an eye on him, Doctor.

(He turns to exit left, but the Doctor is already ahead of him.)

DR. KLYSTER: Sorry. No can do.
                    I have to get home and prepare
          all those . . . er . . . preparations. That. I really must . . . er . . .
          prepare.
          It devolves on *you* to have the underlings bring him to *me.*

(His shuffle has become flight. He speaks over his shoulder to Antiquides.)

ANTIQUIDES: My personal care. He'll be there shortly.

DR. KLYSTER: I'm leaving!

(Reaching the exit, he disappears as Antiquides calls after him.)

ANTIQUIDES: Good-bye!

(With a look at Clueless One, he hobbles to the exit stage left and departs, leaving
his son-in-law alone, upstage center.)

CLUELESS I: No more Doctor.
                        No more Stepdad.
                                Only me.
          Jove almighty, what happened? Why should they drop by
          to declare me insane? Me, of all people? Since I was born,
          I've never been sick a day in my life. I'm, well, I'm a *well* type.
          The people I move among, the people I *know,* are well types.
          "You're looking *well,*" we say. "I hope you're *well.*" "You're
              *Wel*come."
          Or could it be the case that this strange pair, so quick
          to declare me nuts, are wrong . . . *because they're nuts themselves?*
          —So, what's the plan?
                        I want to go home. But Wife says No.

(He gestures at Loveykins's house.)

          And no one over *here* is about to let me in.

(He moves to his own house, before the door.)

          Talk about your decidedly damnable denouements.
          I'll stay right here.
                        I'll be in by dark.
                                At the very least.

(He sits down gloomily directly before his own front door and "freezes," staring out
at the audience. He is, for all intents and purposes, part of the set.)

Act V, Scene 6 [966–989]

(Enter, stage right, Smug. As usual, he is in love with himself. He does not notice
Clueless One, nor does Clueless notice him. He launches into his *apologia pro vita
sua.* First, a recitative.)

SMUG:

KNOW YOUR SLAVES

          Noting, as I start, an axiom that might well be taken as ironclad—
          That Good is Better than Bad—
          I address a burning question of the day which may have bred, in
              some of you, a nagging doubt:
          What is the Good Slave's nature? How can you ascertain the Good
              Slave? or rather, What is SuperSlave all about?
          He is about his master's business, which he plans, scans, arranges,
              changes, facilitates, and superintends
          To his Boss's felicitous ends.
          The acid test occurs when Boss is away,
          And SuperSlave doesn't play,
          But manages to be both magnificent menial and exalted go-getter,
          By functioning just as well as Boss, or indeed, going Boss one better.

(Then a hymn.)

> *Take up your master's matters,*
> *Ye servants of the Boss!*
> *Facilitate his dealings—*
> *He will not suffer loss . . .*
>
> *Your head be screwed on tightly,*
> *Mouth shut and belly sla-ack.*
> *Thus armed, you need not suffer*
> *The lash on legs or back.*

(Another recitative.)

> *SuperSlave's motivation should be supplied by obsessive inspection,*
>   *from hub to nub,*
> *Of the distinctive markings of that SuperSlave antitype, the instant-*
>   *fulfillment sluggard: The Sub-.*
> *SubSlave is stippled with stigmata: striped by the whip's splash on*
>   *back, scarred and scored by manacles*
> *On wrists and anacles,*
> *As he staggers, turning the millwheel with groans and wheezes,*
> *Stooped with exhaustion, shrunk with starvation, stiff with the cold*
>   *endured unclad in the hardest of freezes.*
> *Such, as SuperSlave know'th,*
> *Are the rewards of sloth.*
>
> *And such are what I'm afraid of:*
> *Since I'd rather not show the world at large the shoddy stuff I'm*
>   *made of,*
> *I've made my decision firmly founded on Fear,*
> *And being Super-, not Sub-, is a lifestyle to which I shall firmly*
>   *adhere,*
> *Inasmuch as I prefer flack to whack, eating to beating, filling to*
>   *milling, and mouth's crunch to millwheel's curse . . .*
> *And hence the consumer and not the surce.*

(He sings a Song of Subordination.)

> *And so,*
> *I live with fear*
> *Up to the hilt*
> *And follow orders.*
> *No groans*
> *For Boss to hear,*
> *I get no guilt*
> *Inside his borders.*
> *I'm there*

By Boss's side
Each time he calls
Me in his guy-way.
That's what
Advances me—
HIS WAY Is My Way.

The rest
Can swill their fill—
A motley mob
To be blindsided.
But I
Will do my will
And fill my job,
So I've decided.
Throughout
My stormy life
I've traveled both
Should-way and Is-way,
But now,
To serve my Boss,
I'll do it HIS WAY.

And so I save
My back from scars.
Because for stripes
You get no stars.
At being Good,
If I succeed,
Well—who can tell?—
I might be freed.
Let record show
I took no blow,
But did it HIS WAY.

(Performance over, he looks at the area in front of Loveykins's house and then returns to straight speech.)

And so, pursuant to orders, I have located lodgings,
and there have checked the baggage and checked the men.
Next, I meet him here . . .

(He looks around.)

or rather knock right *here*

(He knocks at Loveykins's door.)

to let him know . . .

(He waits.)

that I've arrived . . .

(He waits some more.)

> to lead him forth

in safety . . .

(Yet more.)

> from this Sump of Despond and Disaster.

(He gives up waiting.)

> Uh-oh.

I fear I reach the field too late.

> The battle's over.

(He sits down dejectedly in front of Loveykins's house.)

Act V, Scene 7 [990–1049]

(Enter, stage left, Antiquides, conducting an awkward squad of four Orderlies. They are large but not, shall we say, especially luminous, nor inclined to come to grips with a madman. Antiquides is somewhat overcome by his role.)

ANTIQUIDES: This is serious business, dammit! Remember who's in command!
I've given you orders; obey them.

> I'm giving you more; obey *them!*

That man's our objective:

> advance, and hoist him on high,

and convey our prey to the Clinic! Immediately—unless
you want your sides and shanks studded with ugly welts!
He'll threaten you, perhaps—don't give it a second thought.
CHARGE!

(The squad does not move, collectively or individually.)

> Immobility? Hesitation? Why?

You should already have him wriggling in air and halfway there!

(The four move, raggedly. Antiquides sighs.)

I'm off to the clinic. Quite easy to find when you get there.

(He exits hurriedly [for him] stage left. The squad of Orderlies swoops on Clueless One, who emerges from his suspended animation and notices them for the first time.)

CLUELESS I: Ooogoddam!

What's happening?

> I seem to be the object of a mad attack.

Who are you, please?

(They reach him . . .)

> What's your intention?

(surround him . . .)

> Why'm I encircled?

(lay hands on him . . .)

Where are you hauling me off to?

(hoist him high in the air . . .)

> Correction: *heaving* me off to?

(as he calls to the audience . . .)

Fellow citizens! Epidamnians! Aid and assistance! Please!

(as he struggles to no avail.)

—Let me down, dammit!

(The foofaraw rouses Smug, in front of Loveykins's house. He takes in the situation at a glance.)

SMUG: Ye Gods! What do I behold?
My master borne away on the shoulders of utter unknowns,
in a fashion that hardly befits his rank or position!

CLUELESS I:

(In extremis, as yet unconscious of a potential deliverer.)

Is there no one ready to risk my rescue?

(Smug leaps to his feet.)

SMUG: Yes, one!
Reckless of my own safety, master, I speed to your succor!

(Before he speeds, he addresses the audience.)

—Epidamnians all, what has become of your civic pride?
Subjecting a tourist of rank to a brutal multiple mugging
in a public street, in a city at peace, in the glare of day?
Disgraceful!

(He shouts to the Orderlies.)

—Let that master *go!*

(He is seen by Clueless One, who is vigorously writhing in midair.)

CLUELESS I: Dear total stranger,
a plea: can you condone this colossal miscarriage of justice?

SMUG:

(As he rushes to bring aid.)

Not I! I fly to aid and abet, and otherwise supply
selfless support.

Never will I consent to your slaughter—
far, far better were mine!

(Almost there.)

Do not go gentle, boss:

(He arrives.)

You break that shoulder hold—grab the guy's eye, and pull!
I'll plant a crop of blows in these faces and raise sheer hell!

(To the Orderlies.)

—Carry my master? You'll pay a bill of lading in blood—
PUT HIM DOWN!

(He attacks, inspiring Clueless One to real action against one of the band of four.)

CLUELESS I: I've got him by the eye!

SMUG: Well, don't
let it go till you see the socket!

(Under his furious assailment, the Orderlies put Clueless One down. Smug attacks them singly, first one . . .)

Bunch of brigands!

(then another . . .)

Squad of savages!

(then a third.)

Mob of muggers!

(They have not yet disengaged but wish to.)

ORDERLIES: Cease and desist!
Enough's enough!

SMUG: Then let him go!

(The three peel off. Clueless One concentrates on the fourth.)

CLUELESS I: Naughty—no touching!

(He perceives Smug at work on the last of the three.)

—Set his skull in cornrows!

(The three are in full flight to the exit down stage left, with Smug close to the last one.)

SMUG: .   Absent thyself—to hell!

(He receives the fourth and last Orderly from Clueless One.)

A straggler? Congratulations, sir—you've won last prize!

(He boots him off. The Orderlies are gone. Smug preens as he stares off after them.)

I've fulfilled my dream: to change the world, one face at a time.

(He looks around for Clueless One and finds him very grateful. They meet down center.)

—Hooboy, boss—I came to your rescue just in the nick.

CLUELESS I: May Heaven bless you much and often, total stranger:
             if you hadn't showed, I'd never see another sunset.

SMUG: Thanks for the blessing, boss . . . but the really *proper* reply
             is manumission.

CLUELESS I: You mean you want me to set you free?

SMUG: Certainly, seeing as I saved your life; that's how it's done.

CLUELESS I: How strange. I fear you're mistaken.

SMUG: Mistaken? Me?

CLUELESS I: I swear by Jove the Father that I am *not* your master.

SMUG: Don't say that; He might hear!

CLUELESS I: I'm telling the absolute truth:
             no slave of mine ever did for me what you just did.

SMUG: You're not my master?

CLUELESS I: I'm not.

SMUG: Well, then, you shouldn't object
             to letting me go free.

CLUELESS I: As far as I'm concerned,
             okay:
                  Be thou free, and go wherever thou wilt.

SMUG: I presume you *bid* me to do this? That's how the formula runs.

CLUELESS I: *By whatever power is vested in me, I* BID *you be free.*

SMUG: I salute you, Honored Patron, formerly known as Master.

(Clueless One, tired of the game, turns away. Smug is nonplussed for only an instant. Acting as another, he shakes his own hand, taps his own head, and addresses himself.)

Congratulations on your liberation, Smug!

(Liking the ritual, he shakes and taps again, and then speaks as to one of a crowd of admirers.)

You, too, sir?

(Same routine.)

And, sir, you?

(Gazing at his imaginary flock of well-wishers.)

> Such sincerity all round!

(Back to reality, he faces Clueless One.)

> —Oh, Patron? One request: Let there be no reduction
> in the orders you give me, former slave though I may be.
> I hereby give notice that I intend to stay at your side.
> Whithersoever thou goest—like *home*—thither go I.

CLUELESS I: Oh no, thou don't.

SMUG: Now go I off to the tavern to fetch
the bags and the cash. The Wallet with all your funds for our trip
is duly stashed away under seal. I'll deliver it here
to you in a moment.

CLUELESS I:

(A lightning reconsideration.)

> A Wallet? Thou'd better get a move on.

SMUG: I guarantee to return the exact amount. Wait for me here.

(He rushes off stage right, leaving Clueless One bemused but, on balance, pleased.)

CLUELESS I: A day for amazing surprises in all sorts of guises and sizes—
my identity stripped and denied, my body barred and excluded,
my person mugged on demand, my longtime sponge gone dry,
my gifts transmuted to thefts—and this by my near and dear.
But then my life is saved by an utter unknown, who insists
that he's my slave—and so I set him free. Of course.
And now he's on his way to fetch me a stash of money.
Well, yes.
> If he brings the money, I'd better *insist* that he takes
his departure *whithersoever he goddam will,* or else
he'll probably come to his senses and demand the money back.
Amazing!
> The doddering duo declared that I was insane;
I'm certainly very confused.
> What does all this madness mean?
No matter what it is, it seems to me like dreaming.

(He shakes his head to clear it and stares at Loveykins's house.)

> And now for another try at the daughter of joy next door.
> Her fury doesn't faze me, provided I can persuade her
> to give me back the Pelisse.
> > I've got to get it back home.

(He slips into Loveykins's house, without knocking.)

Act V, Scene 8 [1050–1059]

(As Clueless One disappears into Loveykins's house, Smug returns, stage right, with Clueless Two. The pair are not happy.)

CLUELESS II: This time you've gone too far. Having the gall to insist
we've met since I sent you off with the sailors!

SMUG: We did *so* meet!

(Indicating Clueless One's house.)

On this very spot, before that house, I rescued you,
I plucked you off the shoulders of four abductors, rough types,
as you were being shanghai'd. I can still hear your scream:
"Ooogoddam!" was the way you put it.
                                I speed to your aid!
I snatch you away!
                    They fight, but I carry the day with my fists!
And as I delivered you, so did you set me free . . .
But when I proposed that I'd go pick up the bags and the cash,
you ran like hell to cut me off and deny you did what you did.

CLUELESS II: I *bade* you depart a free man?

SMUG: True.

CLUELESS II: I'd sooner be sold
as a slave myself than set you free—now, that's what's *true!*

Act V, Scene 9 [1060–1162]

(Clueless One enters from Loveykins's house, shouting back into the closing door.)

CLUELESS I: *Not true!* You can swear till you're blue, but that won't make it true!
I never purloined the Pelisse or the bracelet!

(He turns away from the door and makes in the general direction of his own house.)

                                    Disgusting floozies.

(His face is exposed to the pair downstage.)

SMUG: Undying gods! What do I see?

CLUELESS II: I give up: what do you see?

SMUG: Your personal mirror.

CLUELESS II: And what in the world do you mean by that?

SMUG: Your spit-and-image, down to the least detail.

(He turns Clueless Two to see Clueless One.)

CLUELESS II: Damn!
The more I look at me, the less unlike the likeness.

(Clueless One has noticed the pair. He tries to attract the attention of Smug, who is still engaged with Clueless Two.)

CLUELESS I: —Young man?
                    Hey, Total Stranger?
                                    Oh, you who saved my life—
        Yoo-hoo!

(He advances to Smug. The three are now arranged down center: Smug in the middle, Clueless One on his left, Clueless Two on his right—a configuration they will maintain, roughly, until until the brothers join.)

SMUG: Yoo-hoo to you. Might you reveal your name . . .
        unless it goes against the grain?

CLUELESS I: Oh, hang the grain.
        For all your blessings on me, you deserve to achieve your desire.
        And so: my name is *Clueless*.

CLUELESS II: It isn't! That name is *mine*.

CLUELESS I: From Sicily. Syracuse.

CLUELESS II: My own, my native land—
        my hometown, too!

CLUELESS I: What did I hear you say?

CLUELESS II: The facts.

(Smug inspects Clueless One.)

SMUG:

        (To Clueless One.)

            —You see, I thought *he* was *you*. I bothered him half to death.
        Now, *this* is the one I know. My master. I'm slave to *him*.

        (To Clueless Two.)

            —I *do* apologize, sir, for any stupid remarks
        I may have delivered to you from the depths of my confusion.

CLUELESS II: You're not confused; you're crazy. We disembarked together
        this morning, you and I. Or have you forgotten?

SMUG: Oops.
        Correct as usual, sir. *You* are my master, of course . . .

        (He turns to Clueless One.)

            — . . . and *you* are out one slave. And so,

        (He turns to Clueless Two.)

                                hello to *you*,

        (He turns to Clueless One.)

good-bye to *you.*

(To the audience, as he indicates Clueless Two.)

Take my word for it, *this* is Clueless.

CLUELESS I: No, you take *my* word: *I* am.

CLUELESS II: What flimsy fiction is this?
You're Clueless?

CLUELESS I: So I claim. Legitimate son of Copeless.

CLUELESS II: Son of *my* father?

CLUELESS I: No, not yours. I'm son of my own.
I don't jump claims on fathers. I have one—I'll keep Copeless.

SMUG:

(Advancing downstage, dead center.)

Ye gods in heaven, bring to fruition the expectation
that even now balloons and burgeons within my brain!
Unless this mess miscarries, these are the twins in question.
Names and addresses the same—precisely identical parents.
I'll cut Boss out of the herd.

(He looks upstage at the two Cluelesses.)

—Oh, Clueless?

CLUELESS I AND II: You called?

SMUG: Not both.
Just one: the Clueless I knew on the boat.

CLUELESS I: Not me . . .

CLUELESS II: . . . but *me.*

SMUG: It's you I want, then. Q.E.D. Come over here.

(Clueless Two comes down quickly, at Smug's right.)

CLUELESS II: I'm over here. What's up?

SMUG:

(Pointing to Clueless One.)

You see that man right there?
He's either the acme of con men,
                              or else your long-lost twin.
I have never beheld a man so much a *match* for another.
No bead of liquid is liker—
                              you're two drops of milk in a pod.
You take after him, he copies you—a facsimile set
with sameness of names, and duplicate dads, and homogenous
    homelands.

Our course of action?
>We work in close and probe this double.

CLUELESS II: Now, there is a perfect plan. For this advice, much thanks.
Don't stop your support, I beg you:
>I pledge to set you free
if you can give me proof that this is my mislaid Brother.

SMUG: I hope so.

CLUELESS II: Ditto.
>*Likewise,* I mean.
>Or else, *me, too.*

(Smug turns to Clueless One.)

SMUG: —A word.

(Clueless One advances to Smug. The three are now arranged down center: Smug in the middle, Clueless One on his left, Clueless Two on his right—a configuration they will maintain, roughly, until the brothers join. Smug's air is very official; he is managing things.)

>I believe you claimed your name was Clueless?

CLUELESS I: I did.

SMUG: Well, here's another claimant; *his* name is Clueless, too.
You stated, as Birthplace, Sicily: city of Syracuse—
his Birthplace, too, as it happens.
>Your father, you further averred,
went under the name of *Copeless.* It happens that *his* did, too.
I offer you both a once-in-a-lifetime chance to advance
your personal fortunes—and, at the same time, mine as well.

CLUELESS I: You clearly deserve to get whatever you want from me.
I may be free and clear, but I'm utterly in your debt;
I'll further your aims and whims like merest merchandise.

SMUG: I hope to establish you two as twins, as brothers born
on a single day to a single father and . . . single mother.

CLUELESS I: Another surprise! Your project assuredly gets my backing . . .
if you can bring it about.

SMUG: I can.

(He addresses them both.)

>—What I need from you
is answers. Clear and concise replies to the questions I ask.

CLUELESS I: Inquire when ready; I'll answer, with nothing I know withheld.

SMUG: Your name is Clueless?

CLUELESS I: It is.

    (Smug turns to Clueless Two.)

SMUG: And yours as well?

CLUELESS II: It is.

    (Smug turns back to Clueless One.)

SMUG: You further affirm your father was Copeless?

CLUELESS I: He was.

CLUELESS II: Mine, too.

    (This hastiness earns a frown from Smug, who keeps on interrogating Clueless One.)

SMUG: Your Birthplace—Syracuse?

CLUELESS I: It was.

    (Smug turns to Clueless Two.)

SMUG: Yours, too?

CLUELESS II: Of course.

    (Smug beckons both closer to him, and his tone becomees less formal.)

SMUG: I feel that I can inform you that things are Looking Good.
             But don't slack off.

    (He shoves them back to their former positions. Again the inquisitor, he addresses
Clueless One.)

                              Now cast your mind way back to the past.
             Give me your earliest recollection of your native land.

CLUELESS I: Well, when I left it. Went to Tarentum with Daddy on business.
             Got lost in the crowd.
                                    Kidnapped.
                                          Carried off here.

CLUELESS II: God in the highest, preserve me!

    (This provokes Smug to severity.)

SMUG: No shouting, please! Keep quiet!

    (Back to the interrogation of Clueless One.)

             —And what was your age, when Daddy took you off on that trip?

CLUELESS I: Seven, I think . . .
                        Yes. I was losing my baby teeth.
             I never saw Daddy again.

SMUG: Quite so. And how many sons
            did Daddy have?

CLUELESS I: It's been quite a while . . .

SMUG: Just take your time.

CLUELESS I: Let's see. There was me . . . and another.
                              That should work out to . . .

            (He does it on his fingers.)

                                                    two?

SMUG: And you were the older?

CLUELESS I: No.

SMUG: Then you were the younger?

CLUELESS I: No.

            (An awkward pause.)

            Well, we were both the same age.

SMUG: But how could such a thing happen?

CLUELESS I: Well, we were twins. Of each other.

            (Clueless Two is overcome by this revelation.)

CLUELESS II: Ye gods! Preserved again!

SMUG: —No Interruptions! Shut up, or I shut this inquiry down!

CLUELESS II: I'm shutting.

SMUG: —Moving along:
                              You two twins shared one name?

CLUELESS I: Not, not at all.
                        I had the same name I have now.
            Clueless.
                  But Brother—at least back then—
                              they called him *Bootless*.

CLUELESS II: The clues are all in place!
                        I can't restrain myself—
            it's time for hugs!

            (He lurches toward Clueless One but is restrained by Smug.)

                        —Oh, sibling and twin, a happy hello!
            Remember Brother Bootless?

CLUELESS I: But how did you get my name?
            Why are you Clueless?

CLUELESS II: The news came: You and Daddy were dead,
           And so Grandaddy . . .

CLUELESS I: You don't mean
                                        Grandaddy *Clueless?*
           The Original Clueless?
                               Clueless the First?

CLUELESS II: The very same.
           So that you shouldn't be lost and forgotten,
                                        he called me *you.*

CLUELESS I: That's logical. I believe you.
                               One last question.

CLUELESS II: Proceed.

CLUELESS I: Our mutual Mother's name . . . ?

CLUELESS II: Was Detrimenta.

CLUELESS I: Correct!

     (Smug steps out of the way, and the two brothers embrace.)

           As I behold you after so many hopeless years,
           oh unexpected Brother, a happy hello to you!

CLUELESS II: And another to you, dear Brother, my goal so long sought
           in sorrow and sadness, and just this moment attained in joy!

     (Smug tries to penetrate the embrace with more information.)

SMUG: And this explains the courtesan's reason for calling you Clueless:
           She thought that you were him—
                               the one she'd invited to lunch.

CLUELESS I: I told her to have a lunch prepared at her place . . .
           to keep my wife in the dark about that damned Pelisse
           I stole from her over there and took to the hooker here.

CLUELESS II: I think I've got it.

     (He fumbles in his cloak.)

                          One Pelisse, coming up!

     (He produces the Pelisse.)

CLUELESS I: That's it—
                 the precise Pelisse.
                          But how did it ever get over to you?

CLUELESS II: The hooker did it. She dragged me off to lunch at her place,
           and called it my present to her.
                               A lovely lunch it was,

complete with wine and sex. And then I snatched the Pelisse.
Not to forget this bracelet.

(He produces the bracelet.)

CLUELESS I: Now this, I declare, is bliss—
to be the source of a life of ease to a long-lost Brother!
And I was there, in a way: She invited you only
because she had this idée fixe that you were me.

SMUG: You don't have reservations about my freedom, do you?
I mean, you gave the order . . .

CLUELESS I:

(To Clueless Two.)

                                        And *you* should give it, too.
Oblige me, Brother, and grant with zest this last request.

(Clueless Two shrugs, then taps Smug on the head.)

CLUELESS II: Be thou free.

(Clueless One turns to Smug, and taps him again.)

CLUELESS I: Congratulations on liberation.

(Smug puts out his hand, evidently to receive a gift. Another awkward pause. No
one knows how to end this. Smug lowers his empty hand.)

SMUG: But isn't this rather skimpy? I mean, I'm supposed to be free
for a long time.
                            Isn't there more?
                                        Something *tangible,* maybe?

(Wrapped up with each other, the brothers ignore him.)

CLUELESS II: Well, now, Brother, it all turned out the way we wanted.
What say we go back home?

CLUELESS I: To Sicily, Brother? Sure.
But before I do your bidding, I'll have to hold an auction
and sell my effects and whatever.
                            Until that's over, Brother,
you'll stay at my place.
                            Inside, sib.

(Clueless One and Two begin to move toward the door of One's house.)

CLUELESS II: That's fine with me.

(The two are about to enter when Smug calls out.)

SMUG: Gentlemen, one more request.

CLUELESS I: Which is . . . ?

SMUG: I want to be
your auctioneer.

CLUELESS I: And so you shall.

SMUG: It's not too soon
to make the announcement. When's it scheduled?

CLUELESS I: Week from today.

SMUG:

(Advancing to the audience, he shills loudly as the Twins watch.)

ATTENTION ALL!
Official Announcement Is Hereby Made
of an
AUCTION!!!
Today Week   Dawn till Noon

FOR SALE
The Goods, Effects, & Fixtures,
The Chattels, Dwellings, & Farms,
The Slaves & Stuff
of CLUELESS, late of this city

EVERYTHING MUST GO!!!
TERMS: CASH

BONUS!
One (1) WIFE
—Used, a Fixer-Upper—
NO OFFER REFUSED
That amounts to at least
One-twentieth
of 1%
of 1%
of 1%
of 1%
of any sum
you care to name . . .

(He drops his role completely, solicits the audience as audience.)

—And now, dear audience,
To you from us,
A Fond Farewell.
To us from you,
Thunderous Applause!

(All exit into the house of Clueless One. The play is over.)

Finis

The Wild, Wild Women

BACCHIDES

TITVS MACCIVS
Douglass Parker
PLAVTVS

Introduction to *The Wild, Wild Women*

Bacchides—*The Wild, Wild Women*—is probably a very late play; I would push for a date after 190 B.C. It is also a very *full* play, as if Plautus, when pleased with a given shtick, had hurried to repeat it in variation: *The letter bit works—let's run that again.* Or: *Peeking in the whorehouse door brings laughs once—why not twice, or thrice, or even more?* And so it goes, and grows. And grows.[1]

Does all the swelling come from Plautus? Probably not. *Bacchides* appears to be the one play of his whose source exists in more than inflated flyspecks. Menander's *Double Deceiver* (Δὶς Ἐξαπατῶν) offers some quite substantial fragments and a recoverable plot: A young Athenian man (Moschos = Mnesilochus in Plautus = Intensides in this translation), while off to Asia to collect a debt for his father, falls in love with an already-contracted courtesan (? = Bacchis B/Soror = Bacchis Two/ Sissy) and writes a friend at home (Sostratos = Pistoclerus = Æsygo) to arrange a liaison. Returned home, Moschos is assisted by his slave (Syros = Chrysalus = Nugget) in flimflamming his father (? = Nicobulus = Curmudgeous) out of a large part of the collected money, sufficient to buy out the girl's contract; but the boy refuses it after he sees her identical sister (? = Bacchis A = Bacchis One) in embrace with his friend Sostratos. The slave Syros deceives Moschos's father *again* and achieves the money once more. Both pairs of lovers are united. Tableau. End of *Double Deceiver.*

So far, source and progeny run together very well . . . but we have only arrived at Act IV, Scene 10, of *Bacchides,* which begins with the Clever Slave's soldierly *Gloat:* here, the self-congratulation of a hero is cast in epic terms, very like the Taking of Troy. But the Gloat gets out of hand, inflates to unbelievable proportions, and suddenly starts the fully ended play up again. There is more money to be got from Intensides' father, and Nugget rides again, deceiving Curmudgeous yet once more, changing from Double Deceiver to *Triple Trickster,* by means of another letter. Nor will Plautus end his play with this twist. The sons have been corrupted; why not their fathers? And the two old men finally wind up the rigmarole, shambling eagerly inside with the sisters Bacchis, concluding things in a Happy and Disgraceful Ending.

It is, in all senses, a *vital* play. It will not die, not even if you beat it with a stick. Plautus certainly follows Menander's plotline, but he treats it like a surrealist redoing an heirloom necklace, daubing and coating each pearl on the string with variegated plasticine and broken glass and cold cereal . . . and extending his creation with light rope when it proves too small for his vision. It is a marvelous *deformation,* transforming Menander's smooth *inevitable, see?* into *what the hell next?* So, in grappling with

---

[1] In this version, the play's growth is even more spectacular. I have reconstructed its missing beginning, quite freely and at considerable length, in a "preAct" of five scenes, running between a fifth and a quarter of the remainder's size. This would make it about the equal in volume of *Miles Gloriosus* (*Major Blowhard*), Plautus's longest play. In this preAct, the surviving fragments are underlined. For the rationale and explanation of the reconstruction, see Appendix 1.

this work, the reader will do well to keep some items in mind: (1) Plautus is only occasionally *microconsistent,* often preferring to give an idea, a shtick, or wild language its head in defiance of character, plot, or logic. (2) The same disregard for dramatic niceness may have yielded to the excellences and demands of his players; he must have had a company of virtuoso soloists, each of them to be supplied with chances to shine, often in defiance of the play. Nugget's swelling Gloat is only the most flagrant example; the tutor (Lydos = Lydus = Zeugma) is allowed Nestorian length for his rants. (3) This play, off and on, resembles a modern musical comedy, especially in the monologues in recitative/aria structure that accompany entrances. I have implied existent tunes for some outright songs, but only some, which will make the reader a composer as well.

One more point, an unusual one. If the dating is right, Plautus, at his career's end, may have tried to be an Aristophanes. Roman Comedy rarely deals with current events, but this play is *Bacchides*—the women named after the god *Bacchus.* And in the late 190s and early 180s, the recently introduced worship of that god in Rome was a very hot issue. A cause célèbre was found: the supposed "initiation" into the Dionysiac mysteries of the wealthy young Roman Aebutius, in order to steal his inheritance, brought about senatorial fulminations; these culminated in the law *Senatus Consultum de Bacchanalibus* of 187, which suppressed the cult. A play about Bacchic corruption of young *and* old for money—what might its effect have been in Rome around the year 192, when the crisis was building? Or what furor might it have raised when the scandal was being debated? What we do know is that the title, and maybe the names of the title characters—these were Plautus's choices.[2] Menander's title centered on the Managing Slave, and so did his play.

The Wild, Wild Women, then, is a wild, wild play, a linguistic donnybrook, a politico-comico-tragico-epico-musical gallimaufry, very possibly a monument to self-indulgence, very probably too long. No shorter, certainly, in this translation, which tries to follow the playwright whichever way he twirls.

Names

As in my version of *Menaechmi,* I have renamed Plautus's characters, even as he redid the *Dramatis Personae* of his source. My goal here has been to make statements, euonymic, dysonymic, or descriptive, about the characters themselves. Thus, Mnesilochus of *Bacchides,* a very bipolar young man, is here "Intensides" (pronounced *In-TENSE-id-eez*), which at least catches him on the upswing; his more laid-back counterpart Pistoclerus has become "Æsygo" (pronounced *EAsy-go*). Intensides' choleric father, once Nicobulus ("victorious in counsel," or, less probably but more attractively, "counseling victory"), is now "Curmudgeous"; Æsygo's amiable sire, like son, like father, has become "Æsycome." The tutor, who Plautus set forth as Lydus (that is, "the Lydian"), is a rhetorical figure if ever there was one, and so has acquired the name of one: "Zeugma" (*ZOOG-ma*). The soldier Cleomachus has retained his military attitude as "Major Machismo." Plautus's invaluable Chrysalus, who might have turned out as

---

[2] For more on the pursuit of the Bacchic question, and one way to bring it into relief, see Appendix 2.

"Goldbrick," has become "Nugget" instead. Only the sisters who gave their names to the Latin play, however, have retained their Plautine names: "Bacchis" and Bacchis" (pronounced *BACK-iss*).

Texts and Acknowledgments

This version of *Bacchides* draws from standard editions of the Latin: W. M. Lindsay's *OCT* and Alfred Ernout's *Budé*. Most helpful has been the edition with commentary and prose translation by John Barsby (Aris & Phillips/Bolchazy-Carducci 1986). I owe a great deal to the *Bacchides* translation of James Tatum (Johns Hopkins 1982); he supplied a preAct both instructive and inspiring. My reading of the play depends a good deal on William S. Anderson's *Barbarian Play: Plautus' Roman Comedy* (University of Toronto Press 1993). Greta Ham and Tim Moore have given writings, readings, comments, and conversation. Not least did Deena Berg and William Levitan both pull and push.

DOUGLASS PARKER

Basic Set

House of Bacchis One   Alley   House of Curmudgeous

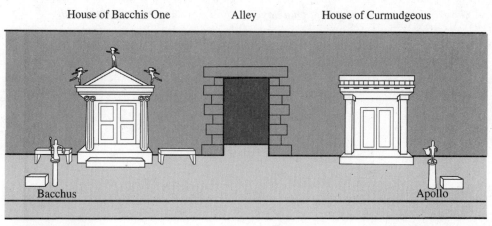

To the harbor   To downtown
(stage right)   *(stage left)*

SCENE: *A quiet middle-class street in the outskirts of Athens, such as might have been found there in the late fourth or early third century* B.C. *Two houses front on this thoroughfare. Stage left, the house of Curmudgeous, a rather wealthy burgher. Stage right, the* maison de joie *of Bacchis One, a youngish enterprising hooker/ madam. Between the two, a separating space that is usually termed an* alley, *but* side street *works better here. These are both substantial dwellings, though they differ widely in functions and status. Curmudgeous's is the locale of Old Money, Bacchis's that of a rather respectable business on the rise.*

There are other differences. Both houses have practical double doors opening directly onto the stage, but Bacchis's doors, at least, are capable of being peered into from the stage without exposing the interior to the audience, a ploy that happens frequently. Curmudgeous's house is rich enough, but forbidding and dull. Bacchis's place is attractive, verging on the gaudy; it also possesses benches (to accommodate overflow) flanking the doors, and, downstage, a small shrine to the god Bacchus—a sculptured head on a stela will do. Downstage from Curmudgeous's house is a like representation of Apollo. Curmudgeous's house, rarely bothered by crowds, needs no benches.

The houses pick up the qualities of the side exits. Offstage left is downtown Athens, the place of Business and Exchange. The wealthy Æsycome lives down that way. Off stage right is the harbor, the way from and to the Great Outside World, route of Returnees, Foreigners, and Fun. The stage symbolism thus resembles that of Epidamnus in Double Bind (Menaechmi), *but with a difference. The Athens of*

Bacchides, *in spite of Curmudgeous's architecture, is a happier and wiser place, where a young man of money might well like to* stay; *it* includes *the demesne of Bacchis.*

One warning: The designer who wishes to take the theme of Bacchic rites into more extended account will be confronted with a dilemma. It was one of the Roman complaints about these mysteries that they took place in the dark and so encouraged every sort of lubricious enormity. Bacchis One's house should therefore convey both *airy enticement* and *supernal lightlessness. Managing this paradox should present a considerable challenge. If choice has to be made, stick with enticement.*

The stage is empty at start.

Dramatis Personae

The Hookers
  BACCHIS ONE (Bacchis A)
  SISSY (BACCHIS TWO) (Soror [Bacchis B])   her sister

The Johns
  ÆSYGO (Pistoclerus)   son of Æsycome
  INTENSIDES (Mnesilochus)   son of Curmudgeous

The Marks
  CURMUDGEOUS (Nicobulus)   father of Intensides
  ÆSYCOME (Philoxenus)   father of Æsygo

The Gofers
  FEARSOME   slave to Bacchis One
  GIZMO (Puer)   page to Machismo
  LICKAS (Parasitus)   parasite to Machismo

The Muscle
  SHAMBLES (Artamo)   overseer to Curmudgeous

The Preacher
  ZEUGMA (Lydus)   tutor to Æsygo

The Capo
  MAJOR MACHISMO (Cleomachus)

The Operator
  NUGGET (Chrysalus)   slave to Curmudgeous and Intensides

The Mob
  FOUR HEAVIES (Lorarii)   slaves to Curmudgeous

The Staff
  ASSORTED SERVANTS (Ancillae, Servi)   maids and servants to Bacchis One
                                             and Bacchis Two

The Wild, Wild Women

preAct I, Scene A

(Bacchis One enters hurriedly stage left, from downtown, where she has evidently been doing some shopping. She looks over her shoulder nervously. Arrived at the door of her house, stage right, she drops her parcels, elaborately motions the audience to silence, and quickly enters the house. A moment, and Æsygo rushes on stage left. He looks around, puzzled, then makes his way unsurely to the door Bacchis has just entered. He raises his hand to knock, but she throws open the door and springs out at him, making a tiger growl and forming her fingers into claws.)

BACCHIS I: Grrrrrrr!

(Startled, and indeed rather frightened, Æsygo backs away to the left.)

[ΔE *FAN* 1]   Look, Junior, this stalking has got to stop *right now!*
You may know who I am, but I don't know *you,*
and I will not have attentions forced upon me
by a Perfect Stranger!
                    What do you think I am?

ÆSYGO: I *know* what you are, ma'am, and that's the reason . . .

BACCHIS I: I have a profession, you know! I am not one
of the ragtag bobtail types that clutter the streets!
I am an independent contractor, owner and sole
proprietor of a well-established business . . .

ÆSYGO: That's very impressive.

BACCHIS I: . . . who specializes in long-term
hookups, one-on-one . . .

ÆSYGO: *You're* very impressive.

BACCHIS I: . . . whose standing in the community guarantees
a certain immunity from the importunities
of any Moschos, Phaedo, or Sostratus
who happens to rub up against me in the market!

ÆSYGO: You're pretty, too.

(She notes the compliment automatically, acknowledges offhand, then plunges back into the tirade.)

192

BACCHIS I: —Thank you, I'm sure.—
            And therefore, I hereby serve you notice:
                                    Get Lost!
            Unless you wish to feel the unwanted attentions
            of a large and powerful bouncer behind that door!

(Æsygo, it is to be feared, has not taken her words in the proper spirit; in fact, he has stood his ground as she advances on him. He sniffs the air.)

ÆSYGO: What's that pretty smell?

BACCHIS I: They call it *Perfume*.

(She relents a little.)

            This one's *Arabian Noon*.   [XX]

(But only a little.)

                            I'm telling you, *go!*
            Depart! Vamoose! and Scram . . .

ÆSYGO: It tickles my nose.

BACCHIS I: . . . unless you care to apply through proper channels,
            of course.

(She pulls a stylus and a small tablet out of her bosom.)

            I think I could work you in . . .

ÆSYGO: You could?

BACCHIS I: . . . tomorrow.

ÆSYGO: Oh, no! Tomorrow'll be too late!

BACCHIS I: Too late? You've made a bet? You're under a spell?

ÆSYGO: No, it's nothing like that.

BACCHIS I: What *is* it like?

ÆSYGO: Well, first, it's not for me; it's for a friend.

BACCHIS I: Heard *that* before . . .

ÆSYGO: And next, I don't want sex . . .

BACCHIS I: Oh-oh . . .

ÆSYGO: . . . but information.

BACCHIS I: What sort of a girl
            do you think I am?

ÆSYGO: A perfectly lovely girl.
            An absolutely . . . *No!* That's not why I'm here!
            I'm trying to find a girl for a friend . . .

BACCHIS I:	I see.

Well, I've left all that behind, of course,
what with being an *entrepreneuse* and all,
but if you think you've found your life's vocation,
[XIX] do let me set you straight on the perils of *pimping:*
Remember, *Price* is the point, and *Pricing Structure*
is what it's all about.
                         Just keep an eye
on *Price,* and perhaps you'll grow up able to make
a proper appointment, and give up accosting Ladies
like me in the market.
                         And then there's *Inventory* . . .

ÆSYGO: I'm *not* a pimp! I'm just a very good friend!

BACCHIS I: You could have fooled *me.*

ÆSYGO: A very good friend
who's wasted nearly a year in combing Athens
to find a girl for my friend.

BACCHIS I: He must be picky.

ÆSYGO: I'm trying to find a *particular* girl. In *Athens,*
which means I've tramped all over this wretched city.
I've gone to the wall for my friend.
                         I've also gone
to the Forum, the temples, the shops, the upscale villas,
the downscale shacks, the public assemblies, and all
the stews, bordellos, and fancy houses in town.
I have *not* found The Girl, and my friend arrives
in Athens *today!*
                         I'm at the end of my rope,
and *you* are my last lorn hope.

BACCHIS I: Perhaps I can help.
This Girl—she has a name?

ÆSYGO: She certainly does.
She must be the only *Bacchis* in town.

BACCHIS I: What say?

ÆSYGO: Her name is *Bacchis.*

BACCHIS I: You're seeking *Bacchis?*

ÆSYGO: I am.

BACCHIS I: You're looking at Bacchis.

ÆSYGO: You mean that Bacchis is *you?*
          And *you* is Bacchis? Oh gosh, how utterly great!

     (He thinks again.)

          Oh god, how completely catastrophic!

BACCHIS I: I seem to
          be getting mixed signals here.
                              Still, what's his name?

     (She readies her stylus and tablet for writing.)

ÆSYGO: Whose name?

BACCHIS I: The name of your out-of-town friend. We'd better
          set up an appointment . . .
                              He does have money, your friend?

ÆSYGO: Why, yes, he . . . Money to make, well, make an *appointment?*
          With *you?*

BACCHIS I: Bacchis he wants, so Bacchis he gets.

ÆSYGO: With beautiful you? With beautiful, sweet-smelling *you?*

     (Aside.)

          What's happened to me? Can I be falling in love?

BACCHIS I: So what's his name?

ÆSYGO: Intensi . . . *no!*

BACCHIS I: Strange name.

ÆSYGO: Let's put it on hold.

BACCHIS I: Then no appointment?

ÆSYGO: N-none.

     (Aside.)

          —Time to fall back in disorder. I'd better regroup.—

     (He slowly begins to effect a retreat.)

          Well, sorry to cause you bother.
                              I guess I'll be going.

BACCHIS I: But it was so *important.* You walked for a *year.*

ÆSYGO: Well, yes, but it was healthy.
                              I'll tell you what:
          when he gets in, I'll send him by.

BACCHIS I: All right,
          I suppose.

There's just one thing:
don't send him today.
I'm closed today.
It's family business. My sister's
coming to visit.
But open bright and early
tomorrow morning.

ÆSYGO: I'll remember that.

(He finally commits himself to leaving.)

And so good-bye.

BACCHIS I: But don't be a stranger. I'd like
to see you again.

ÆSYGO: I'd like you to like that. Well,
good-bye again.

BACCHIS I: Try *au revoir.*

ÆSYGO: Oh gosh.

(He increases his speed. She calls after him.)

BACCHIS I: You didn't tell me your name.

(He answers over his shoulder.)

ÆSYGO: That's right; I didn't.
[XXIII]   Just call me NoName.

(He doesn't break stride but exits stage left. She looks after him, then turns to
the audience.)

BACCHIS I: Oh. Meet plenty of *those*
in this business. People need names of their very own.
Do all these anonymous types hang out together?
But how can they tell each other apart? Oh, well,
it takes all kinds.

(She picks up her parcels and opens the door of her house.)

I'd better put these away
and check how the cleaning's coming. No telling what time
the bunch pulls in from the boat.

(She stops and ponders.)

It's such a pity—
a fresh, delicious, stupid Nice Young Hunk.
With stuff like that, a girl could go Creative.

He *must* have a handle. Every man needs a name.
Even Ulysses. He tried the Incognito shtick,   [XV]
but couldn't keep it up for more than a day . . .
and this boy's no epic hero. Ulysses was troubled
and bothered, and wandered for twenty years before
he found his way home, but Junior here is loster
than Ulysses ever was, and he's home *already*;
he's covered more miles without even leaving town.

(She sighs, then brightens.)

But he'll be back; they always are. A perfect sacrifice
to celebrate the return of sister Bacchis!

(She does the tiger bit again.)

Grrrrrr!

(She waves good-bye to the audience and enters her house.)

preAct I, Scene B

(Bacchis's growl may still be resonating as Æsygo creeps back onstage from
the entrance left. Cautiously, his eyes ever on Bacchis's house, he makes his
way down center, then turns to the audience.)

ÆSYGO: I'm sorry for that exhibition. I didn't mean
to lose control, but I have fallen in love.
I've also taken a header into deep despair,
because my love can never be achieved
unless I sacrifice all truth and honor,
and betray the greatest buddy a man ever had . . .
or else consign myself to dragging out
a sere and withered existence, doubtless ending
my meaningless life in horror and pain quite soon.

Perhaps I'd better explain. My name—*of course*
I have a name—my name is Æsygo.
I am the son and heir of Æsycome.

(He points off left.)

We live over that way, a little nearer Downtown,
in a comfortable house that rather resembles this one.

(He points to Curmudgeous's house, stage left.)

Comfortable. Solid. Stolid. Let's face it, *dull.*
This happens to be the home of my fastest friend,
Intensides. He's *very* fast. And fun.
And often *freaked.* For him, I'd willingly lay
my life on the line . . .

               if not my love. Oh, dear.

(For an instant, he is very sad.)

> He has a bear of a father called Curmudgeous.
> *My* dad takes life as it comes and pretty much lets me
> do the same, but Curmudgeous is something else.
> He never lets up on Intensides, but always
> hassles him hard with the homiletic approach:
> *Early to bed,* and *In my day,* and mainly
> *A drachma saved.*
>   About two years ago,
> Curmudgeous erupted—a wild and costly oat—
> and shipped his prodigal off to Ephesus, over
> in Asia Minor. To collect some debt, he said,
> *To learn the value of Money* . . . but mainly, I think,
> to get him out of town. Why that was supposed
> to quiet Intensides down, I have no idea,
> but I know that the debt in question was *very* substantial.
> Like, *huge.*
>   But Intensides on the loose is still
> Intensides, and some time back he sent me
> a manic letter.
>   Let's see. I have it right here:

(From a fold of his garment, he pulls out a set of tablets, opens it up, and begins to read, quite flatly.)

> "DEAR BEST OF ALL POSSIBLE BUDDIES I HOPE YOU'RE WELL.
> LONG TIME NO SEE HA HA."

(He shrugs.)

>   It *will* get better.
> "LAST NIGHT WE FINISHED THE LAST LEG HA HA AGAIN
> OF OUR TRIP TO EPHESUS ALL THE WAY FROM SAMOS.
> I FELL IN LOVE IN SAMOS. HER NAME IS BACCHIS."

(He stops for a moment to inhale deeply, as if in pain.)

> I know, I *know.*
>   "THIS TIME IT'S THE REAL THING.
> WE'RE TALKING SERIOUS FOREVER HERE.
> TROUBLE IS, BACCHIS IS CAUGHT IN A LONG-TERM HOOKUP
> WITH A MAJOR NAMED MACHISMO. A THUG WHO HIRES
> HIMSELF TO THE HIGHEST BIDDER.
>   I HAD TO LEAVE HER
> BEHIND IN SAMOS. HA HA AGAIN."

[VII]

(He winces and clucks his tongue.)

>   Oh, dear.
> "BUT BACCHIS TOLD ME MACHISMO WAS UP FOR TRANSFER,

WHICH MEANS SHE'LL BE IN ATHENS BEFORE TOO LONG.
SO SPEAKING OF ATHENS, COULD YOU DO ME A FAVOR?
NO SWEAT NO TROUBLE AT ALL."
                              Oh, sure. A breeze.
"FIND OUT WHERE BACCHIS IS STAYING AT IN ATHENS,
AND TELL HER I'M COMING HOME SOON. AND FIX IT UP
SO WE CAN MEET AND WORK THINGS OUT. PLEASE DO THIS
PLEASE. SHE IS THE GIRL OF MY DREAMS. I WANT
TO HOLD HER TIGHT AND NIBBLE HER EAR AND WHISPER . . ."

(He looks straight at the audience.)

        Here comes the good part.
                        "AND WHISPER SOFT AND LOW
'MY HEART MY HOPE MY HEAVENLY HONEY BABE   [XII]
WITHOUT YOU LIFE IS AWFUL AND I CAN'T EAT.'"
Say what you want about Intensides' style,
he *can* pull off a zinger when he's inspired.
"ANOTHER THING I WANT TO DO IS HOLD HER . . ."

(He flips the tablet over and tries to find his place.)

". . . IS HOLD HER . . ."
                        Hold her *what?*

(He finds it.)

                              Oh, wow.

(Directly to the audience.)

                                    It gets
a little *personal* here. Let's cut to the chase.
"PLEASE DO THIS PLEASE OR ELSE I'LL KILL MYSELF.
I'LL MAKE IT A MESSY DEATH.
                        WITH HOPES FOR YOUR
CONTINUED HEALTH, I DO REMAIN YOUR FAITHFUL
FRIEND *NEAR DEATH* UNLESS YOU BAIL ME OUT,
INTENSIDES."
                —That's how I've wasted the year just past,
interviewing every hooker in Athens—
only to find that the Girl of my buddy's Dreams
is the Girl in his own Backyard, the Girl Next Door . . .

(He indicates the house of Bacchis One.)

        and *also* the Girl of *My* Dreams, the incarnation
        of all the fevered fantasies I've ever felt.
        I *can't* give her up. I can't arrive at a full stop
        before I've even *started.* My life would be
        no more than an empty husk around the neck.
        So *no!* Intensides can't have Bacchis—she's *mine!*

I'll never release her! He can go and . . .
>   Naw.
That hothead popoff might just do what he said.
It's more than honor; I'd never forgive myself.
Plus, *messy* he specified; *messy* he must have meant.
And I simply can*not* endure the sight of blood.

So what to do?
>   Go home, and pretend our meeting—
one which I'll never forget as long as I live
—never took place?
>   Or go back to Bacchis and beg—

[XIII]   "Please, ma'am, permit me to love you?"

(He looks up at the statue of Bacchus.)

>   I haven't earned it,
>   but I'd really appreciate some sort of sacred sign.
>   It needn't be large. It needn't even be . . .

(Bacchis One's small slave Fearsome tears onstage from the harbor exit, stage right, screaming.)

FEARSOME: GANGWAYYYYY!

(He bangs on Bacchis One's door.)

>   IT'S HERE!
>   THE MAJOR DOCKED!
>   THEY'RE ON THEIR WAYYY!

(He bangs away. Æsygo is horrified.)

ÆSYGO: The *Major?* The thug who's keeping Bacchis? Oh, *no.*
>   Her personality's winning, her body is stunning,
>   her total impression is spinning me out of my mind . . .
>   but I'm not really ready to fight a war
>   about her, not with a mercenary type
>   who's probably very large.
>   And fierce, to boot.

> *He who loves and runs away*
>   *May be alive the following day.*
> *He who splits the scene in sorrow*
>   *Is pretty sure to see tomorrow.*

Precisely what Zeugma, my Tutor, is always saying:
There is no substitute for ancestral wisdom.
I'll probably survive this.

(He looks longingly at Bacchis One's house.)

>   —Sorry, Bacchis.

(He waves sadly, then sprints off stage left. Fearsome keeps banging away.)

preAct I, Scene C

(Bacchis One, angry at the shouting and banging, suddenly opens the door. This upsets Fearsome, quite literally, but he immediately springs up again.)

BACCHIS I: I'll have you know that I'm a respectable . . .

                                        Oh, it's you.

FEARSOME: SHE'S ON HER WAYYY!

BACCHIS I: Who's on her way?

FEARSOME: YOUR SISTER!

BACCHIS I: SISSY?
           Already?
                          Oh, lord, the house is a mess!
                                        They should have finished
           the cleaning by now!
                          The custodian—where in the world did he get to?

FEARSOME: DON'T ASK ME! I'VE BEEN WAITING . . .

BACCHIS I: STOP SCREAMING!

FEARSOME: I've been waiting
           at the docks all day.

BACCHIS I: He's probably sleeping one off out back.
           <u>Go find that piece of shit and tell him that if he doesn't</u>   [IV]
           <u>fill his bucket and shlep it out front Right Now,</u> the staff
           is due for another eunuch!
                                        —And have the women man every
           available broom on the double!
                                   Cleaning? This place needs *purging!*
           Well? Don't just stand there—*Move!*

(Darting by her into the house, Fearsome risks one last scream.)

FEARSOME: I'M ON MY WAYYY!

(Bacchis aims a roundhouse right at him, but misses.)

BACCHIS I: They'd better get out here soon . . .

(Slowly, the staff, with brooms and all, begins to appear. She greets some of them singly and viciously.)

                                   —Hi there; so nice to see you.
                   —Late night last night?
                          —I didn't mean to disturb your slumbers.

(The last to stagger on is the Custodian, a quivering man with a large bucket and a huge hangover.)

—About that eunuch position: do give it serious thought.
We always welcome *incentive* on the part of the staff,
those who put off their own . . . *concerns* to help the team . . .

(She lines them in front of her, then marches back and forth like a drill sergeant.)

—Dress up that line! And dress up your*selves,* if you get the
   time.
But not before you've *cleaned* within an inch of your life.
You ought to be able to see your face reflected in the floor.

A WOMAN: But it's a dirt floor!

BACCHIS I: I didn't say it was going to be *easy.*
But let's get this place *clean!* We're due for a *Sister's
   Inspection:*
And no one digs for dirt like a Sister—or dishes it out.
No one lusts after dust like a Sister—or musses it up.
And no inspector alive or dead can rival a Sister
at magnifying the measliest smudge until it attains
the inflated status of Crime against Family, Heaven, and Earth!
So ready, set, and GO!

[The company galvanizes into action and joins Bacchis One in her Cleaning Song.][3]
[Tutte.]

[III]

Sweep the floor	*and wipe the dust*
Dig the dirt	*and scrape the rust.*
Whirl the washrag,	*spin the broom,*
Scrub the tubs,	*and ream each room!*
Brush the windows	*flush the walls—*
Today's the day	*when Sister calls!*
Beat the carpets,	*sluice the sashes,*
Scour the copper,	*dump the ashes,*
Shine the tiles,	*grind the grout,*
Get the grime	*and gravel out.*
Whisk the plates	*and chuck the crumbs—*
Today's the day	*when Sister comes!*

[Bacchis sola.]

Brandish broom	*and flourish mop*
Keep on cleaning	*till you drop!*
You can sweep the fug	*beneath the rug*

---

[3] The bracketed stage directions may be used by directors who don't mind being Aristophanic. A choral song is *not* standard Plautine technique, though Plautus does bring a few singing fishermen on in *Rudens.* Those who would hew to the line should disregard the bracketed passages and have Bacchis do the *complete* song as a solo, aiming it at the supers onstage, as Erotium (Loveykins) does in her Cleaning Song in *Menaechmi* (*Double Bind*).

> *When your visitor's merely a Mister . . .*
> *But the only plan   is spick and span*
> *when the visitor is your* Sister . . .

[Bacchis's entire staff gives a locomotive cheer to the mistress.]

BACK US, BACCHIS!
NEVER SACK US!
IF WE LACK THE KNACK, THEN SMACK US!
IF WE SLACK, THEN WHACK US, BACCHIS!
ROCK US! SHOCK US!
KNOCK US!
YAYYYY, BOCCHIS!

(The cleaning done, the staff and Bacchis congratulate each other with hugs and cheers. Then suddenly, from the entrance stage right, comes the voice of Bacchus Two—or Sissy, as we shall call her.)

SISSY: A party? For me? How sweet!
                              You really shouldn't have done it.

(To a woman, the entire staff freezes in horror, and then, as on signal, breaks for the house. The ensuing melee resembles nothing so much as a Boeotian fire drill, but in a surprisingly brief time, every member of the household has disappeared inside—except for Bacchis One, who is left, smoothing and brushing herself as she prepares to greet Sissy.)

preAct I, Scene D

(Enter, stage right, from the harbor, Sissy in full fig, followed by a small retinue of one or two attendants and preceded by Gizmo, Major Machismo's page, an extremely young boy slave with a piping voice. All move close and contemplate the sparkling house and its now rather dingy owner.)

SISSY: Bacchis!

BACCHIS I: Sissy!

(Sissy freezes and pulls up.)

SISSY: Don't call me that.

BACCHIS I: I always did.

SISSY: You call me *Bacchis!*

BACCHIS I: I won't—*I'm* Bacchis!

SISSY: Are not!

BACCHIS I: Am so!

SISSY: Don't you touch me!

BACCHIS I: We'll settle it later—everyone's watching.

(For form's sake, they decide to embrace, and do, rather gingerly. It is a short embrace, even for sisters, because Gizmo, dressed in a very gaudy military uniform and carrying a large scroll, which he handles like a swagger-stick, rushes up and pries them apart.)

GIZMO: *Break!*

(Reading from the scroll, which will become progressively more difficult to manage.)

"NO PUBLIC DISPLAYS OF AFFECTION FOR ANYONE ELSE!"

SISSY: But she's my sister!

GIZMO: I don't care if she's your *mother*— The Scroll says *no!*

BACCHIS I: My goodness—such a cute little boy!

(To Sissy.)

          Yours?

(It is difficult to tell who is more outraged by the question, Sissy or Gizmo, but Gizmo gets in first.)

GIZMO: I am *not* a "little boy." And if I was, I wouldn't be *hers!*
                          I am a Plenipotentiary Vice-Valet and Adjutant to Major Machismo!

BACCHIS I: Very impressive in one so young. But how did it happen?

(This is the signal for a song by Gizmo. Genre: Vo-de-oh-do.)

GIZMO: *I'm a winsome little minion,*   *and I haven't learned to shave.*
[I]   *But the house is my dominion*   *'coz I'm not your av'rage slave.*
              I'm a first assistant lackey—   *accept no substitute.*
              The other slaves are tacky,   *but what I am, is cute!*

              I'm the main man of Machismo   *and I'm never grim or grave.*
              I'm Machismo's little Gizmo,   *'coz I'm not your av'rage slave!*

BACCHIS I: But what's the Scroll?

GIZMO: Your sister's Papers.

BACCHIS I: My sister needs Papers?

GIZMO: Her shore-leave papers. To see that she doesn't get In Trouble. The Major's very thorough.

BACCHIS I: The Major's very thick.

GIZMO: Allow me:
                    "SUBJECT: BACCHIS OF SAMOS, STRUMPET FIRST CLASS.
              ACTIVITY: SIBLING, FEMALE, VISITATION OF.
              SUBJECT IS HEREBY GRANTED LEAVE ASHORE IN ATHENS
              FOR A PERIOD NOT TO EXCEED SIX HOURS . . ."

BACCHIS I: *Six hours!* That's hardly
time for *hello.*

GIZMO: "PROVIDED SUBJECT STRICTLY ADHERES
TO CONDITIONS HEREIN SET FORTH:"

BACCHIS I: *Subject?* Adheres to *Conditions?*

GIZMO: Don't interrupt.
                    "IMPRIMIS: NO PUBLIC DISPLAYS OF AFFECTION
FOR ANYONE ELSE.
                    SECUNDO: SUBJECT IS NOT TO DICKER . . ."

BACCHIS I: You watch your language! I'll have you know . . .

GIZMO: ". . . IS NOT TO DICKER
OR TRAFFIC TO SET UP AN ANNUAL COMPACT WITH ANYONE
ELSE."   [Xa]

BACCHIS I: Restraint of Trade!

GIZMO: "THIRDLY: SUBJECT IS HEREBY ENJOINED
DURING LEAVE FROM INDULGENCE IN ANY SHAPE OR FORM   [Xb]
OF LASCIVIOUS CARRIAGE OR HANKY OR PANKY OR NIK-NIK."

BACCHIS I: *Nik-Nik?*
That's really *kinky.*

SISSY: And don't I know it. Men are such sluts.   [XI]

GIZMO: "NUMERO LAST: SUBJECT IS ORDERED TO COME ABOARD
BY DUSK IN THE STATE AND SHAPE IN WHICH SHE EARLIER
    LEFT."
—And now we have the kicker:
                    "INFRACTION OF THESE CONDITIONS
IN PART OR IN WHOLE RESULTS IN IMMEDIATE FORFEIT OF
    SUBJECT'S
ENTIRE PRORATED RETAINER PLUS GIFTS AND EXPENSES, A
    TOTAL
OF TWO HUNDRED GOLD KAHUNAS."[4]

BACCHIS I: But that's five thousand drachmas!

---

[4] Behind *Kahuna* is a real coin named a *Philip,* or *Philippic.* This international coin was substantial, weighing 1720 grams of gold; two hundred of them would have been worth 48 silver *minas,* or 4800 *drachmas.* I've rounded this equivalence off to five thousand, and then thrown away all pretense of accuracy in renaming *Philippus* as *Kahuna* to indicate something both foreign and large. For largeness is the point here, and I have also often expressed the sum in drachmas to underline the *expensiveness* of the whole affair. A year with Bacchis Two costs Major Machismo more than the free-and-clear price of a house—in Plautus's *Trinummus,* 40 *minas,* or 4000 *drachmas.* (*Kahuna,* so far as I know, is the first Hawaiian word ever used to name a Greek coin.)

GIZMO: Arithmetic quite correct.

BACCHIS I: Who sees that she keeps the Conditions?

GIZMO: The Adjutant.

BACCHIS I: *You,* MightiMite? *You're* riding herd on *Sissy?*

SISSY: That's *Bacchis!*

BACCHIS I: Sorry.
                                —You're in charge of Bacchis's behavior?

GIZMO: You have a problem with that?

BACCHIS I: Why no. No problem at all.
              I welcome it, in fact.

    (Turning on an ominous charm.)

                                Come in and take your ease.
              There's lots to do. We specialize in cute little boys.

    (Sissy joins in.)

SISSY: Ve haff vays. Mysterious vays.

BACCHIS I: With no dull moments.

    (Gizmo is becoming very nervous and backs away as the sisters bore in on
    him.)

                        You look quite *sturdy;* that's good.

SISSY: And stoic at standing pain.

BACCHIS I: Subject to frequent fainting?

SISSY: Giddy when upside down?

BACCHIS I: Allergic to leather?

GIZMO: Just a minute . . .

SISSY: A speedy healer?

    (Gizmo is backpedaling with increasing speed. The sisters advance.)

GIZMO: There's really no need . . .

BACCHIS I: The whip!

GIZMO: . . . for hands-on methods.

BACCHIS I: The rope!

GIZMO: I can just as easy come back.
                                Or send somebody else . . .

    (Bacchis One unsheathes her claws at him.)

BACCHIS I: Grrrrr!

GIZMO: I guess I'd better . . .

(Sissy follows suit.)

SISSY: Roarrrr!

GIZMO: . . . be going. Good-bye!

(He rushes offstage in terror. They look after him.)

BACCHIS I: Too bad. He could have been fun.

SISSY: He wouldn't. He's just a toad.

BACCHIS I: About the name.

SISSY: It doesn't matter. I've just got used
to *Bacchis* while I'm on retainer to Major Machismo.
But what was Mom thinking of?

BACCHIS I: Incurably pious, I guess.
I'll never forget the day she told me, "Look here, Bacchis.
This is your little sister. Her name's the same as yours.   [VI]
Kiss sweet little Bacchis, Bacchis."

SISSY: She told that to *me*. I'm older.

BACCHIS I: No, *I* am.

SISSY: No, it's me. I think.

BACCHIS I: No, *me*. I think.

SISSY: Well, one of us has to be older.

BACCHIS I: Then one of us has to be younger.

SISSY: Unless we're twins.

BACCHIS I: Which we're not.

SISSY: Obviously.

BACCHIS I: And no one in her right mind would give her *twins* the same
          name.

SISSY: Which brings us back to Mom.

BACCHIS I: We simply *can't* be twins.

SISSY: Look, do we really have to go through all this again?

BACCHIS I: It's called *exposition*. Lets the audience know what we know.

SISSY: But we don't *know* a single thing.

BACCHIS I: Well, there you have it.

SISSY: I'm sick of this. Just call me *Bacchis* in public, okay?

BACCHIS I: Okay, Bacchis it is.
                                              And we've got other worries.
                    What's with your Major Machismo? The retainer's pretty hefty.

SISSY: There's nothing left. And he wasn't worth it.

BACCHIS I: Tell me about it.

      (This is the signal for a song by Sissy. Genre: Bluesy Narrative.)

SISSY: *Lemme tell you my story*   *bout Major Machismo,*
                    That absolute whiz at   *militarismo.*
                    He promised me excitement   *and joie de vie . . .*
                    But Machismo has a heart about   *as big as a pea.*

                    My life is a dream with   *Machismo the Playboy.*
                    That troglodytic, paralytic   *home-tonight-we-stayboy.*
                    He buys me dresses fit to start   *a riot or a rout,*
                    Then shuts me in the house   *and never lets me go out.*

                    The Major nets me necklaces   *and fits me out in fashion,*
                    But the Major is a Minor when   *it's time for passion:*
                    He drags me to the bedroom   *and throws me on the floor . . .*
                    And then I lie awake all night   *and listen to him snore.*

[VIIIa]   *Machismo's a windbag,*   *Machismo's a bellows,*
                    Machismo's got more wind   *than forty other fellows.*
                    He gusts the covers off the bed   *from midnight to noon,*
                    Then blasts off the mains'l—   *a human typhoon!*

BACCHIS I: No redeeming qualities?

SISSY: None that I've ever noticed.
[II]   He's world-class cruel, too; his methods of managing slaves
                    are clubbing and binding and working till dropping, and getting
                        worse.
                    Except for Gizmo, of course—his bite-sized bobolink boy.

[VIIIb] BACCHIS I: What's his provenance? That could explain his habits.

SISSY: Sometimes
                    he says he's from Thebes. He's stupid enough, but the accent's
                        wrong.
                    And no one who comes from Argos toots his own horn that
                        much.

[VIIIc] BACCHIS I: I bet it's Praeneste.

SISSY: Praeneste certainly breeds the best boasters—
a bump in the road that deserves its reputation—but it's   [IX]
over in Italy. Out of the mainstream.

BACCHIS I: Which would make him
an out-of-it blowhard rube.

SISSY: Sounds like Praeneste for sure.
—Let's get to the point. How can we pry poor, pitiful Bacchis
out of the Major's clammy clutches?

SISSY: We need a plan.

BACCHIS I: Agreed, but we need money more. Two hundred Kahunas
in solid Gold. We need a sponsor.

SISSY: A sugar daddy.

(Bacchis One addresses the statue of Bacchus.)

BACCHIS I: Mayhap Dionysus incline to send us a Savior soon!

(They do not have long to wait, because . . .)

preAct I, Scene E

(. . . on rushes Æsygo, stage right. It is not a concerted rush; he stops and
addresses the audience. He does not see the Sisters Bacchis.)

ÆSYGO: I'm back. I know I swore that I'd stay away,
and never betray my buddy tried and true,
but I can't stand it. The blasted prospect of Life
that lacks a Bacchis racks me, body and soul.

—But what would I do if I got her? My Tutor never
covered that little detail.

(He shrugs.)

                                           One thing at a time.

(Across the stage, the sisters have been seeing (though not hearing) him with
considerable fascination.)

SISSY: What have we here?

BACCHIS I: Oh, lord. It's *him* again.

SISSY: Who's *him?*

BACCHIS I: Can't say. He didn't leave his name.

SISSY: Everyone has a name.

BACCHIS I: Not *NoName* here.

SISSY: No name at all?
                              You know if he has any money?

BACCHIS I: He didn't say.

SISSY: He's good at that.

BACCHIS I: He *might.*
                His clothes are nice enough.

SISSY: Well, let's get closer.

(They do. Æsygo still doesn't see them.)

ÆSYGO: What can I tell Intensides? *I'm sorry, chum?*
                —I ripped your darling off?
                                          —Too bad about Bacchis—
                lost at sea, they say?
                                I can't endure this.
                Oh, Bacchis, why didn't Heaven create you *double?*
                A pair of Bacchises—Bacchides? damn those plurals.—
                Then I could have Bacchis *One,* and Intensides
                could maybe renew his thing with Bacchis *Two,* and . . .
                Hear me, Heaven. Grant me Bacchis in *sets!*

(The girls, still with no idea what he's saying, move to him.)

BACCHIS I: Pardon me, sir . . .

SISSY: . . . we have a proposition.

(He sees them.)

ÆSYGO: A brace of Bacchides!? Thank you, thank you, God!
                Blessings and Gratifications for making me
                the happiest wannabe traitor that ever lived!

                    The woeful world's   a paradise.
                    God works in ways   so neat and nice:
                    To solve a mess,   He makes it twice!

(He scrutinizes the sisters.)

                Which one do I take?
                                But why does it matter? I heard somewhere,
[V]   One drop of milk is just the same as another drop.
                And so I guess I'll take the one that's not so dusty.

(He rushes to Sissy and embraces her.)

                Bacchis belovèd—I'm back!

SISSY: You better watch it, buster!

(She clouts him one. He reels backward, then launches himself at Bacchis One
and embraces *her.*)

ÆSYGO: Bacchis belovèd—I'm back!

BACCHIS I: You're actually pretty forward,
          but you seem rather attractive.
                                   How are you fixed for funds?

ÆSYGO: For what?

BACCHIS I: For *fun,* I said. Just for fun, are you ready
          to tell me your name?   [XVI]

ÆSYGO: I'm sorry. Of course. It's Æsygo.
          the son of Æsycome.

BACCHIS I:

          (Pointing off left, towards downtown.)

                              Would that be Æsycome,
          the rich and prosperous merchant who lives down that way?

ÆSYGO: The same.

BACCHIS I: How very nice.
                    Let me introduce my sister—er, *Bacchis.*

ÆSYGO: It had to be. There stands the woman who's buried my buddy   [XVII]
          and me in bother.
                              —We have a mutual friend. Do you
          recall *Intensides,* by any chance?

          (Sissy clutches her heart and rolls her eyes.)

SISSY: My long-lost truest love!

ÆSYGO: My soon-to-be-found best friend.
                              He sent me a letter suggesting
          that you and he might get together when he got back.
          And he gets back today.

SISSY: Can such things be?

ÆSYGO: They can.
          So wait right here, and I'll run down to the docks and find him.

SISSY: Alas! It's not so simple.

BACCHIS I: Alas! It's not so easy.

ÆSYGO: Alas! I should have known this might have been the case.
          So what's the trouble?

SISSY: A Major disaster.

BACCHIS I: A mess about Money.

SISSY: The abysmal Major Machismo refuses to set me free . . .

BACCHIS I: . . . unless she pays him the sum of Two Hundred Gold
                Kahunas.

ÆSYGO: Two Hundred Gold Kahunas? Boy, that's a mess of mazuma—
                that comes to five thousand drachmas!

BACCHIS I: Arithmetic quite correct.
                Where can we seek a Savior?

SISSY: A parfit gentil Hero?

BACCHIS I: Who rescues my Sister may have his way with me . . . for free!

SISSY: A pretty fair bargain, you know.

(Bacchis One glares at Sissy and gives her a sideways aside.)

BACCHIS I: —Let's not overdo it, *Bacchis*.

(She turns back to ÆSygo.)

                I implore you, Mister . . . Æsygo, couldn't you tell us where
                we might locate a man who's filled with compassion and
                power?

SISSY: Someone to liberate . . .

BACCHIS I: . . . rescue . . .

SISSY: . . . assist . . .

BACCHIS I: . . . and possibly help?

(In spite of himself, Æsygo plays up in the Earnest Simpleton mode.)

ÆSYGO: Gosh, ladies, why not *me?*

SISSY: Why, what a perfect idea!

BACCHIS I: Why didn't we think of that?

ÆSYGO: I may not look like much,
                but I can tell right from wrong . . .

BACCHIS I:

(An agonized aside.)

                                . . . Oh, *no!*

ÆSYGO: . . . and this looks *right.*
                This way, I can help my buddy and heal the hole in my heart
                with no waste effort. Killin' two birds with one stone, y' might
                say.

BACCHIS I:

   (A wry aside.)

      —I didn't know pigeons threw stones.

ÆSYGO: Just tell me what I can do.
    I don't have that kind of money, but I'll sure help where I can.
    So what should I do? Just point me straight, and I'm your man.

BACCHIS I: You certainly are.
                      Excuse us for just a moment, would you?
    We have to devise a plan of action—Girl Talk, you know.
    I'll rush right back, dear Hero!

ÆSYGO: You do that, little darlin'.

   (The sisters depart down left from him and huddle out of earshot. Æsygo comes
to himself, with an almost audible jerk.)

    I can't believe I said that; my mind is melting in mush.
    Supposing she rushes back to enfold me, how do I hold her?
    Zeugma never touched on practical items like that
    in his lectures. *How to Tell If It's Love or Loathesome Lust*—   [XIV]
    that was his drift. But which was which . . . well, I forget.
    Still, she's a *hooker.* And hookers *hook.* And I'd better cover
    whatever it is they hook you in.
                      I'll go . . .

   (He starts to the right, then takes a look a Bacchis One and stops.)

                        . . . I'll stay.

   (Aside, the sisters huddle and discuss their potential deliverer.)

BACCHIS I: So what do you think?

SISSY: You know him. You go first.

BACCHIS I: He seems a nice enough type. I wouldn't award him a trophy
    for brains . . .

SISSY: There are better things than brains.

BACCHIS I: . . . and he's not exactly
    built . . .

SISSY: There are better things than brains and build.

BACCHIS I: . . . nor does he
    look *rich* . . .

SISSY: There are better things than brains and build.

BACCHIS I: And so?

SISSY: Let's face it; he's *nada.*

BACCHIS I: I wouldn't say *that*.

SISSY: What would you say?

BACCHIS I: He seems a nice enough type . . .

SISSY: Oh, god . . .

BACCHIS I: and he's all we've got . . .

SISSY: Oh, god *again*.

BACCHIS I: and so, unless you want to spend your
declining years as a one-woman Veterans' Aid Branch Office,
I think . . .

SISSY: I'm afraid . . .

BACCHIS I: we'd better . . .

SISSY: you're right . . .

BACCHIS I: give him *The Treatment*.

SISSY: Okay.

        (Beat. Then, in confusion.)

        Which one? The *Change-Your-Luck?*

BACCHIS I: No, no. He's *pure*.

SISSY: Too bad.
        Well, what? *The Chicken Inspector?*

BACCHIS I: No, that's for farmers.
Our boy's a townie.

SISSY: God save Athens. *The Hole in the Wall?*

BACCHIS I: No time.

SISSY: *The Monkey on the Roof?*

BACCHIS I: Needs too many props.

SISSY: I've got it—
Double-Your-Fun!

BACCHIS I: Not really; monogamous type.
                Now, look:
We don't have to get *baroque*. He's already with us in spirit,
sad as he is. We'll have to *Make Do*.

SISSY: Don't know that one.

BACCHIS I: It isn't a *one;* it's a frame . . .

SISSY: Oh. Like for rape?

BACCHIS I: A frame of *mind*.
    Examine him closely. He's ready to fall.

SISSY: You mean . . . ?

BACCHIS I: I do:
    High-Low.

SISSY: Of course! Which part do I take?

BACCHIS I: Whichever you want.

SISSY: Oh, my.

    (She ponders.)

        In these long-term hookups, a girl gets out of practice.
    And you're so good at *High*. I swear, <u>you could charm the
        toughest</u>   [XVIII]
  <u>customer</u> into a cuddly cup of custard.
                        But tell me,
    who does what? I'm a little rusty.

    (Segue directly into Act I, Scene 1.)

Act I, Scene 1 [35–108]

    (The two sisters are conversing apart, to the discomfiture of Æsygo.)

BACCHIS I: How does this strike you?
    You do tacit, I'll do talk.

SISSY: I love it. Let's.

BACCHIS I: And if I dry up, you'll be right there to fill me in.

SISSY: Well, I don't know about prompting. What if *I* blow up in *my* lines?

BACCHIS I: Poor nightingale—afraid she might forget her song.
                      —Come on. Quick march.

    (They return to the bemused Æsygo.)

ÆSYGO: Here comes the company: Bacchis & Bacchis, unlimited,
    Sex Our Specialty, Interchangeable Arts & Parts,
    A Family Firm. And what are they up to now?
                    —Hi, there!
    I hope the Executive Session turned out all right?

BACCHIS I: Just fine.
    No trick to it.

ÆSYGO: That must be quite a change.

    (A glare from the sisters.)

                Sorry.

(Bacchis One adopts a classic pose of grief, and Sissy slumps in sympathetic sorrow.)

BACCHIS I: What Is More Woeful Than Woman?

ÆSYGO: Search me. You got any suggestions?

BACCHIS I: I am about my sister's business. She beseeches me
               to procure a Savior to succor her, to take her part,
               to fix that soldier—I'm sorry, I can't go on.

     (She goes on.)

                                                          Someone
               who, when she's fulfilled her contract and her hitch is up,
               will waft her back to her sweet little home on Samos.
                                                          Please, Sir,
               I beg you, take her part!

ÆSYGO: Which part do you want me to take?

BACCHIS I: To effect her safe return home, and stop that odious creature
               from prisoning her permanently on his staff as a . . . *tweeny.*
               She Is A Good Girl, Sir. If only she had The Money
               to buy out her contract now, she'd be thrilled to pay him off.

ÆSYGO: This Major—where is he now?

BACCHIS I: In the near vicinity, Sir.
               He may well turn up any moment.

     (Change in tone.)

                                             And so our house
               would be the perfect place to confront him. Yes,
               you could take a load off your feet while waiting, and have a drink
               in the bargain, and, after your drink—and that's in the bargain,
                   too—
               I'll personally top off the drink with this world's sweetest kiss.

ÆSYGO: Your mouth drips honey, but it's nothing but glue!

BACCHIS I: I beg your pardon?

ÆSYGO:

     (A little insane.)

               You don't fool me! Fowl play—two poachers stalking their prey!
               One lone, lorn . . .

BACCHIS I: Loon?

ÆSYGO: . . . as I was about to say, *pigeon.*
               —I'm a goner . . . here comes the glue. Right where the feathers
               are short.—
                          A pretty plot, but let me inform you, female,

it's not the sort of affair that I should associate in . . .

er, with.

BACCHIS I: Why not, pray tell?

ÆSYGO: Well frankly, Bacchis, I quake at *Bacchae*—
those wild, wild women who produce Bacchanalian orgies
charged with backache and backbite and backstab. I blanch at
    debauches.

BACCHIS I: But what's to be afraid of? You're scared of lying down for supper?
Can't you abide a bed?

ÆSYGO: By itself, a bed's not bad . . .
But a bed turns bawd when it bodes a bod,
                         and that's bad.

BACCHIS I: I see.

ÆSYGO: An Endangering Species, that's what you are! I decline to recline
in your lurid, lightless lair. It's not my sort of affair;
it leads to the worst kind of LUST!

BACCHIS I: If it leads to any LUST
in *my* den, darling, I'll be the one to turn you off.
You've got it all wrong: there's only one reason I want you inside,
and that's to amaze the Major:
                         When you're with us—chaperoning—
neither Sissy nor I can suffer extortion, assault, or abduction.
You'll be our defender, and do your buddy his promised favor:
Three birds with one stone!
                         There's more, of course:
                         When the Major comes,
he'll have to conclude that I'm Your Mistress!
                         How does that strike you?

(Dead silence.)

No comment?

ÆSYGO: How smooth and sleek those syllables sound when you say them!
But when the crunch comes, reality's in, and Life's on the line—
just watch those pear-shaped tones break out in spikes . . . and
    BANG!
an estate shot full of holes, a heavily honeycombed heart,
my career all raddled to tatters, my Good Name gouged!

SISSY: But what's to be afraid of from *her?*

ÆSYGO: Again that question!
When a lad of my tender years can make his unguarded way
into her erotic rumpus room, her pit of obscene calisthenics,
to writhe into wrong, to drip his fame and fortune away

            in gouts of sweat?

BACCHIS I: The *nicest* way of putting things.

ÆSYGO: A place to trade my manly sword for a dicky bird,
my casque for a barrel, my plate for a dish, my bow for a belle,
my buckler for supper, my lance for lunch, my cuirass for kisses,
my sling for a drink, my poleax for pillows, my horse for a whore!
AWAY! GET THEE BEHIND ME! LEST I BE UNMANNED.

BACCHIS I: You really are a compulsive. Hard case.

ÆSYGO: I look out for myself.

BACCHIS I: You'd better look out for me. You need to be melted down—
a service I'm glad to perform. It goes like this . . .

      (She puts her arms around him.)

                              Want more?

ÆSYGO: You're really too expensive . . .
                      I can't afford your service . . .

BACCHIS I: Pretend. Act like you love me.

ÆSYGO: What school of acting? Method?
Ham? Sincere, or devil-may-care, or highfalutin?

BACCHIS I: Just follow directions. Now, when the Major enters, you put
your arms around me—*so*—and embrace me madly—*thus.*

      (An affectionate pose is arranged and held. At length Æsygo recovers his voice.)

ÆSYGO: Is this really required? I don't see the point.

BACCHIS I: You will. It's this:
I want the Major to *see* us. Don't worry; I know what I'm doing.

ÆSYGO: That's just what I'm worried about.
                     There *is* one thing . . .

BACCHIS I: Now what?

ÆSYGO: A Good Soldier always looks out for the unforeseen. Suppose,
inside your house, things take a swift and unexpected change?

BACCHIS I: Such as?

ÆSYGO: A sudden lunch. An ad lib dinner. An orgy.
Oh, I'm no fool. I know what goes on in human anthills.
So, if that happens, where . . .

BACCHIS I: Where *what?*

ÆSYGO: Well, where do I sit?

BACCHIS I: You *recline* by me. Hard by the hostess. Like with like,
              and nice with nice. Your place is reserved, no matter the hour,
              no matter the day. When a nice time's your aim, drop in and
                  whisper,
              "Can you fix me up?" And I'll fix you up, with the nicest spot
              in the house, right next to the fixer. Me.

ÆSYGO: I'd better be careful.
              A river, a raging flood like this, is hard to ford.

BACCHIS I:

    (Aside.)

              And even harder to cross without loss, intrepid voyager.

    (Up.)

              Hand, please. In we go!

ÆSYGO: Oh, no, not there. Not on your life.

BACCHIS I: You have an objection?

ÆSYGO: It's all too perfect. It might be designed
              to trap a lad of my tender years:
                                        Strong Wine, Loose Women,
              and Staying Up Late.

BACCHIS I:

    (Exasperated.)

                             That's *it*. Do you think I'm taking this trouble
              for any other reason than you, lover, *you?* So the Major makes off
              with my sister—she'll get over it. It's up to you. Don't come
              a step inside that house unless you really want to.

ÆSYGO:

    (Aside.)

              And now it's the moment of truth, and my vaunted strength of will
              sits down and waves good-bye . . .

BACCHIS I: Something new to be afraid of?

ÆSYGO: Nothing important . . .
                                    Madam, I make myself over to you,
              free and clear. I'm yours. To command. At your service.

BACCHIS I: You're sweet,
              and here's your very first service:
                                        I'm giving a welcome-back dinner
              for Sissy here today . . .

    (A quite convincing fumble.)

Now, where did I put that money?
Of course, it's inside. I'll have it brought out, so you can take it
down to market and spare no expense in providing us splendid
provender.

ÆSYGO: Oh, no, I insist. My treat. It's Man the Provider.
I wouldn't have any manhood left if my hostess served me
out of the goodness of her heart with such a lavish hand
and footed the bills for it, too.

BACCHIS I: I'd really rather you didn't.

ÆSYGO: As a favor? For me?

BACCHIS I: Very well. If you insist. A favor.
I can't deny you a thing. But do *me* a favor: be quick.

ÆSYGO: I'll be back before my love for you has time to cool.

      (He strides off left, in proud confusion. A pause.)

SISSY: You certainly do know how to lay out a banquet, Bacchis.

BACCHIS I: And why do you say that, Bacchis?

SISSY: Fresh fish. In my estimation,
you've just landed quite a catch.

BACCHIS I: And what's a hooker for?
But now that I've got mine, I have to give you some help
in gaffing Intensides, Bacchis. That way, you can net pure profit
here in Athens, rather than back on the road with the Major.

SISSY: That's exactly what I desire.

BACCHIS I: And service will be provided.

      (A call from the house.)

The water's hot. We'll go in now. You can take a bath.
What with a sea voyage and all, you must be a bundle of nerves.

SISSY: Yes, you might say that.

BACCHIS I:

      (Looking off left.)

                              And here comes somebody noisy,
bent on raising a row. We'd better get out of his way.
Come on inside, and get refreshed with a soak and a nap.

      (The sisters exit into Bacchis One's house.)

Act I, Scene 2 [109–169]

(Enter Æsygo, followed—or preceded; *n'importe*—by a procession of slaves bearing
goodies, followed—*et ça importe*—by Zeugma, who is making an extremely bad
job of trying not to look as though he were skulking—which he is.)

ZEUGMA: Aha!

ÆSYGO: I beg your pardon?

ZEUGMA:

(Ever the schoolmaster.)

                                        Long time ere this,
              young Æsygo, have I held my tongue,
              on tacit tiptoe trailing this crazy column
              of conspicuous consumption, no effort sparing to spy out
              your possible motives. This show could corrupt Lycurgus
              the Spartan, lead him hell-bent for leather down
              the primrose path. And so, my question: whither
              do you betake yourself with this parade?

ÆSYGO:

(Pointing to Bacchis One's house.)

              Oh, here.

ZEUGMA: Oh, here.

(Beat. Take. Then, savagely:)

                                   Where's *here?* Whose house is that?

ÆSYGO: That is the temple of Love, Desire, and Lust,
              of Joys and Ease and Sprees, Divertissement,
              of Pleasure, Leisure, Hijinks, Chat, and Mwah!

ZEUGMA: *Chat?* Who's that?

ÆSYGO: The God of Civilized Intercourse.

ZEUGMA: And *Mwah?*

ÆSYGO:

(Putting his palm to his mouth and bringing it away suddenly.)

                         Mwah—the goddess of prolonged osculation.

ZEUGMA: You take your business elsewhere; I never heard
              of such a goddamned god.

ÆSYGO: But only villains
              vilify virtue, and here you are defaming
              deity, panning the pantheon.
                                        It's just not right.

ZEUGMA: You're trying to tell me there IS a god named *Mwah?*

ÆSYGO: You're trying to tell me you never knew there was?
              Zeugma—oh, the shame of it—you're just not civilized!

My tutor, the man who knew more than the pre-Socratics—
or so I thought—turns out to have less knowledge
than an unwashed, underage Italian primitive!
Big as you are, and not know the names of the gods!

(Scanning the procession.)

ZEUGMA: I do not like this shoddy outfit at all.

ÆSYGO: Well, nobody fitted it out for you, now, did they?
They fitted it out for *me*. And I like it. All.

ZEUGMA: And has it come to this? You launch a series
of flip smartass ripostes at ME? Oh, NAY, boy!
E'en had you ten stout tongues, far better 'twere
to stay shut up!

ÆSYGO: *In school we cannot fitly bide us
through every stage of life*—now can we, Zeugma?
Besides, my mind's preempted with one large worry:
Will the cook's finesse do this provender proud?

ZEUGMA: Oh, the waste of it! You've ruined yourself,
and me, *and* all my selfless effort. My constant
moral instruction has been to no avail.

ÆSYGO: For what it's worth, I wasted my efforts as much:
Your instruction seems to be a bust for us both.

ZEUGMA: Hard words, and harder heart!

ÆSYGO: And hardest head.
Frankly, Zeugma, you bore me. Now shut your mouth
and come on in with me to Bacchis's house?

ZEUGMA: Will you look at that? This stripling calls me *Zeugma!*
No tittle remains of my tender title "Tutor."

ÆSYGO: I appeal to decorum: it is neither right nor fitting
for Man the Provider to provide the feast, to sink down
on the couch entwined in his mistress' embrace, to give her
a lingering kiss, to accept the cheers of the other
guests, and then, with the party clustered round,
to say, "Oh, by the way, folks, this is my *Tutor.*"

ZEUGMA: Party? An *orgy,* you mean! Is that the goal
of all these piles of provender?

ÆSYGO:

(Piously.)

                                        We can but hope.
The gods it is who mold man's puny wishes.

ZEUGMA:

>(A sudden realization.)

>>A mistress? *You?*

ÆSYGO:

>(Grabbing him by the arm.)

>>>Well, seeing *is* believing.

ZEUGMA:

>(Breaking away.)

>>No! I refuse to see, nor will I allow it!
>>I'm going home!
>>>(And you know what *that* means.)

ÆSYGO:

>(Catching him by the arm and dragging him back.)

>>None of that, Zeugma, or You'll Be Sorry.

ZEUGMA: A threat?
>>I'll be sorry? Just what does this mean? Be *sorry?*

ÆSYGO: Let's say I've graduated from your jurisdiction.

ZEUGMA:

>(In a frenzy.)

>>THE PIT! WHERE IS THE PIT?

ÆSYGO: Across town.

ZEUGMA: OH, PIT!
>>How gladly might I now possess me of you,
>>and you, you of me! Let me have life behind me,
>>no more before me! Did ever pupil stoop
>>to muscles and threats against his trusted *teacher?*
>>No more will I instruct the red-blooded boys,
>>when this young blood endeavors to spill my blood,
>>which I haven't got.

ÆSYGO: What say we do a play?
>>The hero Hercules wasting his teacher Linus?

ZEUGMA: Far better might I play the reverend Phoenix,
>>announcing to his father the death of Achilles—
>>i.e., *you.*

ÆSYGO: Enough of ancient history.

ZEUGMA: Behold him! His shame is shattered, his respect is ruined!

What profiteth it you? A gain that matches ill
with your tender years: unblushing insolence!

(Playing on the heartstrings.)

Think, lad: does it never more come to your mind
that you have a Dear Old Father?

ÆSYGO: Now, look here, Zeugma:
which one of us is *really* the slave to the other?

ZEUGMA: What base preceptor taught you that, you viper?
It was not I. But now you've found your level:
you have a talent, an inborn gift for orgies,
but none for my ethics and morals—oh, woe, no!
To waste my service on such a sneak as you,
hiding away the traces of lust from me, your Tutor.
And from your Daddy!

ÆSYGO: Zeugma, as a favored slave,
you've had a certain limited freedom of speech.
It's now revoked!
                              Quick march! Get in that house!

(Into the house of Bacchis One, he ushers the laden servants and drags the protesting
Tutor.)

Act II, Scene 1 [170–177]

(Enter Nugget stage right, from the harbor, looking recently nautical. He looks
around him with pleasure, then strikes an attitude whose theatricality parallels that of
his address.)

NUGGET: Oh, blessed birthplace of my boss, how y'awl?
I trust you're well. And I, who now behold
your blissful vista barely twice twelve months
since I departed hence for Ephesus—let me
now sincerely swear I'm glad to see you.

(To the statue of the god Apollo by Curmudgeous's house.)

Another hearty hello to *you,* Apollo,
the god next door, pronounced with reverence deep.
From you I beg a boon:
                                    could you possibly fix it
so old Curmudgeous, our household's doddering codger,
stays out of my way until I've had a chance
to chat with Æsygo, the chum and buddy
of my young master Intensides? You see,
he sent this Æsygo a letter about
the girl he wants to live with, Bacchis . . . Anyway,
please don't forget the name. That's *Æsygo.*

Act II, Scene 2 [178–234]

(There is no crash of thunder; lightning does not flash; there is not a suspicious brightness in the air; horses do not break into irrational whinny . . . but, as if on cue, Æsygo emerges from the house of Bacchis One. Rather lingeringly, true: Bacchis One is evidently on the other end of a tender farewell.)

ÆSYGO: There's really no need for all these tears and entreaties.
                Of course I'll come back; I couldn't leave you now
                if I wanted to. Which I don't. Love's got me leashed
                with an ironclad lease; my heart's tied hand and foot.

NUGGET:

(Erstaunt.)

                Talk of divine intervention! Whom do I see
                but Æsygo!
                          Hello there, Æsygo.

ÆSYGO:

(Breaking away from the door.)

                Hello there, Nugget.

NUGGET: Allow me, Sir, to effect you
                a savings in words and effort in the lengthy ritual:
                Point One: You're glad I'm back.
                                    Point Two: I believe
                your gladness.
                          Point Three: You pledge me the run of your house
                and dinner, as per the rules for greeting and treating
                a traveler from abroad.
                          Point Four: I accept that pledge,
                and pledge my appearance.
                                    Point Five: I say my piece,
                bring you best wishes from your trusted buddy.
                                              Point Six:
                You will, of course, inquire as to his location.
                I reply: Among The Living.

ÆSYGO: But Intensides . . . well,
                he *is* All Right?

NUGGET: I was rather expecting that *you*
                could inform me on that, Sir.

ÆSYGO: Me? But how would I
                know that?

NUGGET: If you don't, no one else does.

ÆSYGO: Explain.

NUGGET: Quite simple. It concerns his girl. Attend:
               location, location, location—and a little logic:
               If she's been found, his state of health is huge.
               If she's still lost, he's sick, he's left for dead.
               The lover's life lies in the lovée. If she's away,
               then he's long gone, a cipher. But if she's here . . .
               his money's gobbled, geshpent—and he's an insolvent
               wreck.
                              So how have you handled the job he gave you?

ÆSYGO: Am I the sort to shirk performing a favor
               duly requested, to greet my friend
               on his return with "Sorry, not done yet"?
               I'd rather serve my time in the swamps of Hell.

NUGGET: You mean that you found Bacchis?

ÆSYGO: The Bacchis from Samos.

NUGGET: An import? That Samian schlock is HANDLE WITH CARE.
               And keep it THIS END UP, or it goes to pieces.

ÆSYGO: Always with the jokes.

NUGGET: Oblige me, please:
               precisely where can Bacchis be found at the moment?

ÆSYGO:

     (Pointing to Bacchis One's house.)

               Right here.
                              The house I just left.
                                             You saw me come out.

NUGGET: How deft—a handy neighbor, the girl next door.
               She *does* recall Intensides, I suppose?

ÆSYGO: Recall? She *dotes*.
                              What's more, she thinks he's unique—
               the only wonderful one-of-a-kind in the world.

NUGGET: Well, whaddya know?

ÆSYGO: What's more, you wouldn't believe
               the depth of her feelings. Authentic love, the whole bit:
               deprived, frustrated, wretched, nauseous . . .

NUGGET: That's great!

ÆSYGO: What's more, the eentsiest instant doesn't click by
               when she doesn't call him by name . . .

NUGGET: And feels immensely
               better. Of course.

ÆSYGO: What's more . . .

NUGGET: What's more, I think,
      is my imminent departure.

(He turns to go off, probably stage right.)

ÆSYGO: And miss the chance
      to hear your master's lovely luck in detail?

NUGGET: The script's okay—but your acting gives me heartburn.

(He turns to the audience.)

      Isn't this always the way? Take Plautus's hit
      Epidicus—that's my favorite piece. I love it
      better than *me*. But give the title role
      to Pellio,[5] and that play plummets to last on my list.

(He shrugs, and turns back to Æsygo.)

      And where would you class this Bacchis? Under *buxom?*

ÆSYGO: *Buxom?* Oboy.
                          I'd judge her a Juno . . . if only
      I hadn't graded *my* Bacchis a Venus, and Venus,
      you see, isn't Juno's sister, and so . . .

(He would dither on, but Nugget cuts him off.)

NUGGET: *Thank you.*

(A call to his absent master.)

      Attention, Intensides!
                      As near as I can
      assess the plot, your Object Of Love is ready.
      Your Means *To* Love, however, needs some work.

(Back to Æsygo.)

      —I rather gather Gold's needed to further this business?

ÆSYGO: It is. Gold *sterling.* Coin of the realm.

NUGGET: I gather
      Gold's needed *soon?*

ÆSYGO: What's more, Gold's needed *now.*
      Soon is the time the Major arrives.

NUGGET: The Major?

ÆSYGO: He's coming to get the Gold and give up Bacchis.

---

[5] For "Pellio," those who produce this play may wish to substitute the *real* name of the actor who
performs the role of Nugget . . . and who is, in fact, uttering this line.

NUGGET: Then let him come. He can choose the time. Provided
he doesn't keep me waiting. The wherewithal
is herewithal.
              Do I feel frightened? *No.*
Do I go down on my knees to any man?
No again.
           My strength is as the strength of ten
because my heart is *dirty.*
                 —Get back inside;
I'll handle matters out here.
                   Let Bacchis know
Intensides surfaces soon!

ÆSYGO: You command; I obey.

(He exits into Bacchis One's house.)

NUGGET: The Gold Rush is going down, and it's up to me.
The Ephesian venture yielded capital returns:
we've brought along twelve hundred Kahunas in Gold—
that's thirty thousand drachmas, more or less.
One of the locals repaid Old Master a debt.
My task for today is skulduggery: somehow devise
a device and fix a hoax to coax and shift
some share of that stash of cash to underwrite
Young Master's *amour.*

(He turns toward Curmudgeous's house, stage left.)

                The door—*our* door.
It creaked. Here comes somebody. I wonder who?

Act II, Scene 3 [235–367]

(Curmudgeous, in a paroxysm of perturbation, emerges from his house. He does not immediately see Nugget.)

CURMUDGE.:   Now, down to the docks to check the recent arrivals:
did any Ephesian freighter put in to Piraeus?
I'm alarmed. My son's been dawdling too long in the decadent
East. I'd better see that prodigal soon.

NUGGET: A lovely prospect for unravelment, strand by strand . . .
god willing, of course. No dozing—duty calls.
The Gold's on the block, Nugget; so hit your mark,
and Presto, make a few passes, and Change-o, behold!
Transform that fogy into a glistening ram,
and give his golden fleece your closest shave,
trimmed to the skin, till all but the horns are shorn!

(He approaches Curmudgeous and addresses him in a Jeevesian superior-deferential mode, well adapted to the faithful servant.)

          To Curmudgeous, high and mighty, Nugget the worm
          extends a lowly hello, with extreme best wishes
          and deep servile concern for his master's welfare.

CURMUDGE.:   What the hell did you do with my son?

NUGGET: Tut, Sir.
          Return my greeting; that's a good boss.

CURMUDGE.:   So Hi.
          Intensides—where the hell *is* he?

NUGGET: Alive.
                          And lively.

CURMUDGE.:   He's *here?*

NUGGET: He's here.

CURMUDGE.:   That came like a splash of cold water.
          Best of health since he left?

NUGGET: Ready for the ring:
          Fettle, fine. Tail, bushy. Oats, felt.
                        He's quite the athlete.

CURMUDGE.:   And what about IT?

NUGGET: What IT?

CURMUDGE.:   The IT I sent him
          to Ephesus after! Did he collect the Gold
          from my longtime buddy, Prestigius?

(Nugget doubles up and goes into a small but interesting fit.)

NUGGET: *WHINNNGGG!*[6]

(He regroups.)

          That name! Whenever I hear it in the merest
          whisper, I suffer immediate headsplitting heartburn.
          You'll have to face it, Sir: your buddy's a baddy.

CURMUDGE.:   But how can this be?

NUGGET: Because the Fearsome Foursome,
          the Holy Quaternity—Fire, Moon, Sun, and Day—
          have never shone on a more nefarious felon.

CURMUDGE.:   More nefarious than *Prestigius?*

(Nugget doubles up.)

---

[6] The continuation of this standard burlesque/vaudeville bit, known as "Martha Washington" or "Pocomoco," goes beyond the text, but the initial pretended headache/stomachache is there.

NUGGET: *WHINNNGGG!*

(Manfully mastering the fit, he rises to a reply.)

Than Pres . . . than *him,* Sir. Yes.

CURMUDGE.:   But what did he do?

NUGGET: Try "What did he leave undone?" *That* answer's easy.
He led off his litany of lies with flat denial,
flung in the teeth of your son: He owed you nothing,
not the half of a drachma. Intensides countered
crisply: he summoned an *authentic* family friend,
the venerable Paleozóïdês, in whose presence
he delivered the *Receipt* to Pres . . . to the aforesaid.

CURMUDGE.:   The Receipt?

NUGGET: The Receipt you commissioned your son to deliver.

CURMUDGE.:   How did he react when he received the Receipt?

NUGGET: He fudged, Sir. Affirmed it was fake—a deceitful Receipt.
And followed this falsehood with pecks of invective against
your guiltless son, Sir. Who, the villain charged,
had led a career of crime as a major forger.

CURMUDGE.:   You got the Gold? Just tell me the bottom line.

NUGGET: The court appointed a board of assessors, which found
against your friend, compelled him to pay the sum
of thirty thousand drachmas, twelve hundred Kahunas.

CURMUDGE.:   Precisely the sum he owed.

NUGGET: That's not quite all.
So listen. He had a roundhouse punch in reserve.

CURMUDGE.:   That's not quite all? There's *more?*

NUGGET: Just pay attention.

(Aside.)

And now the mighty hawk poises above his prey . . .

CURMUDGE.:   Ruined. I'm ruined. Loaned Gold to the Father of Lies.

NUGGET: —The *God*father, Sir. Do listen.

CURMUDGE.:   Great Friend of the Family!
Oh, what a judge of character . . .

NUGGET: Duly receiving
the gold, we decamped, and loaded the bullion on board,
smit with longing to fare forth homeward at last.
(Almost like a line from Homer, Sir, don't you think?)

As it chanced, I was seated high on the poop of our sloop,
engaged in a casual scan of the bay, when I spied
some villains rigging a cutter, raked and scraped,
a thoroughly vile vessel, Sir, Up To No Good.

CURMUDGE.: That cutter'll scuttle me right at the waterline!

NUGGET: Would it help to know that your Great Friend went halves
in this cutter with a band of pirates?

CURMUDGE.:   I must have the mind
of a mushroom. To loan my gold to a man whose very
name, Prestigius . . .

NUGGET: *WHINNNGGG!*

CURMUDGE.:   proclaimed he'd nick me
for every last lone nugget I dared to loan him!

NUGGET: The cutter is clearly intending to ambush our sloop.
I commence to cast a cool eye and determine their tactics.
Meanwhile, our sloop weighs anchor and leaves the harbor.
Once we leave its safety, the pirates ply oars,
skim toward us speedy as birds, madly as wind.
Well, now, when I perceive their little game
I devise a counter. We heave to. Stop there. Dead.

CURMUDGE.: You stopped?

NUGGET: Of course.

CURMUDGE.:   And what did the pirates do then?

NUGGET: They see us perform that daring diversion—dead stop—
and panic. Break ranks, right there in the harbor.

CURMUDGE.:   *One* ship
breaks ranks?

NUGGET: Of course.

CURMUDGE.:   But can they do that?
                                                And then
you what?

NUGGET: Obvious tactic: We nipped back inside
the harbor to port.

CURMUDGE.:   A very sage maneuver.
Which the pirates followed by . . .

NUGGET: Retreat.

CURMUDGE.:   *Retreat?*

NUGGET: Back to the dock where they started. Along about evening.

CURMUDGE.: Their guilt was clear: To see you were gulled of the Gold.
The only possible reason for such an action.

NUGGET: I wasn't beguiled, Sir; I understood. And reacted
With the only proper reaction. Fear and trembling.
We see they're rabid for ravage. Goal: our Gold.
No delay. We assay our options.
Next morning at sunup,
we unload our mother lode down to the last yellow speck,
in the presence of our enemies. Its gilded glinting
glared on the gangsters' guild as we bore it by them,
open, aboveboard. They deserved to know the facts.

CURMUDGE.: Oh, clever!

NUGGET: I thought so.

CURMUDGE.:   And what did they do then?

NUGGET: One look at us as we strode to the town with the Gold,
and they paled on the spot, waggled their heads in defeat,
bailed out their cutter and beached her. And we . . .

CURMUDGE.:   Yes? Yes?

NUGGET: We deposited every last drachma of your Gold, Sir,
in the vaults of *Plutocrates,* deacon and vicar of holy
Diana, Goddess of Ephesus.

CURMUDGE.:   WHO THE HELL IS
PLUTOCRATES?

NUGGET: The son of Magnanimus, Sir.
Today in all Ephesus there exists no man
of greater worth.

CURMUDGE.:   And worth a great deal more,
if he diddled me out of all that Gold.
My Kahunas!

NUGGET: Not to worry. Your Gold is secure in escrow
within Diana's Temple at Ephesus, Sir,
where every Ephesian eye looks after your fortune.

CURMUDGE.: Hear the last words of your dying victim: *That* Gold
would be one hell of a lot better watched by two *eyes
here in Athens*—MINE!
Unless . . . You couldn't
have chanced to bring just a bit of the Gold back home?

NUGGET: Well . . . yes, I guess. But I really don't know how much.

CURMUDGE.: What do you mean, you don't know?

NUGGET: I mean that your son
            Intensides handled that end of the business. He made
            a secret call on Plutocrates that night,
            and neither to me nor to anyone else in the crew
            was he feeling trustful. So that's what I mean when I say
            I do not know what pittance your son brought back.
            Certainly can't have been much.

CURMUDGE.:   As much as half?
            In your estimation, of course?

NUGGET: *I simply don't know!*
            But it couldn't have been that much. I hardly think so.

CURMUDGE.:   A third, then—could he have a third?

NUGGET: I certainly
            don't think so . . .
                              Of course, I really don't know.
            The bottom line on Gold is this: the only
            thing I know is, I know nothing at all.
            For the nonce, it's up to you: secure a ship
            and sail to Ephesus. That way, *you* make the withdrawal,
            and ferry your Gold back home from Plutocrates.

(He makes to shove Curmudgeous off right, to the harbor.)

            And so, fare . . .

(He stops.)

                              Wait! One thing before you go.

CURMUDGE.:   What's that?

NUGGET: Do not, under any circumstances,
            forget to take *The Ring.*

CURMUDGE.:   What *Ring?*

NUGGET: Your son's *Ring.*
            Intensides' *Ring.*

CURMUDGE.:   And why do I need his *Ring?*

NUGGET: It establishes your ID. Plutocrates
            will release the Gold to the man who presents that *Ring,*
            and him alone.

CURMUDGE.:   I won't forget. That's very
            apt advice. But this Plutocrates, now:
            Is he, well, rich?

NUGGET: Is he rich, you ask?

CURMUDGE.:   I do.

NUGGET: A man who uses Gold to sole his shoes?

CURMUDGE.: That seems a little tasteless.

NUGGET: Sheer necessity.
            The man's so rich, so loaded with Gold, he can't
            find places to put it.

CURMUDGE.:   He might try putting it here.
            I have some ideas . . .
                             Oh. Who were the witnesses
            when the Gold was deposited with Plutocrates?

NUGGET: Everybody in town was a witness. There's not
            a single Ephesian who doesn't know, first-hand.

CURMUDGE.: I have to admit that my son did this one thing,
            at least, with a certain amount of sense. If he had
            to leave the Gold with someone, he chose a rich man
            to keep it for him. I should be able to effect
            withdrawal immediately.

NUGGET: No worry at all,
            and not the slightest chance of delay. You should
            be able to cart it away the day you arrive.

CURMUDGE.: Urrrgh.
            I really believed that I'd escaped the rigors
            of life at sea, that at my age I was
            disqualified for any more bounding on boats.
            But now I see that any choice I might have
            is nonexistent. Great Family Friend Prestigius

(A very slight shudder from Nugget.)

            has certainly fixed me up!
                             —Just one last thing:
            where's my son now?

NUGGET: Intensides?

(The merest pause for thought.)

                             Oh, he went—
            that's it—he went *downtown* to greet the gods
            and say hello to his friends.

CURMUDGE.:   No need to wait here.
            The closer I get to my boy, the quicker I'll meet him.

(He exits briskly—for him—stage left. Nugget watches him waddle off.)

NUGGET: And the stately lugger puts out, awash to the gunwales.
            —The web's begun: I spin, I spin . . . not bad,

if I do say so myself. I'm stringing the thread
of my Young Master's life on the paths
of freely funded fornication, enabling him
to employ to that end as much of the Gold as he wants . . .
and refund to his father as much as he's inclined to.
Old Master, bound for the balance, sloshes East . . .
while here in Athens the Golden Age returns
for the two of us, unless, of course, dear Daddy
refuses to leave us, and shanghais me and and his son
along to the East.
    But why be gloomy? Think
of the hell I can raise in Athens!
          Just one worry:
what happens when Daddy discovers that he's been duped,
been seasick East and West on a trumped-up Gold strike
while we've run through his precious Kahunas at home—
what happens then? He calls me Nugget now . . .
as soon as he's back, he'll change my name to Tombstone.
Oh, well, if push comes to push, I can always seize
the golden opportunity: Flight. Escape.
But if I'm caught? Well, then, the hell with him!
He'll wish he hadn't! Out on that farm of his
he may have whips, and rods, and clubs, but I
have close at hand—at home, in fact—my back!
I'll show him the stuff I'm made of!
          All over the place.
—And now to work: First find Intensides,
then fill him in on the plot about the Gold,
and give him the news that his darling Bacchis is found.

(Exit, purposefully, stage right, to the harbor.)

Act III, Scene 1 [368–384]

(A violent hammering from inside Bacchis's house. The voice of Zeugma, raised in terrified consternation, is heard through the shaking door.)

ZEUGMA: Open! Broach! Employ all speed, I beg, I implore you:
     Unplug these gates of hell!

(The door bursts open, and he jets on stage, in some dishevelment, to the accompaniment of raucous laughter and impolite music. The door slams shut, stopping the sound.)

          And hell it is, I assure you.
No mortal enters that chasm without abandoning hope,
all hope, of ever attaining Moral Niceness.
          Those sisters!
Bacchis and Bacchis they call them, but what they are is
  BACCHAE!

(This last word should be pronounced something like "bockh-eye," with heavy
aspiration.)

> The wild, debauched devotees of the god of wine and lust!
> Get ye behind me, sisters, who suck the blood of men!

(Changing tone, he continues his address to the audience.)

> That whole establishment is naught but a whited and whetted
> engine designed to effect complete and speedy Corruption!
> I took one horrified look—well, two—or possibly three—
> and instantly fled away from the scene with all heels and speed.
> But shall I suppress my findings? Conceal these dealings? Keep
>   mum?
> Ah, Æsygo, am I the man to deceive your Daddy,
> withhold from him a detailed retailing of all your sins,
> your ruinous losses, obscene desires, that mort of misconduct
> with which you strain to stain the name of your father, and me,
> and your nearest and dearest friend, and, not to forget it, yourself,
> with Disgrace, and Loss, and *Sin?* I ask you, am I that man
> to eclipse the slips with which you cast your father, and me,
> and your friends, and relations, as accessories in shame?
> I ask you, am I that man?
>   Well, let me dissolve your doubt:
> this instant, before you can escalate your tale of scandal,
> *I'll tell your Daddy! now!*
>   I shall divest myself
> of all connection *with* and responsibility *for*
> this fetid affair, and furnish the facts to the poor lad's father.
> Doubtless *he* can effect some speedy extrication
> of his errant son from the sullied muck he wallows in.

(Exit stage left, to Forum.)

Act III, Scene 2 [385–404]

(Enter Intensides from the habor, stage right, followed by a train of slaves with
baggage, some of it obviously quite heavy. He stops. They stop.)

INTENSIDES: I've thought my theory thoroughly through, I think, and tho—
     and *so*—I present it now:
>   Nothing in nature surpasses
> a friend who deserves the name . . . except the Gods, of course.
> I've tested and proved this truth by my own experience.
> I left for Ephesus just about two years back,
> and on my arrival, I sent a letter to Æsygo,
> my friend, my buddy, my pal: *Please find my lovely Bacchis.*
> And find her he did, or so, at least, I understand
> by the news that Nugget brought.
>   Nugget, my clever slave.
> *Consistently* clever. He's really up to his standard this time:

what a plot he's prepared to separate Pop from that GOLD
and use it to underwrite my upcoming relationship!
[But here he comes now![7]

(Curmudgeous, in utter and absolute fury, storms onstage left. He does not, repeat
NOT, see Intensides at all but is making for his house.)

Hi, Daddy—I'm back!

(Curmudgeous, still not breaking stride, reaches his own front door and opens it.)

It's me: Your son . . .

(SLAM! And Curmudgeous disappears inside.)

   . . . Intensides?

(He shrugs and directs a last pro forma call at the closed door.)

I'll catch you later.

(He turns back to the audience.)

—AS I WAS SAYING:]
Ingratitude is worse than a social lapse; it *costs*.
Be a . . . oh, be a . . . good-deed-doer. That's it. Whatever.
Remember *Thank you* and *pay back:* they are the Way of the World.
Forgive your enemies, and the best and brightest raise your praises;
but stiff your friends, and even the bastards put you down.

What it all comes down to is this: I'd better watch myself,
conduct my comportment with caution and care.
This is the test,
Intensides, the great divide, the symptom that shows
the state of your soul. Are you the man you ought to be?
Bad, or Good in every way?
Just, or Unjust?
Cheap, or freehanded? Well-bred chum, or son of a bitch?
You can't let a slave outstrip you in . . . good-deed-doing.
No matter what you do, you'll do it on public view.

(He looks offstage left.)

But here they come—the Dad of my chum, and his tutor to boot.
I'll be discreet and catch their drift from over here.

(He presses against the wall of Bacchis One's house. This position will hardly conceal
him, and there is also the train of baggage handlers, but he has the established
convention of New Comedy to rely on: *People onstage are invisible until noticed.*)

---

[7] Who *he?* In context, the pronoun would appear to indicate Nugget or Curmudgeous. Since
neither appears at this point, the words are generally taken to be the relics of an attempt, by some
early producer or director, to shorten the play. But Nugget won't be back for 250 lines, and
Curmudgeous is offstage for almost 400. A cut to either entrance would seriously eviscerate
the plot's development. Just possibly—and the minimal likelihood of this solution must be
stressed—Curmudgeous *does* enter here from the Forum, fulminating to such a degree over the

Act III, Scene 3 [405–499]

(Enter an outraged Zeugma and a reluctant Æsycome stage left. They do not notice
Intensides.)

ZEUGMA: And now, sir, we shall examine the state of your heart: do you
                 possess the prerequisite piss and ginger?
                                                      Walk this way.

(Bent on leading him to Bacchis One's house.)

ÆSYCOME: Walk *what* way? Where are you taking me now?

ZEUGMA: To her, sir, *her*—
                 the siren who so savagely soiled and sullied your sole son!

ÆSYCOME: Gracious, Zeugma. Temper your temper: *Nasty
                 but nice* is the path of prudence.
                                          The real miracle's when
                 an adolescent *doesn't* indulge in . . . what you said.
                 Why, take my case: I sowed an oat or two myself
                 when I was that age.

ZEUGMA: Oh damn—that's it! You permissive parents
                 spoil the boys!
                            Without your milksop meddling, I could have
                 prodded the lad to pursue a life of rectitude
                 along the straight and narrow. But you and your overindulgence
                 have pampered and petted Æsygo into a profligate punk!

INTENSIDES: *Æsygo?*
                            —the name of my friend! What does it mean—
                 Zeugma the Tutor on Æsygo's case? What could have happened?

ÆSYCOME:

    (Aside.)

                 It doesn't last, this lust to indulge the whims of the flesh:
                 a little time, and he'll relapse into proper self-loathing.
                 As long as my boy's behavior remains this side of disgusting,
                 just cut him some slack.

ZEUGMA: Some *slack!* To wreck his life?
                                                           Never!
                 No nick of slack will I cut, as long as there's breath in this body!
                 How can you mount a ringing defense of a son on the skids!
                 Was *that* your primary education—*First Steps in Sleaze?*
                 No. Until you touched twenty, you couldn't move a foot
                 outside the house with your tutor more than an inch away.

---

nonappearance of his long-gone son that he doesn't see Intensides at all, but charges straight into
his house to nurse his cholera. Admittedly, this play gets Curmudgeous back into his house,
whence he will enter next. For those who think such neatness is vital, I have supplied a brief
nonconfrontation, indicated by brackets.

You got to the exercise grounds before the sun came up,
or the coach-in-charge imposed a *gig,* a penalty swift and severe,
its impact increased by disgrace to pupil and teacher alike.
Next, exercise:
                    the Race and the Wrestle,
                                        the Discus and Spear,
        the Boxing and Ballplay,
                            topped off with the Jump!
                                        —in a logical system
of body-building, not beset with Whoring Around
and Osculation for Time.
                        (Yes, life was lived outside
in those days, far from the fug and the fog of disgusting dives.)
Then, home from the track and the ring, in the presence of your tutor,
spruce in your skivvies and perched on the very tip of your chair,
you started to read your book:
                        One syllable slurred, and your back
broke out in messier spots than the gown of a cross-eyed wet nurse.

INTENSIDES:

   (Aside.)

        I'm the source of my friend's misfortune—it tears me apart.
        My blameless buddy's besmirched, he staggers beneath a stigma—
        it's all my fault!

ÆSYCOME: Standards aren't what they used to be.

ZEUGMA: I'm perfectly well aware of that!
                                In the good old days,
        a youngster had been elected to public office before
        he ceased to accord his Tutor's pronouncements respectful
            submission.
        But now, when your charge is six at most, you brush against him,
        and WHAM! immediate backlash: the toddler takes up his tablet
        and rearranges your skull.
                            You stagger your way to his father
        to lodge a complaint . . .
                            and father chucks son under chin, and chortles:
        "Standing up in self-defense? That's Daddy's boy."
        But Tutor receives correction: "Look here, you no-account ancient,
        you do not touch my son for brave assertive action!"
        Verdict in force, and court in recess, and Tutor in shock,
        departing the scene in gloom, snuffed out like a limpwick lantern.
        Can a Tutor maintain any discipline under these conditions?
        When beatings are on the docket, he always leads the list.

INTENSIDES:

   (Still aside.)

        Now, there's a complaint that's *felt.* A little analysis shows
        that Æsygo's been raining tattoos on his tutor's skull.

(He has been moving closer to the pair; he is now level with Curmudgeous's door. Zeugma sees him.)

ZEUGMA: And who just hove into view over here by the door?
                                                              Behold!
             What an arrival! The greatest epiphany ever could never
             pleasure me more!

ÆSYCOME:

             (Squinting.)

                         Who's that over there?

ZEUGMA: Intensides.
             Best buddy and chum to Æsygo your son—remember?
             A lad, I might add, quite far removed in essential nature
             from that sad specimen, presently cuddled in yonder bordello.
             Happy Curmudgeous! What a masterwork he's turned out!

(Intensides approaches the pair. Eventually, the three work down left. The audience sees an open triangle: Zeugma stage left, Intensides center, Æsycome right.)

ÆSYCOME: Welcome back, Intensides. Good to see you safe.

INTENSIDES: Bless you, Æsycome.

(He is rather pointedly ignoring Zeugma, who is not, however, to be put off. He extends a displaying hand and treats Æsygo as an exhibition.)

ZEUGMA: Lo! the reply to a father's prayer—
             a son who fulfills the prescription: Departs on sea voyage? *Check.*
             Furthers family business? *Check.*
                                         Manages household?
             Check.
                     Complies and conforms with father's way and will?
             Check and double-check!
                                  Æsygo's chum since boyhood;
             the two aren't three days apart, if you reckon age by Time:
             but figure Character in, and this lad's thirty years ahead!

(This invidious comparison moves the normally mild Æsycome to flash out something like anger.)

ÆSYCOME: You watch yourself.
                              Enough of this guff about my boy—
             it isn't fair!

ZEUGMA: In brief, *shut up!* Avoid compounding
             your folly in raising the boy with pity at the ugly result.
             I'd keep him away from drachmas and put him in charge of disasters.

ÆSYCOME: How so?

ZEUGMA: Whatever he touches is due for steady shrinkage.

INTENSIDES: But you're subjecting my pal to pretty pitiless vilification.

Why, Zeugma? I mean to say, you *are* the tutor who taught him.

ZEUGMA: Your pal has passed away . . .

INTENSIDES: God, no!

ZEUGMA: . . . past decency.
It's purest truth, and not second-hand.
                                        I beheld it myself.

INTENSIDES: Beheld *what?* Give me the facts.

ZEUGMA: Your pal is ignobly ensnared
in the claws of a *hooker* . . .

INTENSIDES: You cut that out!

ZEUGMA: a hooker in a lather.
Halfwoman, half whirlpool. No mere male can skirt her orbit:
she slurps the sucker down.

INTENSIDES: This whirlpool has an address?

(Zeugma points to Bacchis's house.)

ZEUGMA: Right here.

INTENSIDES: This whirlpool has a source?

ZEUGMA: From Samos, she says.

INTENSIDES: She has a name?

ZEUGMA: Yes. Bacchis.

INTENSIDES: No trouble, Zeugma;
you've made a simple mistake, is all. Trust me: I know
the affair from top to bottom.
                              You castigate Æsygo wrongly.
My buddy's blameless. He's not a letch, he's a surrogate,
an agent performing an . . . *errand* for . . . Someone Else . . . for a
   friend.
A friend who extends to his pal the best of heartfelt wishes,
because he's a fervent agent, this pal, who'll accomplish
   commissions
with utmost zeal.

ZEUGMA: I agree about zeal; your friend's a fanatic.
But did his instructions really prescribe such acts of passion?
Should an agent recline with a woman and clasp her eagerly to him?
Does "zeal" include, say, copping a feel? Or specify there
the girl on his lap, his hand on her breasts, their lips englued?

(Intensides is very shaken.)

That hanky-panky's for starters:

                                    I could go on, of course,
increasing the tawdry toll of disgusting subgarment maneuvers,
shamelessly carried out, that I was forced to observe.
But modesty rules it out,
                                    and besides, you get the idea.
In sum: your chum, my charge, and this man's Daddy's boy
has passed beyond. Is *dead*. To any sense of shame.
You get the idea. Though I could have stayed to garner *detail*
of the really revolting skill he displayed. But close inspection
was hardly proper for me. And even less proper for him.

INTENSIDES:

(Overcome.)

                    Who's dead is *me*. Thanks, Pal!
                                    Well, keep a good thing going.
Death to my heartless girlfriend! I'd sooner die myself—
with substantial pain—than stay one down to a *femme fatale!*
Is nothing sure in this world? Must subjects of trust and faith
forever be objects of blind conjecture?

ZEUGMA: Just what I was saying:
Add altruism to the list. And observe the utter agony,
undergone for the sake of his friend, his chum, his pal,
your degraded son! A soul in torment for Someone Else!

ÆSYCOME: Please, Intensides, a favor? I beg you.
                                    Preserve his soul?
And bring his baser nature under some control?
You're not just preserving a pal, you're restoring a son to his father.

INTENSIDES: It's what I want to do . . .

ZEUGMA: It might be all for the best
if you left me to stay with him here.

ÆSYCOME: He can handle it by himself.

ZEUGMA: Attention, Intensides! Take this loser in charge! Go forth,
and righteously dress the dastard down for the shame he has
           showered
on you—and me, of course, and the rest of his friends as well—
by these unspeakable actions!

ÆSYCOME: Just one more little thing:
the entire weight of this catastrophe rests on your shoulders.
—And now let's go, Zeugma. Walk this way.

ZEUGMA: I am.

(Zeugma and Æsycome plod off stage left to their home.)

Act III, Scene 4 [500–525]

(Left to himself center stage, Intensides tries to sort things out.)

INTENSIDES: Enemies. Those I've got, but which is the worst?
           My pal of pals, perhaps?   .
                           My mistress, maybe?
           I haven't the slightest idea.
                         She did, of course.
           Idolized him ahead of, instead of me.
           Well, he can take her. Clearly the best solution.

(The facade of sweet reason cracks into pieces.)

           —Oh, DAMN!!!
                     She's done me wrong, and she's gonna hurt . . .
me,[8] of course!
                    May no one ever trust
      the truth of an oath I swear, if I should fail
      to take that girl and exercise tireless twists
      of perverted planning to utterly . . .
                         love her to pieces!
      I guarantee she won't put me up as a target
      for putdowns; no, sir! I'm leaving for home this instant—
      to loot my Daddy's stash and find her a present!
      How can I hurt her? Let me count the ways:
      reduced to begging, empty-handed, I see . . .
      my Daddy again!

(He stops and shakes his head.)

                    —I must be going crazy
      to stand here spinning cheap fiction about the future.
      Oh, damn—I guess I'm in love.
                      I'm *sure* I'm in love.

(The implications of what he has just said sink in.)

      But that doesn't mean that I intend to employ
      the dinkiest flake of my newfound Gold to fatten
      that woman's assets. I'd rather win the cup
      for Pauper of the Year.
                    She will not live to make
      an after-dinner anecdote out of *this* boy!
      Because—this just occurred; remember, you heard it here—
      I've formed a foolproof plan to save me from seduction:

---

[8] This follows the reading *meo* at line 504 rather than *suo*. It is sometimes suggested that the speaker is engaging in irony when he slips into the floutings of expectation that stud these lines. I disagree. Intensides (Mnesilochus), a standard Roman Comedy stripling, given to deep feeling and shallow thought, is incapable of irony, but not even he is blind to self-knowledge.

I'm refunding every bit of that Gold to
                                    Daddy!
Coin by coin!
                    Then let that slinky deceiver
lisp her wheedles and whisper enticements to *me—*
the neediest flat-broke down-and-outer in town!
Like delivering lectures on Graceful Living in the tomb.

[(He rehearses his recent eloquence, but doesn't get it quite right.)

Take it from the top:[9]
                    I do not intend to employ
the dinkiest flake of my newfound Gold to fatten
that woman's assets. I'd rather grind out my life
in want, from hand to hand!
                                    (Or something like that.)]
My mind's made up—the Gold goes back to Daddy!

(He turns to the implications of this decision.)

With a really impassioned request for him to go easy
on Nugget. For my sake.
                    I'll jolly him out of the rage
he's bound to feel when he finds he's been finagled.
For my sake.
            I mean, it's only fair for me to plead
and save the life of the man who told him a lie
or two.
            For my sake.

(To the porters, who have been waiting patiently for quite a while.)

                    Attention!
                            Follow my lead!

(He leads them in to Curmudgeous's house, stage left.)

---

[9] The three lines of Latin that the bracketed passage translates and extends do not occur in the oldest manuscript of Plautus. Further, as inspection shows, they are a near-perfect repetition of three lines occurring shortly before. In short, they are perfect candidates for ejection from the text, on the grounds that they were inserted by some late director of the play, to serve the special circumstances, whatever they might have been, of his production. This interpretation is probably right. And yet there remains a minor possibility that the lines occurred in the original and that Intensides is repeating himself, quite possibly deliberately. He is *proud* of the self-knowledge he's won through to here. He recapitulates it, rolls it over on his tongue . . . and, predictably enough, messes it up. For such as feel that this view may possess a minimum of viability, I have preserved the lines, and flanked them with comments to guide the interpretation. One may use them or not, as one prefers.

Act III, Scene 5 [526–529]

(As the last of Intensides' porters disappear into the house, Æsygo enters from Bacchis One's house. Dressed for a party, he is, shall we say, somewhat disheveled. His wreath is askew, chiton disarranged, his cloak slung carelessly over a shoulder. He is rather happy, and, we realize by his stammer, rather drunk. He first calls back through the door to Bacchis—one of them—inside the house. She does not appear.)

ÆSYGO: No worry, Bacchis. I know my p-priorities p-perfectly p-plainly.
My wish is your c-command. First f-find Intendises,
then bring him back to B-Bacchis.

(He closes the door and turns front.)

I find his dep-portment puzzling:
Presuming he laid an eye on my letter . . .

(He staggers but recovers his balance.)

what's holding him up?

(He turns toward Curmudgeous's house.)

I'll drop in there and p-pay my respects.
He might be home.

(He sets off shakily to his left, but does not get very far, because . . .)

Act III, Scene 6 [530–572]

(Intensides, flushed with pride, enters from Curmudgeous's house. The sight stops Æsygo dead in his tracks, but Intensides does not see him immediately.)

INTENSIDES: I did it!
All the Gold to Daddy.
I am Flat Broke—
ready to thumb my nose at the coldest shoulder in town.

(He preens.)

Daddy *loathed* reprieving Nugget. It went down hard,
but he snuffed his huff at last . . . and he did it all for *me!*

(He sees Æsygo. The two goggle at each other.)

ÆSYGO: Is this my *b-bon ami?*

INTENSIDES: Is this my enemy?—
I can't believe my eyes.

ÆSYGO: It has to be him.

INTENSIDES: It's him.

ÆSYGO: Now, s-step right up to my buddy and give him a huge hello.
Welcome b-back, Intensides! B-blessings upon you!

INTENSIDES: Hi.

ÆSYGO: To celebrate your safe return from foreign parts,
             it's P-party T-time!

INTENSIDES: I don't go to parties that turn my stomach.

ÆSYGO: You contracted a touch of nausea, maybe, on your return?

INTENSIDES: That's it. Acute.

ÆSYGO: But how?

INTENSIDES: It began with a so-called friend,
             a louse I had always believed to be my bosom buddy.

ÆSYGO: Isn't that always the way? Lots of those guys around,
             character, none. Just when you think you've got a f-friend,
             the truth comes out—your friend's a f-fiend of . . .

    (He thinks.)

                                          f-f-falsimony!

(He gets into his stride, with Intensides nodding vigorously at each new calumny.)

             Tongue, busy; hand, lazy.
                            Palaver that never delivers.
             A lackey lacking in loyalty.
                            Why? He's jealous, that's why.
             But very careful, oh yes, that nobody's jealous of *him*.
             Who envies a sluggard stuck in his sloth? He's lazy *on purpose!*

INTENSIDES: You seem to have done exhaustive research on the matter at hand.
             But let me make one addition:
                            Since Wicked Wicked Wreaks,
             this fiend befouls himself.
                            A friend to none, he finds
             his world is full of *foes!*
                            This utter idiot fancies
             he's flouting the others—he's not flout*ist,* but flout*ee!*

             This bastard bears a striking resemblance to the man I mentioned:
             the one I *thought* was my friend—my alter ego, in fact.
             He exhausted his talents formulating the greatest foulness
             that he could do me, to dupe me out of whatever I had.

ÆSYGO: That guy has got to be the supremest son-of-a bitch!

INTENSIDES: My thoughts precisely.

ÆSYGO: God almighty!
                            Please, I'm begging:
             tell me his name!

INTENSIDES: It's someone you know. You like him, in fact.
             That's why I hesitate to beg you in turn to apply your talents

to that blasted bastard's complete destruction.

ÆSYGO: Just tell me his name!
I'll do him grievous bodily harm in some way or other,
or else you can call me a faithless sluggard stuck in his sloth!

INTENSIDES: Well, I don't know. He's worthless, he's scum, but he also happens
to be your friend—and damn, what very good friends you are!

ÆSYGO: That makes it worse. I can't continue to value the friendship
of some disgusting nogoodnick. Tell me his goddam name!

INTENSIDES: I admit you do have a point. Well, no help for it. I guess
I'll have to disclose his name.
                                              Æsygo.

     (A pause.)

ÆSYGO: Yes?

INTENSIDES: That's *it*—
Æsygo. *You* have annihilated your comrade and friend,
namely, *me.*

ÆSYGO: What do you mean?

INTENSIDES: What do you mean,
"*What do you mean?*" Look, did I, or did I not, send you
a letter from Ephesus, requesting you to discover my mistress?

ÆSYGO: You did, I confess it. But add that I *found her.*

INTENSIDES: *Found* isn't the word.
I asked you to turn her up, not *on!* Athens is chockful
of *hookers.* Why choose the one I said to take under your wing
to get in a flap about, to fall for her and trip me up?

ÆSYGO: You're out of your mind.

INTENSIDES: You can't deny it. You're found out, down
to the ground. Your Tutor blew your cover.
                                              You've wiped me out.

ÆSYGO: Why try to rile me? Is all this smearing your own idea?

INTENSIDES: Oh, no. You're in love with Bacchis.

ÆSYGO: Well, yes, but we have a *pair.*
Two Bacchises. Right inside.

INTENSIDES: A pair of Bacchises? *Two?*

ÆSYGO: And sisters. Both. Of each other.

INTENSIDES: Deliberate meaningless jabber!

ÆSYGO: It all comes down to this: You stop degrading my friendship,

or else I hoist you up on my shoulders and haul you away
to see for yourself.

(He grabs Intensides.)

INTENSIDES: No, don't!
                                        Just wait a minute—I'm coming!

(He breaks loose, but Æsygo grabs at him again.)

ÆSYGO: I will not wait. My name's at stake!

(Intensides pushes him off and indicates willingness to obey.)

INTENSIDES: I'm right behind you.

(He follows Æsygo into Bacchis One's house.)

Act IV, Scene 1 [573–583]

(The Major's Parasite, Lickas, enters stage right from the harbor, dragging the tiny
page Gizmo behind him, and speaks directly to the audience.)

LICKAS: I play your standard Parasite. Sponsored, of course,
               by a perfectly worthless bastard.
                                        A *military* bastard.
               The very bastard who shipped his popsy along
               from Samos to Athens. The Major's sent me on a mission:
               first find the girl, and then find out her decision:
               is she buying out her contract or sticking with him?

(He looks in confusion from one house to the other.)

               Oh, god.

(He turns to Gizmo, who has lost his earlier self-confidence and is cowering behind
him.)

                        —Hey, weenie! You got stuck with her
               this morning. Go up to the house—whichever it is—
               and knock.

(Gizmo continues to cower.)

                        On the door.

(Same bit.)

                                        On the double!

(He shoves Gizmo towards the door.)

                                                Knock quick!

(Gizmo makes a small tentative tap on Bacchis's door.)

               Come back here!

(Gizmo walks slowly back.)

      Budge it, midget!

(Gizmo arrives.)

            Send a minnow
to do a man's job. You can snarf a loaf of bread
that's taller than you, but *knocking?* You haven't a clue.
Now, listen:

(He steps to Bacchis's door and shouts.)

      Anyone home?

(As he says this, he beats tattoo on the door: *Shave-and-a-haircut, two-bits.* There is no answer, but Gizmo gets the idea and returns to the door. He calls out.)

Gizmo: Hey! Anyone here?

(He accompanies this with his own tattoo: *Paradiddle, paradiddle, flam, flam, flam.* Again no answer. Lickas returns to the fray.)

Lickas: Anyone working the door?

(His tattoo this time is noisier and more baroque, a florid fusillade ending in this: *Wopbabaloobop, awopbamboom.* Again, no answer. Gizmo steps up and begins a "Wipeout" phrase, very loud and long, behind his call.)

Gizmo: Is anyone coming . . .

(Bacchis's door flies open, disclosing a very angry Æsygo. Gizmo freezes.)

  . . . out?

(He scuttles out of range behind Lickas.)

Act IV, Scene 2 [583–611]

(Emerging in anger, Æsygo confronts Lickas.)

Æsygo: What the hell's going on out here?
Why the percussion recital? An attack of palsy?
You want to work out? Go use your own front door!
You damned near broke the slab right off the hinge.

(Trying to pull himself together.)

What can you possibly want?

Lickas: Good day, young sir.

Æsygo: Well, same to you . . . but whom did you come to see?

Lickas: Bacchis.

Æsygo: That all? Which Bacchis?

Lickas: Just Bacchis—there's more?
Here's the miniversion: Major Machismo
sent me to *Bacchis*: either she buys out her contract—

refunds him two hundred Kahunas in Gold—or else
she leaves with him today for Super City.

ÆSYGO: She isn't going.

(Lickas stands his ground but puts out a hand, palm up.)

She refuses to go.

(Lickas stays, palm still up.)

Absolutely.

(The same bit continues: Lickas imperturbable, Æsygo's anger increasing.)

Back off and make your report.

Go tell the Major
She Loves Another.
Not Him.
So take a hike!

LICKAS: Temper, temper.

ÆSYGO: Temper? It's only a sample.
Your face is only a hand span away from disaster.

(He clenches his fists and lifts them to head level, advancing slowly.)

My mighty Malocclusion-Inducers twitch
in lust to realign your putrid profile!

(Stepping back in cautious alarm, Lickas speaks an aside that seems to come from a tragedy.)

LICKAS: Translated, these mumblings appear to indicate
that I must needs take heavy heed, to avoid
the forced extraction from my mandibles
of these my Goober-Reducers.

(To Æsygo.)

I'll give him the message,
but you're the one at risk.

(Æsygo moves to him. They are now in each other's face, but really don't know how to do this.)

ÆSYGO: What did I hear?

LICKAS: I said, I'll tell him.

ÆSYGO: Just for the record, who are you?

LICKAS: My Major's Integumental Sheath.

ÆSYGO: His what?

LICKAS: His Second Skin.

ÆSYGO: Only a minor Major
          could hide his hide behind such vile veneer.

LICKAS: He's coming—he'll swell to alarming proportions!

ÆSYGO: I hope
          he splits. Both skins.

     (The confrontation, such as it is, is at an end.)

LICKAS: Well, sir. Will that be all?

ÆSYGO: Out of here! Git!
                              I stress the need for speed.

LICKAS: My best to you, oh great Malocclusion-Inducer.

ÆSYGO: And mine to you, Integumental Sheath.

     (He turns to the audience as Lickas and Gizmo exit stage right, to the harbor.)

          I've arrived at complete confusion. What sort of advice
          do I give my buddy about his Bacchis? No clue.
          His fury forced him to refund the Gold to his daddy
          in toto; there isn't a single plugged drachma left
          to pay the Major . . .

     (A creak from Bacchis's door.)

                         But hark! A creak from the door!
          I'll sneak over here, keep out of sight.

     (He slips into the alley between the houses, with an announcement to the audience.)

                              New scene:
          From Bacchis's house, Intensides enters, in gloom.

     (From Bacchis's house, Intensides enters, in gloom.)

Act IV, Scene 3 [612–639]

(But Gloom is hardly the word. Intensides is in a passion of depression, a positive whirlwind of self-disesteem. He storms onstage and slumps in front of the house, then produces, as Æsygo watches, a song of Utter Depression. Genre: Self-destructive Moan, such as might be sung on a Gloomy Sunday.)

INTENSIDES: *I'm*
          Brutal, unbridled, and brash   *in a rashly irrational manner;*
          No tint of respect or restraint,   *of decency, fitness, or honor.*
                Out of control, no class or attractiveness,
                At human relations no hint of effectiveness,
                Given to tirades of crazy invectiveness . . .
                         · **Born Nasty.**

          I'm
          Wild, disagreeable, beastly,   *and testy and crass and demented;*

Call me whatever you will,   I'll still be worse than I'm painted.
Selfish proclivities working to gum me up,
Insensitivity rushing to numb me up,
Put them together, here's one phrase to sum me up:
Born Nasty.

(He moves into a recitative that takes stock of his wretched existence.)

WHEREFORE:
    Surpassing all rivals in mindless strife
    I've earned this share of the Good Things in Life—

Blessings:	*Nada.*
Profits:	*None.*
Friendships:	*Not a bloody one.*
Deep Affection:	*Not a bit.*
Satisfaction:	*Not a whit.*
Reputation:	*Less than aught.*
Luck, The Breaks, and Fortune:	*Naught.*

On the other hand, my impossible habits
have credited me with the following debits:

Reproach and Rebuke,	*Disfavor and Flak,*
Tarnish and Smirch,	*Being left in the Lurch,*
Aversion, Aspersion,	*and Vituperation,*
Discredit, Misuse,	*and Verbal Abuse, or*

           Just Say Loser.

Thrown by throes of passion,	*I wasted Nugget's work*
And ruined all my prospects,	*because I am a jerk.*
A nothing.	

    A nix.

       A no-go à go-go . . .

(He would go on, but Æsygo has witnessed enough self-torture.)

ÆSYGO: Our boy needs comfort and cheer, so let's get to it.

(He moves down to Intensides and begins a doomed attempt at cheer, which quickly fritters away. The two impinge on each other in an antiphon.)

            Well, friend, how does it . . .

INTENSIDES: *I'm destroyed.*

ÆSYGO: go today?

INTENSIDES: *I'm null and void.*

ÆSYGO: God help you find . . .

INTENSIDES: *Bested. Basted.*

ÆSYGO: a better way.

INTENSIDES:	*Worsted. Wasted.*
ÆSYGO:	Stop your whines!
INTENSIDES:	*Eradicated.*
ÆSYGO:	Shut the *hell* up!
INTENSIDES:	*Devastated.*
ÆSYGO:	Something nice may . . .
INTENSIDES:	*Squáshed under fóot.*
ÆSYGO:	still develop.
INTENSIDES:	*Blitzed. Kapútt.*

(Æsygo gives up.)

ÆSYGO: Frankly, friend, you've lost it.

INTENSIDES: Correction, please:
I've *had* it.
I'm undergoing internal upheaval. It's sour and sharp.
How did I get that angry? Accusing an innocent friend
of a baseless abomination!

ÆSYGO: Just get a bit of backbone.

INTENSIDES: Who's selling? And how could I buy it? A corpse has more ready
cash.

ÆSYGO: The Major's parasite just dropped by to collect the refund.
I turned my tongue to account and managed to drive him away
from house and *her.* He won't show his face on *this* street again.

INTENSIDES: That hardly helps *my* case.
So how do I deal with this?
I'm broke, and Bacchis goes back to the Major. Depend on that.

ÆSYGO: Depend on *this:*
If I had money, I promise I wouldn't
offer *you* any. No, *sir.*

INTENSIDES: Oh, yes, you would. I know you.
I trust your friendship because I know you're a lover, too.
But by that token you're stuck in your *own* thick muck of trouble.
Besides, you're as broke as I am. No aid and comfort from *you.*

ÆSYGO: Will you kindly just *shut up?* I'm sure one god or another
will bail us out of this soon.

INTENSIDES: Hot air. Good-bye.

(He slowly begins to trudge stage left, to the downtown exit. Æsygo looks off right,
towards the harbor.)

ÆSYGO: Hang on.

INTENSIDES: What's up?

ÆSYGO: It's Nugget—your bank is on the way!

                                                       Keep still.

(They conceal themselves in the alley as Nugget, no worry in the world, strides on stage right from the harbor.)

Act IV, Scene 4 [640–760]

(Preening, Nugget moves down center, to deliver his Lesser Brag. He does not see the young men.)

NUGGET:

(First a recitative.)

> *Ecce homo—*
> *The Major Domo!*
> *Which is to say ME, who now comes in triumph at you,*
> *Fully deserving of weighing in Gold, and watching said metal*
>   *melt and mold into a highly visible statue,*
> *Inasmuch as I today have achieved a double exploit,*
> *Daringly adroit*
> *And generating such repute*
> *As to haul off a double helping of spoils and loot.*
> *Behold a slave who can serve two masters, and then some,*
> *In a manner not to be described as less than elegant, or even*
>   *downright hensome.*
>
> *Take the Old Master, definitively duped and shafted,*
> *His gaffer's craft upset by a craft more cunningly crafted,*
> *Quelled, impelled, and superpropelled ineluctably ahead*
> *Into omnifarious gullibility to everything I said.*
> *This superannuated blatherskite—*
> *Him I served Right.*
>
> *I've served another master, however, and him I served Well —*
> *Old Master's passionate son, the lover under a spell*
> *With whom I've swallowed and swilled and loved and lost,*
> *By winning a way to defray for such employments the staggering*
>   *cost—*
> *Supplying an immense and commodious cache, with regal panache,*
> *Of Gold, fresh-minted as cold hard cash.*
> *My pet hates, of course, are the Standard Comic Slaves, those*
>   *archaic hacks*
> *Who preen onstage when they salvage a measly hundred drachs:*
> *Disgraces to the profession, in action hidebound and crude,*
> *Who pale before the New Slavery, which I term Creative Servitude.*

(Then to a Song of Himself. Genre: Strut.)

Your Standard Slave is worthless,   a waste, a loss, dead weight.
The only slave worth keeping's   the Slave that can Create.

His mind is free and fertile,   it's never trapped or locked;
There's no effective limit   to what he can concoct.

For every crunch he offers   resources to be tapped;
To every varied challenge,   our hero can adapt.

It's broad and universal,   his virtuosohood:
Among the bads, he's badder;   among the goodies, good.

Among the clean, he's squeaky,   an unpolluted saint;
Among the soiled, he's tawdry,   with smudge and spot and taint.

With grifters, he's a grifter,   and hones his gift for graft.
With felons, he's a felon,   a master of the craft.

In every plight or pickle,   his talents are profuse,
He turns the opposition   any way but loose.

The tightest squeeze can't hold him,   he's never cul-de-sacked,
This Mogul of the Gambit,   this Artist of the Act!

But I digress. Moving on to the matter at hand . . .

What chunk of the Gold   did Junior withhold?
What divvy for Dear Old Dad?
A dutiful son   splits nine for one,
and Dear Old Dad should be glad
At an increment   of ten per cent—
for a father, a tithe's not bad.

(He finally sees Intensides and Æsygo. They steadfastly avoid his gaze.)

But lo and behold, before me precisely the person I seek!

(Neither acknowledges him. They keep staring at the ground.)

—But why so downcast? I hope you didn't drop any Gold?

(Neither looks up. Nugget moves near and peers closely at Intensides' face.)

Nothing here but pathos, depression, and gloom?

(The silence continues. Nugget tries an aside)

Looks bad. What's worse, it's *motivated.*

(He tries again.)

—Reply requested.

INTENSIDES: I've had it, Nugget.

NUGGET: The Gold? You maybe kept too little?

INTENSIDES: Too Little I'd love. For me, Too Little is lots.

It's *loads.*

NUGGET: You're incomprehensible, dimwit! I mangle my manhood in labor,
               risk stretchmarks to bring to birth this instant approach to profit—
               any conceivable sum for the taking—and what do you do?
               Scoop with both hands? Not you—you stick in two fingers and
                   pinch.
               Has it escaped you that chances like this don't come along often?

INTENSIDES: You're wrong.

NUGGET: No wronger than you. You should have dug down deep.

INTENSIDES: Well, fire away. That's mild, compared with what you'd be saying
               if you really knew what I really did.
                                            I'm done for.

NUGGET: Why does
               that simple formula fill me with fear of disaster to come?

INTENSIDES: I've had it.

NUGGET: Some details, please.

INTENSIDES: Well, about that gold . . .

NUGGET: Yes?

INTENSIDES: Every last flake. To Daddy. I made. A total refund.

NUGGET: A *refund?*

INTENSIDES: A refund.

NUGGET: Total?

INTENSIDES: Teetotal.

NUGGET: We're done for. Both.

        (He searches for words, which, when they come, are rather mild.)

               What prompted you to commit catastrophe on that scale?

INTENSIDES: Frankly, Nugget, I blew it. An alleged allegation was lodged
               and nudged me into believing my Bacchis and Æsygo here
               had set me up. So, angry and stunned, I refunded the Gold
               to Daddy *in toto.*

NUGGET: And did you chance to add a few words
               to your Daddy on that occasion?

INTENSIDES: Why, yes. I mentioned how promptly
               Prestigius presented the Gold when I him asked about it.

NUGGET: Of course.
               The very words to reduce your faithful Nugget to rubble.
               As soon as your Daddy finds me, I'm hustled off to the Proper

Authorities. I'll make a fine display, spread-eagled and flayed.

INTENSIDES: I really brought Daddy around.

NUGGET: Oh, sure. To sending me under.

INTENSIDES: Oh, no. To agreeing to keep you from grievous bodily harm . . .
not to mention his frightening fury. Now, that took effort.

(After a fairly awkward pause, he decides on brisk cajolery.)

Well, Nugget: here's a new job for you.

(Nugget is not impressed.)

NUGGET: What new job is that?

INTENSIDES: It's back to the front—another sortie against the Old Guy.
Combine, devise, and cobble together a tactic or two,
Outfox the fox once more, and bring that Gold back home!

NUGGET: It can't be done. I *know*.

INTENSIDES: Just make a start, and you're home free.
It's easy.

NUGGET: *Easy?* I don't think so. Your Daddy trapped me
red-handed in a barefaced lie. My credibility's nil.
If I went down on my knees, I couldn't make him believe
a single thing I said . . . not even *not* to believe me.

(He is in the depths.)

INTENSIDES: I'm glad you didn't hear his pointed remarks against you.

(Nugget scents like a hound.)

NUGGET: What remarks are those?

INTENSIDES: He said that if you swore the Sun
up there was the Sun, he'd have to believe it was the Moon,
and so the Day would be the Night.

(Nugget is suddenly alive and eager.)

NUGGET: He actually said that?
It's too good to go to waste.
                                Well, time to diddle Daddy:
I'll wipe the Old Guy out!

ÆSYGO:

(Silent on the periphery for some time, he is happy to join in.)

Marvelous! How can we help?

NUGGET:

(To both of them. He is expansive, in Managing mode, and they are his creatures.)

Just keep on loving. And that's an order!
                                                      And when in need
of money, apply to me, your Source of Supply, for any
sum, since how can I justify the name I bear
except by deeds? To start, how big is the bagatelle
you need this time around?

INTENSIDES: A whole two hundred Kahunas.
To buy out Bacchis's contract.

NUGGET: The Source will gladly Supply it.

INTENSIDES: And then there's our overhead . . .

NUGGET: Whoa! Please, not so fast.
One trifle at a time works best. We attend to Bacchis first,
and then we adjust your expenses.

(He turns master strategist.)

                                          Two hundred Kahunas calls for
a frontal maneuver best effected by long-range bombardment.
I'll wind the catapult up to the max and breach the battlements,
shatter the tower. *Then* comes the frontal assault to invade
and invest that rickety city-state . . . and *div*est it as well.

(A touch of the epic mode.)

     An I win through, ye twain bear off to your ladies fair
     Gold in huge hampers heaped as high as your hearts' desire.

(Intensides follows suit.)

INTENSIDES: *Our fate is in thy hands, brave Nugget.*

NUGGET:

(All business again, to Æsygo.)

                                          Inside to Bacchis,
Æsygo; come back quick with . . .

ÆSYGO: What?

NUGGET: Whatever we need
to write a letter. A stylus. Some tablets. Some wax and thread.

ÆSYGO: I'll bring them out pronto.

(He hurries into Bacchis One's house.)

INTENSIDES: So what's next on your list?
If I might ask, of course.

NUGGET: Is dinner ready yet?
How many at table? You and him and your girlfriend—three?

INTENSIDES: You've got it.

NUGGET: Æsygo, though—no girl for him?

INTENSIDES: No—*yes!*
I love one, he loves the other.

NUGGET: What other?

INTENSIDES: The other
sister, of course. Her name is Bacchis. Just like mine's.

NUGGET: What's that you say?

INTENSIDES: I said we'd be four for dinner.

NUGGET: No, wait.
There's a double dining couch?

INTENSIDES: Why, yes.

NUGGET: Precisely where
did they set it up?

INTENSIDES: Why did you ask that question?

NUGGET: *Because*
I wanted to know the answer! That's the way I am!

You have no idea of the thrust and size of the enterprise
on which I'm embarking. So where's the couch?

INTENSIDES: Hand, please.
Now walk this way to the door . . .

  (He conducts Nugget to Bacchis One's door.)

                          and see for yourself.

(He opens the door, but not so wide that the audience can see within. Nugget makes
a frame with his fingers and peers through it.)

NUGGET: Oh, Yesss!
                 It's perfectly framed—the exact location I need.

(Æsygo rushes out of the door, carrying the writing materials.)

ÆSYGO: Your order's ready. Quality orders to quality staff
prepared on the spot and the dot.

NUGGET: And what have *you* prepared?

ÆSYGO: Each item you specified, sir.

NUGGET:

  (To Intensides.)

                          Quick, now! The stylus—take it!

And grab these tablets—they're for you, too.

(Intensides obeys.)

INTENSIDES: Okay. What next?

NUGGET: Next write what I tell you to write. And Why, you ask? Because
            I want your father to recognize your writing when
            he reads it.
                         Write!

INTENSIDES: Write *what?*

NUGGET: First wish him the best of health.
            And use your own words; be distinctive.

(Propping the tablets, Intensides starts writing. It is not what he does best.)

ÆSYGO: Shouldn't he wish him
            disease and sudden death? It seems more pertinent, really.

NUGGET: *Refrain from interrupting!*

INTENSIDES:

(Showing the face of the tablets.)

                              There's what you wanted, in wax.

NUGGET: Please read your version aloud.

INTENSIDES: DEAR DADDY: I HOPE YOU'RE WELL.

NUGGET:

(Beat. Take.)

            It'll have to do; no time.
                         Now write this underneath:
            NUGGET KEEPS NAGGING ME, DADDY. HE'S ALWAYS ON MY CASE
            BECAUSE I REFUNDED THE GOLD AND DIDN'T CHEAT YOU ONE BIT.

(Intensides writes.)

ÆSYGO: Slow down—give him time.

NUGGET: Nothing's faster than the fingers
            of a man in love.

ÆSYGO: At fumbling away the family funds,
            but not at writing.

(Intensides looks up.)

INTENSIDES: I've finished that bit. Dictate away.

NUGGET: SO THEREFORE, DADDY DEAR, BE SURE TO WATCH OUT FOR NUGGET.
            HE'S GOT A HOAX ON THE BLOCKS TO MULCT YOU OUT OF THE
            MOOLAH,

AND SWEARS AN OATH ON THAT SCAM.

(Scribble, scribble.)

                                     Careful. That has to be clear.

(Intensides finishes.)

INTENSIDES: More words!

NUGGET: WHAT'S MORE, HE'S PROMISED TO GIVE ME THE GOLD,
TO HAND OVER TO WHORES AND WASTE IN VISITING SUMPS OF SIN,
AND EVEN, DADDY, IN LIVING LIKE A GREEK.
                                PLEASE, DADDY,
TAKE SPECIAL CARE TODAY THAT HE DOESN'T ROB YOU BLIND.

(More writing. Intensides looks up.)

INTENSIDES: I'm ready.

NUGGET: All right. Add this . . .

(He thinks.)

INTENSIDES: Just tell me what to write!

NUGGET: BUT, DADDY, I BEG YOU ON NO ACCOUNT TO FORGET THE PROMISE
YOU MADE TO ME: DON'T BEAT HIM!
                        BUT TRUSS HIM UP TIGHT AT HOME,
AND KEEP HIM UNDER YOUR PERSONAL WATCH.

(Intensides finishes. Nugget turns to Æsygo.)

                                  Quick, now: give him
the wax and thread.

(To Intensides, as he receives the materials.)

                Okay. First tie it together,
                          then seal it.

(Intensides obeys. Æsygo breaks in.)

ÆSYGO:[10]   Excuse me, but how can this document possibly further
the matter at hand? Just what conceivable good can come
from telling him not to trust you, but truss you up tight at home?

NUGGET: *It's just my little whim!*
                    Can't you attend to your own
concerns and leave me completely alone?
                        Look: I'm the prop
of this project. Mine is the risk that carries it through to the end.

---

[10] This speech is usually assigned to Intensides, but I give it, and Intensides' next one, to Æsygo, who has made an earlier suggestion and is very probably eager to participate more centrally in the plot.

ÆSYGO: That's fair enough.

NUGGET:

    (Turning back to Intensides.)

                So give me the tablets.

INTENSIDES: Take them; they're yours.

NUGGET: All right, now, men: ATTENTION!

    (He draws them up before him in military fashon.)

                Intensides!
                        Æsygo, too!
Now, here's your agenda.
               Direct your steps, and those
of your respective mistresses, to the double couch
located within this house, there each by each to recline
and commence . . .
              DRINKING!

ÆSYGO: Anything else?

NUGGET: One further point:
once deployed at dinner, you are not to shift location,
until such time as you perceive my official signal.

ÆSYGO: Now, *there* is a excellent general.

NUGGET: You're two drinks down already.

INTENSIDES: We're out of here.

    (He and Æsygo rush into the house. Nugget looks after them.)

NUGGET: You do your duty, and I'll do mine.

Act IV, Scene 5 [761–769]

    (Left alone, Nugget reflects.)

NUGGET: This venture I've entered upon is dementedly vast . . .
maybe too huge to conclude in a single day.
And that's one worry.
               Another's the subject himself:
I need him *fierce,* I need him *savage* and *bestial,*
or else my plan's a bust. A deceit of this sort
just couldn't stomach a peaceful geezer who didn't
go up in flames the moment I came into view.
My plan? I'll spit him and parch him, set him revolving
above the blazing fire, until he's braised
as tough to the touch as a roast garbonza!
                      And now

I'll wend my leisurely way to the door, and wait
in perfect position to meet him issuing forth
and shove the letter inside his hot old hand.

(He establishes his position upstage, immediately stage left of Curmudgeous's door.)

Act IV, Scene 6 [770–798]

(Curmudgeous enters stage left from downtown, in his usual choleric fury.[11] He does not see the surprised Nugget.)

CURMUDGE.:　How could I let that no-good Nugget escape?
It's torn me apart! It's ruined my whole damned day!

NUGGET:

(Aside.)

He's riled! He's raving!
　　　　　　　　　　　　Such luck—I'm saved by the bile.
This seems the perfect time to approach.

CURMUDGE.:　　　　　　　　　　　　Hey? Someone's
talking.
　　　　And near at hand.
　　　　　　　　　　　　And—who could doubt it?—
　Nugget!

NUGGET:

(Aside.)

Into the jaws of battle . . .

(He moves to Curmudgeous, whose fury has acquired sarcasm.)

CURMUDGE.:　　　　　　　　　　At your service,
oh best and bravest of Slaves! You bring new news?
An early departure date for my Ephesus trip,
to recover my long-lost Gold from Plutocrates?

No word?
　　　　Oh, how too bad!

　　　　　　　　　　If I didn't dote
on my son so much that I grant him whatever he asks for,

---

[11] Curmudgeous, it will be remembered, went off stage left to downtown in Act II, Scene 3. He has not been back since—unless one adopts his silent (and ill-attested) return in Act III, Scene 2. There are three options here: (1) For those who adopt the return, he appears here from the house, since that's where he is. For those who don't, he may either (2) enter from downtown, stage left, because he hasn't returned home yet, or (3) enter from the house, since there's no point in being overprecise about these things, and Nugget *says* he'll see him in the house. But Nugget has not yet *been* in any house, and his plan to catch Curmudgeous does not succeed. Plan (2) seems best.

        I swear that the lying hide that covers your sides
        would present a perfect example of slash and burn,
        riddled and raddled to ribbons with rods! What's more,
        you'd now be grinding away the shank of your so-called
        existence in rigid restraint as you spun a millwheel.
        I've found you out! Intensides divulged
        the list of your high crimes and low behavior!

NUGGET: An allegation?
                    How great—I'm officially Evil.
        Authentic Scapegoat and Sinner.
                          A word of warning:
        only believe what you *see*.
                       And that's my final
        word on the subject.

CURMUDGE.:   Transgressors shouldn't make threats.

NUGGET: You want to know what your boy is like?

(He hands Curmudgeous the tablets.)

                       For quick
        enlightenment, read this letter. He sent it by me,
        with a special request for you to carry it out.

(Curmudgeous grabs the letter.)

CURMUDGE.: I'll take that.

NUGGET: You'll notice the seal's completely intact.

CURMUDGE.: I notice, I notice.
                But where's he now?

NUGGET: Don't know.
        I'm a slave, and so I'm not supposed to know
        a single thing. And so I forgot what I know.
        And all I know is, I'm a slave . . . which means
        I don't even know what I *do* know.
                     Know what I mean?

(Curmudgeous tries to make sense of this, but gives up shortly and reads the letter.
Nugget indulges in an aside.)

        I've set the trap, and inserted the worm, and stretched
        the cord, and now my pretty thrush is due
        to be hung up high before the sun goes down.

(Curmudgeous finishes the letter with mounting agitation and makes cautiously for
his front door.)

CURMUDGE.: Don't move.
        Stay right here.

> With you shortly, Nugget.
>
> Back in a flash.

(He enters the house, leaving Nugget to indulge briefly in a bit of Distressed Maiden shtick from melodrama.)

NUGGET: Oh goodness gracious me—I am being *tricked!*
            What does this scoundrel intend?
                        What *can* he be up to?

(He abandons the bit.)

> He's gone to get some thugs to tie me up.
> Ahoy! The dreadnought's shipping water, but
> the brave little raft is riding the top of the crest!
> Silence on deck! I think I hear the door.

Act IV, Scene 7 [799–841]

(A feisty Curmudgeous enters from the house, ushering a rough crowd of slaves and porters, headed by their overseer Shambles. They advance on Nugget.)

CURMUDGE.: Tie his hands up, Shambles! Look sharp about it!

(Nugget's hands are tightly bound. The gang of porters keeps hands on him.)

NUGGET: What did I do?

CURMUDGE.:   The slightest mumble earns him
            a high, hard hook to the head!
                        —What's in this letter?

NUGGET: Why are you asking me? This letter stayed shut
            and sealed from pickup from him to drop-off to you.

CURMUDGE.: Oh damn—it's all here!

(He swoops into interrogation, with constant reference to the letter.)

> So tell me, true or false:
> You NAGGED my son and heir, kept ON HIS CASE
> because he REFUNDED THE GOLD?
>   You declared you had
> A HOAX ON THE BLOCKS to MULCT ME OUT OF THE
> MOOLAH?

NUGGET: Well, did I say so?

CURMUDGE.:   You did.

NUGGET: Can you present
            the person who says I said so?

CURMUDGE.:   You shut your mouth!
            There *is* no person.

(He brandishes the letter.)

                                This letter, the very letter
that you delivered in person, this letter indicts you,
this letter convicts you, this letter condemns you to be
TRUSSED UP in bondage!

NUGGET: I'd say your son was revising
traditional fiction: The Doomed Delivery Boy.
"Once on a time, a messenger, name of Nugget,
messed himself up with his missive . . ."
                                                    Give it a miss.

CURMUDGE.: I'll teach you to—lost my place—to seduce my son
into sharing your sins and LIVING LIKE A *GREEK!*
O Fiend Than Whom!

NUGGET: O Fogy Than Which!
                                                      Why can't
you understand that you're *on sale* today?
Displayed on the block, beside the auctioneer.

CURMUDGE.: Oh, yeah?

NUGGET: Oh, yeah!

CURMUDGE.:   Well, tell me this . . .

(He fumbles for the crusher, but misses.)

                                              Who's selling?

NUGGET:

(A spiel to the audience in his auctioneer mode.)

        You folks recall the proverb—*God's dearly belovèds
        succumb in their prime.* Before they have to surrender
        their stamina, senses, and *sense.* Well, this loss leader
        bears no such burdensome baggage. If any god ever
        took a shine to him, he'd have been underground
        for at least ten years.
                          (Do I hear twenty?)
                                              These days,
        he mainly takes up space.
                                  I place in offer
        the Onus of the Earth!
                              His price? The going rate
        for one dessicated toadstool, spotted with rot.

CURMUDGE.: Is that your considered judgment—*the Onus of Earth?*

(To Shambles and the porters.)

        Cart him away!

(The gang grabs Nugget very roughly. Curmudgeous suddenly reconsiders and stops
them.)

No! Tote him inside and rope him
up tight to something heavy—a pillar!

(He restrains them from immediate performance of this, to gloat over Nugget.)

Now hear this:
Never will you MULCT ME OUT OF MY MOOLAH!

NUGGET:

(Moving into his Oracular mode.)

Yea, for as a gift thy moolah cometh.

CURMUDGE.:   A *gift?*

NUGGET: *Thy gift to me. Then, of thine own free will,*
wilt thou much and mightily sue for mulcting,
when thou behold'st mine accuser in peril and risk,
beset by terminal jeopardy.

CURMUDGE.:   *Jeopardy?*

NUGGET: Yup.
Then wilt thou strain to bestow on Nugget his freedom,
whereto I'll counter:
                    Never! Cart it away!

CURMUDGE.: Tell me, unspeakable scumbag: *What jeopardy?*
Intensides at risk? What risk is that?

NUGGET:

(Indicating Baçchis Two's house with a shake of his head.)

Just walk this way. You'll have the facts in a jiffy.

CURMUDGE.: Long trip?

NUGGET: Three steps at most.

CURMUDGE.:

(As they move to Bacchis Two's door.)

                              Ten steps, at least.

NUGGET:

(Into his Languid Aristocrat mode.)

Shambles, old man, be a dear and open the door
a teeny tad?
                    Be *gentle*: We don't want it *creaking,*
do we?
          How perfect!

(He drops the mode and addresses Curmudgeous, waggling again at the door.)

—I want *you* over *here.*

(Curmudgeous clumps over to the door and, directed by Nugget's nods, puts his eye to the crack in the door.)

Get a good view of the dinner?

CURMUDGE.:   Why, yes. Oh, look:
Æsygo's sitting with Bacchis.

NUGGET: Indeed he is.
And who, pray tell, do you see on the other couch?

CURMUDGE.:

(Struck by the vision.)

Write me down as *deceased.*

NUGGET: Recognize the male?

CURMUDGE.:   I certainly do.

NUGGET: Now be so kind as to furnish
your take on the female's beauty. Lovely or not?

(Curmudgeous keeps his eye glued to the door.)

CURMUDGE.:   A looker!

NUGGET: And what's her occupation? A hooker?

CURMUDGE.:   Of course.

NUGGET: Oh, that's too bad. You were doing so well.

CURMUDGE.:   No hooker? Then what the hell *is* she?

NUGGET: Observe and deduce . . .
because you sure as hell won't find out from *me.*

(Off right, a mighty roar wells up and out, as from a male behemoth deprived of its mate.)

Act IV, Scene 8 [842–924]

(Enter, stage right, the source of the yawp: Major Machismo, the puissant primitive. He addresses the audience, advancing, ultimately, to take up a position down center. He does not see the considerable crowd onstage, even though he wheels around fairly often. When this occurs, Nugget, Curmudgeous, and even the servants engage in elaborate scrambles to avoid his line of sight. They are always successful, though barely; never, until Nugget, released, confronts him directly, does Machismo have any idea that anyone else is onstage. His asides, as they might be termed, are delivered *fortissimo.* Curmudgeous moves Nugget and the porters to the alley.)

MACHISMO: *My Woman's a captive! She's cooped up under guard
by a weasly wimp—*
                            Intensides, son of Curmudgeous!

Dat ain't no way to behave!

CURMUDGE.:   Wh-who's this? *What's* this?

(Nugget does not answer but indulges in an aside.)

NUGGET: The Major's right on the dot. I call that timing.

MACHISMO: *What's wrong wit' dis Intensides? Does he t'ink dat I'm*
              a lady *what can't defend hisself an' his?*
              First time I meet dat guy, I let all his air out,
              I raise my sword and cut off his future, or else
              I lose my standing wit' Mars and da Goddess of Combat.

CURMUDGE.:   That man intends Intensides harm. Who *is* he?

NUGGET: You saw the girl your son's wrapped up in? Her husband.

CURMUDGE.:   Her *husband?*

NUGGET: The same.

CURMUDGE.:   Oh, god—you mean she's *married?*

NUGGET: You'll find out soon.

CURMUDGE.:   Oh agony, agony! Now
              I'm *really* dead.

NUGGET: And I'm still Nugget the no-good?
              No problem: truss me again and apply to your son
              for advice.
                         I *said* you'd learn the boy's true nature.

CURMUDGE.:   What *do* I do this time?

NUGGET: Well, disentwine me, for starters.
              I'm free in a flash, or your son the adulterer's set
              for a sudden seizure. In *flagrante.*

MACHISMO:

(He has not yet noticed the group.)

                                   No amount
              of money can warm duh cockles of my heart as much
              as catching dat pair horizontal, spread out on duh couch.
              Don't want no cash; I want blood!

NUGGET: You heard his words.
              Will you let me loose or not?

CURMUDGE.:   All right!
                                   Untie him!

(As Shambles and the gang turn Nugget loose.)

              I'm frozen stiff with fear! In fact, I'm dreadlocked!

MACHISMO: *I'll fix dat woman—she spreads her body around*
  the low-rent district, but she is not *gonna claim dat*
  duh man she latched onto's a patsy for her to pooh-pooh!

(Nugget is now free.)

NUGGET: You might effect some sort of arrangement by spending
  a little spare change . . .

CURMUDGE.:   So arrange! Effect! And spend
  whatever you want, to preserve my son and heir.
  Don't let him be caught in the act and cut down young!

MACHISMO: *If I don't get two hundred Kahunas in Gold,*
  I puncture that pair and let their souls out slow!

CURMUDGE.: An offer! Go make whatever arrangement you can.
  Get on this, *please!*

NUGGET: I'll give it my very best shot.

(He moves quickly down to Machismo, center, and confronts him head on, bawling
as loudly as he does.)

  What's all the shouting for?

(Machismo is rather startled but keeps on shouting.)

MACHISMO: *Take me to your master!*

NUGGET: *Who knows where he is? Not me!*

(He shepherds Machismo away from Curmudgeous, whose curiosity leads him to
sidle closer. Nugget speaks in a low tone.)

      Now how would you like
  a definite pledge of your Kahunas this instant?
  You'd be able to stop this howling hullabaloo.

MACHISMO: *Dere's nothin' I'd fancy more!*

NUGGET: One qualification:
  I'd like your permission to sully your name, and blacken
  your nature beneath a flood of verbal besmirchment?

MACHISMO: *Be my guest!*

(This howl is heard by Curmudgeous.)

CURMUDGE.:   The rat has a golden tongue.

(Nugget indicates Curmudgeous to Machismo.)

NUGGET: Now, that's Intensides' daddy. Let's go over.

(He mutters as they move to meet the old man.)

  Just ask for the Gold.

(Archly and quietly.)

For that other stuff, 'nuff said

CURMUDGE.:   What news?

NUGGET: I drove him down to two hundred Kahunas.

CURMUDGE.:   Esteemed redeemer—you have preserved my person!
How soon do I say *I'll pay?*

(Nugget ranges the two before him.)

NUGGET: No sweat. A simple
verbal contract.

(He turns to Machismo.)

You start this off. *You* ask . . .

(Machismo indicates confusion. Nugget points at Curmudgeous.)

Ask whom? Ask *Him.*

(He turns to Curmudgeous.)

And then *you* pledge . . .

(Curmudgeous shakes his head. Nugget points to Machismo.)

To *him,* of course!

(Things seem well-arranged, until Curmudgeous jumps the gun.)

CURMUDGE.:   I promise!

(Nugget withers him with a glance and turns to Machismo.)

NUGGET: Start asking *now.*

MACHISMO: *I ask for pure Gold coin, to the sum of two
hundred Kahunas. Will you pay it?*

(Silence from Curmudgeous, who is still puzzled.)

NUGGET: Well?
Just say, "The sum will be paid."

(Light dawns.)

CURMUDGE.:   *I'll pay! I'll pay!*

(Handclasp. Tableau. Shortly, Nugget launches his invective against a smiling
Machismo, who does not seem inclined to leave.)

NUGGET: Well now, disgusting person, what comes next?
More debts to collect? More refunds?
                              Stop hassling him.
And no more threats of death—he's petrified.
Not that you'll get off easy. He and I

make quite a fearsome pair.
                        You have a sword?
So what? We have a *spit* in the kitchen. The man
who riles me's liable to perforation—I'll fill you
fuller of holes than a mouse-and-pea kebob!

(Machismo still has not moved, and suddenly Nugget figures out why.)

I knew it all along! You're eaten up
by suspicion:

(Pointing to Bacchis One's house.)

                    is *he* in there with your Woman?

Machismo: *Damn right he is!*

Nugget:

(In his Pious mode.)

> *I hereby take my oath*
> *By all the gods that I know and you know—*
> *By Jupiter, Juno,*
> *By Ceres, Latona,*
> *Minerva, Pomona,*[12]
> *By Mercury, Hercules,*
> *Deified Virtue*
> *Hypostatized Hope,*
> *And personified Property . . .*

(A stop for breath, and he charges on.)

> *. . . By Castor and Pollux,*
> *By Mars and by Venus,*
> *And even Summánus,*
> *And geezer Saturnus,*
> *Including the Sun*
> *Plus every one*
> *Of the gods I've been forced to omit—*
> *Intensides isn't*
> *Embracing or kissing,*
> *Reclining, entwining,*
> *Or taking an innocent walk*
> *That might cause people to talk*
> *Or engaged in activities*
> *Only too human*

---

[12] I should point out that the goddess Pomona is included in the translation only for the rhyme, which is as much reason as some of her companions have, especially Summanus, god of nighttime lightning.

With
Your
Woman!

CURMUDGE.:

(Touched by what he regards as self-sacrifice.)

Now, *there* is an oath!
Pyramid perjuries, piled
on high to preserve me!

MACHISMO: *He ain't inside da house?*
Where is *da boy?*

NUGGET: He's been relocated, down
on the farm. And as for your Woman, she went to visit
Minerva's temple.
It's just reopened. You might
drop down and see if she's there.

MACHISMO: *Dat's downtown, right?*
I'm off to da Forum.

NUGGET: You're off to hell, I hope.

MACHISMO: *Do I get da Gold today?*

NUGGET: You do. *With luck,*
you get hung as well!
Don't go thinking we need
anything else from you, you walking zilch!

(Machismo, still in the best of humor, strides off stage left, to downtown. Nugget
turns to Curmudgeous.)

—He's out of here.
Now, master—and this request
I beg by the gods, who never die—allow me
to go in here and see your son.

CURMUDGE.:   In there? But why?

(Nugget goes into his Zeugma mode.)

NUGGET: Moral instruction, sir. I beg your leave
to chastise that rascal at considerable length
for his indulgence in such shameless behavior.

CURMUDGE.: My leave? No, I beg yours!
And one more thing:
Do not go easy, please! You whale away
in withering words!

NUGGET: No need to direct me, sir.

I've already planned an omnibus castigation
surpassing the best the comic stage has to offer.

(He jauntily enters the house of Bacchis One.)

CURMUDGE.:   That slave's an infection. Who needs, or wants, or *misses*
a sty in the eye when it's gone? But get one and bang!
it *matters*; your sty's a *crux,* never out of touch.
Such luck that Nuggest was festering here today—
or else the Major would have astonished my son
and his wife in the very depths of the dirty deed
and diced them with sword and dagger. But thanks to Nugget,
I've bought my boy! He may cost a couple of hundred Kahunas,
but least he's all in one piece.

            Still, two hundred Kahunas!
I'd better inspect the cargo before I fork over
that sort of cash and entrust my money to Nugget.

(He looks suspiciously at the letter.)

I'm inclined to give this a Second Reading: if you can't
trust a sealed letter, what *can* you trust?

(Clutching the letter, he enters his house, stage left.)

Act IV, Scene 9 [925–1075]

(Enter, from Bacchis One's house, stage right, Nugget in his glory. He is carrying
what is clearly *another* letter. He moves to stage center, turns to the audience, and
declaims . . .)

NUGGET'S GLOAT[13]

NUGGET: Top Spot in the Roster of Human Achievement—Number One Seed
in Best of Breed—is assigned, in a tie, to the mighty Atrídae:
They toppled the hapless towers of Troy, and flattened its god-built
battlements . . .

          expedited, of course, by corps and divisions
of can-do stalwarts, tons of ordnance, masses of horses,
a full flotilla . . .

          and all it took was Ten Long Years.

---

[13] The following intertextual extravaganza is unusual in the extreme—a slave delivering, in
terms of the Trojan War, a Soldier's *brag* that will not quit. On the altered pearl necklace that is
Bacchides, we suddenly encounter the Zircon as Big as the Ritz. Its *function* seems clear: under
guise of ending the play, it cannons it on to the next 200 Kahunas, and the corruption of the aged
in Act V. But its length and incoherencies prove too much for some, who excise considerable
swatches as interpolations by later producers/actors, expansions of a favorite's turn. This is
surely possible . . . though *Bacchides* is hardly the play from which to trim excesses. I've given
the whole speech its head and added, in the stage directions, a slight surface motivation—
Waiting for Curmudgeous. This passage has doubtless been swollen by generation upon generation of producers. The modern director is invited to prune.

> This is *History?*
A puny bunion on the Toe of Time, compared with the epic
heroics that *I* am about to embark on: the extirpation
of one mean, grasping master . . . alone, unpropped, and unaided.

(He moves into his Barker mode.)

> I beg your attention, friends: there's nothing stuffed in my mufti:
Behold: no corps concealed, and nary a sloop or a troop.
[Only experience. Not so long ago, I pillaged
the *pater* and funded the Son with the golden fruit of the booty.][14]

(He looks impatiently over his shoulder at Cumudgeous's house and shrugs.)

> Please excuse the brief delay. We're waiting for Priam,
my prey, who's still offstage. I'll fill the gap till his entrance
with a standard, plangent tragic lament.

(He stands firmly center, musses his hair, beats his breast a few times, and wails.)

> *Alackaday!*
> *O Woe and Pity and Wail for Troy the Land of the Father!*
> *O Plaint for Pergamum's Passing!*

(He cheats towards Curmudgeous's house and shouts louder.)

> *O Knell for Priam now nil . . .*
> *O Old Guy, doomed to the looting of* four *hundred gold Kahunas!*

(Nothing from the house. He shrugs again, holds up the tablets, and returns to his Barker mode.)

> Subject the object I hold in my hand to scrutiny, folks.
What is it?
> 　　　　Waxed tablets of pine—officially tagged
and sealed with a signet . . .
> 　　　　　　　—A letter, you say?
> 　　　　　　　　　Oh, tut, folks, tut!

(He waggles the tablets.)

> Behold a HORSE—
> 　　　　the very Wooden Horse you ought
to beware of Greeks even bearing which.

(In the Pedantic mode:)

> 　　　　　　To guide the perplexed:
inspect the intertext.
> 　　　　A simple allegory yields

---

[14] In the original, the bracketed passage (= line 931) is extremely hard to use without either (a) an insert or (b) an orgy of cutting. The distant paraphrase here offered allows it to fit *in situ,* but contains more mortising than it should, and imports a minor break in such flow as there is.

startling equivalents. Thus we derive by substitution
Æsygo matching *Epeíus* the joiner, who furnished the staples
to build the Horse. *Intensides* equals the crafty *Sínon,*
who lay in wait on Achilles' tomb to betray the city . . .
though Intensides is Sporting inside on a couch with Sissy
and isn't *waiting* at all. This Sínon cuddled a spark
to signal the waiting Greek, but our lad blazes with passion,
a one-man conflagration.
                        Ulysses, planner supreme,
works out to *Me,* who produced and directed the whole shebang.

(Another futile glance at the house. He peers inside the letter.)

The letters inscribed inside the letter I hold in my hand here
are veterans chucked in the breach, broadside to the arsenal's
        buttress,
lying like troopers, a scrappy cadre mustered, *not*
to force the fence of the fort, but take their toll of the till,
when H-O-R-S-E spells breakup, and breakdown, and washout
of a ga-ga Old Guy and his GOLD.
                        This foggy fogy, *ill*-witted,
ill-brained, *ill*-natured, deserves and receives the name of ILL-ium.
The *Major* whose darling deserted? That's *Menelaus,* of course,
leaving me to double the role of stout *Agamemnon* . . .
plus always the foresaid shifty Ulysses, son of Laërtes.
Intensides will appear as Paris, the peerless impairment
of all ancestral assets, now graced with a *Helen* to waste them.
She's the reason I levy this siege on well-heeled Ilium.

(An awkward pause, but he soldiers on.)

At Ilium once did Ulysses, that dogged caitiff, they say,
riot in brazen brashness, I do the same right here.
Compare us: I've been caught in the toils of my very own trap;
he, camouflaged as a tramp to spy out Troy's intentions,
blew his cover and damn near died. A parallel plight
befell me today, but I worked loose with a dose of deception,
freed by fraud like Ulysses from durance degrading and deadly.

(A desperate look at the house stage left. No Curmudgeous.)

Moving right along . . .
                        The countdown to Ilium's smashup
consisted, I hear, in the ordered occurrence of three disasters,
or DOOMS.
                        DOOM ONE: Athénê's statue stolen from Troy.
DOOM TWO: The Trojan hero Troilus sundered from life.
DOOM THREE: Atop Troy Gate, the lintel splintered to admit
one Wooden Horse.
                        And equal to these are the final fates

of *Curmudgeous,* our own homegrown, outdated *Ilium Two.*
HOME DOOM ONE: A bit ago, I spun for the codger
a whopper containing a greedy host, and Diana's temple,
and a pirate cutter . . . well, that works out to my theft of the statue:
I ripped off Pallas from the palace . . .
                                        leaving two DOOMS before
I brought down our own Ilium Two in urban sprawl.

And what was HOME DOOM TWO—our match for Troilus'
    murder?
Why, LETTER the FIRST, informing the father his son was sunk
in hanky-panky with the wedded wife of a raging Major.
I barely got out alive. Compare the sticky minutes
Ulysses spent when harlot Helen saw through his clothing
and hauled him off for disposal to *Hecuba,* Queen of Troy.
But Ulysses wheedled the Queen to let him slip off and away,
and even so I rose to my ruses and gaffed the Old Guy.
and blithely escaped the scrape, my skin intact, by craft.
I then crossed words with the blowhard Major, the downer of towns
by verbal flak. Unarmed except for my tongue, I licked him . . .
then mixed it up again with the Senior Citizen. Yea,
I sacked that burgher, laid him out flat with a lie to the jaw,
and now he'll purvey the promised purse to the dominant Major,
TWO HUNDRED KAHUNAS IN GOLD!

                                And so to the final hurdle:
HOME DOOM THREE!
                        There's never enough Kahunas, of course.
We need TWO HUNDRED more, to furnish victorious troops
with a ration all round of grog, of wine infused with honey,
to toast their taking of Troy and its Ilium-gotten gains.

(A sidewise look at Curmudgeous's house. Does he hear something?)

The present Priam is quite an advance on the Priam of legend,
the sire of fifty measly sons. *Our* Priam possesses
FOUR HUNDRED—golden boys in mint condition—
and on this day I'll dispose of every single one.
Two sharp shocks, and they'll be utterly spent.
                                        And Priam?
Well, if I can find a market for dirty old men, I'll *sell* him.
Yes, up he'll go on the block to cap the city's collapse.

(A squeal from the hinges of Curmudgeous's front door.)

Lo! I descry old Priam before the portals deploying.
I make my way to him, and shall address him.
                                        —Ahoy!

(Enter Curmudgeous from his house. The ensuing encounter begins in schizoid fashion: Nugget, in his hero mode, raves on in a rococo epical-tragical diction, while poor Curmudgeous makes his way in something like standard speech.)

CURMUDGE.: The sound of a voice. It's somewhere near. Whose might it be?

NUGGET: *All hail, Curmudgeous!*

CURMUDGE.:   What is going *on?* The job
I gave you—did you do it?

NUGGET: *You ask? Approach!*

CURMUDGE.:   I'm 'proaching.

NUGGET: *From out my matchless store of eloquence and revilement,*
I chid and steered the churl till he dissolved in tears.

CURMUDGE.: What did he say?

NUGGET:

(Holding the new letter high.)

> *No word emitted he, but wept,*
> *gave hearken to my message, drew his stylus forth,*
> *and speechless wrote reply and silent sealed it up,*
> *and bade me bear it here.*

(He hands Curmudgeous the letter with a flourish.)

> *But have a care; this missive*
> *is hardly like to sing a tune that's new.*

(He drops the epic diction for a moment.)

                              Inspect the seal.
Be sure it's his.

(Curmedgeous obeys.)

CURMUDGE.:   It is.

(He holds the letter away from himself.)

                              Now, *this* is a letter I want
to analyze closely.

NUGGET: Analyze away.

(Uttering an epic aside, he starts to move away.)

> *—And yea,*
> *now cracks the gate in twain, now yawns the way to Troy,*
> *now rolls the Horse within, and havoc high evokes.*

(Curmudgeous calls him back, and they move into a rapid exchange.)

CURMUDGE.:	*Nugget, you're needed.*
NUGGET:	*I'm needed? How so?*
CURMUDGE.:	*Stay here while I read it.*
NUGGET:	*I'd only impede it.*
CURMUDGE.:	*I'd like you to know* *The news in this letter.*
NUGGET:	*Not knowing is better;* *I'm going away.*
CURMUDGE.:	*No, dammit, you stay!*
NUGGET:	*But why should I stay so?*
CURMUDGE.:	*The reason?* I say so!
NUGGET:	*I guess that I'll stay.*

(A pause while Curmudgeous opens the tablets.)

CURMUDGE.:	*Such miniature writing.*
NUGGET:	*Oh, no; it's the sighting.* *In letters, the size* *Depends on the eyes:* *For old eyes, they're small;* *For young eyes, they're tall.*
CURMUDGE.:	*Just stick to the point!*
NUGGET:	*I think that I won't.* *It's useless to do.*
CURMUDGE.:	*I command you to!*
NUGGET:	*Slave does what he must?* *That sounds fair and just.*
CURMUDGE.:	*Just do it, I say!*
NUGGET:	*All right, then.* Okay. *Read on and fire away.*

(The fit is over, and normal speech is in order.)

No doubt young ears can help make out those letters.

CURMUDGE.:	This thing is *huge*. Such wear and tear on the stylus—

and god, what a waste of wax!
No help for it.
I'll read it through to the bitter end.
"DEAR DADDY:
UNLESS YOU'D RATHER SEE YOUR ONLY SON

IN A VERY SAD STATE OF HEALTH—NO, MAKE THAT *DEAD*—
GIVE NUGGET TWO HUNDRED GOLD KAHUNAS."

                                        But didn't
I *do* that?
          Oh Damn and Damn and Triple God*damn!*

NUGGET: Permission to interrupt?

CURMUDGE.:   All right. What is it?

NUGGET: Check through the letter. *Your* state of health—
no word of concern?

(Curmudgeous checks.)

CURMUDGE.:   Can't find a single one.

NUGGET: A very bad sign. The counsel of wisdom is this:
don't pay him that amount on any account!
BUT if you insist on taking this senseless course,
you find yourself another delivery boy!
I will not make that drop, sir! No command,
no say-so can compel me to risk my tattered
reputation, or stick my innocence back
in the line of fire! Who needs more battle fatigue?

CURMUDGE.:   Just *listen,* dammit! Let me read this through.

NUGGET: Disgusting letter, sir! From its very inception,
no hint of *shame!*

(Curmudgeous reads again.)

CURMUDGE.:   "SHAME ON ME, DADDY! I BLUSH
TO SHOW MYSELF IN YOUR PRESENCE, NOW THAT YOU KNOW
THE HEIGHT AND DEPTH OF MY DISGRACEFUL AFFAIR
WITH THE WEDDED WIFE OF THAT MAJOR FROM OUT OF TOWN."
—You got *that* right. Ashamed? I've been *embarrassed*
to the tune of a whole two hundred Kahunas in Gold
to ransom your beleaguered butt out of scandal
alive and well!

NUGGET: The tenor of my remarks
to your son and heir was strikingly similar, sir.

CURMUDGE.:   "I BLEW IT. NO BRAIN AT ALL. BUT PLEASE, DEAR DADDY
DON'T CAST ME OUT AND AWAY FOR A STUPID MISTAKE.
I FOLLOWED THE LUSTFUL LEAD OF A HEART IN HEAT;
I COULDN'T KEEP MY EYES ON THE STRAIGHT AND NARROW.
THESE ORGANS SEDUCED ME INTO AN ACT WHICH NOW
AFFORDS ME NOTHING BUT *SHAME.*"
                      You should have tried
A little less SHAME now, and more SENSE then.

NUGGET: What a coincidence, sir—my very words
to the worthless, immature rogue.

CURMUDGE.:   "DEAR DADDY, DO
APPRECIATE THE THOROUGHNESS OF VICIOUS
CASTIGATION, THE SHEER VARIETY
OF USEFUL MORAL INSTRUCTION EMPLOYED BY NUGGET,
OUR FAITHFUL SLAVE, TO MAKE ME A BETTER BOY.
YOU ARE, AND FOREVER SHOULD BE, IN HIS DEBT."

NUGGET: He wrote that? Show me where.

CURMUDGE.:   See for yourself.

NUGGET:

(He goes to his knees, hands clasped.)

The new ex-rascal, fresh from rehab, falls on
his knees to acknowledge the agents of his reform.

CURMUDGE.:   "IF I RETAIN THE MEREST VESTIGE OF A RIGHT
TO BEG A BOON, DEAR DADDY, THIS BOON I BEG:
ANOTHER TWO HUNDRED KAHUNAS IN GOLD."

NUGGET: No.
Show some sense, sir! Not a single drachma!

CURMUDGE.:   I'm reading this—will you please let me finish?
"AND WHY, YOU ASK? I SWORE MY SOLEMN OATH—
NO LOOPHOLE LEFT AT ALL—TO PAY THAT WOMAN
THAT SUM BEFORE THE SUN GOES DOWN, AND SHE
DEPARTS FOREVER.
              I CANNOT FACE THE DISGRACE
OF A BROKEN OATH. I'D SOONER—WELL, YOU KNOW.
DEAR DADDY, FREE YOUR BOY FROM THE BITTER BONDS
OF PERJURY, SET HIM LOOSE FROM THE GRASPING EMBRACE
OF THAT AWFUL WOMAN, WHO DRAGGED HIM DOWN TO THE DEPTHS
OF SIN AND EXPENSE, AT EARLIEST CONVENIENCE!
AND DON'T OBSESS ON THOSE TWO HUNDRED KAHUNAS;
I'LL PAY THEM BACK A THOUSAND TIMES . . .
                  PROVIDED, OF COURSE,
THAT I STAY ALIVE.
              GOOD-BYE FROM YOUR BOY, WHO TRUSTS
FOR SWIFT COMPLETION OF THIS, HIS LAST REQUEST."
—So, Nugget, what course of action? Any ideas?

NUGGET: You're asking me for *advice?* Try again tomorrow.
I will not give you the chance to claim that whatever
might happen to go awry was my suggestion.
But still, let's suppose that I were the father involved.
My considered judgment then would be payment in full,

not let my one son wallow his life away
in disgrace and besmirchment.

                My point? You're stuck between
two stools. So, either you lose the money, or else
you cause your son to ruin his life, because of
a broken oath that he swore in the heat of passion.
The matter is up to you. I take no sides,
I grind no axe, I urge neither A nor B.

CURMUDGE.: I'm sorry for him.

NUGGET: You should be; he's your son.
Some people might consider it better to lose
a little more money, and not supply a screaming
scandal to downtown gossip's tender mercies.
But me, I'm neutral.

CURMUDGE.:   Oh, damn. I wish he'd stayed
in Asia, alive and well, and never come home.
That I could deal with.

               But now he's safe at home,
and what the hell do I do?

                 If 'twere to be lost,
'twere well to lose it as fast as 'twere possible, so
away inside for two hundred Kahunas, *times two:*
the fee for the Major's mangled marriage, *plus*
hush money needed to fill an adulterous oath.
Nothing like ethics.

          —Nugget, stick around.
Back out in a minute.

NUGGET: *Tall Troy collapses in ruin,*
and Pergamum buckles and truckles beneath the blades
of assembled chiefs. I *knew* I'd be the boy
to destroy the topless towers, and leave Troy void!

(To the audience.)

I know someone among you will now assert
I deserve to be trussed and hung up high for
an atrocity on this scale.

            —Well, sir, I wouldn't
bet you're wrong. But still, such lovely confusion!
—There goes the door—a creak and squeal announcing
the loot forthcoming from Troy!

             But shut up, Nugget.
Silence is Golden now.

(Curmudgeous emerges from his house, struggling under the weight of two equally
heavy sacks of Gold. He puts one down and attempts to hand the other to Nugget.)

CURMUDGE.:   Here, Nugget, take it.

This one goes to my son. Deliver it, please.
The other goes to settle up with the Major.
I'll take it down to the Forum straight away.

(Nugget backs away.)

NUGGET: Sorry, but no can do. In fact, no *will* do.
You'd better locate another packhorse. I simply
refuse to incur an obligation like this.
The Trust involved is more than I can endure.

CURMUDGE.:   Don't be a bloody bore; just take the bag.

NUGGET: I will not take the bag!

CURMUDGE.:   Oh. Pretty please?

NUGGET: NO! I've made my attitude perfectly plain.

CURMUDGE.:   Come on, you're making me late.

NUGGET: I'll try this again:
I won't be put in charge of any Gold!

(A pause, while he appears to think it over.)

Well, if I am, put someone in charge of *me*.

CURMUDGE.:   Look, this is difficult enough.

NUGGET: There's no way out?
Oh, all right. Give me the bag.

(Curmudgeous, very relieved, hands him the bag in question.)

CURMUDGE.:   So while I'm gone—
and I'll hardly be gone at all—take care of this.

(He picks up the other bag and moves off stage left as fast as he can, given its
weight. Nugget, hugging his bag, gazes after the departing Curmudgeous.)

NUGGET: I've already taken care . . . of you. I've made you
the most benighted old bastard that ever got bilked!
Behold, from modest beginnings, a denouement
imbued with style and class!

(He manages to march in pattern and do the manual of arms with the bag of Gold at
one and the same time.)

Forward, *Harch!*
The action debouches in glory, the victor advances,
laden with lashings and loads of beautiful booty!
Myself preserved, the city razed to the ground,
I now conduct my soldiers safely home—
two hundred elite troops, and not one lost!

(Directly to the audience.)

> I know what you're saying out there, that such colossal
> conquest calls for a proper parade. But Official Triumphs
> occur on every corner these days; they're—well, they're *trite*.
> Not worth my time.

(He reaches into the bag and pulls out a fistful of golden coins.)

> This doesn't mean, however,
> that worthy fighters such as these will lack
> a proper reception upon their safe return,
> where wine and honey will flow . . .

(Short pause for thought. He shrugs.)

> . . . like honey and wine.
> And now to deliver the loot to the sergeant at arms.

(Hoisting the Gold-bag high, he strides without knocking into the house of Bacchis
One.)

Act IV, Scene 10 [1076–1085][15]

(Enter Æsycome from town, stage left.)

ÆSYCOME: The more meditation I mull on the messes my son is making,
    the lifestyle and modes of existence he jackknifes into headfirst,
    the more I incline to worry—to absolute terror, in fact:
    might he not be sprinting along the road to ruin?
    I know, I was his age once, and the things he does, I did—
    but at least I managed somehow to preserve a sense of *proportion*.
    I had the affairs, the whores, the drink, the expense . . . but not all
     the time!

(Moving to his right, he is struck by another thought. He stops.)

> What's more, I'm very disturbed at the general state of relations
> that fathers have with their sons. As a matter of principle, I
> have supplied my son with the wherewithal to indulge his wishes;
> I think it only fair. But still, am I indulging his sloth too much?

(He is now down center and has passed the home of Curmudgeous and Intensides.)

> So now I'm turning my steps to Intensides' place, to learn
> how far, if at all, he has progressed, as per my request,
> in constraining my son to the paths of virtue and dullness. I know
> that if opportunity came his way, he *must* have succeeded.

---

[15] This translation endeavors to provide some ease of location by strictly indicating the acts and
scenes to be found in the standard editions. It should be noted that *this* scene, labeled as the last in
Act *Four*, in fact supplies a beginning to the action that occupies Act *Five*—which is to say, the
final deception of the old men, not by Nugget, but by the Sisters Bacchis.

He's the boy for the job:
>
> virtuous and dull since birth.

(In his usual fog, he wanders upstage, right, to the house of Bacchis One. Fascinated, he soon becomes lost in wonder before it.)

Act V, Scene 1 [1086–1119]

(Curmudgeous, in his standard frenzy, returns from the downtown, stage left. He does not see Æsycome, who is staring at Bacchis One's house. Nor does Æsycome see him—or, what may be more surprising, hear him as he harangues the audience.)

CURMUDGE.: Oh, Dammmn!

Of all the addled idiots and downright drooling dunces,
of all the muttonhead morons and noncompos nincompoop clods,
of all the veritable vegetables that have ever existed on earth
or ever *will* exist on earth, I TAKE THE CAKE!
Winner by twenty lengths in the freestyle stupidity sweepstakes.
Oh, Dammmn!

(He moves to center stage and sets up shop for a tirade.)

The chagrin is too much to bear. How could this happen to me?
How could any male attaining to my mature years
be cleaned out so completely in such a ridiculous manner,
not once but *twice?* I can't root it out of my head, and the more
I mull, the madder I get at the mess my son has made!
I have been crushed to earth, and then jerked out by the roots,
and then ripped hither from yon in every conceivable way.
All shapes of evil pursue me; I die and die again,
working down the list of really revolting deaths.
Who cut me to bits today?
>
> The answer's Nugget, of course.

Who laid me low and stripped the body?
>
> Nugget again.

I have been shorn. Of my gold. Who did it?
>
> Nugget once more.

The knave connived to knife the naive one, every which way.
And oh, I bit! He convinced me the girl was the Major's wife:
But now the Major informs me the girl is a whore, with a load
of corroborating detail! He'd rented her for the year,
but then her remaining contract—all prorated of course—
was bought out with the money promised to save my worthless son
by me, the ninny of ninnies. And this, this is what pierces
straight to the floor of my heart: this is the ultimate torture,
the last indignity for me, a male of my mature years,
to be hornswoggled and made a butt in the bargain, and then,
in the depths of my shame, be *expurgated* out of my gold.

Oh, Dammmn!

To have a slave, *my* slave, with such contempt for my status!
It's not the money involved; it's the principle of the thing:
I could lose more Gold any other way and mind it less.

(At length, Æsycome, waking from his scrutiny of Bacchis One's front door,
perceives to his surprise that something is going on.)

ÆSYCOME: Methought I heard a voice. Methinks it's near at hand.
Mewonder *Whose?*

(He looks around and sees Curmudgeous.)

Of course—it's Æsygo's buddy's daddy's.

(He moves to Curmudgeous, center. Curmudgeous finally sees *him.*)

CURMUDGE.:   Oh, good! Another destroyed depressive to share the load.
Hello, Æsycome.

ÆSYCOME: Hi. And where in the world did *you* come from?

CURMUDGE.:

(Pointing off left.)

Downtown—home of the downer.

ÆSYCOME:

(Indicating the audience.)

No better here. So welcome
to uptown—home of the uptight.

CURMUDGE.:   What a coincidence—
same age, same lousy luck.

ÆSYCOME: Amen to that. But what's
the matter, precisely?

CURMUDGE.:   Precisely the matter that matters with *you.*

ÆSYCOME: You're sick about your son?

CURMUDGE.:   No, no. Sick *of* my son.

ÆSYCOME: I feel your pain. Mine catches me right around the heart.

CURMUDGE.:   That paragon Nugget's the source of infection for my affliction:
destroyed my son, demolished my assets, dismantled *me.*

ÆSYCOME: But what's gone wrong with your boy?

CURMUDGE.:   Pay close attention: He's gone
down the primrose path with *yours*—they've both got *mistresses!*

ÆSYCOME: Oh. How do you know?

CURMUDGE.:   I *saw* them!

ÆSYCOME: You did? Well, golly.

    (Aside.)

                                               Damn.

CURMUDGE.: No time for standing around. Assault and batter that door,
               and pull that pair of perverts out by the roots!

ÆSYCOME: Yes, let's.
    Right away. Of course.

(Curmudgeous immediately marches up to the door and bangs away. Æsycome
hangs back.)

CURMUDGE.:   AHOY THE WHOREHOUSE! BACCHIS!
    I'm asking you pretty please, BACCHIS! Undo this door . . .
    unless you want it split to flinders.
                        Including the frame!

(He continues banging.)

Act V, Scene 2 [1120–1211]

(The door bursts open, revealing a very annoyed pair of Bacchises, Bacchis One and
Sissy, primed for a fight.)

BACCHIS I: Who bellows *Bacchis?* Who thwacks my dwelling? Who cracks the
            welkin?

CURMUDGE.: I do!
         Him too.

(The women stride out and take up a position down right. The men do the same
down center. Each pair surveys the other. Bacchis One turns to Sissy. [Until
Curmudgeous calls out to the women, the sisters will converse loudly, the old men
sotto voce.] It should be clear that the sisters are carrying out a planned routine.)

BACCHIS I: But what in the world can this mean?
    Some nameless shepherd appears to have left us a pair of sheep.

CURMUDGE.:

    (To Æsycome.)
    Sheep! No decent women would call us that.

SISSY: But *sheep?* Are you sure?

    (The sisters go into a sheep song.)

BACCHIS I:	*They are raddled old rams that have lost their way,*	*Baa, Baa, Baa.*
SISSY:	*They are little slack sheep that have gone astray,*	*Baa, Baa, Baa.*
BOTH:	*Cut from the flock to wander free,*	
	Aged just less than eternity,	
	Lost past hope of recovery,	*Baa, Baa, Baa.*

(The old men notice and confer.)

ÆSYCOME: Do we put up with derision?

CURMUDGE.:   We do. They're digging their own grave.]

    (The sisters continue the song.)

BACCHIS I: *Oh, your standard sheep is cruddy,*
        And its fleece is full of grease,
        And its matted wool supplies a dull display . . .
SISSY: *But the sheep in front of our house*
        Have a glisten and a gleam,
        And the bigger one's been shorn two times today.

ÆSYCOME: I suppose we deserve all this. We didn't *have* to come here.

SISSY: *They were prodigal once, but they lost it all,*   *Bleat, Bleat, Bleat.*
BACCHIS I: *They were spenders, but can't pay the cost at all,*   *Bleat, Bleat, Bleat.*
BOTH: *Losing their wool to the clips and shears,*
        Dropping their drive to the rush of years,
        All they could possibly bring in here's   *Bleat, Bleat, Bleat.*

    (The sisters confer again.)

SISSY: They're hardly a threat. Let's herd them inside.

BACCHIS I: But what's the point?

    (Back into the song.)

BACCHIS I: *Oh, their wool is nonexistent,*
        And they're not designed for milk,
        Their potential is perpetually on hold.
SISSY: *And they've shed their leaves and acorns,*
        And their fruit dropped off to rot,
        And they couldn't do a thing inside our fold.
BACCHIS I: *They are poor withered wethers who've lost their bleat,*   *Bye, Bye, Bye.*
SISSY: *They are mum-stricken mutton, quite obsolete,*   *Bye, Bye, Bye.*
BOTH: *Customers nobody sane would choose,*
        Rams who forgot what to do with ewes,
        Bring them inside here? Well, please excuse . . .   *Bye, Bye, Bye.*

BACCHIS I: All right, Bacchis. Back in the house.

    (The sisters make as if to do that, with a good-bye wave at the fathers. Curmudgeous
finds his voice.)

CURMUDGE.:   You HALT in your tracks!
    These sheep have a bone to pick with you!

SISSY: Why, gracious me—
    a miracle! Sheep calling out to us, in human voices!

    (The men [Curmudgeous striding, Æsygo reluctant] approach the women.)

CURMUDGE.:   These sheep owe you a flock of trouble, and intend to pay it.

BACCHIS I: Whatever you owe is forgiven. You keep it; I do not want it.
           But just out of asking, why do we deserve these threats?

ÆSYCOME: A report's gone out you've penned our little lambkins up.

CURMUDGE.:   And that's not all. You've snatched my nasty brute of a mastiff.
           Unless you produce this livestock, deliver it over to us,
           we metamorphose into *Rams,* and levy an instant attack!

BACCHIS I: —Bacchis, a word in private.

SISSY: So?

(The sisters move down right, out of earshot.)

CURMUDGE.:   Where are they going?

(The old men crane after the sisters, who converse in low tones.)

BACCHIS I: I hereby deed you full rights to the farther father,

(Indicating Æsycome.)

                                 in trust
that you'll tranquilize him even further.

(Indicating Curmudgeous.)

                     Myself, I'll sally forth
to god's angry ram over here. Inveiglement ought to work.

SISSY: No problem; I'll hold my end up. Though I have to confess
         I loathe this Service to the Dead.

BACCHIS I: Regardless, do your job.

SISSY: Oh, hush. You grapple with your trouble, and I'll perform as promised.

CURMUDGE.:

(Puzzled, to Æsycome.)

         A private conference—why?

ÆSYCOME: Could we have one of those?

CURMUDGE.:   You're trying to tell me something?

ÆSYCOME: It's hard to put into words.
         Fact is, I'm embarrassed . . .

CURMUDGE.:   And why should you be embarrassed?

ÆSYCOME: . . . but you're a good friend. So, I've decided to let you in

on my deepest and darkest desires. And, well, here goes:
I'm *Worthless*.

CURMUDGE.:   You are.

ÆSYCOME: An absolute *Nothing*.

CURMUDGE.:   That checks.

ÆSYCOME: *No Good*.

CURMUDGE.: What else is new?
                          But kindly explain *why* you're *No Good*.

ÆSYCOME: I'm stuck in birdlime; I'm pierced by a dart to the root of my heart.

CURMUDGE.:

    (Aside.)

            Your anatomy's off; you mean you're gored to the core of your crotch.

    (To Æsycome.)

            —But what can you mean?

    (Aside.)

                                    I have a fairly close idea what's up.
                    But still, I'm agog to hear it firsthand.

ÆSYCOME:

    (Pointing to Sissy.)

                                        You see that girl?

CURMUDGE.: I do indeed.

ÆSYCOME: Not bad, huh?

CURMUDGE.:   Wrong. For what she is,
                Bad is the word.
                                And you're *No Good,* and . . .

ÆSYCOME: Keeping it short,
                I love her.

CURMUDGE.:   You love her?

ÆSYCOME: *Va-va-voom!*

CURMUDGE.:   A male like you,
                mature in years, in *Love?* It's disgusting! How could you *do* it?

ÆSYCOME: Why shouldn't I fall in love?

CURMUDGE.:   At your age, it's disgraceful!

ÆSYCOME: I refuse to argue the matter. And I'm not mad at my son;
              don't you be, either.
                                   They're in Love, and so they're Wise.

BACCHIS I:

      (To Sissy.)

              Come over here.

      (The sisters move back left towards the men.)

CURMUDGE.:   And finally here they are again,
              the alluring, enticing seductresses.
                                   —So, what's it going to be?
              Do you hand over our sons and servant all nice and easy?
              Or do I come on strong and throw my weight around?

ÆSYCOME: I think you'd better go. Completely tasteless behavior
              to such a Luscious Young Thing . . . You can't be a man any more.

BACCHIS I:

      (Snuggling up to Curmudgeous and working her wiles.)

              O most most reverend ancient who art on earth, do let me
              prevail on you for a boon. Call off this stubborn siege
              against your son's peccadillos.

CURMUDGE.:   No matter how luscious you are,
              you leave me alone, or else I'll make big trouble for you!

      (He brandishes a fist. Bacchis One doesn't move.)

BACCHIS I: I welcome the tiniest touch of those big, strong, masterful hands.
              How could they hurt?

CURMUDGE.:   *Sweet talk!*
                                   I'm feeling fear. I'm lost.

      (We now have two mixed couples, well separated, in different stages of relationship.
      Bacchis and Curmudgeous are still at the confrontational stage, but Sissy and Æsycome
      are verging on closeness.)

SISSY:

      (To Bacchis One, indicating Æsycome.)

              Mine's not so frisky, somehow. Really. A perfect lamb.

      (Bacchis One is still hitting on Curmudgeous, with steady increments of success.)

BACCHIS I: You come inside with me, and punish your son in there . . .
              If that's what you really want . . .

CURMUDGE.:   Oh, dammit, leave me alone!

BACCHIS I: Do let me . . . prevail upon you, precious.

CURMUDGE.:   *Prevail* upon me?

(Attention turns to the other couple.)

SISSY: I can sure prevail the hell out of this one here!

ÆSYCOME: No need:
               I'll prevail on you to take me inside.

SISSY: A man of wit.

ÆSYCOME: But only on my conditions, which are . . .

SISSY: To be with me.

ÆSYCOME: The total sum of all my desires—you got it in one.

(He enfolds her, attracting the comment of Curmudgeous, who is losing his battle.)

CURMUDGE.:   I've seen my share of Worthless No-Good Nothings, but never
               a No-Gooder Naught than you.

ÆSYCOME: You've got it—me to an N.

BACCHIS I:

(Persisting with Curmudgeous.)

               Just come along inside—and it's nothing but wall-to-wall *class*.
               Vino and victuals and *nard* in abundance.

CURMUDGE.:   Enough already!
               I am up to here with banquets; entertain me or not,
               it makes no difference at all.
                                    MONEY is what it's about:
               My son and Nugget relieved me of four hundred Gold Kahunas,
               and I refuse to relinquish nailing Nugget up on the cross,
               even if it costs me another four hundred to put him there!

BACCHIS I: But put the case the boys give half of it back, well, *then*
               will you come along inside . . . and forgive their tiny trespasses?

(This attracts a contribution from Æsycome.)

ÆSYCOME: HE WILL!

CURMUDGE.:   He certainly WON'T! It's not the thing I do.
               Just let me alone. All I want is vengeance. In full.

ÆSYCOME: Talk about your No-Good Naughts. You'd really better be careful:
               the gods will rescind your blessings . . . and who's responsible? You.
               They're giving you half the money. Take it, and have a drink or two
               and a roll or two with the hooker. Come on and celebrate!

CURMUDGE.:   So what do I celebrate when I take a drink in the spot,
               the very spot, where my only son's life was ruined?

ÆSYCOME: Just drink.

CURMUDGE.:   Oh, well. The way of the world. No matter how utterly shameful,
disgraceful, *and* disgusting it is, I'll steel myself
to the task. *I shall endure.*

(An awkward pause, then timidly to Bacchis One.)

One question: when you and my son
get down on the couch, do I *watch?*

BACCHIS I: God, no! The Guest is *you,*
beside me, fully entitled to every kiss and embrace.

CURMUDGE.:

(Aside.)

What now? My head's started itching. Oh, damn. It's really a strain
to say NO over and over.

BACCHIS I: Haven't you noticed that Life
is highly abridged and condensed, even for those who enjoy it?
Last Chance, buster. Chuck it away today, and your gusto
is lost forever. Going, going . . .

CURMUDGE.:   So what's my option?

ÆSYCOME: Questions, questions . . .

CURMUDGE.:   Well, I'm afraid.

BACCHIS I: Of what?

CURMUDGE.:   Of losing
clout to my son. And that slave.

BACCHIS I: Poor baby, what's with *clout?*
The boy's your son: so where does he get his money, except from
the sums you choose to disburse *at your whim?*

(The crusher. Curmudgeous goes into an aside.)

CURMUDGE.:   Right through to the marrow.
Does this mean she's prevailing over firm convictions,
the sanctions I sunk in stone?

(The struggle over, he relaxes into Bacchis One's arms.)

—Oh, well. My disrepute
is complete, and through your efforts.

(He thinks this over for a beat, then, happily:)

It's all *your fault!*

BACCHIS I: It would be a little nicer, if you expended *some* effort,
rather than leaning on me.

(Curmudgeous cooperates in the embrace.)

                                        But I'm to take this, then,
              as your fixed conviction?

CURMUDGE.:   What I say once, I never change.

BACCHIS I: It's getting late. So go inside. The couch is waiting.
              Also your sons, who long . . .

CURMUDGE.:   To see us breathe our last, *toute de suite.*

SISSY: And evening is nigh. So, gentlemen, right this way.

CURMUDGE.:   You lead,
              we follow. Your downcast, insolvent slaves.

BACCHIS I:

              (To the audience.)

                                        An elegant outcome:
              the dads lay traps for their boys, but bag themselves instead.

(Sissy leading, the two couples move into Bacchis One's house. A pause, and the
Producer, the leader of the company, appears, to speak the Moral Epilogue.)

PRODUCER: The Management's Standard Disclaimer:
                                        These fathers were certified
              rotten from earliest youth,
                                or else they wouldn't have acted
              in such a revolting fashion as set forth here today.
              In fact, if we hadn't observed before, with our very own eyes,
              delinquent daddies jostling with sons at houses of shame,
              we simply would have refused to produce this play.
                                                    Spectators,
              we hope your health is sufficient to accord us hearty applause.

Finis

The Mother-In-Law

HECYRA

PVBLIVS
Deena Berg
TERENTIVS AFER

Introduction to *The Mother-in-Law*

As confessed by Terence in his prologues, the first two productions of *The Mother-in-Law* (*Hecyra*), in 165 and 160 B.C., were disasters. Based on a Greek original by Apollodorus, the script could not withstand the immediate competition of tightrope walkers and gladiators. A repeat performance in 160 B.C. was, however, well received.

Some critics have taken the first two fiascoes as proof that the play was, and still is, a flop. Not so. If the ancient audience swallowed the eloquent, tongue-in-cheek legal defense delivered by Lucius Ambivius Turpio prior to the third performance, so should we. But *The Mother-in-Law* is not the usual fare we expect from Roman New Comedy—not even from Terence. Only the brilliant rendering of the muddled family communication keeps the comic from teetering into the tragic.

Blame is the driving force of the play, hurled in rapid succession between characters uncharacteristic of New Comedy. Sostrata, the title role, is far from the meddlesome nag that comes to mind when mothers-in-law are mentioned. She seems, in fact, to be a loving wife, mother, and mother-in-law. These qualities do not stop her husband Laches from blaming her when their new daughter-in-law runs back home. Laches is so convinced by his own sputtering accusations and self-righteous rhetoric that he does not need to stoop to questions or facts. When Pamphilus arrives, he takes up where his father leaves off and shifts the blame back to his new bride Philumena (who never appears onstage). Enter Phidippus, Philumena's father, who then turns around and blames the girl's mother, Myrrina. Even Parmeno, the family slave who by New Comedy standards should be the all-seeing genius behind the solution, assumes blame needlessly and wanders in the dark. When the finger is finally pointed at Pamphilus (the right place for the wrong reason), he too runs away. The only individual who seems to be self-aware, communicative, and nonjudgmental is Bacchis, the hard-nosed prostitute whom Pamphilus was forced to give up. In New Comedy's most ironic ending, she is the one who resolves the family's problems.

The play deals with serious issues: mistrust between husband and wife, miscommunication between parent and child, rape and responsibility. In this regard, Terence has echoes in modern semiserious situation comedies, such as Norman Lear's *All in the Family.* In *The Mother-in-Law,* a "feel-good" ending, with the traditional revelation of all the facts, would be unthinkable. Even Pamphilus expresses his relief that such a finale does not take place:

> *placet non fieri hoc ititdem ut in comeodiis*
> *omnia omnes ubi resciscunt.*
> (No need for one of those comic endings where everyone
> finds out everything.)

The audience cannot help but wonder whether justice has really been served and whether understanding and trust will ever arise within and between the two families.

Set and staging are remarkable for the lack of gimmickry. Subtle details differentiate the three houses, but the usual gap between "fun-loving-house-of-pleasure" and "sober-domain-of-upright-citizen" should not be as pronounced.

Eavesdropping and asides are kept to a minimum; the play depends upon intimate conversations—gossip, deal-making, confession—which require a special venue, and who better than Venus to provide such a place. A statue of the goddess stands between the houses of Laches and Bacchis, so that under the watch of Love herself the frayed knot of romance is repaired—for the moment.

Texts and Commentaries: I relied on the Oxford text edited by Robert Kauer and W. M. Lindsay, *P. Terenti Afri Comoediae,* "Oxford Classical Texts" (Oxford: Clarendon Press, 1926; repr. 1979), and the commentary by T. F. Carney, *Hecyra P. Terenti Afri,* "Proceedings of the African Classical Associations, Supplement, no. 2." (Classical Association of Rhodesia and Nyassaland, 1963).

Deena Berg

Basic Set

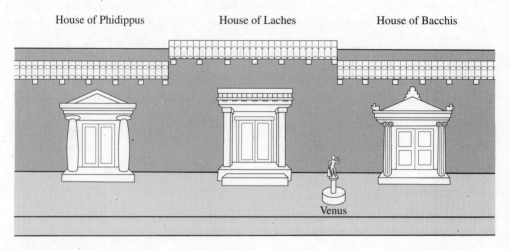

House of Phidippus   House of Laches   House of Bacchis

Venus

To the harbor
(stage right)

To downtown
(stage left)

SCENE: *A street in Athens, fronted by three houses. Center stage is the house of Laches, a wealthy but conservative residence, with a small flight of steps leading up to the door. Stage right is the house of Phidippus, also respectable but less opulent. Stage left is the house of Bacchis, not terribly ornate, but flashier than its neighbors. Between the houses of Laches and Bacchis is a statue of Venus on a pedestal, which is surrounded by a circular base suitable for sitting. Stage right leads to the harbor. Stage left leads downtown.*

Dramatis Personae

PHILOTIS (*fill-OH-tis*)   a young courtesan

SYRA (*SEAR-a*)   an old courtesan

BACCHIS (*BAH-kiss*)   a young courtesan, ex-girlfriend of Pamphilus

TWO SERVANTS TO BACCHIS

PAMPHILUS (*PAM-fill-us*)   a young husband

LACHES (*LAH-keys*)   Pamphilus's father

SOSTRATA (*SOS-tra-ta*)   Pamphilus's mother

PARMENO (*PAR-men-o*)   the family servant

TWO BAGGAGE BOYS

PHILUMENA (*fill-u-MEE-na*)   Pamphilus's young wife (does not appear)

PHIDIPPUS (*fi-DIP-pus*)   Philumena's father

MYRRINA (*MERE-in-a*)   Philumena's mother

SOSIA (*SO-si-a*)   the family servant

The Mother-in-Law

Prologue I [1–8]

Today's performance is titled the *The Mother-in-Law.*
An unprecedented portent upstaged the premiere
and created such a disaster, the play was neither
seen nor heard: to wit, an ominous flock
of funambulists appeared overhead, leaving
the audience awed and utterly dazed in amazement.
The present version is totally new to ensure
a pristine production: the author had no intention
of doubling his earnings by staging a twice-told tale.
You've seen the rest of his plays; please watch this one, too.

Prologue II[1] [9–57]

Ladies and Gentlemen:
Forget for the moment my actor's attire and let me play
the attorney. May the court permit a successful appeal,
and grant me, despite my years, that same due process of law
I once enjoyed in my youth, when I rehabilitated
unpopular plays and let them grow old with our plaudits, instead
of grow mold with their playwrights.
                              Recall, if you will, those early works
by Caecilius,[2] performed and produced by me. At times
I was booed off the boards; at times I barely clung to the curtain.
But knowing that showbiz is fickle at best, I redoubled my efforts
despite my doubts, and restaged the aforementioned flops. I carefully
bolstered—not bludgeoned—the poet's burgeoning ego, ergo
ensuring new plays to produce.
                              Yes, thanks to my efforts, these works
were seen by the public: once given fair hearing, favor was instant.
And so I restored to his proper place a poet almost
debarred by the barbs of his foes, a poet poised to abandon
his calling, his craft, his theatrical career. But IF
I had scorned his scripts in that very moment of crisis, IF
I had chosen to quash his zeal, to make him retire instead
of rewrite, I could have easily put the kibosh on his work.
And now, for my sake, consider this case with open minds.

---

[1] Presented by Lucius Ambivius Turpio, a famous actor and producer of the play, in 160 B.C.

[2] Caecilius Statius, an early comic poet.

I bring you—yet again—*The Mother-in-Law,* a play
so stifled by strife, NOT ONCE have I finished my lines
in peace. But YOUR good taste, protectress of our production,
will muffle such hubbub.
                                Forget, if you will, Premiere Number One.
First, fanfare goes up for a heavyweight match. Then word runs
        round
that the Fabulous Flying Flavians are about to walk the ropes.
Fans flood in, women cry out,
                                I exit unheard.
But holding fast to my long-standing motto "Never Give Up,"
I try again.
                Let us also forget Premiere Number Two.
A triumphant first act, then someone hollers "Gladiators!"
The wild-eyed throngs converge: they shove, they shout,
they wrestle over the seats while I barely escape with my own.

Today we have no roiling rumpus, just peace and quiet.
I have plenty of time to perform, and YOU have the chance
to festoon this season's festive stage with praise and glory.
Forfend that comedy fall to the hands of only a few:
as backers and boosters of art, let YOUR weight lend weight to
        MINE.
My business never has been to fatten my bottom line;
I made up my mind long ago to reap my greatest reward
by serving your greater interests. In return, I ask the court
to grant my humble petition:
                                Protect this playwright, whose work
now lies in my custody, and whose fate now rests in your hands;
do not let his jaundiced detractors deride and condemn him unjustly.
Take this case to heart, for my sake, and give it your ear,
that others might take up their pens, thus paving the way in the
        future
for me to produce new plays paid out of my own private pocket.

Act I, Scene 1 [58–75]

(Philotis and Syra enter from the house of Bacchis and sit down on the statue base.)

PHILOTIS: Honestly, Syra! You have to look high and low
                in this business to find a man who won't cheat on you now.
                Just take this guy Pamphilus: over and over he swore
                to Bacchis—and so straight-faced you had to believe him—

(She places her hand on her heart.)

                "Upon my honor, I'll wed no woman 'til death
                do us part." Then poof! He's a married man.

SYRA: And THAT
        is why I constantly warn you, constantly badger you,
        NOT TO PITY THE CLIENT!
                                    Once you take 'em
        captive,
                    it's whack 'em,
                            hack 'em,
                                and sack 'em!

PHILOTIS: With no
        exceptions?

SYRA: None. A man's surrender is always
        conditional. The hearts and flowers are merely
        a ploy: his real objective is maximum whoopee
        at minimum price. So tell me, why not return
        the favor? Strike back first with a sneak attack!

PHILOTIS: But heck! It's not nice to treat them all the same.

SYRA: NOT NICE to wreak havoc upon the enemy line?
        NOT NICE to swindle the troops with the very same swizz
        they use on you?
                        Such a pity, the waste! If only
        I had your youth, your looks. Or you had my brains.

Act I, Scene 2 [76–197]

(Parmeno enters from the house of Laches, still speaking to someone inside.)

PARMENO: Be sure to tell the old man—IN CASE he comes looking—
        I've just gone down to the docks to see when Pamphilus
        might ship in. You got that, Scirtus? You tell him
        ONLY if he asks. If he doesn't ask,
        then don't volunteer; let's keep this excuse nice and fresh
        for the next time.

(Aside, as he notices the women.)

                        Is that Philotis I see? Where on earth
        has she been hiding?

(Aloud.)

                        Philotis, how lovely to see you!

(He rushes over to kiss her hand.)

PHILOTIS: Oh, Parmeno! Nice indeed to see you too!

SYRA: A helluva pleasure, Parmeno.

(She extends her hand to be kissed.)

PARMENO:

> (he pauses and then shakes Syra's hand heartily.)

> > > And dammit, Syra,
> > the same to you.

> (An awkward silence. Parmeno clears his throat until Syra gets up and goes back into the house of Bacchis. He then sits down and snuggles up to Philotis.)

> > > So tell me, Philotis, dear,
> > where have you been amusing yourself these days?

PHILOTIS: I wasn't amused the least tiny bit. I went off
with that beastly baboon of a captain, and next thing I knew,
I was cooped up in Corinth. Two whole years I suffered
that man. It was awful, just awful.

PARMENO:

> (As he pats her hand.)

> > > > Good god! My poor
> > Philotikins! I bet you were itching for Athens
> > half the time! You must have kicked yourself
> > for not being pickier.

PHILOTIS: I can't tell you how desperate I was
to dump old soldier-boy and thumb a ride back.
My heart ached for friends,
> > > freedom,
> > > > and decent hors d'oeuvres.
There it was always "Permission to speak, sir"—and only
whatever he wanted to hear.

PARMENO: Tsk, tsk. Your charming
chitchat smothered by all that official hoo-ha.

PHILOTIS: But what's going on with Pamphilus? Bacchis herself
just gave me the news inside a few moments ago.
I never imagined he'd ever stoop to marry
another woman as long as SHE

> (She nods toward the house of Bacchis.)

> > > was around.

PARMENO: Oh, can you REALLY call it a marriage?

PHILOTIS: What do you mean?
He did get married, didn't he?

PARMENO: He did. But I fear
the blessed union is teetering on the rocks.

PHILOTIS: May the merciful gods send down a divorce—whatever will help our Bacchis. But Parmeno, make me believe you.

PARMENO: It's not for public knowledge. Don't twist my arm.

PHILOTIS: Just because you don't want it out in the open?
I swear to god, I have no intention of breathing
a word. I promise. I just want a little something
—strictly hush-hush—for my own peace of mind.

PARMENO: A promise
from YOU? That's hardly a reason to risk my patootie.

PHILOTIS: Come now, Parmeno, don't play hard to get.
This secret is killing you even more than me.

PARMENO:

(Aside.)

She's right about that. I'm a pathological blabber.

(To Philotis.)

Okay. If you swear you'll keep quiet, I'll tell you.

PHILOTIS: Now THAT'S
the old spirit! I promise. So spill.

PARMENO:

(He looks around and leans toward her.)

                                                     Listen up.

PHILOTIS: I'm listening.

PARMENO: Pamphilus HAD been as wildly in love as ever
with Bacchis, when Laches—his father—began to give him
the standard "When are you going to get married?" routine.
With all the classic fatherly lines, including:
"I won't live forever";
                              "You ARE my only son";
and, "A grandchild before I die—that's all I ask."
"Forget it," was Pamphilus's first reaction. But Laches
really sat on him hard, and Pamphilus started
to waffle, torn between love and his duty to Daddy.
The old man hammered and hounded and got what he wanted:
namely, Pamphilus engaged to the girl next door.

(He nods toward the house of Phidippus.)

Pamphilus shrugged it off with no second thought.
And then, his wedding day dawns.
                              The buffet arrives.
He suddenly sees there is nowhere to go but the altar.

Heartsick, he fumbles through. I think Bacchis herself
—had she BEEN there, of course—would have pitied the sight.
Whenever he had a minute alone, he'd come
and cry on my shoulder:
                              "Oh, Parmeno, why did I do it?
Could I have dug my grave any deeper? I just can't
go on. I'm done for, Parmeno. Doomed. Destroyed."

PHILOTIS:

(She shakes her fist at the house of Laches.)

O, curse you, Laches, and all of your nagging!

PARMENO: In short,
they got married. Their wedding night, he didn't touch her.
Next evening, nothing again.

(He leans in further and pauses.)

                              She's still a virgin.

PHILOTIS:

(She shoves him away.)

You CAN'T be serious. All those half-drunk hormones
between the sheets, and he's able to turn down a virgin?
NOT very likely. I think you're lying.

PARMENO: I thought
you'd say that. *You* have eager and ready buyers;
but SHE was a forced acquisition.

PHILOTIS: So then what happened?

PARMENO:

(He draws Philotis closer.)

A few days later he pulls me aside—away
from the house—and tells me the girl is still a virgin.
Before the wedding, he'd hoped that the marriage might work.
"But Parmeno, boy," he says, "I've made up my mind.
I just can't live like this any longer, dangling her
like a plaything. For her sake as well as mine,
I have to do what honor demands and give her
back to her parents—just the way I found her."

PHILOTIS: So according to YOU, he's devoted and decent at heart.

(She turns away. Parmeno pulls her back.)

PARMENO: "On the one hand," he says, "it won't do ME any good
to let any of this get out. On the other hand,

I can't return a perfectly normal girl
to her father—he'll think I think she's not good enough.
All I can hope is that once she figures things out
and sees I'm off-limits, she'll finally pack up and go."

PHILOTIS: And what happened meanwhile? He kept seeing Bacchis?

PARMENO: Daily.
                    But—you know how these things go. Alienation
                 of affection did not sit well with Bacchis.
                 She got very nasty and raised her rates on the spot.

PHILOTIS: Dear god, I'm not surprised.

PARMENO: But what REALLY unhitched
                 the two happened next: he started thinking.
                                                        Deeply.
                 First, about himself;
                                and then about HER,

(He nods toward the house of Bacchis.)

                 and then about the girl at home.

(He nods toward the house of Laches.)

                                                He contrasted
                 their habits, compared their styles. The one at home
                 was shy and modest, just as a lady should be.
                 She swallowed her husband's snubs and slights, kept all
                 of his nasty tantrums quiet.
                                        In part overcome
                 by pity for his wife,
                                in part overwhelmed
                 by his lover's lack of compassion,
                                                he started to slip.
                 Little by little his love turned from Bacchis to home
                 and settled at last on his soul mate.
                                        Meanwhile, his uncle
                 drops dead on the far-off island of Imbros. The estate
                 goes straight into probate, demanding the family's presence.
                 Pamphilus—now the loving bridegroom—resists.
                 But his father insists on shipping him off. The girl
                 stays here with her mother-in-law. The old man goes back
                 to the farm and hardly ever comes to town.

PHILOTIS: So where's the rocky marriage in all of this?

PARMENO: I'm about to tell you. At first things were fine—both mother
                 and daughter-in-law got along for several days.
                 But during that time Philumena—that's the new bride—

began despising Sostrata—that's her in-law.
Extremely peculiar behavior. Never a quarrel,
never an accusation.

PHILOTIS: What went on?

PARMENO: Whenever Sostrata tried to sit down and chat,
Philumena suddenly vanished. Refused to talk.
She finally couldn't stand any more and ran home.
Pretended her mother needed her there for some sacred
celebration. Day after day goes by,
and Sostrata sends for the girl. They send back some flimsy
excuse. She sends again: no answer. Frequent
requests ensue: they claim the girl is sick.
Then Sostrata goes to visit but can't get in
the door.
            The old man—my boss—found out, and rode back
from the farm last night. Approached Philumena's dad
for a man-to-man chat right away. I don't know what happened.
However, I'm deeply concerned about this turn
of events.
            Well, there you have it. The entire story.
I'd better go now. I have a boat to meet.

PHILOTIS: Me too. I have a business appointment. A foreign
client.

PARMENO: May the gods bless your every transaction.

PHILOTIS: See you later.

PARMENO: You too, Philotis, dear.

(Parmeno exits stage right. Philotis exits stage left.)

Act II, Scene 1 [198–242]

(Laches enters from his house, followed by Sostrata.)

LACHES: In the name of god and every decent man
alive!
            It's a plot!
                    Women!
                            What a conniving
species!
            They WANT the same things, they HATE the same things.
Not the slightest degree of deviation between
any two. Mothers-in-law hate daughters-in-law—
no exceptions.
            The same damn rule applies to their husbands:
each must be opposed with exactly the same

unflagging pigheaded zeal.
                           And why? I have
a theory: it's due to the fact that they share the same
alma mater—"Our Lady of Marital Discord"—headed,
of course, by that shining beacon of bile: MY WIFE.

SOSTRATA: My goodness gracious, what are you blaming ME for?
I can't imagine!

LACHES: Hah! You "can't imagine"?

SOSTRATA: I haven't a clue! May heaven have mercy, Laches,
my dear, and let us grow old as one!

LACHES: God forbid!

SOSTRATA: Your accusations are groundless. One day you'll wake up
and see.

LACHES: I'm wide awake. And as for grounds,
I have plenty. Words can't begin to describe what you've done.
You've besmirched yourself, your husband, your whole family tree!
You've filled your son's life with woe!
                          You've made enemies out of
his in-laws—OUR FRIENDS—who judged him a nice enough boy
to trust with their only daughter. With no help at all,
YOU and your shocking behavior have mucked up this marriage.

SOSTRATA: ME?

LACHES: Yes, I mean you! The woman who thinks
my skull is so full of boulders, there's no room for brains!
Or is it you think I spend so much time on the farm
that I'm not aware of what you're up to? In fact,
I'm far more aware of the goings-on here than what's on-going
out there. And I'll tell you precisely why: what YOU do
in private directly affects my public image.

Yes, I've known it a while: Philumena can't stand you.
I'm not the least bit amazed—quite the contrary.
If indeed she could, I'd be far more surprised. But I hardly
guessed that she'd hate the whole household! Had I but known,
then SHE'D be at home, and YOU'D be out on your ear.

Just look at the grief you've caused! I deserve so much better!
I'm out on the farm pushing production for your sake,
still laying out income so you and the boy can live high
on the hog. I haven't let up, despite the fact
I should have retired years ago. And what
do I get in return? You couldn't care less how I'm hurt.

SOSTRATA: I swear, this isn't my fault. I had no stake in this whatsoever.

LACHES:
           I beg to differ. Quite the opposite.
YOU were the only one here, so it's ALL YOUR FAULT!
You're stuck with it, Sostrata! Don't you remember our deal?
I relieved you of all obligations save one: that you stay
and handle things here. Now aren't you ashamed of yourself?
A woman your age picking fights with a teenage girl!
Are you trying to tell me, in fact it's HER fault?

SOSTRATA:
                                      Laches,
sweetheart, that's hardly what I said.

LACHES:
                          I'm damn glad
to hear it, at least for our son's sake. You, of course,
have nothing to lose by being offensive.

SOSTRATA:
                              Laches,
darling, how do you know that she isn't pretending
to hate me? Maybe she just wants to spend more time
with her mother.

LACHES:
                 How can you say that? How much proof
is required? Yesterday not a soul would let you
come in when you tried to see her!

SOSTRATA:
                       They said she was terribly
sick. And THAT is the reason they wouldn't let me
come in.

LACHES:
            A chronic case of "in-law-itis,"
I gather. Due to your noxious nature more
than anything else. I'm hardly surprised. You women
spend your days cajoling your sons into marriage,
providing, of course, that YOU get to make the match.
You nag, and he drags the girl across the threshold;
you nag, and he drags the very same girl out the door.

Act II: Scene 2 [243–273]

(Phidippus enters from his house, still speaking to his daughter Philumena inside.)

PHIDIPPUS:
Philumena, I know I have every right to make you
do as I say, but I can't fight my fatherly feelings.
Do what you want. Daddy won't stand in your way.

LACHES:
I believe I see Phidippus coming! Excellent
timing! He'll help me get to the bottom of this.
Phidippus, I know I'm prone to indulge my nearest
and dearest in all of their whims, but not to the point
of letting my sunny and flexible nature spoil

their characters. Now, if you followed my example,
both of our houses would be better off. But I see
your females have you wrapped around their pinkies.

PHIDIPPUS: That so?

LACHES: Last night I came over on serious business,
the subject—your daughter. You sent me away no less
confused than when I came. It just isn't nice
to keep your grudge all bottled up—that is,
if you want this marriage to last. If we did something wrong,
speak up! We'll straighten it out or apologize.
You be the judge as to how we should make amends.

On the other hand, if you're keeping the girl away
because she truly is sick, and you fear she'll receive
inadequate care in my home, I feel most grossly
offended. As long the loving gods smile upon me,
I'll never admit—despite the fact that you ARE
her father—that you wish her hale and hearty more than
I. Yes, I do all the more for the sake of my son,
who hardly thinks less of her than he does of himself.
I'm sure it will hit him hard—no secret there—
if he happens to find that his wife has gone home. And THAT
is why I'm anxious for her to come back before he does.

PHIDIPPUS: Laches, you and family have shown us constant
concern and ready kindness. I'm sure what you say
is just as you say. I'm taking it all to heart.
And I want you to trust me when I tell you, I'm EAGER
to send her back, if there's any way I can do it.

LACHES: What's in your way? Oh ho! Don't tell me she's blaming
her husband!

PHIDIPPUS: Not at all. You see, I started
to nudge her harder, to pressure her into returning.
But then she swore up and down that as long as Pamphilus
was away, she wouldn't set foot in your house.
We all have our faults; I'm afraid I was born easygoing.
I can't say no to my family.

LACHES:

(To Sostrata.)

          Now WHAT did I tell you,
Sostrata?

SOSTRATA: Mercy! This doesn't look good.

LACHES:

   (To Phidippus.)

                                 That's it?

      Are you sure?

PHIDIPPUS: I guess—at least for now. Something else?
        I need to go downtown.

LACHES: I'll keep you company.

   (Laches and Phidippus exit stage left.)

Act II: Scene 3 [274–280]

SOSTRATA: Heaven have mercy! Because of a few wayward wives
           who make all women look equally bad, our spouses
           saddle the bulk of us with unequal justice.
           As far as my husband's accusations go,
           I swear by the blessed gods, I AM NOT GUILTY!
           But clearing my name won't be easy. Men are stuck
           on the notion that mothers-in-law are unjustifiably
           evil.
               But I'm not like that at all, by god!
           I've always treated the girl just like my own daughter!
           I don't understand how this could happen to me!
           And I hope and pray that Pamphilus comes home soon.

   (She exits into her house.)

Act III, Scene 1 [281–335]

   (Pamphilus and Parmeno enter stage right.)

PAMPHILUS: Has any man's path been plagued by more bitter pitfalls
           of love?
                I think not.
                    Poor me.
                        For this I clung
        to my slender thread of life?
                      For this I champed
      at the bit to come home?
                    Hardly.
                        Far better to spend
        the rest of my days in the wilds of somewhere or other,
        than find myself stuck in this tragic mess, staring misery
        right in the eyes. Adversity strikes anytime,
        anywhere; for us, the afflicted, those prior moments
        of ignorant bliss are all we have in the bank.

   (He sits down on the statue base.)

PARMENO: But look at it this way: the sooner you find out what happened,
             the sooner you dig a way out. If you hadn't come back,
             the deadly looks might have flared into open warfare.
             I'm absolutely positive, Pamphilus: the moment
             they see you, they'll both think twice. You'll sift through the facts,
             smooth out their feathers, and have them chatting away
             in no time. You've burdened your bosom with nothing but fluff.

PAMPHILUS: Why try to console me? Can anyone—name any city—
             lay claim to a greater web of woe? Before
             I brought THIS girl home, I was completely in love with another.
             I gave her my heart. But Daddy got pushy. I didn't dare
             turn down his choice. My situation was patent,
             my grief—though silent—clear to the casual observer.
             Scarcely had I disengaged myself
             from my first true love and sorted through my feelings,
             scarcely had I started to fall for the new girl,
             when LO AND BEHOLD! A new crisis rears up to drag me
             away from HER.
                                   It has to be SOMEBODY'S fault—
             I presume I'll find it's my mother's—or my wife's.
             And when I DO pin the blame, what's the net result?
             Instantaneous wretchdom and sorrow.
                                                 I have to shrug off
             my mother's conduct, Parmeno—duty demands it.
             But I'm also in debt to my wife: she put up with my insults
             so sweetly, and never let out a peep to the world.
             Whatever it was, it must have been truly enormous,
             Parmeno. Big enough to split them apart
             and keep them angry a very, very long time.

PARMENO: Oh nonsense! It's teensy at most, I swear to god.
             Apply, if you will, a bit of basic logic:
             major hysteria does not imply major harm.
             Assume minor offense "A"; the cool-headed type
             —let's call him "X"—will shrug it off with a smile;
             but "Y"—the crotchety sort—will hold a grudge for life.
             Yes, youngsters squabble over the silliest things,
             and why? Because their tender young minds are wobbly,
             bobbing around like rudderless ships.
                                                 Those women
             are just as childish: thoughts like mush. One word
             was probably all it took to fire them up.

PAMPHILUS: Go inside now, Parmeno. Tell them I'm back.

   (Muffled chaos is heard from inside the house of Phidippus.)

PARMENO: Whoa! What's all this?

PAMPHILUS: Shut up. I hear some kind
    of commotion—people running back and forth.

PARMENO: Come on. I'll sneak up to the door.

(More noise and screaming from inside.)

                            Hey, did you hear THAT?

PAMPHILUS: Would you stop with the blabber? My god, I heard a scream.

(He leaps up from the statue base.)

PARMENO: Oh, *I* can't talk, but it's fine for you.

(More moaning, then shushing noises.)

MYRRINA:

(From within.)

                            Philumena,
    sweetheart, keep quiet! I beg you!

PAMPHILUS: That voice! It sounds like
    Philumena's mother. I'm sunk!

PARMENO: Why's that?

PAMPHILUS: I'm doomed!

PARMENO: How come?

PAMPHILUS: No doubt about it, Parmeno.
    They're hiding something big and awful from me.

PARMENO: They did say something was giving your wife the shakes.
    Maybe that's what's going on. Just a guess.

PAMPHILUS: I'm double doomed! Why didn't you say so before?

PARMENO: I can't spit it all out at once!

PAMPHILUS: What does she have?

PARMENO: I don't know.

PAMPHILUS: How's that? Didn't anyone call a doctor?

PARMENO: I don't know.

PAMPHILUS: Well, why I am dawdling here instead
    of dashing inside to find out? Philumena, my love,
    in what shattered state shall I stumble upon you? Whatever
    threatens your life will have to take my life too.

(He runs into the house of Phidippus.)

PARMENO: No point in me going after him. My hunch

is those people can't stand us. Yesterday no one
invited Sostrata in. If the girl gets much sicker—
I hope not, of course, for the sake of my boss—but they'll say
that Sostrata's slave was inside,

                  that it's ALL MY FAULT,
that *I* was the one who brought in some sort of a plague
to ruin everyone's health and welfare, and made
the girl even worse. Then Sostrata gets all the blame,
and I find myself up to my neck in hot water.

Act III, Scene 2 [336–360]

(Sostrata emerges from the house of Laches.)

SOSTRATA: I've been listening to all of the fuss next door for goodness knows
how long! Oh, dear me! I'm afraid Philumena's
condition has taken a turn for the worse.

                        Ye gods
of Health and Good Hygiene, I pray, do not let this happen!
I'll go see her now.

(She heads towards the door of the house of Phidippus.)

PARMENO: Ahem. Sostrata, ma'am?

SOSTRATA: Who's that?

PARMENO: They'll just lock you out in the cold again.

SOSTRATA: Oh Parmeno, is that you? I'm utterly lost.
Tell me, what's a poor mother to do? I can't go
visit Pamphilus's wife, who's lying here sick
next door?

PARMENO: Go visit? Don't even send someone
to visit for you. Loving a person who finds you
vile—in my book that counts for two dumb mistakes.
For the former party, a waste of good effort; for the latter,
a big fat annoyance.

             Besides, your son went in
right when he got here to find out how she's doing.

SOSTRATA: What's that? Did you say Pamphilus? Here?

PARMENO: Just arrived.

SOSTRATA: Oh, thank heavens! My goodness, once more I feel hope
in my heart. What a load off my mind!

PARMENO: Which is why I don't want you
going inside. As soon as they have a moment
alone—assuming Philumena's pain
lets up a bit—I'm sure she'll spill all the details

about your rift and how the hostilities started.
Lo and behold! I see him coming out now!
And boy, does he look depressed!

SOSTRATA: My dear sweet son!

(Pamphilus emerges from the house of Phidippus, sniffling and wiping his eyes.)

PAMPHILUS: Oh. Hello, Mother.

SOSTRATA: I'm so happy you're safe and sound.
Philumena? Is SHE doing better?

PAMPHILUS: Well, just a smidge.

SOSTRATA: May heaven help her! But why are you crying, if that's
the case? Son, why do you look so sad?

(She takes out a handkerchief and dabs at his eyes.)

PAMPHILUS: It's nothing,
Mother.

SOSTRATA: Then what was all that uproar? Tell me!
A sudden stab of pain?

PAMPHILUS: Uh, yes. That's it.
That's exactly what happened.

SOSTRATA: What does she have?

PAMPHILUS: A fever.

SOSTRATA: Daily?

PAMPHILUS: That's what they say. But please go inside now,
Mother. I'll be there soon.

SOSTRATA: All right.

(She exits into the house of Laches.)

PAMPHILUS: Parmeno,
go find the baggage boys and give them a hand
with my luggage.

(He turns away and weeps into the handkerchief.)

PARMENO: Why should I? Can't they find their OWN way
home?

(Pamphilus blows his nose, and turns back to Parmeno.)

PAMPHILUS: Well, what are you waiting around for? MOVE!

(Parmeno exits stage right. Pamphilus paces back and forth in front of the statue.)

Act III, Scene 3 [361–414]

PAMPHILUS: I can't even begin to describe what happened. A bolt
right out of the blue. My eyes and ears couldn't take any more.
I had to get myself out and fast—I almost fainted
right there on the spot.
                              Just moments ago
I rushed in, afraid—no, convinced—I would see my wife
writhing in pain, wracked by some OTHER
affliction than that upon which I stumbled.
                                              Poor me.
When the servants saw I was back, they were totally caught
off guard. All at once they burst into cheers and yelled
"He's here!"
                    And then I noticed they suddenly all
turned pale—my timing couldn't have been any worse.
Meanwhile, one of them scurried off to announce
my arrival. Dying to see my wife, of course,
I charged straight in.
                          And then, when I got to her room,
the diagnosis was instantly clear.
                                        I'm cursed.
They had no chance to cover it up; what else could she do
but moan and holler, given her condition?
And then—right after I had an eyeful—I said:
"OH! SHAME ON YOU!"
                            and tore myself away,
my cheeks wet with tears, my emotions topsy-turvy
because of this heinous, shocking event.
                                          Her mother,
Myrrina, came right behind me; when I reached the door,
she fell to her knees, and HER cheeks were wet with tears.
Poor thing—I just had to have pity. There's no doubt about it,
in my opinion: whether we're haughty or humble,
it's all in how the cookies crumble.
                                    And then
she made the following speech:
                                  "Oh, Pamphilus, dear,
you see why she had to leave you. Some shameless cad
—I don't know who—had his way with her before
her wedding. She's hiding out here, to keep the birth
a secret from you and everyone else."
                                      When I think
of her words, I can't help but weep. OH GOD, WHY ME?
And then she said:
                        "In the name of whatever fate

that brought you here today, in the name of justice,
in the name of god, we beg you—the both of us—
please keep this accident secret and don't tell a soul.

Oh, Pamphilus, dear, if you ever felt her tender
feelings for you, all she asks is for you to return
the favor—is that so much trouble? As for taking her back,
you do what's best for you. No one but you
even knows she's gone into labor; no one but you
knows you're not the father. They tell me two months went by
before you slept together, and now it's seven
months all told since the two of you were married,
and—I'm sure you know how to count.
                                    Oh, Pamphilus, dear,
if it's in any way possible, I very much want—
and I'm doing whatever I can—to make sure that her father
and everyone else is clueless about the birth.
But if there's no way to keep them from finding out,
I'll say she lost the baby. I'm sure that no one
will be suspicious; they'll naturally assume that it's yours.
We'll give the baby away as soon as we can.[3]
None of this will be any bother to you;
all you'll have done is covered up the outrageous
insult done to my innocent daughter."
                                    I promised
not to talk. And I'm determined to show
I'm a man of my word.
                      But take her back? In MY
opinion, it goes against all sense of honor—
although the loving moments we spent together
do weigh on my mind. I weep at the thought
of my days ahead, a life of inconsolable
solitude. O Fortune, how briefly you smile!
But previous heartache has taught me the hardships of love:
I gave up Bacchis by choice; and now I must turn
to the task of forgetting Philumena.

(He glances right.)

                                    Here comes
Parmeno, baggage boys in tow. Well, no need
in the least for him to find out: he's the only one
who knows I avoided my wife for weeks right after
the wedding. I'm afraid if he hears her shrieking again

---

[3] The practice referred to by Terence is actually exposure *(expositio),* the practice of putting infants out in the wild to die or be picked up by strangers. This might be used in cases in which the child was deformed or was the product of rape or incest.

and again, he'll figure out she's in labor. I need
to send him off on some goose-chase, until she delivers.

(He walks over and paces in front of the door to Laches' house.)

Act III, Scene 4 [415–450]

(Parmeno enters with Sosia, stage right. The baggage boys follow.)

PARMENO: You say the trip was something less than comfy?

SOSIA: Dammit, Parmeno! Words can't describe the utter
nightmare of sea travel.

PARMENO: That bad?

SOSIA: You lucky dog.
You've never been to sea: you have no idea
what misery you've missed. But I'll skip the minor horrors
and get to the worst part: there I was, on board
for thirty days—maybe more—waiting for death
with every wave. Our weather was that lousy.

PARMENO: Nasty stuff.

SOSIA: Don't tell me. If I ever found out
I had to go back, I swear I'd run away.

PARMENO: That's hardly a threat. Far limper excuses have forced you
to similar action, Sosia.

(Pamphilus coughs and continues pacing.)

                 Wait! I see Pamphilus
hanging around our front door.
                      Inside, everyone!
I'll go find out what he wants.

(Sosia and the other servants exit into the house of Laches. Parmeno approaches
Pamphilus.)

                   Still out here, sir?

PAMPHILUS: Indeed. I've been waiting for you.

PARMENO: What for?

PAMPHILUS: It's urgent!
I need someone to run to the temple.

(He indicates something very high offstage right.)

                 That temple
up there, on top of the hill![4]

---

[4] Terence refers to the holy district of the "high city" (acropolis), which usually required a good
climb.

PARMENO: What someone?

PAMPHILUS: You.

PARMENO: Way up there? What for?

PAMPHILUS: To find Callidemides—
my host on the isle of Mykonos. We sailed together.

PARMENO:

(Aside.)

It'll kill me. This boy must have sworn he'd give me a hernia
if Neptune would grant him safe trip home.

PAMPHILUS: Well, hurry!

PARMENO: What do you want me to tell him? Or perhaps
you want me to stand at the door and wave my fingers?

PAMPHILUS: No, of course not. I made an appointment to meet him
today. You tell him I can't, so he won't wait around.
Now, fly like the wind!

PARMENO: But I've never seen the man's face!

PAMPHILUS: Oh, I'll tell you what he looks like. Tall, uh, six feet.
Reddish face. Uh, curly hair. Uh, biggish
build. Uh, eyes—pale blue, washed out. In general,
he looks like a corpse.

PARMENO:

(Aside.)

Ugh. May the gods put him six feet
under before I get there!

(To Pamphilus.)

What should I do
if he doesn't show up? Just wait around until dark?

PAMPHILUS: That's fine. Now run.

PARMENO: I can't. I'm flagging already.

(He exits stage right.)

PAMPHILUS: He's gone. Now what do I do? O heaven, why
have you cursed me like this? I have no idea whatsoever
of how to keep secret what Myrrina
begged me not to tell: HER DAUGHTER IS HAVING
A BABY!
           I really do pity the woman. But still,
I must do what I can to do right by my mother and father.

Parents before passion—it's only the proper thing.
Oh no! Oh yes! I see Phidippus and Daddy—
they're coming this way! I don't know what to tell them.

Act III, Scene 5 [451–515]

(Laches and Phidippus enter stage left.)

LACHES: Didn't you say just now that your daughter was waiting
around for my son?

PHIDIPPUS: Yes, I did.

LACHES: They say he's returned.
So make her come back.

PAMPHILUS:

(Aside.)

                              What excuse can I give my father?
I don't know how to tell him I can't take her back.

LACHES: I just heard mumbling. Who's there?

PAMPHILUS:

(Aside to himself.)

                              Steady, now.
No changing course. Full speed ahead.

(He moves forward.)

LACHES: Ah, here's
the man himself.

PAMPHILUS: Hi, Daddy.

LACHES: Hello, Sonny Boy!

(He embraces Pamphilus.)

PHIDIPPUS: It's good to have you back here, Pamphilus. More
importantly, safe and sound.

(He shakes Pamphilus's hand.)

PAMPHILUS: Whatever you say, sir.

LACHES: Just got back?

PAMPHILUS: Just moments ago.

LACHES: So tell me,
what did cousin Phania leave us?

PAMPHILUS: Gosh.

To tell you the truth, old Phania was deeply devoted
to pleasure right up 'til the end. Not a second thought
about his heirs. In fact, his tombstone read,
"He lived to live it up."

LACHES: Is that all you brought back?
An epitaph?

PAMPHILUS: We made a little profit.

LACHES: Ah, but such a great loss. I wish he were still
alive and well.

PAMPHILUS: It's a pretty safe bet that wish
won't come true. He looked exceedingly dead.

(Aside.)

And I'm sure you like him better this way.

LACHES: Phidippus here
made his daughter come home to visit last night.

(He nudges Phidippus.)

                                   Tell him

you made her do it.

PHIDIPPUS:

(To Laches.)

             Stop poking me.

(To Pamphilus.)

                          Yes, I did.

LACHES: But now he's sending her back.

PAMPHILUS: Of course. I know
exactly what happened. I heard it all the minute
I landed.

LACHES: Damn those evil, loose-lipped old gossips!

PAMPHILUS:

(To Phidippus.)

    Sir, it is my belief that I've always avoided
giving your family any grounds for complaint;
in fact, if I felt like recalling how devoted, how kind,
how gentle I've been to your daughter, I certainly could—
but of course, I'd rather you heard it from her than from me.
Your faith in me will only be confirmed
when the woman who's done me such wrong admits that I've always

done right by her.
                              It wasn't my fault, I swear
to god. This breakup had nothing to do with me.
It's Philumena. SHE thinks she's too good to put up
with Mother's habits. The girl has no self-restraint,
not a whit of respect for her in-law's routine. And peace
cannot be restored by any other means
than separation: Phidippus, I'm forced to choose
between my mother and wife. My pursuit of personal
pleasure must yield to my sacred duty to Mother.

LACHES: Uh, Pamphilus, boy, my ears are pleased as punch
at what you've just said. It's great to know you have
your priorities straight; you've put all else but your parents
in second place. BUT you're angry, Pamphilus. Why not
cool off before you make such a rash decision?

PAMPHILUS: Angry, Daddy? Why would I be so unfair?
She's never done a thing against my will;
in fact, she often filled my every wish.
I love her, adore her; and I want her very badly:
I know firsthand just how nice she is.
But duty insists she be ripped perforce from my arms:
I hope and pray she lives out the rest of her life
with a man who is far more fortunate than I.

PHIDIPPUS: It's all in your hands to stop it.

LACHES: Assuming you had
any sense. Insist that she come back.

PAMPHILUS: I won't.
I've made my decision, Daddy: Mother comes first.

(He exits into the house of Laches.)

LACHES: Hey, where are you going? Wait a minute, I asked
you a question! Where are you going?

PHIDIPPUS: Why's he so stubborn?

LACHES: I told you so, Phidippus! Didn't I say
he would handle this badly? That's exactly why
I begged and begged you to send your daughter back.

PHIDIPPUS: For heaven's sake! The boy's a mule. I never
thought he could act so ugly. He thinks I'm going
to beg him? Hah! If he wants to get his wife back,
fine! If he doesn't, then let him hand over her dowry!

LACHES: Look at this! Now the both of you are gnashing
your teeth and ranting.

PHIDIPPUS:

> (He yells at the house of Laches.)

          TOO BIG FOR YOUR BOOTS NOW, PAMPHILUS!
WHAT A NICE WAY TO COME BACK HERE!

LACHES:

                              Angry though he
may be—and who can blame him?—this too shall pass.

PHIDIPPUS: That so? One itty-bitty inheritance
and boom: you're suddenly hoity-toity.

LACHES:

                      So now
you want to fuss at ME?

PHIDIPPUS:

                   He has until sundown
to think it over. And then I need an answer:
does he want her or not? If she can't be his,
then let her belong to somebody else.

> (He exits into his house.)

LACHES:

                    Phidippus!
Hold on a minute and hear a few words!
                      He's gone.
Oh, why do I care? Let the two of them thrash it out
'til they're finally happy. Neither he nor my son
have any respect for my wishes; they simply toss
my words away like trash.
                I know—I'll go inside
and take this out on my wife. This plot, after all,
is completely her fault. Yes, onward! To vent my spleen!

> (He exits into his house.)

Act IV, Scene 1 [516–576]

> (Myrrina enters from the house of Phidippus.)

MYRRINA: Eek!
        Am I in the soup!
                So now what to do?
And where to go?
              And what do I tell my husband?
I'm doomed!
          I think he heard the baby cry!
He suddenly ran into Philumena's room
without saying a single word!
                 But if he finds out
that she's given birth, what excuse do I give him now
for keeping the whole thing a secret? Heaven have mercy!

I haven't the faintest idea!

What's that creaking?

The door! He must be looking for me. I'm doomed!

(She grabs a broom and starts to sweep and whistle. Phidippus enters from his house.)

PHIDIPPUS: As soon as I ran to my daughter's side, my wife
ran straight out the door.

Aha! I see her now.

Well, Myrrina, what have you got to say?

(Myrrina whistles louder.)

Hey there! I'm talking to YOU!

MYRRINA: To ME, hubby dearest?

PHIDIPPUS: "Hubby dearest"? That so? I actually rank
as high on your list as "husband"—maybe even
up there with "human being"? If you ever thought
I was either one—"wifey poo"—you wouldn't have made
such an ass out of me with all your little—activities.

MYRRINA: Which ones?

PHIDIPPUS: As if you have to ask! Our daughter
has just had a baby!

(He pauses for Myrrina to answer; she doesn't.)

Your lips are sealed, eh?

WELL, WHOSE IS IT?

MYRRINA: That's NOT a nice thing for a father
to ask! God strike me dead as I stand here! WHOSE,
pray tell, do you think, but her lawfully wedded husband's?

(She points the broom at the house of Laches and glares at Phidippus.)

PHIDIPPUS: That's what I thought.

(He gives Myrrina a peck on the cheek.)

Ha ha. What else would a father assume?
But I'm very confused. Why did you go to the trouble
of hiding the birth from us all? Especially when
the baby popped out so healthy. And promptly too![5]

---

[5] According to the clues in the play, the baby is born seven months after the marriage. Phidippus has trouble reconciling the healthy appearance of the full-term baby with the math. He is perhaps in denial, not well-versed in female matters, or simply not all that good with numbers. The same applies to Pamphilus.

(He counts on his fingers, shakes his head, counts again, shakes his head, and then shrugs his shoulders.)

> You know very well the child would place our friendship
> with THEM

(He nods at the house of Laches.)

>   on a firmer foundation. Is the heart that pounds
> in your breast so stubborn you'd rather pitch the poor creature
> than see your daughter joined to a man you don't like?
> And there I was, heaping piles of blame on them,
> when the truth is, IT'S ALL YOUR FAULT!

MYRRINA:

(Aside.)

>   Oh doom doom DOOM.

PHIDIPPUS: If only I could remember what you said—
> Ah, now I know! You once said something about this,
> the day we welcomed the boy as our son-in-law.
> You said you couldn't stand to see your daughter
> go off with a man who was still in love with some floozy.
> How did you put it? "A man who sleeps out, not in."

MYRRINA:

(Aside.)

> Whatever excuse he wants—but not the truth!

PHIDIPPUS: I knew he had a girlfriend long before YOU did,
> Myrrina; still, I never held that goof
> against him—it's normal teenage behavior. By golly,
> he'll rake himself over the coals for it someday.
>   But YOU—
> as soon as you dug in your heels, you never stopped trying
> to snatch your daughter away and botch up my deal.
> Your intentions are perfectly clear from what happened today.

MYRRINA: Do you think my maternal instincts are twisted? If good
> were to come of this marriage for us, how could I think that?

PHIDIPPUS: Are you a judge or a prophet? How can you know
> what's good for us?
>   Maybe you heard some gossip:
> someone saw Pamphilus coming and going from what's-her-name's
> house. So what? As long as he was discreet—
> and didn't do it too often—wouldn't it
> be nicer for us to pretend we didn't notice,
> rather than nose around and make him hate us?

After all, he'd been dating the girl for quite a while.
If he suddenly dumped her without a second thought,
I don't believe he'd be a decent person,
much less a decent husband.

MYRRINA: For goodness sake,
will you put the boy and all you think I've done wrong
aside for a moment? Go talk to him—alone—
and ask him whether or not he wants his wife back.
If he says "yes," then send her over; but if
he doesn't, I did what was right for my daughter's future.

PHIDIPPUS: Even if that's the case, Myrrina, that HE
rejected her first and you were aware of his failings,
still, I was here. And I should have made
the decision. I'm hopping mad! I can't believe
you did this without even asking! You can't take the baby
outside this house. Wherever you want to take it,
you can't.

(He stomps toward the house of Laches and pauses.)
(Aside.)

                    I'm a bigger dope if I think if she plans
to pay attention! I'll go inside and order
the servants not to let the child out of sight.

(He exits into his own house.)

MYRRINA: Great gods above! Has any woman alive
reaped such a harvest of heartache?
                              No news to me
how he'll take it, if he finds out what really happened.
This little matter made him foam at the mouth,
and I don't know how to change his mind.
                                        And now
the only thing left to go wrong will go wrong,
if he makes me keep the child. We have no idea
who the father is. When my daughter's honor was plundered,
it was dark: she couldn't see the man's face; she wasn't
even able to snatch a clue.
                    But HE,
however, tugged the ring right off her finger
before he ran away.
                    I'm afraid that Pamphilus
won't keep his promise when he finds out we're keeping the child.

(She goes into the house of Phidippus.)

Act IV, Scene 2 [577–606]

(Sostrata and Pamphilus enter from the house of Laches.)

SOSTRATA: Pamphilus, dear, I know you're trying your best
to hide the way you feel, but you can't fool your mother.
I know you suspect that Philumena left
because of the way I acted. For the love of god,
I hope you'll grant me this:
                        I swear I have never
given the girl the tiniest reason to hate me.
It's not my fault.
              I've always believed you loved me;
and now you've deepened my trust. Your father told me
all about how you chose to side with me
instead of the love of your life. And now I must
return the favor—I want you to know that you'll always
come first with your mother. Pamphilus, dear, I feel
I should do what's best, what's best for the two of you
and for my reputation.
                 I'm going back to the farm
to live with your father. I'll be out of your way,
and your wife won't have a reason not to come back.

PAMPHILUS: I beg you, what kind of ridiculous plan is that?
Submit to her silly whims? Say good-bye to the city
and live in the sticks? I won't let you do it, Mother!
Nor will I let foul gossip tarnish our name!
I'll make it known that my brash determination
—not your gentle nature—is solely at fault.
Have you leave your family and friends for my sake? No,
I just won't have it! Besides, it's the holiday season.

SOSTRATA: Goodness gracious, I don't enjoy those things
anymore! I did when I was younger, but now
I've had enough of the social whirl.
                       As I enter
old age, all that matters is not to become
a burden to you or anyone else: I don't want
people counting the days 'til I turn up my toes.
I see that I'm hated here—despite the fact
that it's not my fault—so my time has come to go.
It's best this way, since I'll quash all complaints on both sides:
I myself will rise above all suspicion,
and still please our neighbors. People pigeonhole women
in nasty ways: I beg you, let me go!

PAMPHILUS:

(Aside.)

> How can I be so lucky in everything else
> but this? To have HER for a mother, but HER for a wife!

SOSTRATA: Pamphilus, dear, now can't you put up with one little
annoyance, whatever it is? If everything else
about her is just what you want—and that's how she looks
to me—then do your mother this favor. Take her
back.

PAMPHILUS: Oh god, is this painful!

SOSTRATA: It hurts me too,
Pamphilus, dear. My heart aches no less than yours.

Act IV, Scene 3 [607–622]

(Laches enters from his house.)

LACHES: I was standing behind the door, and I heard every word
you said, my wife. It's simply common sense,
to bend when you must, where you must.
           Yes, take
the bull by the horns today, and not by the tail
tomorrow.

SOSTRATA: Let's pray that turns out to be true.

LACHES: Then off
you go! To the farm! Where I'll put up with you,
and you'll put up with me!

SOSTRATA: My goodness, I hope so.

LACHES: Now go inside and pack whatever you want
to take.

(He pauses.)

    That's all I have to say.

SOSTRATA: All right.
As you wish.

(She exits into the house of Laches.)

PAMPHILUS: Now hold on, Daddy.

LACHES: What is it, Pamphilus?

PAMPHILUS: Mother leave here? I think not!

LACHES: And why exactly
do you think not?

PAMPHILUS: Because I haven't decided
what to do with my wife.

LACHES: What do you mean?
What else do you want to do besides take her back?

PAMPHILUS: Of course, I want her back. I can hardly contain
myself. But I can't undermine my own decision.
I'm determined to expedite this matter, and I think
the two will more likely make up if I DON'T take her back.

LACHES: WHAT? You don't know that. And it's none of your business what
the two of them do, once your mother is gone.
People our age are a pain in the neck to youngsters.
It's time we got off this stage, my boy: in the end
we play nothing but wheezing old geezers and doddering hags.
But here comes Phidippus, right on schedule. Come on.

Act IV, Scene 4 [623–726]

(Phidippus enters from his house, still speaking to his daughter inside.)

PHIDIPPUS: I'm just as angry with you, Philumena! Heck,
I'm REALLY angry! That was a very naughty
thing, goshdarnit—although you have the excuse
that your mother made you do it. But there's no excuse
for her.

LACHES: Ah, Phidippus! What luck! You couldn't have come
at a better moment.

PHIDIPPUS: And how is that?

PAMPHILUS:

(Aside.)

                                Oh, what
in the world should I say? Oh, how do I break the news?

LACHES: Give your daughter this message: my wife is moving
back out to our farm. Philumena can now come home
and not feel cramped.

PHIDIPPUS: Ah, but YOUR wife is not to blame.
The problem, in fact, is MY wife. It's all been HER fault.

PAMPHILUS:

(Aside.)

    . THAT's a new twist.

PHIDIPPUS: Yes, Laches, SHE'S the cook
who's been stirring the pot.

PAMPHILUS:

(Aside.)

                                   Let them stew all they want, as long
          as they don't make me take her back.

PHIDIPPUS: Two families tied
          forever by friendship, Pamphilus. THAT's what I'd love
          to see, if it's possible. BUT, on the other hand,
          if you happen to have different feelings, just take the child.

PAMPHILUS:

          (Aside.)

          THE CHILD? He knows there's a child? Dear god!

LACHES: THE CHILD?
          WHAT CHILD?

PHIDIPPUS: We have a grandson. Born today.
          When Philumena left your house, she was pregnant.
          I didn't know until now the girl was expecting.

LACHES: Bless my soul! Isn't this a joyous announcement?
          I'm delighted that mother and child are both doing well!
          But your wife—what kind of woman is SHE, habitually
          holding back information? For months she pulled
          the wool over us. Words fail me! It's such bad taste!

PHIDIPPUS: I don't like it any better than you do, Laches.

PAMPHILUS:

          (Aside.)

          I may have had my doubts before, but not now—
          no, not if she comes with another man's child in tow.

LACHES: That settles the whole discussion, Pamphilus. Right?

PAMPHILUS:

          (Aside.)

          I'm doomed!

LACHES:

          (To Pamphilus.)

                        Oh, how your mother and I have yearned
          for this day: to hear a little voice of your own
          call you "Daddy!" And now that day is here.

          (He kneels.)

                                             YE GODS,
          I WISH TO EXPRESS MY THANKS.

PAMPHILUS:

> (Aside.)

> I wish I were dead.

LACHES:

> (To Pamphilus.)

> Now take your wife home, and don't talk back.

PAMPHILUS:

> Look, Daddy,
> I'm sure she wouldn't have kept the baby a secret
> from me—which I know for a fact she did—if she REALLY
> wanted to have my children or be my wife.
> But since I feel she's given me the cold shoulder
> —and I doubt that things will ever warm up between us—
> why should I take her back?

LACHES:

> She's young! Her mother
> made her do it! Is that so amazing? You think
> you can find a wife who doesn't have any quirks?
> Or perhaps you think husbands don't have their little lapses?

PHIDIPPUS: Laches! And you too, Pamphilus! Work it out
> among yourselves: do you want to give her back
> or bring her home? My wife is out of my hands—
> she'll do as she pleases. But either way, you won't
> have trouble from us.
> > But what should we do with the baby?

LACHES: What a ridiculous question! Whatever happens,
> you turn it over to Pamphilus here, of course!
> So WE can raise the child.

PAMPHILUS:

> (Aside.)

> Its own father left it;
> why on earth is it MY job to raise it?

LACHES:

> (To Pamphilus.)

> What's that?
> Oh, now we shouldn't raise the child, eh Pamphilus?
> Tell me, what DO you suggest? We leave it out
> on some doorstep?

(Pamphilus shrugs yes.)

> WHAT? ARE YOU TOTALLY OUT OF YOUR MIND?

Goddammit! I just can't stifle myself anymore!
I don't want to say this in. front of HIM,

(He nods at Phidippus.)

but you've pushed me

too far!
    You think I'm some ignoramus? I know
exactly why you've been sobbing and moping around
like this!
        The first excuse you gave was your mother:
as long as she was here, you couldn't allow
your wife to live under our roof. And so your mother
offers to leave. But when you saw THAT excuse
swept away, you latched onto another one: that "nobody
told you about the baby."
            If YOU think I'm out
of touch with whatever goes on inside that head
of yours, you're sadly mistaken.
                The years I gave you
to cuddle and coo with

(He points to the house of Bacchis.)

that cupcake!

The years I gave you

to come to your senses and face your connubial duty!
The bills I paid with a smile while you lavished that tart
with trifles and baubles! I begged, I pleaded for you
to marry; I said, "It's time to grow up!" I tugged—
you toppled and took your vows. Back then you deferred
to my wishes and did the right thing. But now your brains
are brimming with thoughts of

(He points to the house of Bacchis.)

whatshername again!

By deferring to   •

(He points to the house of Bacchis.)

HER, you've grossly offended

(He points to the house of Phidippus.)

HER!

Bah! Regressed to your former lifestyle, that's what I see!

PAMPHILUS: Me?

LACHES: YES, YOU! What you've done is simply outrageous!
Conjuring up all sorts of phony excuses
to fan the flames of familial discord! And why?

so you could shack up with

(He points to the house of Bacchis.)

                                    HER the very second
you ditched your only witness—

(He points to the house of Phidippus.)

                                    HER! Oh yes,
your WIFE is on to you. Why else would she leave you?

PHIDIPPUS: The man reads minds! THAT'S exactly what happened!

PAMPHILUS: I swear that none of it's true. Upon my honor.

LACHES: Well, then take your wife back. Or tell us why not.

PAMPHILUS: I don't think this is the time.

LACHES: THEN TAKE THE BABY!
It isn't HIS fault! I'll deal with the mother later.

PAMPHILUS:

   (Aside.)

   All is lost! I'm dead! The battle is hopeless!
   Outflanked by Daddy on every side! No ground
   to gain if I stay. Retreat is my only option.
   I don't think they'll take the child in without my blessing—6
   especially not if my mother-in-law backs me up!

(He exits stage left running. Laches follows him for a few steps.)

LACHES: Are you running away? Hey! Aren't you going to answer?

   (To Phidippus.)

   Does he seem a bit unstable to you?
   Well, let him go. Hand over the baby, Phidippus.
   I'll raise the child myself.

PHIDIPPUS: By all means. No wonder
   my wife had her hackles up. Yes, women are like that.
   They don't take things lightly. Once they go sour, they STAY sour.
   THAT's why Myrrina was angry. She told me herself.
   To be honest, I didn't want to say so with Pamphilus
   here; in fact, I didn't believe it at first.
   But now it's very clear. He's scared to death
   of marriage. He's simply not cut out for it.

---

6 A Roman father formally recognized an infant as his own by picking it up off the ground when it was first presented to him.

LACHES: So what should I do, Phidippus? Any advice?

PHIDIPPUS: Ah, what should you do?

> Well, first of all, I think
> we should make arrangements to speak to

(He points to the house of Bacchis.)

> that temptress next door.
> We'll start off by begging.
> Then we'll shame her.
> And if THAT
> doesn't work, we'll resort to force. We'll threaten to do something
> serious if she fools with him in the future.

LACHES: I'll follow your prescription.

(He calls into his house.)

> You there! Boy!

(A servant appears in the doorway.)

> Run next door to Bacchis, our OTHER neighbor.
> Tell her to come here. I want a few words with her.

(The servant runs into the house of Bacchis. Phidippus turns to leave.)

> Phidippus, please! I beseech your support in this matter.

PHIDIPPUS: Ah, Laches, I've said it before, and I'll say it again:
I wish with all my heart to cement the ties
that bind us. If, that is, it can actually happen.
And which, I hope, will certainly happen. But do you
really want me around when you let her have it?

LACHES: Of course not! You go find the child a wet nurse.

(Phidippus exits stage left.)

Act V, Scene 1 [727–767]

(Bacchis exits from her house, accompanied by her servants, to whom she is still
speaking.)

BACCHIS: So Laches wants to see me? Not for nothin',
I bet. I've got a pretty good hunch what it is.

LACHES:

(To himself.)

> Steady, now! Can't let myself get all
> worked up and come away empty-handed. Must not
> overdo the job. Must not undermine my position.
> All right. Now here I go.

(He takes a deep breath.)
(Aloud.)

Hello there, Bacchis!

BACCHIS: And Hello to you, Laches.

(She flashes a dazzling smile at him and sits down on the statue base. He is
momentarily dazed.)

LACHES: Uh, by Jove, I guess you're wondering
why I had my servant summon you out here.

BACCHIS: By Jove, I sure am.

(She crosses her legs.)

And it makes me a teeny bit antsy,
considerin' my chosen profession. You might be a little
on guard against girls like me in this line of work.
But let me assure you: I'm very ready and willin'
to defend the way I conduct my business.

(Laches coughs and composes himself.)

LACHES: Woman,
as long as you tell the truth, you have nothing to fear
from me. I'm too old to be forgiven for foolish
blunders: hence, I take extra care and pains
so as not to leap to any rash conclusions.
Therefore, if you conduct yourself—either now
or in the future—as a nice young lady should,
it would hardly be fair for me to insult you by making
some oafish remark you didn't yet deserve.

BACCHIS: Well, thank you very kindly! By golly, I'm simply
overwhelmed with gratitude! You know,
it wouldn't help me at all if people said,
"I'm sorry!" AFTER they actually insulted me.
Do tell me, what's the problem?

(She pats the statue base, gesturing for Laches to sit down. He does so cautiously.)

LACHES: My son. You persist
on keeping him a returning customer.

BACCHIS: Hardly!

(She turns away and pouts.)

LACHES: Now let me speak! I put up with your little affair
before he got married.

(Bacchis starts tapping her foot.)

Hold on! I haven't made

my point yet!

(Bacchis turns back and gives him her full attention.)

Ahem. So now he has a wife.
And thus it behooves you—while you have the chance
to consider your own best interests—to find a steadier
steady.
His feelings toward you are fleeting at best;
and YOU won't stay a perky spring chicken forever.

BACCHIS: Just who's been sayin' all this?

LACHES: His mother-in-law.

BACCHIS: About ME?

LACHES: Your very self. And because of you,
she rustled her daughter off, and wanted to give
the baby away—the one her daughter just had—
in utter secrecy.

BACCHIS: Laches, by Blessed Venus
—and if I knew a way to convince you aside
from swearin' a solemn oath, I promise I'd use it—
I've given your son the cold shoulder ever since
the day he got hitched.

(She pouts and looks sad. Laches scoops over and gives her a pat on the back.)

LACHES: You delightful thing, you!
But you know what would make me very happy? Please?

BACCHIS: What is it? Do tell!

(She scoots in closer to Laches.)

LACHES: Step in and repeat that oath
to these women. Give them the same guarantee. You can smooth out
their feelings, and wipe the smudge off your name.

BACCHIS: Well, all right.
But nobody else in this business would do such a thing,
by golly. Plead a man's case to his wife? Unheard of!
But I don't want your son to be under suspicion because
of some empty rumor. And I sure don't think it's fair
for you to call him a cheat when he actually isn't.
After all, you ARE his family. Help
is what he deserves. I'll do what I can to oblige him.

LACHES: That tongue of yours has me eating right out of your hand!
I must admit, the women were not alone
in their fears—I also thought the gossip was true.
But now I see that our earlier views of you

were off the mark.

(He takes her hand in his.)

Make sure that you don't change a bit—
and thus you'll enjoy our family's lasting friendship.
Do anything else—

(She pouts.)

I'd better hush up. No need
to offend you. But let me give you one piece of advice:
it's better to toy with my good side instead of my bad.

(She gives him a little peck on the cheek.)

Act V, Scene 2 [768–798]

(Phidippus enters stage left leading a wet nurse, to whom he is still speaking.)

PHIDIPPUS: I'll be glad to see that you get all you need at our house.
But as soon as you fill up on food and drink, make sure
to fill up the baby.

LACHES: I see my fellow in-law
coming now. He's found a nurse for the baby.

(Phidippus mutters more instructions to the nurse, who exits into his house.)

Phidippus, Bacchis has given her solemn oath—

PHIDIPPUS: So THIS is HER?

(He stares in disbelief at Bacchis, who is now fondling Laches' ear.)

LACHES: The one and only.

PHIDIPPUS: Heck,
she doesn't look the god-fearing type. I imagine
the gods don't put too much stock in her sort, either.

(Bacchis waves her hand at Phidippus.)

BACCHIS: Here, take my servants. Torture them all you like
if you want the truth. You have my fullest permission.
But this is where things stand: it's up to me
to make Pamphilus's wife come home. And if I succeed,
I won't regret when it ruins my reputation,
that I performed an act that would make other women
of independent means turn tail and RUN!

LACHES: Well, Phidippus? We found out we were misinformed
regarding the role of our wives in this matter; let's put
Bacchis on trial right now. If your wife discovers
she fell for a groundless charge, she'll drop her grudge.
On the other hand, if my son is miffed because

your daughter had her baby in secret, that's minor:
he'll cool down quickly. No doubt about it,
there's nothing bad enough to warrant divorce.

PHIDIPPUS: My god, I certainly hope so.

(Bacchis pats the statue base and beckons to Phidippus to join them.)

LACHES: Examine the witness.

(He holds out Bacchis's hand for Phidippus to take.)

Here she is. Just let her answer your questions
until you're satisfied.

PHIDIPPUS:

(He steps back.)

                                   Why are you telling ME this?
Didn't you already hear how I stand on the matter,
Laches? The two of YOU go and put their minds at ease.

(He exits stage left in a hurry.)

LACHES: In the name of god, I beg you, Bacchis. Keep
that promise you made me.

(He stands up, still holding her hand.)

BACCHIS: You want ME to go inside
and bring up the subject?

LACHES: Go on. Smooth their feathers.
Make them believe you.

BACCHIS: I'll go, but I'm pretty darn sure
they'd soon as spit on my sandals as look at my face.
When a groom steps out on his bride, she tends to view
his mistress as some sort of monster.

LACHES: They'll be your allies—
as soon as they find out your reason for coming. I promise,
those very same women will turn into friends when they know
the truth. You'll disperse the cloud of doubt and suspicion.

BACCHIS: Consolin' Philumena, a customer's wife!
I could die of shame!

(Laches helps her to her feet. She snaps her fingers at her servants.)

                              You two! Now follow me in.

(She struts into the house of Phidippus, followed by her servants.)

LACHES: I could only wish for the sort of windfall that dropped
into Bacchis's lap! To ingratiate herself

and do me a favor without a thing to lose!
If it's true she tossed Pamphilus out on his ear, she knows
the deed will bring her fame;
                                    fortune;
                                              glory!
She'll be thanking him and befriending us!

(He exits into his house.)

Act V, Scene 3 [799–840]

(Parmeno enters stage right.)

PARMENO: Honest to god! My boss sure puts a pretty
            puny price on my time and worth. To think,
            sending me off to sit on my hands all day—
            and for what?
                        NOTHING!
                                ABSOLUTELY NOTHING!
            There I was, hanging around the temple
            door for "CALLIDEMIDES, THE HOST FROM MYKONOS."
            Like an ass I camped out all day, lunging
            up at whoever walked by with:
                                    "Excuse, young man,
            but tell me, are *you* a Mykonian?"
                                    "I'm not."
                                              "Your name
            isn't Callidemides?"
                        "No."
                                "No friend in town
            by the name of Pamphilus?"
                                    Answer negative. Same
            every time. In my opinion, he doesn't exist.
            I finally got so damned embarrassed, I left.

(Bacchis enters from the house of Phidippus.)

            But why do I see Bacchis coming out
            of the house next door? What was she doing in THERE?

BACCHIS: Parmeno! A good thing you're here. Go and find Pamphilus!

(Parmeno remains motionless.)

            Come on! Snap to it!

PARMENO: What for?

BACCHIS: Tell him I BEG him
            to come.

PARMENO: To you?

BACCHIS: Not me. Philumena.

PARMENO: What's up?

BACCHIS: Just poke your nose right back out—it's none of your business.

PARMENO: That's it? No other message?

BACCHIS: Add this: that Myrrina
                recognized the ring he once gave me. It belongs
                to her daughter.

PARMENO: Message received. Is that all there is?

BACCHIS: That's all. He'll zip back as soon as you open your mouth.

    (Parmeno still doesn't move.)

                Well, why are you standin' there, coolin' your heels?

PARMENO: COOLING?
                I never get the chance! I've been burning up ground
                for most of the day with all this rambling and scrambling.

    (He ponders which way to go for a moment, then hobbles off stage left.)

BACCHIS: My work today is goin' to make that Pamphilus
                one satisfied boy!
                            Could I bring in happier news?
                Could I haul off a heavier load?
                                    I rescued his baby!
                The child, who, thanks to those women and even his father,
                was almost done for!
                            I rounded up his wife!
                The girl he thought he would never hold again
                in his arms!
                        And as for his daddy's and in-law's suspicions,
                poof! Thanks to me, he's entirely off the hook.
                Yep, this ring yanked the cat right out of the bag!

    (She holds out her hand and admires a ring on her finger.)

                I remember—about ten months ago, I think—
                it was just after dark, when Pamphilus—pantin' wildly
                out of breath—came staggerin' through my door
                all alone, with his snoot full of wine and this ring in his fist.

                I was scared to death. "My Pamphilus, honey!" I said, ·
                "You're as pale as a ghost! For goodness sake, please tell me
                what happened? And where in the world did you get that ring?"
                He dawdled around, tryin' to act nonchalant.
                I saw right through his act, and then I started to get suspicious.
                I twisted his arm and made him talk. He finally confessed
                that he'd had his way with some girl passin' by on the street.

While they wrestled, he told me, he happened to pull a ring
off her finger. Myrrina spotted the ring just now
while I had it on my pinkie. She asked me where
it had come from. I told her all I knew, and the facts
just spoke for themselves: HE was the one who knocked
Philumena up, which makes the baby HIS child.
He's blessed with joy and all because of me—

(Her eyes brim with tears of joy. She pulls out a handkerchief to dab her eyes.)

I'm so very happy—
                              although the rest of the girls
in the guild do frown on this sort of thing: the happily
married man is bad for business. But hell!
I won't use dirty tricks just to keep the cash
flowin' in. It was nice as long as it lasted. To me
he was always generous, charmin', and kind, and from my point
of view, his marriage was certainly quite a setback.
But praise be to Venus, my conscience is clear: I did nothin'
wrong to deserve it. I received a whole lot of good,
and it's only fair that I get my share of the bad.

(She walks over and waits in the doorway of Laches' house.)

Act V, Scene 4 [841–880]

(Parmeno enters stage left, followed by Pamphilus.)

PAMPHILUS: Parmeno, PLEASE make sure you have the details
absolutely straight. Don't leave me to flounder
around in a fleeting world of futile hopes.

PARMENO: I'm sure.

PAMPHILUS: Completely?

PARMENO: Completely.

PAMPHILUS: I've joined the immortal
gods, if it's true.

PARMENO: You'll see for yourself.

PAMPHILUS: But wait
a minute. Please. I'm afraid what I THINK you're saying
and what you might be saying are not the same thing.

PARMENO: I'll wait.

PAMPHILUS: So this is what you said—I think:
that Myrrina saw that Bacchis had her ring.

PARMENO: A fact.

PAMPHILUS: The ring I once gave her. And SHE sent you off
to tell me. Is that a fact?

PARMENO: That's just what I said.

PAMPHILUS: Could Fortune smile on any man more kindly?
Could Venus pile her bounty any higher?

(He hugs Parmeno.)

What can I give you to thank you for bringing this news?
Say what! I ask you, what? I just don't know!

PARMENO: But I do.

PAMPHILUS: What's that?

PARMENO: Absolutely nothing.
As far as I can tell, you've haven't gained
a bit of good from the news—or from me, for that matter.

PAMPHILUS: ME let YOU get away without lavishing gifts
at your feet?
                    O you, who snatched my hopeless soul
from the very portals of Hell; you, who warmed
my lifeless corpse in the dazzling rays of the sun?
What kind of ungrateful clod do you think I am?

(He notices Bacchis.)

But wait! I see Bacchis standing next to the door.
She's waiting for me, I guess. Well, gotta go.

BACCHIS: Why, hello, Pamphilus!

(Pamphilus rushes over and takes her hand.)

PAMPHILUS: Bacchis, my own dear Bacchis!
My goddess of sweet salvation!

BACCHIS: A pleasure to help.

(They walk over to the statue base and sit down. Parmeno leans in the doorway to
Laches' house.)

PAMPHILUS: I can't help but believe you, you good-deed do-er.
You've really kept up those delicious looks—you haven't
changed a day. It's always such a delight
to visit with you, to hear your voice, to watch
you coming my way down the street, no matter where.

BACCHIS: And YOU, golly gee, have kept up those cute little ways
of yours: there isn't a man alive more charmin'.

PAMPHILUS: Ha ha ha. So now you tell me?

BACCHIS: You did
             the right thing by fallin' in love with your wife. I never
             saw her before today—at least I don't think—
             but she seems like, in my estimation, Pamphilus, quite
             a classy lady.

PAMPHILUS: Come on now. Tell me the truth.

BACCHIS: Oh, Pamphilus! Cross my heart. It's true.

PAMPHILUS: And tell me,
             did you mention any of this to my father?

BACCHIS: Nothing.

PAMPHILUS: Whew. And no reason to breathe a word.
             I'd rather avoid those slapstick endings where everyone
             finds out everything. Those who need to know
             already know; and those who don't—don't.
             They won't be any the wiser.

BACCHIS: And even better:
             I'll give you another tidbit to help you relax
             and trust that it's all a secret. Myrrina took
             my word of honor—that's what she told her husband—
             so he thinks she thinks you're Mr. Nice Guy again.

PAMPHILUS: That's perfect! I hope it all goes according to plan.

(Bacchis gives him a kiss on the cheek and exits into her house. Parmeno
approaches Pamphilus.)

PARMENO: Boss, with your permission, what good did I do you
             today? And what were the two of you chatting about?

PAMPHILUS: Permission denied.

PARMENO: Well nonetheless, I've got
             a hunch.

       (Aside.)

                    I "snatched his lifeless body from Hell"—
             but how?

PAMPHILUS: You're clueless, Parmeno. How much help
             you gave me, or how much woe you saved me, you'll never
             know.

PARMENO: Not true. I knew all along. I never
             fumbled a moment.

PAMPHILUS: I have no doubt.

(He rises and gives Parmeno a pat on the back.)

PARMENO: I mean ME?
                Parmeno? Not there on the job before he's needed?

PAMPHILUS: Come on, Parmeno. Let's go inside.

(He exits into the house of Laches.)

PARMENO: I'm coming.
                Go figure. I've done more good accidentally today
                than I've ever done on purpose.
                                        So give me a hand!

Finis

The Adelphoe Brothers

PVBLIVS
Deena Berg
TERENTIVS AFER

Introduction to *The Brothers*

Presented in 160 B.C., *The Brothers* (*Adelphoe*) was the last of Terence's plays, as well as his best. Based on an original by Menander, its dialogue is witty, its characters and plots well-crafted. But the lasting appeal of this play lies in the universal question at its core: how does one rear a decent human being? With an iron fist? Or kid gloves? *The Brothers* tackles this dilemma—and simultaneously wrestles with the issue of sibling rivalry—by pitting brother against brother in a parenting match. Defending the liberal position is Micio, who adopted his brother's first-born son, Aeschinus. A bachelor to the bone, Micio is wealthy, urbane, and irritatingly logical. He spouts theories on child psychology that are so "hands off" as to make Dr. Spock's seem repressive. In the conservative corner is Demea, Micio's brother and Aeschinus's natural father, who raises a second son, Ctesipho. Worn out by his life and wife on the farm, Demea is as volcanic as Micio is smugly serene, and the stage explodes when the opposites collide. By virtue of his money, charm, and rhetoric, Micio maintains the upper hand for most of the play. Demea finally "concedes," but by applying his brother's own tactics, forces Micio into a draw.

While their fathers cling to their extreme positions, the two sons manage to bring home their objects of desire through such "respectable" means as kidnapping and premarital pregnancy. The plots intertwine nicely, thanks to Syrus, Micio's self-indulgent slave, who neatly disposes of anyone blocking the paths of true love and fine food.

One very small snag, for which Terence has been skewered through the ages, is the first scene of Act II. Terence freely admits in the prologue that he borrowed this scene from another play. Sannio, the outraged pimp from whom the lute-girl has been stolen, arrives on stage before Aeschinus does, begging for help. From Demea's description in Act I, the event seems already to have taken place, or else time has slowed to a sudden crawl. The action needs some careful staging to make it seem plausible, but ultimately the scene does add an important element, in that the audience immediately sees the output of Micio's and Demea's parenting: Aeschinus the Smart Aleck Scofflaw, and Ctesipho the Spineless Sneak. Both children have their better sides, but neither lives up to his father's claim of a "model citizen." The subtle touches in all the characterizations give the play a remarkable realism and account for its enduring popularity.

The stage should instantly convey the differences between Micio's wealth and Sostrata's lack thereof. I have suggested two special architectural flourishes for Micio's house—a balcony and a garden gate—which further the impression of Micio's economic success and assist the blocking. As Ctesipho's love nest, the balcony provides a plausible perch for asides in Demea's presence. The garden gate, a trellised affair that occupies the customary central opening of the stage, does not actually serve as an entrance or exit; it does, however, afford a convenient spot for eavesdropping.

Moreover, when the two houses are "joined" in Act V, the glimpse of wall-bashing and bride-smuggling adds a nice touch of irony to Micio's protestations against marriage.

Texts and Commentaries: I employed the text edited by Robert Kauer and W. M. Lindsay, *P. Terenti Afri Comoediae* "Oxford Classical Texts" (Oxford: Clarendon Press, 1926; repr. 1979). Additional help came from R. H. Martin's commentary, *Terence: Adelphoe* "Cambridge Greek and Latin Texts" (London: Cambridge University Press, 1976; reprint 1988), and the notes to A. S. Gratwick's *Terence: The Brothers* (Warminster: Aris & Phillips, 1988).

DEENA BERG

Basic Set

House of Micio   Garden of Micio   House of Sostrata

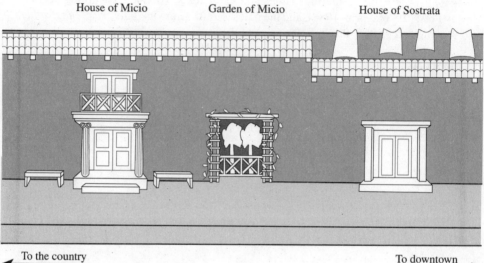

To the country
(stage right)

To downtown
(stage left)

SCENE: *A street in Athens. Stage left, the house of Micio, a two-story affair with a balcony. Marble benches flank the front door. Stage right, the house of Sostrata, a modest one-story structure. Its roof terrace is festooned with laundry. At center stage is a gate, slightly recessed and shaded by a trellis with a vine, which provides a glimpse into Micio's garden. Stage left leads downtown and to the port; stage right leads to the countryside.*

Dramatis Personae

Micio (*MIH-key-o*)	a middle-aged gentleman residing in Athens
Demea (*DEE-me-a*)	Micio's brother, a farmer
Aeschinus (*EE-skin-us*)	Demea's elder teenage son, adopted by Micio
Ctesipho (*KTEH-si-fo*)	Demea's younger teenage son
Syrus (*SEAR-us*)	Micio's head house slave
Parmeno (*PAR-men-o*)	Aeschinus's slave and muscle
Dromo and Stephanio (*DRO-mo*) (*ste-FAH-nee-o*)	Micio's other slaves
Sostrata (*SOS-tra-ta*)	an impoverished Athenian widow
Pamphila (*PAM-fill-a*)	Sostrata's very pregnant daughter
Canthara (*KAN-tha-ra*)	Sostrata's aged nurse
Hegio (*HEG-ee-o*)	Sostrata's distant but doting male relative
Geta (*GET-a*)	Sostrata's devoted slave
Sannio (*SAH-nee-o*)	a pimp
Bacchis (*BAH-kiss*)	a lute girl

The Brothers

Prologue[1] [1–25]

It has recently—and often—been brought to our author's attention
that a number of contemptuous critics—no need for names—
no longer content with panning his previous plays,
are already hacking away at his newest piece,
which we are even now about to present.
Therefore, the playwright would like to entrust the case
to you, the audience—an impartial jury—let YOU
accordingly give the verdict—thumbs-up or thumbs-down.

Exhibit A. Diphilus wrote a comedy in Greek
entitled *Mort à trois,* which Plautus adapted
and labeled *Three's a Shroud.* The original has a bit
at the start wherein a young man snatches a call girl
away from her pander. Plautus saw fit to leave
this scene on the shelf, untouched and gathering dust;
our author decided to help himself and insert
the incident, word for word, in his all-new version
of Menander's hit, *The Brothers,* today's premiere.
So examine the facts if you will, and YOU be the judge
of whether this action constitutes theft or merely
honest appropriation of abandoned goods.

Exhibit B. The Prosecution further charges
that local luminaries—no need for names—
have aided, abetted, and, horrors! collaborated
in these productions.[2] The author maintains said charge
should be considered distinction, not detraction.
Why, it's a positive honor finding favor
with those very men who find favor with you, the public;
the very men whose services everyone seeks
when needed in war, in peace, in daily business,
without being thought the least bit highfalutin.

With the court's permission, there's no synopsis. The plot
unfolds in Act I: the old men give the gist
and act out the rest.

---

[1] This prologue preceded the play's first presentation at the funeral games of Aemilius Paullus.

[2] The reference is presuambly to, among others, Scipio Aemilianus Africanus, Terence's well-known literary patron and one of the sponsors of the funeral games.

                    May your open minds encourage
        our playwright and ipso facto up his output.

Act I, Scene 1 [26–80]

(Micio, looking worried, enters from his house.)

MICIO: STORAX!
                    Where is that houseboy?
                                Aeschinus—my son—
            STILL isn't back from that little soiree last night;
            and the servants—what escorts!—THEY didn't come back either.

(He sighs.)

            Just as they say, if you're ever held up, far better
            to suffer whatever scenario a seething wife
            concocts, than the mishaps imagined by a doting parent.
            A wife, if you're late, will chalk it up to flirtation,
            fornication, intoxication, and every
            form of self-gratification, sure that you're having
            the time of your life while she's stuck by herself at home.
            But parents—
                    I fret and pace if my son is late,
            I'm fraught with worry: maybe he came down with a cold?
            Or fell in a ditch? Or broke a leg or something?

(He sighs again.)

            Only a fool would open his heart and care
            for anything more than his very own hide. My god,
            the boy's not even my own—he belongs to my brother.
            And what a brother! He's nothing like me at all:
            our tastes haven't been the same ever since we were little.

            I, on the one hand, took up this leisurely urban
            existence, a casual lifestyle. And as for a wife,
            what some folks consider a blessing—I never had one.

            But HE—completely the opposite—chose the farm
            and opted for rustic drudgery and hardship—he married.
            He had two sons but couldn't afford to raise both,
            so I adopted the elder, who was only a toddler
            at the time. I think of him as my own, my pride,
            my joy.
                    He's the dearest thing in the world to me,
            and I have taken pains to ensure our mutual
            love and respect. I indulge his whims, overlook
            his boo-boos, and don't demand that he do things my way.

The result?

          While other youngsters distrust authority
and tend to conceal their little pubescent pranks,
MY son is completely and utterly candid with me.
It's this way:

                   the child who habitually lies to his father
or dares to sneak around behind his back
is more than prone to do the same to others.
I'm firmly convinced that shame and self-respect,
when carefully instilled by generous and sensitive treatment,
go further than fear in eliciting healthy behavior.

These tender nuances of child-rearing are, of course,
completely lost on my brother. He's always moaning,
"Micio! What are you doing? Why do you ruin him?
Why do you let the boy cruise,

                   booze,

                         run amok?
Why the vast allowance, the endless wardrobe?
YOU are a grossly permissive liberal dupe!"

But HE'S a severely repressive, tightfisted rube,
misguided in his belief that respect is more deep
and durable when it's coerced than when cemented
by friendship. *I* myself adhere to the theory
that the child bullied by punishment does right only
if he fears he'll be caught; but take such fear away,
and PRESTO! he's back to his old naughty self in no time.
But if you let kindness be the tie that binds,
he'll act sincerely, he'll WANT to return the favor,
and his behavior will be the same at home
or away. A parent simply must encourage
virtue for virtue's sake, and not make it hang by a threat.
Yes, THAT'S the line dividing dictators from dads.
And whoever denies it—THERE is an unfit father.

Speaking of whom—is that him now?

(He squints.)

                               It is.
Looks grim, I'm afraid—he's doubtless in some sort of snit.

(He sighs again.)

I guess we're due for the usual brotherly rhubarb.

(He forces a smile and faces stage right.)

Demea, nice to see you safe and sound.

Act I, Scene 2 [81–154]

(Demea enters right, frowning.)

DEMEA: And just in the nick of time! I've been looking all over for you.

MICIO: But why the scowl?

DEMEA: With *your son* Aeschinus on our hands,
           you ask me, "Why the scowl?"

MICIO:

     (Aside.)

                                   You see what I mean?

     (Aloud.)

                                   So what has he done?

DEMEA: Done? The boy who knows no shame, who knows no fear,
           who snorts in the face of law and order? Forget all prior
           offenses; what has that devious mind hatched now?

MICIO: Well, WHAT?

DEMEA: Breaking and entering; beating the owner and his household staff
           within an inch of their lives; nabbing some girl he's got
           the hots for. The entire town is outraged. People stop
           in the street just to tell me the lurid details, Micio. EVERYONE
           is talking about it.
                         If he needs a model to follow, why not
           his brother Ctesipho? Now there's an honest, hard-working boy,
           devoted to leading a thrifty and sober life on the farm.
           But Aeschinus? Your boy? No, he's nothing like that at all.
           But, Aeschinus, hell! I really mean YOU, yes, Micio, YOU.
           YOU let him sink to this depth of depravity and degradation.

MICIO: I'll tell you the height of injustice—an out-of-it know-it-all,
           who knocks whatever he hasn't tried.

DEMEA: And the point of that?

MICIO: The point is, brother dear, you are hardly a competent judge.
           It's no crime for a youngster to crash the occasional brothel,
           have a drink, knock down a door now and then—that's not
           the case. If WE never did such sorts of things, it was
           because we couldn't afford it. Do you think it's fair to take credit
           for all the virtue bestowed on you by Lady Hard-luck?
           Had WE been given the wherewithal, we would have done likewise.
           And if YOU would join the human race, you might let your boy
           act like a boy while he IS a boy, instead of stifling

his puberty till middle age, when he finally gives your carcass
a long awaited heave-ho.

DEMEA: Of all the chuckleheaded—
dammit, Micio, you drive me crazy. Not a crime
for a boy to do this?

MICIO: Now listen. Repeated pounding will get
you nowhere. You gave me your son to adopt, and now he's mine.
If he does something wrong, he does it to me, Demea. *I* bear the
    brunt.
The dinner parties, the trendy colognes—they're out of MY pocket.
And as for girls, well, the money is there for as long as it lasts;
when it's gone, just maybe he'll find himself locked out in the cold.
But a door in pieces? That can be fixed. A dress in shreds?
I'll call my tailor. Just thank goodness the wherewithal
hasn't yet proved to be a problem.
                                        And one last item—
either you quit the carping or call in a referee.
I may be wrong, but it's easy to show that YOU are wronger.

DEMEA: For god's sake, Micio! Learn what parenting is from a REAL parent.

MICIO: Your parenthood was blind instinct. Mine was planned.

DEMEA: YOU?
PLAN ANYTHING?

MICIO: Once more, and I go.

(He turns as if to retreat to his house. Demea grabs his sleeve.)

DEMEA: How can you treat me this way?

MICIO: How long do I have to hear you harp on the same old subject?

DEMEA: But I worry—

MICIO: And so do I. But, Demea, why don't we each
just mind our own business? You manage your son, I'll manage
    mine.
When you fuss over both, it almost seems as if you want me
TO GIVE THE BOY BACK.

DEMEA: Ah, THAT old line.

MICIO: Well, it LOOKS that way.

DEMEA: Oh, what's the use? Go right ahead if it makes you so happy.
Let him spend
                    and squander
                                        and wallow in moral squalor;
what's it to me? But if I hear one more word after this—

MICIO: What's that? You'll throw another tantrum?

DEMEA: Have you no trust?
                Have I asked you to give him back? It's hard on me, that's all.
                I'm not some stranger. If I object—

(Micio takes a step toward his house.)

                                                All right. I give up.
                You want me to look after mine, so be it. I just thank heaven
                he's all I could ask for. But one day that boy of yours will see—
                No. I won't say anything worse. Not at least about Aeschinus.

(Demea exits stage right.)

MICIO: He's not entirely wrong about this—although
                he's not entirely right. I mean, not that I'm not
                upset by the news, but I couldn't let HIM see that.
                I know him too well: to disarm him, you need resistance,
                steadfast deterrence—still then he's barely human.
                Heaven forbid I should fan the flames of his wrath—
                we'd both be raving loons.
                                        However, truth is,
                this time Aeschinus did us no small disservice.
                What whore has he NOT besnuggled? With whom has he NOT
                shared his wealth? It was just the other day—I was sure
                at last he was bored with it all—he mentioned marriage.
                What joy! I had hoped for so long the fervor of youth
                would finally simmer down. But now it's starting
                all over.
                                Still, whatever the story, I want
                the facts. I'll see if the boy is somewhere downtown.

(He exits stage left.)

Act II, Scene 1 [155–208]

(Sannio enters stage right, running backwards. He stops at center stage.)

SANNIO: HELP! I beg you, noble citizens! Defend the defenseless!
                Help the hapless! An innocent man has been wronged!

(Aeschinus, leading Bacchis with his right hand, enters right. Parmeno follows a few
steps behind.)

AESCHINUS:

(To Bacchis.)

                                                                Relax.

(He swings her around to his left side, so that she faces him, and he takes her left
hand.)

                Stay right over here and—

(Bacchis turns to glare at Sannio.)

Why are you looking over your shoulder?

(Bacchis nods her head at Sannio, who glares back.)

All bluff. He won't dare touch you while I'm around.

SANNIO: She's mine!
          I'll get that female back if it's over my dead body!

(He takes a step forward.)

AESCHINUS: He's nasty, yes, but not nasty enough to provoke a beating
             TWICE IN ONE DAY.

(Sannio takes a step back.)

SANNIO: My character, Aeschinus—just for the record,
          in case you try to claim ignorance—
                              PIMP I may be—

AESCHINUS: I know.

SANNIO: —but a Pimp of Principle. If you think you can wipe the slate clean
             with a little apology—HAH! I fully intend to prosecute.
             Trust me, you won't talk your way out of this tort. I've heard that
                  old line:
             "Sorry, Sir. I swear you deserved better treatment"—meanwhile,
             I'M stuck with unjust deserts, not to mention bruises.

(Aeschinus motions for Parmeno to advance.)

AESCHINUS: What are you waiting for? Hurry up and get the door!

(Parmeno lumbers over and opens the door to Micio's house.)

SANNIO: I'm not getting through to you, am I?

AESCHINUS: Time to go inside.

(He faces Bacchis toward the door and gives her a pat in that direction.)

SANNIO: NO! I'll die first!

(He steps in her way.)

AESCHINUS: Hey Parmeno! Come here!

(Parmeno releases the door and moves a few steps forward.)

                                                   That's still too far.
          Stand here, right next to him.

(Parmeno takes up his position between Bacchis and Sannio.)

                              Good. Now keep your eyes glued to mine,
          and don't hold back; if I wink, you punch him right in the mouth.

SANNIO: Just let him try!

(He gingerly grabs Bacchis's arm.)

AESCHINUS: Hey! Unhand that woman!

(Parmeno socks Sannio in the eye. Sannio releases Bacchis.)

SANNIO: OWWW!
               It's outrageous! Criminal!

AESCHINUS: Careful, he'll make them both a matched set.

(Parmeno socks Sannio in the other eye.)

SANNIO: The pain!

AESCHINUS: I didn't signal, but better early than never.

(He points Bacchis toward Micio's door again.)

               Now YOU head that way.

SANNIO: What is this, Aeschinus? Your little kingdom?

AESCHINUS: If it were, I'd deck you royally like you deserve.

SANNIO: -   But what do you have against ME?

AESCHINUS: Not a thing.

SANNIO: Then what's going on?
               Don't you know the sort of person I am?

AESCHINUS: I don't care.

SANNIO: Have I ever touched anything of YOURS?

AESCHINUS: Bad luck if you did.

SANNIO: Then why should you make off with the girl I paid for? Well?
               Answer me!

AESCHINUS: Now look! You'll be a lot better off
               if you stop making all this commotion in front of our house.
               But, if you insist on being a nuisance, I'll have to have Parmeno
               drag your fanny inside and flog you to death.

SANNIO: FLOG A FREEMAN?
               FATALLY?

AESCHINUS: No fooling.

SANNIO: Despicable! Here, where freemen are equal—
               or so they say?

AESCHINUS: Look, PIMP. If you're done with your little rampage,
               how about listening up now?

SANNIO: MY? You say MY little rampage?
What about YOURS?

AESCHINUS: Forget it. Let's get back to business.

SANNIO: Business? What's to get back to?

AESCHINUS: A little deal that might be
of interest—would you like me to tell you?

SANNIO: I'd love you to tell me—
so long as it's on the level.

AESCHINUS: Hah. A pander demanding
fair-trade practice.

SANNIO: I'm a pimp—I admit it—a perennial pox
on puberty, a perjurer, a pest. But I've done nothing to you.

AESCHINUS: Hell, not yet.

SANNIO: Get back to the subject, Aeschinus—please.

AESCHINUS: You purchased the girl for two thousand—

      (Aside.)

                                        And may you never see
the teeniest profit on that investment!

      (Aloud.)

                                  I'll buy her at cost.

SANNIO: Suppose I don't want to sell? Will you make me?

AESCHINUS: Of course not.

SANNIO: Whew.
You had me scared for a minute.

AESCHINUS: No, I don't believe
you should sell a girl at all—not if she's freeborn. Put it
THIS way:

(He touches Bacchis on the head and assumes a mock-solemn tone.)

          By right of touch I proclaim this lute girl FREE.
So consider your options, PIMP:
                                  you can take the money or find
yourself a lawyer. Think it over while I'm gone.

(He marches Bacchis into the house. Parmeno follows.)

SANNIO: Great god almighty! It's no wonder that victims of crime
go stark-raving mad!
                          He drags me from house and home,

         assaults my person,
                     purloins my property,
                                 and as payment
he wants me to sell her at cost! He did throw in
some five hundred lashes, which leaves me one body sorely
depreciated.
                 For that he deserves a reward?

(He sighs.)

        So be it. He wants to make up the rules? That's fine,
as long as he makes the payment.
                           But wait! A vision!

(He smites his forehead.)

        Oh foolish me! NOW I see what he's up to.
Just as soon as I agree to the deal,
 he pulls out a witness to swear, "SANNIO? THE PIMP?
He sold the girl to Aeschinus ages ago."
And my money? Poof. A dream. "Soon," he'll say,
"come back tomorrow."
                    I could take the abuse, if only
he'd give me the cash. In this line of work, adolescents
present a professional hazard: all you can do
is put up and shut up.
                 But no one is going to PAY up.
Why bother doing accounts? It's all so pointless.

Act II, Scene 2 [209–253]

(Syrus enters from Micio's house, still talking to Aeschinus within.)

SYRUS: Shush! I'll handle the man myself. When I'm through, he'll be
           DYING
         to settle; in fact, he'll even swear that he got a bargain.

(He spots Sannio and assumes a sympathetic expression.)

         —Sannio, what's this I hear? A little bout with the boss?

SANNIO: A lopsided match. I've never seen anything worse in my life:
         I tell you—my whimpers, his wallops—we wore each other out.

SYRUS: It's all your fault.

SANNIO: What else could I do?

SYRUS: Indulge the kid.

SANNIO: I loaned him my face as a punching bag—so who could do more?

SYRUS: Come on, you know what I mean. Why haggle over small change
         when you can bag the big mazuma? I don't believe it. You really

were scared if you bent a little and humored the boy, he wouldn't
repay you with interest? Sheesh. If they handed out prizes for
   sapheads—

SANNIO: I don't plunk down cash on pipe dreams.

SYRUS: You'll never make it in business,
Sannio. Give up. You don't know how to dangle the bait.

SANNIO: I suppose you have a point. I never had that sort
of savvy. I'd rather make off with as much as I can for the sake
of short-term gain.

SYRUS: Look, I know you. I know how your mind works.
Now what's a couple of thousand to get on his good side?
And rumor has it you're on your way to Cyprus—

SANNIO: Ahem.

SYRUS: —you've already chartered a ship, your cargo is packed and
   waiting—
no doubt a heavy load on your mind. When you finally make it
back—I can only hope—well, then you can deal with this trifle.

SANNIO: I'm not budging.

   (Aside.)

               Damn! I'm sunk! It's a plot!

SYRUS:

   (Aside.)

                             He's scared—
he's breaking out in nagging doubts.

SANNIO:

   (Aside.)

                      It's a dirty swindle,
don't you see? He pulled the old squeeze play! I just stocked up
on females and other stuff; they're all set to sail to Cyprus.
Unless I get them to market, they'll spoil—an incalculable loss.
On the other hand, if I wait and put this off, it's over,
my assets frozen, forgotten forever—
                        "Oh, NOW you show up,"
he'll say. "What happened? Where were you?"
                            Better to quit
while I'm still behind. Beats wasting my time around here or in
   court.

SYRUS: So what's the bottom line?

SANNIO: Is this what he's got for self-

respect? Did he stoop to this to start with? A sneak attack
to carry her off?

SYRUS:

(Aside.)

He's tottering.

(Aloud.)

My final offer. See
how you like it. Rather than playing for all or nothing, split
the cost between you. A thousand? No problem. He'll scrape it up
  somewhere.

SANNIO: Hasn't my interest suffered enough? Now I have to
defend my principal?

Has he no shame? He loosens my teeth,
he beats on my head till it looks like a truffle, and to top it all,
he double-deals by going halfsies?

I won't go—ever.

SYRUS: Suit yourself. Anything else, or mind if I leave?

SANNIO: Leave? Don't be silly. Dammit, Syrus, all I ask
is let bygones be bygones. Rather than dragging this thing into court,
I just want what's mine—or at least my initial outlay.

Syrus,

I know up till now we haven't exactly gotten along,
but my friendship can offer some real fringe benefits.

(He winks and gives Syrus a nudge.)

You'll find I'm a man
who never forgets a favor.

SYRUS: I'll do what I can.

(Off-key singing is heard from offstage right.)

There's Ctesipho.
That girl has him tickled pink.

SANNIO: But what's with our deal?

SYRUS: Just wait.

(He conceals Sannio next to the garden gate.)

Act II, Scene 3 [254–264]

(Ctesipho enters stage right, singing somewhat off key.)

CTESIPHO: *When you're in danger, help from a stranger*
                    Is reason enough to rejoice;

> *But given my druther, none but my brother*
> *Would rescue the girl of my choice.*
> *What praise can I sputter? I'm too awed to utter*
> *The glory your virtue is due;*
> *There's no one who's greater, O Aeschinus frater—*
> *There's no other brother like YOUUUUUUUUU.*

SYRUS: Hey Ctesipho!

CTESIPHO: Syrus! Where's Aeschinus?

SYRUS: Inside. He's waiting for you.

CTESIPHO: Oh golly!

SYRUS: What's the matter?

CTESIPHO: What's the matter? Syrus,
that man saved my life. What a guy! He's willing to sacrifice all
for my comfort.
               Slurs!
                    Gossip!
                         Robbery!
                              Fooling around!
He's taking the rap for everything! You can't beat that.

(The door to Micio's house begins to open.)

                                        The door!
          It's creaking! Who's there?

(He hides behind Syrus.)

SYRUS: Hang on, hang on—it's just your brother.

Act II, Scene 4 [265–287]

(Aeschinus enters from Micio's house, looking for Sannio.)

AESCHINUS: Where's that godless scofflaw?

SANNIO:

(Aside.)

                                   He must mean me. But say,
          what's in his hands? Oh damn, they're empty!

(Syrus pushes Ctesipho out where Aeschinus can see him.)

AESCHINUS: What a coincidence!
          Ctesipho! Just the guy I wanted to see. How's it going?
          Your sweetheart is safe in the bag, so no more moping around.

CTESIPHO: Moping? Hardly. I mean, how can I mope when you're my brother?
          Aeschinus, YOU are fantastic—but I'm afraid to say more.

You might think I'm kissing up instead of saying thanks.

(Aeschinus ruffles Ctesipho's hair.)

AESCHINUS: Go on, you silly dope! As if we don't know each other
by now. You deeply wounded my feelings. I almost found out
too late. And almost when things had gone to such an extreme
that no one, no matter how much he wanted to, could have helped.

CTESIPHO: But I was ashamed.

AESCHINUS: Ashamed? Insane, more like it.
                                        To think,
a little thing like that could make you run away
and leave your country? God forbid. It's too awful to mention.

CTESIPHO: I'm sorry.

AESCHINUS:

(To Syrus.)

                    And Sannio?

SYRUS: Soft and willing.

AESCHINUS: I'll go downtown
to pay him off.

(To Ctesipho.)

                    YOU go in and see your girlfriend.

(Ctesipho goes inside. Aeschinus sits down on one of the benches and stretches
contentedly.)

SANNIO:

(He whispers loudly.)

        Syrus! Give him a push!

SYRUS:

(To Aeschinus.)

                    Let's go.

(He lowers his voice.)

                                I think the pimp's in a hurry
to get to Cyprus.

(Sannio emerges.)

SANNIO: Not half as big a hurry as YOU'd
like to see. I'll just lounge around here and wait.

(He sits down on the other bench.)

SYRUS: Don't worry, you'll get
    your money.

SANNIO: He'll pay in full?

(Syrus looks at Aeschinus. Aeschinus looks at Sannio, shrugs his shoulders, and
nods yes to Syrus. Aeschinus then rises and exits stage left.)

SYRUS: IN FULL. Now shut up and come on.

SANNIO: I'm coming.

(Sannio exits left. Syrus starts to follow. Ctesipho appears on the balcony.)

CTESIPHO: Psst! Syrus!

SYRUS: Now what's the matter?

CTESIPHO: PLEASE pay off
    that filthy pimp as soon as possible, would you? If he gets
    any madder, news might leak out to my dad. In which case I'm
      dead.
    Permanently.

SYRUS: Not a chance. Buck up. Have fun.
    And tell the boys to set out the snacks and comfy couches.
    As soon as I swing this deal, I'll be back with the fish du jour.

(He exits left.)

CTESIPHO: What a day, eh? It can't get much better! This calls for a party.

(He disappears inside.)

Act III, Scene 1 [288–298]

(Canthara hobbles out from Sostrata's house, pursued by a nearly hysterical
Sostrata.)

SOSTRATA: I beg you, Canthara—you're our nurse—just how is she doing?

CANTHARA: You want to know how she's doing? For heaven's sake, she's going
    to be just fine—

(Pamphila moans loudly within.)

        —I hope. It's only the first few contractions,
    dear. Her labor pains have barely begun.

(Sostrata begins to weep.)

        Don't tell me
    you're already getting worried! You're acting as if you've never
    seen a baby born before! You had one yourself,
    remember?

SOSTRATA: It's just that I feel so helpless. There's no one to turn to.
We're all alone except for Geta. And he's not here.
There's no one to get the midwife, no one to send a message
to Aeschinus.

(She bursts into tears again.)

CANTHARA: Lordy, I'm sure he'll be here any minute.
You know that never a day goes by that he doesn't come.

SOSTRATA: He's the only cure for what ails us.

CANTHARA: Given what happened, Ma'am,
you have to admit that things could hardly have turned out better.
Once you overlook the seduction, he's quite a catch:
he's kind, got character, comes from a comfortable family—

SOSTRATA: I know.
You're absolutely right. May heaven protect our savior.

Act III, Scene 2 [299–354]

(Geta enters stage right, unaware of Sostrata and Canthara.)

GETA: NOW he's done it! And nothing at all a body can do
to undo it! THIS is the final end for mother, daughter
—hoo boy!—and me.
                              We're under siege! Completely surrounded!
Rapine at every rampart;
                              Squalor at every portal;
Injustice, Disgrace, and Desertion hammering every flank!
What's with today's generation? A parade of pirates and perverts!
Especially that two-timing snake!

SOSTRATA:

(To Canthara.)

                              Heavens! I think I see Geta—
but what's put him in such a rush? And in such an awful tizzy?

GETA: Honor, vows, compassion! Did THAT hold him back or change
his mind? Or the impending patter of little feet, the result
of his own brutal rape—poor girl!—did THAT even stop him?

SOSTRATA:

(To Canthara.)

                                                            What
does he mean? I don't get it.

CANTHARA:

(To Sostrata.)

                                        Please, Ma'am, why don't we move in
a little closer?

GETA: Dammit, they've got me smoldering now;
My brain is so full of bile there's no room left to think.
Hoo boy, how I'd love to get my hands on that household and belch
my wrath on them all while my spleen's still seething. Agony,
     torture,
and death—nothing fancy—as long as I get to inflict it myself.
First, the Old Man:
                              I'd snuff him out for raising that hoodlum.
Then Syrus, the ringleader:
                                   HIM I'd rip to ribbons for starters.
Next I'd grab his belly, I'd fling him upside down,
then finally splatter his cerebellum all over the sidewalk.
At last the brat himself:
                              I'd gouge out his eyes and push him
off something high.
                         The rest I'd beat, I'd batter, I'd bash,
then I'd litter the ground with stiffs.
                                   But what am I doing? There's no time
to waste! I must share the bad news with Sostrata.

(He runs to Sostrata's door and knocks.)

SOSTRATA:

(To Canthara.)

                                                       Let's go grab
his attention.

(Aloud.)

                         Geta!

GETA: Back off, whoever you are.

(Sostrata taps him on the shoulder.)

SOSTRATA: It's me.
          It's Sostrata.

GETA: Sostrata? Where?

(He turns around.)

                              I've been looking all over for you.
God knows how long I've been waiting. What an incredible stroke
of luck you finally showed up.

(He starts to shake.)

                         Oh Sostrata, Ma'am—

SOSTRATA: What's the matter?
              Why are you trembling?

(He drops his head in his hands.)

GETA: Horrible, just horrible!

CANTHARA: Why the hysteria
              Geta, dear? Now, pull yourself together.

GETA: We're utter—

SOSTRATA: "We're utter"? We're utter WHAT?

GETA: —ly done for, finis, kaput—

SOSTRATA: I beg you, please! Explain!

GETA: now that—

SOSTRATA: Now that WHAT, Geta?

GETA: Aeschinus—

SOSTRATA: Aeschinus WHAT? Spit it out!

GETA: He's a total stranger.
              He dumped us.

SOSTRATA: We're doomed! What happened?

GETA: He fell for another woman.

SOSTRATA: Heaven have mercy!

GETA: Not even discreet. He stole her away
              from her pimp in broad daylight.

SOSTRATA: Geta, you sure about this?

GETA: No question.
              Saw the whole thing myself.

SOSTRATA: Oh god, what a wretched existence!
              Who can you trust nowadays? What can you put your faith in?
              Our Aeschinus! Think! Our lifeline! Our only source of hope!
              OUR ONLY SOURCE OF INCOME!
                              Didn't he SWEAR he would die
              if he went a day without her?
                              Didn't he promise over
              and over he'd place the child on his father's lap and beg
              permission to marry?

(She bursts into tears.)

GETA: You can't cry now, Ma'am. You've got to make plans.

(Sostrata nods and blows her nose.)

Do we take this lying down or tell somebody?

CANTHARA: Good grief,
you must be crazy, man! You want to hang out a sign
and tell the world?

GETA: Who ME? Not at all. For starters, it's clear
that he's written us off completely. If we go public, I'm sure
that he'll only deny it. And that's the end of your reputation
as well as your daughter's life. But even if he confessed,
a lot of good it will do the girl now if he's still in love
with another woman. Either way, we ought to keep mum.

SOSTRATA: To heck with what people say! I refuse to cover this up!

GETA: But what will you do?

SOSTRATA: I'll expose him!

CANTHARA: Sostrata, dear, do you know
what you're getting into?

SOSTRATA: Things can't get any bleaker. First,
she has no dowry. As for the next best thing—well, she's been
divested of that. We can't marry off a used virgin. THIS
is all that's left.

(She pulls out a ring from her garment.)

If he tries to wriggle out, we'll put
the engagement ring on the stand! My conscience is clear. No money
changed hands. We have nothing to hide. To court! On breach of
promise!

GETA: What can I say? You've made your case.

SOSTRATA: Now Geta, you run
as fast as you can to Hegio—our distant uncle—and tell him
the story from top to bottom. He and my poor departed
Simulus cherished a lifelong friendship. He doted on us.

GETA: By god, a good thing! No one else gives a damn.

(He exits stage right.)

SOSTRATA: And Canthara, dear,
you run get the midwife. That way she'll be here when we need her.

(Canthara shuffles off stage left. Sostrata goes into her house.)

Act III, Scene 3 [355–446]

(Demea enters right.)

DEMEA: He's digging my grave! I just heard my own son Ctesipho

is in cahoots with Aeschinus! Whore-nabbers the both!
What next? What evil lies ahead for poor papa
when bad leads good to perdition? Where do I look
for him now? I bet he's held hostage in some kind of fleshpot,
lured by his vile older brother.

(Sounds of sloshing from offstage left.)

                            Who's that? It's Syrus!
And heading this way. Ah, the chance to find my boy!
But dammit, they're all as thick as thieves. If he sees
what I'm after, the weasel won't talk.
                                   I'll have to act casual.

(He hides by the garden gate. Syrus enters stage left with two buckets. Dromo and Stephanio follow, each with an enormous bundle.)

SYRUS: —so we told the old man everything, just how it happened. I've never
seen anyone listen with so much relish— oh boy, what a grin!

DEMEA:

(Aside.)

Oh god, what an idiot!

SYRUS: First, he patted his son on the back,
and then he thanked me, of course, for coming up with the plan.

DEMEA:

(Aside.)

I may explode!

SYRUS: Then after he gave us the cash on the spot,
he threw in fifty more for assorted expenses, now wisely
invested at my discretion.

(He nods at the buckets. Demea emerges from his hiding place.)

DEMEA:

(Aloud.)

                         Yup, here's the man to see
when you want things done right.

SYRUS: Whoops! Demea! I almost didn't see you.
How's it going?

DEMEA: "HOW'S IT GOING?" I can't help but marvel,
the way you people do business here.

SYRUS: God knows it's foolish.
Frankly, even ridiculous.

(He holds out one bucket to Dromo.)

                              Dromo! Gut these fish!
But NOT the enormous eel. Let him splash around a bit longer.
Bone him when I get home, but NOT any sooner than that.

(Dromo takes the bucket and exits into Micio's house.)

DEMEA: Completely indecent.

SYRUS: Look, you think I enjoy this? I bitch
to the management all the time.

(He holds out the other bucket to Stephanio.)

                              These anchovies, Stephanio—
make sure they get a nice little soaking.

(Stephanio takes the other bucket inside.)

DEMEA: For heaven's sake!
Does he do it on purpose? Maybe he thinks he'll win a prize
for making his child a delinquent? It kills me!
                                  I can just see it now.
The day when the boy has finally reached the end of his rope.
Penniless, hopeless, feckless, he runs off and joins the army!

SYRUS: THAT'S the sign of a sage, sir. Seeing what lies in the future
as well as what's under your nose!

(Strains of lute music waft from the house.)

DEMEA: Whoa! That lute girl's set up in the house
already?

SYRUS: Indeedy, she is.

DEMEA: He isn't planning to KEEP her
in there—or is he?

SYRUS: I'm inclined to think he will—where madness
leads, he follows.

DEMEA: Shocking!

SYRUS: His father's bungling indulgence—
a sort of depraved permissiveness.

DEMEA: My very own brother
fills me with shame and disgust.

SYRUS: The gap between you gapes,
dear Demea, sir. A virtual gulf. And I'd swear to that statement
behind your back.
                  Just look at you: pound for pound, you're NOTHING
if not solid wisdom.

                        But him? A slave to whimsy, pure fluff.
        You'd never let YOUR son engage in such things, now would you?

DEMEA: Let him?
        I would have sniffed out this plot six months before it hatched.

SYRUS: No need to tell me. I know you don't miss a trick.

DEMEA: If only
        HE could stay like he is right now, that's all I ask.

SYRUS: May each son be made to his father's orders.

DEMEA: And say, what about him?
        You haven't seen him today—or have you?

SYRUS: YOUR son?

        (Aside.)

                                                It's time
        this old boy went back to the boonies.

        (Aloud.)

                                        I believe he's out on the farm,
        doing chores or something. Been at it quite awhile.

DEMEA: Are you sure
        he's there?

SYRUS: Of course. I took him myself.

DEMEA: The best news I've heard.
        I was worried he might be sticking 'round here.

SYRUS: He was all riled up, too.

DEMEA: But why?

SYRUS: A big fight downtown with his brother. It all began
        with that lute girl.

DEMEA: You're kidding!

SYRUS: The heck I am. He pulled no punches.
        Just as the money was counted out, he let out a holler:
        "AESCHINUS! Stooping to sin and soiling the family crest—
        HOW COULD YOU?"

DEMEA: I'm going to cry, I'm so happy.

SYRUS: "It isn't the money
        you're wasting—IT'S YOUR LIFE!"

        (Demea dabs his eyes.)

DEMEA: Oh bless the boy, there's hope.
          A chip right off the old block.

SYRUS:

          (Aside.)

                                        Oh sure!

(Demea blows his nose.)

DEMEA: Still full of his forefathers' pith,
          eh, Syrus?

SYRUS:

          (Aside.)

                              Yuck.

          (Aloud.)

                              All due to having that special someone
          at home to ply him.

DEMEA: I take pains. I overlook nothing. I mold him.
          I force him to peer into other men's lives—as if into a mirror—
          and learn by example. I tell him, "DO THIS—"

SYRUS: Good thinking.

DEMEA: "—NOT THAT."

SYRUS: How clever!

DEMEA: "THIS is Nice—"

SYRUS: So true.

DEMEA: "—and THAT is Nasty."

SYRUS: Bravo.

DEMEA: And furthermore—

SYRUS: Goshdarnit! I DO wish I had
          the time to hear—but I don't. As guardian of several choice
          and tender fillets, I'm obliged to make sure they don't spoil. You
                see,
          it's as great a crime for slave as master, Demea, to ignore
          that set of precepts you just laid out. I do my best
          to direct my fellow menials in very much the same manner:
          "THIS one? Too salty."
                              "THIS one? Too charred."
                                        "And THIS one? Totally
          tasteless!"

"But THAT one? Perfection. Make note for future reference."
I take pains to advise them; I share what fruits of wisdom I have;
I force them to peer into pots and pans—as if into mirrors—
and learn how to use 'em!
       Yes, our behavior is silly—I know it—
but what can you do? Fish gotta swim.

(He turns to go into Micio's house.)

            Did you want something else?

DEMEA: More sense in this house would be nice.

(He turns as if to exit right.)

SYRUS: Are you going back to the country?

DEMEA: Directly.

SYRUS: Why not? After all, what good can you do around here?
No matter how well you hand out advice, there aren't any takers.

(He exits into Micio's house.)

DEMEA: You bet I'm leaving: my only reason for coming
to town has gone back to the farm. He's my sole concern,
my only reason to worry. If Micio wants it
this way, then HE can go deal with the other one.

(He looks offstage right.)

Who's that I see way off in the distance? It isn't
Hegio, my fellow lodge member? Bless my eyes
if I'm seeing straight—it's him all right. Yessir!
We go way back—been friends ever since we were boys.
Tarnation! If only men with his sense of civic
duty hadn't all dried up now; HE still believes
in old-fashioned virtues like loyalty, trust, and honor.
HE wouldn't dream of causing a public scandal.
What a treat! Whenever I see what's left
of our generation, I feel glad to be alive.
I'll wait here so we can say hello and chat.

(He sits down on one of the benches.)

Act III, Scene 4 [447–516]

(Hegio and Geta enter right, both unaware of Demea.)

HEGIO: May heaven have mercy! That's simply outrageous, Geta! Shocking!
I can't believe what you're saying!

GETA: It's fact, no doubt about it.

HEGIO: Such criminal, callous behavior—and coming from such a family!
               Dammit, Aeschinus! THAT you didn't get from your daddy.

DEMEA:

     (Aside.)

               Of course! The kidnapped lute girl! He must have heard! No kin
               to us, and still he's cut to the quick. But the boy's own father?
               Couldn't care less! God help me, if only Micio could hear this.

HEGIO: They have to do the right thing. They won't get away with it.

GETA: Our hopes are riding on you now, Hegio—you're all we have left.
               You're our guardian, godfather. Yes, when the old man gasped out
                  his last,
               he willed our welfare to you. If YOU turn your back, we're goners.

HEGIO: Bite your tongue! I wouldn't dream of abandoning you.
               When it comes to kinfolk, I just can't do enough.

DEMEA:

     (Aside.)

               Here goes.

     (He rises from the bench to greet them.)

                          Well, hey there, Hegio! What's say? Been fine, I hope?

HEGIO: Ah, just the man I wanted. Hello, Demea.

DEMEA: What's wrong?

HEGIO: Your elder son Aeschinus? The one you let your brother adopt?
               He's shrugged off his role as a gentleman, shed all concern—

DEMEA: Now wait—
               just what do you mean?

HEGIO: ·   Remember Simulus, our old pal and crony?

DEMEA: Sure. So what?

HEGIO: Your son has debauched his daughter.

DEMEA: DEAR GOD!

HEGIO: But hang on, Demea—you haven't heard the worst part.

DEMEA: THERE'S WORSE?

HEGIO: Much worse. Now THAT we could take. We could have made
                  excuses:
               "The night was dark,"
                          or, "He was in love,"
                                       or, "Too much to drink,"

or, "Puberty—it's just a phase."
                                    The boy's only human.
But no. When he realized what he had done, he went on his own
to her mother, crying, begging, pleading, promising, SWEARING
on solemn oath to marry the girl and take her home.
And what did he get? Forgiveness. Silence. Absolute trust.
But thanks to that encounter, she's pregnant—nine months and
    counting.
Meanwhile, our fine young man, bless his soul, has left her high
and dry to shack up with some little lutist.

DEMEA: You're sure about this?

HEGIO: Her mother has made the story public. As for the girl,
    her condition is clear. And then there's always Geta, downright
    honest as slaves go. Not some scheming slacker. He takes
    good care of the ladies; in fact, he supports them all by himself.
    Arrest him. Rattle some chains and ask him what happened.

GETA: Why hell,
    you can pull out the thumbscrews, Demea. Torture me all you like
    if it isn't the truth. He'll spill his guts in the end when he looks me
    straight in the eye.

DEMEA: I'm so ashamed. What to do, what to say?
    I just don't know.

(Pamphila moans and shrieks from inside Sostrata's house.)

PAMPHILA: OWEEEEEEEEEEE! The contractions are going to kill me!
    Juno, Great Goddess of Childbirth, HELP ME, PLEASE! I BEG
        YOU!

HEGIO: Good grief! She can't be in labor already?

GETA: She's certainly starting,
    Hegio.

HEGIO: You hear that, Demea? She's calling upon the honor
    of you and your family. Force could be used to make you fix
    this mess, but better you act of your own free will. I pray
    to heaven you'll do what's right, but in case you have other notions,
    Demea, *I* will personally defend this girl and her dear
    departed daddy with force if I have to.
                                    That man was family.
    We grew up as friends. Together in school, inseparable
    in war, and indivisible in peace. We split everything,
    not to mention poverty. I'll go as far as I have to:

I'll go to bat, I'll go to court, I'll even go
to my grave before I think of deserting these women.

So what
do you have to say for yourself?

DEMEA: I'll go and find my brother.

HEGIO: All right, Demea, but YOU still keep this in mind: the easier
you have it because you're rich,

and successful,
and upper-class, and have more weight to throw around, that's ALL
THE MORE REASON
it's up to you to play fair and do what's right.

Assuming,
of course, you WANT to seem respectable.

DEMEA: Rest assured.
Whatever by rights needs doing, consider it done.

HEGIO: It's only
decent. Come now, Geta. Take me inside to see Sostrata.

(He exits with Geta into Sostrata's house.)

DEMEA: What did I tell you? Did I predict this would happen?
If only this were the end! But all that excess
is bound to turn out big and ugly. I'll find
that brother of mine and drop this mess in his lap.

(He exits left; Hegio enters from Sostrata's house, speaking to her within.)

HEGIO: There, there, Sostrata. Do your best to cheer up
and give the girl some comfort. I'll look for Micio—
maybe he went downtown—and give him a full
account of the day's proceedings. And if he's ready
to act responsibly—as he should—then fine,
he can go right ahead. But if he has other ideas,
well, in that case he answers to me. The sooner
I see what he's up to, the sooner I plan our next move.

(He exits stage left.)

Act IV, Scene 1 [517–539]

(Syrus enters from Micio's house, peeling a vegetable. He is followed by Ctesipho.)

CTESIPHO: You say my father went back to the country?

SYRUS: Oh, hours ago.

CTESIPHO: Come on, tell me more.

SYRUS: He's down on the farm, knee-deep, no doubt,
in some momentous endeavor.

CTESIPHO: Boy, I should be so lucky.
NOT that I want him to hurt himself or something. Just wear
himself out so he couldn't get up for, say, the next three days.

SYRUS: Not bad. Though worse is better.

CTESIPHO: True. To spend tonight
like today, in uninterrupted bliss—I'm so willing it hurts.
I don't really hate the farm. I just want a farther farm,
too far for father to find his way here before it's nightfall.
But when he gets home and sees no me, he'll run right back,
I just know it. Then he'll grill me: "WHERE THE HELL HAVE
    YOU BEEN?
The cows have been home for hours." What do I say to that?

SYRUS: You haven't thought of ANYTHING?

CTESIPHO: No. I never do.

SYRUS:

    (Aside.)

    At best he's pathetic.

    (Aloud.)

                                        Don't you have people in town?
    Business associates? Family? Friends?

CTESIPHO: Sure. So what?

SYRUS: You say you were helping them out.

CTESIPHO: When I wasn't? You mean tell a LIE?
I can't do that.

SYRUS: Oh, sure you can!

CTESIPHO: Well, that covers today.
But Syrus, what if I spend the night here? What's my excuse?

SYRUS: That's tricky. Too bad there's no local tradition of late-night charity
work.
        Look, YOU lean back and relax. I know your old man—
this case is purely routine. If he starts to boil over—Presto!
I'll have him meek as a lamb.

CTESIPHO: But how?

SYRUS: He loves to hear you
praised. I'll make you a god in his eyes, I'll sing your virtues—

CTESIPHO: MY virtues?

SYRUS: YOURS. In no time at all, he'll be blubbering for joy like a baby.

(He looks offstage left.)

Uh oh. Watch out.

CTESIPHO: What is it?

SYRUS: The big bad wolf.

CTESIPHO: My father?

SYRUS: None other.

CTESIPHO: Syrus, what are we going to do?

SYRUS: You hide.

(Ctesipho hides next to the garden gate.)

No, INSIDE. I'll see what he wants.

CTESIPHO: If he asks, you never
saw me. Syrus? You hear me?

SYRUS: Can't you lighten up?

(Ctesipho disappears into Micio's house.)

Act IV, Scene 2 [540–591]

(Demea enters left, speaking to himself, without noticing Syrus.)

DEMEA: I swear I'm cursed. To start with, I can't find my brother. Then,
              while I'm out still looking, I run into one of our hired hands
              who tells me Ctesipho is NOT on the farm. Now what?

(Ctesipho appears on the balcony.)

CTESIPHO: Psst, Syrus!

SYRUS:

(Aside to Ctesipho.)

What's wrong?

CTESIPHO: He isn't looking for me, is he?

SYRUS: Yes!

CTESIPHO: I'm dead.

SYRUS: Don't panic.

DEMEA:

(Still to himself.)

Why such lousy luck? I just don't get it.
Misery, hardship, and woe—decreed by fate at my birth.

I'm always the first to sniff out a mess; the first with the facts;
the first to report the fiasco—and the only one who suffers.

SYRUS:

(Aside.)

He slays me! HIM? The first to know? He hasn't a clue!

DEMEA: I'll check again. Maybe Micio is back by now.

CTESIPHO: Hey, Syrus!
PLEASE don't let him barge in here!

SYRUS: Pipe down! I'm doing my best.

CTESIPHO: Good god, the whole night's at stake! You can't be trusted. I'll lock
myself up with the girl in a closet for maximum safety.

SYRUS: You do that.
I'll try to lose him.

(Ctesipho retreats into the house. Syrus steps forward, smiting his forehead with the
vegetable.)

DEMEA:

(Aside.)

Look! It's Syrus, that cesspool of sleaze.

SYRUS:

(Loudly to himself.)

For crying out loud! I swear to god that no one on earth
can survive in this type of surrounding—it stifles the will to live.
Would somebody tell me just how many masters one slave
can have?
          And why do they all insist on dishing out
such rotten treatment?

DEMEA:

(Aside.)

What's HE whining for? He must be up
to something.

(Aloud.)

Hey there, old boy! Is my brother at home?

SYRUS: "OLD BOY?"
For pity's sake! Is that a nice way to address the deceased?

DEMEA: What's wrong?

SYRUS: You have to ask? Your Ctesipho came this close to pummeling me and that lute girl to death.

DEMEA: What's that? You're kidding!

SYRUS: Damned if I am—you shee how he shplit my lip?

DEMEA: But why?

SYRUS: He claims the girl was bought at my urging.

DEMEA: But didn't you just now say that you took him back to the farm?

SYRUS: And so I did—
—but then he came back! Delirious, merciless, beating up the aged without any shame! To think I cradled that boy in my arms, a tiny little tad, no bigger than that—

DEMEA: Congratulations, Ctesipho! Just like your father, you are! Conducted yourself like a man!

SYRUS: Congratulations? Next time he'll keep his hands to himself, if he's smart.

DEMEA: A courageous act.

SYRUS: Why's that? Because he trounces some helpless girl and a little old slave like me who won't hit back? Sure, give him a medal.

DEMEA: He couldn't have done any better. Besides, I agree—I think you headed this scheme. But tell me, is Micio home?

SYRUS: 'Fraid not.

DEMEA: I wonder where I can find him.

SYRUS: I know, but I'll never tell.

DEMEA: That so?

SYRUS: You betcha.

DEMEA: What if I use your face to plow a couple of hectares?

SYRUS: As I said, I don't know the name, but I'm sure of the place.

DEMEA: So tell me.

SYRUS: You know the arcade next door to the market? The one down THAT way?

DEMEA: What do you think? Of course.

SYRUS: Go past it. Now, keep going straight down the street until you come

to the end; when it starts to snake around, you follow the down
    slope.
On THIS side you'll see a little chapel; smack after THAT
there's an alley.

DEMEA: Which one?

SYRUS: The one with the fig tree. The really big one.

DEMEA: It sounds familiar.

SYRUS: Go straight through the alley.

DEMEA: But that's a dead end!

SYRUS: You're right, by golly! Sheesh! It's a wonder I call myself
a man! My mistake.
                The arcade. Yes, let's start back from there.
I know a shortcut—much less chance of your getting lost.
You know the mansion owned by that filthy rich Cratinus?

DEMEA: I've seen it.

SYRUS: Go past it. Then take a left at the cross street. Go straight
to Diana's temple, and then make a turn to your right. Now before
you get to the city gate—the big arches there by the pond—
you'll see a little bakery. Just in front is a workshop.
He's there.

DEMEA: In god's name, what for?

SYRUS:

(He looks around and spots the benches.)

                    Furniture. Patio furniture.
Custom lounges. Special order, with carved wooden legs.

DEMEA: For one of your orgies, I bet. I'd better hurry and catch him.

(He exits stage right.)

SYRUS: DO, BY ALL MEANS!
                You deserve a workout, you dried-up old buzzard.
What in the world is keeping Aeschinus? Lunch is wilting.
And Ctesipho's all wrapped up in his girlfriend.
                        That just leaves me
to take care of. First order of business: a snack. I'll sneak some
    tidbits
to nibble, strictly the tastier morsels. Then wash those down
with a few nice sips of wine while I savor the afternoon.

(He exits into Micio's house.)

Act IV, Scene 3 [592–609]

(Micio and Hegio enter stage left.)

MICIO: Hegio, I see no reason for heaping praise. This crisis
             began in my family. *I* am the one who has to fix it.
             You think I'm the type to feel insulted or take offense
             when somebody lodges a grievance that's just? That I'm the kind
             who would get defensive and try to throw the blame right back?
             Because I haven't behaved like a bastard, you think you should
                   thank me?

HEGIO: Oh no, not at all! I've never thought of you any other
             way! But please, Micio, YOU come along and talk to the mother.
             Explain to her as you did to me that they have the wrong suspect.
             Tell her his BROTHER is having the affair with that lute girl, not
                   him.

MICIO: All right. If YOU think it's best and we need to, I say let's go.

HEGIO: You're performing a great act of kindness. This visit will really lift
             her spirits: between labor and heartache, she's taken quite a beating.
             Besides, you'll have done your duty.
                                          But if you'd rather not,
             I can give her the message myself.

MICIO: No, no, I insist. I'll go.

HEGIO: It really is kind of you, Micio. A general rule of thumb:
             the less you have,
                                   the more you mistrust. And the more you're prone
             to get miffed. It's poverty—makes you feel hedged in. That's why
             you ought to make amends in person: she'll be more forgiving.

MICIO: Very true. Good point.

HEGIO: They live right here. Follow me.

MICIO: Of course.

(He follows Hegio into Sostrata's house.)

Act IV, Scene 4 [610–635]

(Aeschinus enters left.)

AESCHINUS: Rip my heart out! Why didn't I see it coming!
             What do I do?
                       Where do I go?
                                 I don't know.
             My knees are all wobbly, my stomach is tied in a knot,
             and my mind has turned to mush. Oh, how the hell

am I going to get out of this one?

                  I've been accused
of breach of promise. Why not? It all adds up.
Her mother thinks I bought that girl for myself,
a bit of info I managed to catch from the nurse.
I caught her as she was rushing to get the midwife.
I run up and ask,

           "How's Pamphila? Has labor started?"
She YELLS back,

           "BEAT IT, Aeschinus! Hit the road!
We've had enough of your talk, your unkept promises!"
So I say,

           "Hey! Just what do you mean by that?"
and she says,

           "You want the little tart? Then keep her.
Good-bye and good riddance."

                  I suddenly realize
I'm falsely accused, but I have to play dumb. If that gasbag
knew about Ctesipho's love life, she'd tell the whole world.

So what's my next move? Admit the girl belongs
to my brother? A lot of good it will do if THAT
gets out. On the other hand, it might be too late
for the truth. I'm afraid that no one will ever believe me.
All the evidence points in the same direction:
I grabbed her,

        I bought her,

                I put her up in my house.
Oh, it's all my fault, I admit it. I should have told
my father the story, no matter how bad it got.
I should have BEGGED him to let me marry Pamphila.
Now where am I? Nowhere.

                Come on, Aeschinus,
get a grip!

        Step One: Go clear myself with her family.
Step Two: Walk up to the door.

(He approaches the door and hesitates.)

                I'll never make it.
Just knocking gives me the shivers.

(He takes a deep breath and knocks.)

                Hey! Wake up!
It's me, remember? Aeschinus! Somebody open
the door!

(The door swings open.)

                    Oh no! They're coming! I'll hide over here.

(He hides next to the garden gate.)

Act IV, Scene 5 [636–712]

(Micio enters from Sostrata's house, still speaking to her within.)

MICIO: Just do as I told you, Sostrata. I'll find my son and explain
                the arrangements. But who was that knocking?

AESCHINUS:

          (Aside)

                                        Oh no. It's Daddy.
                                                  I'm doomed.

MICIO: Aeschinus?

AESCHINUS:

          (Aside.)

                    What is he doing in THERE?

MICIO: That YOU who knocked?

          (Aside, after a lengthy silence.)

                A man of few words. But why not twist his tail a bit?
                It just might do him some good, since he wasn't willing to trust me.

          (Aloud.)

                Well, aren't you going to answer?

AESCHINUS:

          (As he emerges casually from his hiding place.)

                                        Not THAT door, as far as I know.

MICIO: Oh really? I was indeed wondering what sort of affair could possibly
                bring you here.

          (Aside.)

                    He's blushing—there's hope.

AESCHINUS: So tell me, Daddy.
                What, as a matter of fact, brings YOU here?

MICIO: Oh, nothing to do
                with me. A friend dragged me back from downtown to act as a
                witness.

AESCHINUS: Any reason?

MICIO: I'll tell you. A couple of women live here.
Poor little things. I'm sure you haven't met them—they only
moved here recently.

AESCHINUS: And?

MICIO: So this nice girl lives with her mother—

AESCHINUS: Go on.

MICIO: —and since this girl lost her father, my friend here, her next
of kin, is legally bound to marry her.

AESCHINUS: My life is over.

MICIO: What's that?

AESCHINUS: Forget it. Keep going.

MICIO: He's come to take her away.
Let's see. I do believe he's residing now in Miletus.

AESCHINUS: You can't be serious! Take her away?

MICIO: That's right.

AESCHINUS: Really?
All the way to Miletus?

MICIO: That's right.

AESCHINUS:

        (Aside.)

                                        I feel sick. Very sick.

        (Aloud.)

        And these women? What do THEY say?

MICIO: Well, what do you expect?
They can't really argue.
                              The mother INSISTS there's a baby fathered
by some other man—of course, she won't tell us his name—but
    keeps
insisting that whatshisface got there first and my friend has no claim
on the girl.

AESCHINUS: Aha! You see?
                              I mean, don't you think that's fair,
all things considered?

MICIO: No.

AESCHINUS: But Daddy, why not? He's really
taking her with him?

MICIO: No other option.

AESCHINUS: How COULD you be
SO CALLOUS?
            SO HEARTLESS?
                        SO—
                        frankly, Daddy—SO INSENSITIVE!

MICIO: What do you mean?

AESCHINUS: You have to ask? Now what do YOU think
will happen to that miserable, heartsick wretch who fell in love
with her first? That unfortunate victim of fate who for all I know
is gnashing his teeth at this very moment? How will HE feel
when HE sees her swiped from under his nose and swept right off
the horizon?
            It's outrageous, Daddy. Criminal.

MICIO: By whose brand of logic?
Who promised to bless the marriage? Who gave away the bride?
Where was the groom?
                        And when was the wedding?
                                    And who led her on?
And why did he get involved with another man's woman?

AESCHINUS: A big girl
like that is supposed to sit around and wait for some distant
uncle to show? Now THAT was the point you should have argued,
Daddy. You should have fought back.

MICIO: That's absurd. Attack the man
I came to defend?
            It's none of our business anyway, son.
Who cares? Let's go.

(Aeschinus begins to sniffle.)

                        What's wrong? Are you crying?

AESCHINUS: Listen, Daddy.
            PLEASE!

MICIA:

        . (As he pulls a handkerchief out for Aeschinus.)

            I heard the whole story, Aeschinus. All the details.
But I love you. THAT makes me care all the more what you do.

AESCHINUS: Oh, Daddy!
          I want to deserve that love for as long as you live—just as much
          as I wish I could wipe out this whole ugly business. I feel so rotten.

MICIO: Yes, I'm sure you do. Deep down, I'm convinced,
          you're a decent, well-meaning boy. But all of this wild
          behavior scares me. What kind of place do you think
          this is? You seduced a girl you had no right to touch.
          That's a pretty big boo-boo to start, but at least it's human:
          other good men have made their share of mistakes.
          But after it happened, did you look around for help?
          Or look ahead so as to plan the inevitable outcome?
          Granted, it would have been painful to tell me yourself—
          but how else was I to find out? You just sat there and dawdled
          for nine long months.
                              And now you've let down yourself,
          your girlfriend, your baby—all your dependents. Why?
          Did you think the gods would fix things up while you slept?
          A bride in your bed with no thanks to you? I hope
          to god you never dither around like this again!

          Now cheer up. You're getting married.

AESCHINUS: What?

MICIO: I said, "Cheer up."

AESCHINUS: You're just fooling, Daddy—aren't you?

MICIO: Me fool you? Why should I?

AESCHINUS: I don't know. It's just that I want it so badly I'm afraid to believe it.

MICIO: Go home. You'd better ask the gods for some marriage counseling—
          your wife-to-be is waiting. Scoot!

AESCHINUS: My wife? Right now?

MICIO: Right now.

AESCHINUS: So soon?

MICIO: As soon as possible.

AESCHINUS: Jupiter strike me,
          Dad, if I don't love you more than anything else.

MICIO: Even her?

AESCHINUS: Well, just as much.

MICIO: How generous.

AESCHINUS: Hey! And that man from Miletus?

MICIO: Shipped out, set sail, skedaddled. Why are you stalling?

AESCHINUS: YOU go,
        Daddy. YOU pray instead. You're so much nicer. I'm sure
        the gods will listen to you.

MICIO: No, *I* am going inside
        to get things ready. And YOU will do what I said, if you're smart.

(He exits into his house. Aeschinus waits until he is gone and then lets out a
whistle.)

AESCHINUS: Pretty great stuff, this father/son business. Could friends
        or brothers do any better? Don't you just LOVE him?
        Don't you just want to pick him up in your lap
        and HUG him?
                        Uh oh. He's been so incredibly nice,
        he's got me worried. What if I do something dumb
        and ruin his mood? I'll have to be more careful.
        I'd better go in. I'm holding up my own wedding!

(He skips into Micio's house.)

Act IV, Scene 6 [713–718]

(Demea enters right, panting.)

DEMEA: I'm pooped—from all—this running—around.
                                                May heaven blast you,
        Syrus, and all of your damn directions too. I crawled
        from one end of town to the other: to the gate, to the lake. You name
            it,
        I saw it. I found everything BUT the workshop. And no one has seen
        my brother. Well, I'm not budging. I'll blockade the house 'til he
            comes.

(He sits down on one of the benches.)

Act IV, Scene 7 [719–762]

(Micio opens his door, still speaking to someone within. He is busily attaching
flowers to a headband.)

MICIO: I'll go right over and tell them we're ready.

(Demea leaps up from the bench.)

DEMEA: Aha! There he is!
        I've been on your trail for hours, Micio.

MICIO: And why, dare I ask?

DEMEA: More crime to report—bigger and better crime. And all
        the work of your wonderful boy.

MICIO: How shocking!

DEMEA: Fresh forms of outrage,
major offenses—

MICIO: That's enough.

DEMEA: Ah, YOU don't know
what lurks in his heart!

MICIO: I think I do.

DEMEA: You dope! Wake up!
I don't MEAN the musician. He knocked up a nice girl—a
CITIZEN!

MICIO: I know.

DEMEA: OH HO!
                You know? And you just let it slide?

MICIO: There's no other choice.

DEMEA: What's wrong with you, Micio? No ranting, no raving—

MICIO: No, though I wish—

DEMEA: But there's a BABY!

MICIO: Bless him.

DEMEA: The girl is broke!

MICIO: And so I've heard.

DEMEA: There won't be a dowry!

MICIO: That's obvious.

DEMEA: So what's going to happen now?

MICIO: We meet the crisis head on.

(He tries the garland on his head for size and then takes it off.)

                 The girl moves from THERE—

(He points a flower to Sostrata's house.)

                            —to HERE.

(He points to his own house.)

DEMEA: For heaven's sake, what kind of solution is THAT?

MICIO: What else
do you want me to do?

DEMEA: What else? If this doesn't upset you REALLY,
the least you could do is act like a human being and FAKE IT!

MICIO: I'm giving the bride away myself; the rift has been mended.

There WILL be a wedding, there's nothing to stop it. Act? Pretend?
This is BEING a human being!

DEMEA: But Micio, are you happy?

MICIO: No! If I could change things, I would! But since I can't, I cope.
Life is a gamble, a crapshoot: if luck doesn't roll your way,
you compensate with a little skill.

DEMEA: HA! "A little skill"
set you back two thousand. Try and get compensation for THAT.
You'll have to take a loss, or give her away for free.

MICIO: You're wrong on both counts. I have no intention of selling the lute
         girl.

DEMEA: Then what will you do?

MICIO: I'll let her come live at our house.

DEMEA: Great Jove
have mercy! Whore and housewife under one roof?

MICIO: Why not?

DEMEA: Is this the voice of reason?

MICIO: Sure sounds like it to me.

DEMEA: God help me, this stupid behavior of yours makes me swear you
         bought her
on purpose. What is it? You wanted a playmate to sing duets?

MICIO: Why not?

DEMEA: And the blushing bride? She'll make it a threesome, no doubt?

MICIO: No doubt.

DEMEA: A daisy chain, eh? You bouncing around in the middle?

MICIO: That's it.

DEMEA: It is?

MICIO: You're available, of course, if we need a fourth?

(He swings Demea by one arm while crowning him with the garland.)

DEMEA: OH, HAVE YOU NO SHAME?

MICIO: Oh, Demea! Why don't you lighten up?
Stop frothing at the mouth, and try to look cheerful and happy,
like you're supposed to. Your son is getting married. I'm going
to gather the bride's side together, and then I'll be right back.

(He goes into Sostrata's house. Demea walks to center stage.)

DEMEA: You call this living? You call this morality? I call it insanity.

The daughter-to-be has no dowry,

                                     a whore is tending the home fire,

spending is out of sight,

                         the kid is out of control,

and the old man is out of his mind.

                            Our Lady of Mental Health

could never save this family—even if she wanted.

Act V, Scene 1 [763–775]

(Syrus, tipsy, appears in the doorway of Micio's house.)

SYRUS: Syrus baby, you've done yourself proud. You served yourself
like a master.

(Modestly, stepping aside and answering himself.)

                     Aw, get out of here. But seriously, things
are a wee bit crowded inside.

(He burps loudly, then steps back to answer himself.)

                           Then what's say we take a strolly-
wolly out here?

(He yawns and stretches, and then sits down on one of the benches.)

DEMEA: See that? Some model of self-restraint.

SYRUS: Well, what have we here? It's Demea, one of our favorite oldies.
What's the matter, Demea? Tell Syrus why so glum.

DEMEA: You're vermin.

SYRUS: A miracle! Think! The font of Holy Wisdom
spouting right here in our neighborhood!

DEMEA: If you belonged to me—

SYRUS: Why Demea, you'd be rich! Your financial empire solid!

DEMEA: —I'd really make an example of you.

SYRUS: But what have I done?

DEMEA: You have to ask? Right in the thick of this horrible muddle,
when everything's still in a hideous snarl and nothing's been settled,
there you are pickled, you shameless louse, as if there were
      something
to CELEBRATE!

(He takes the garland off his head and throws it at Syrus.)

SYRUS: This is NOT the reception I had in mind.

Act V, Scene 2 [776–786]

(Dromo appears on the balcony of Micio's house.)

DROMO: HEY, SYRUS! Ctesipho wants you to come back inside!

(Syrus waves Dromo away frantically.)

SYRUS: Get lost!

(Dromo retreats into the house. Demea turns around.)

DEMEA: Did he say something about Ctesipho?

SYRUS: Nope.

DEMEA: Now look, you two-bit
goon, is Ctesipho in there?

SYRUS: Of course not.

DEMEA: Then why did he mention
his name?

SYRUS: Another Ctesipho. Itty-bitty one.
He hangs around here all the time. You know him?

DEMEA: We'll soon find out.

(He starts for the house; Syrus grabs him.)

SYRUS: Hey! Where do you think you're going?

DEMEA: Let go!

SYRUS: The hell I will!

DEMEA: You get your nasty hands off! Or maybe you'd like me to crack
your noodle in two?

(He pulls himself free and marches into Micio's house.)

SYRUS: I lost him. Poor Ctesipho—his party is pooped.
A change of plans is clearly in order:
                              One—lie low
until this blows over.
                        Two—reconnoiter secluded corner
to sleep off impending hangover.
                              Yes, an excellent strategy.

(He sneaks into Micio's house.)

Act V, Scene 3 [787–854]

(Micio enters from Sostrata's house, still speaking to her within.)

MICIO: We're all set to go on our side, just like I told you, Sostrata.
You give the word and—

(A loud noise is heard from Micio's house.)

WHO is banging down my door?

DEMEA:

(As he bursts out of Micio's house.)

THE SHAME OF IT ALL!

Oh, what do I do?

Oh, how can I stand it?

Do I scream? Do I yell? Do I simply drop to my knees in prayer?

(He drops to his knees.)

Heaven! Earth! Ye Waters of Neptune! DO SOMETHING!

MICIO:

(Aside.)

Oh boy.

He's figured the whole thing out. No wonder the flap.

(He sighs.)

That's it.

More bickering. Time to step in.

(He approaches Demea.)

DEMEA: Aha! There he is! The child-warper!

Ruined them both, now, haven't you?

MICIO: First you suppress your hostility.

Settle down. Then we talk.

DEMEA:

(As he stands up and takes a deep breath.)

I'm settled down. All suppressed.

And no more swearing, I promise. But face the facts. Didn't
we promise—on YOUR suggestion—that I wouldn't meddle with
    your boy?

And you wouldn't meddle with mine? Well, answer me!

MICIO: We did.

I don't deny it.

DEMEA: Then why is my son half-drunk on your couch?

Why shelter him, Micio? Why buy him a mistress? It's okay to bend
the rules to MY disadvantage? I don't interfere with your boy;
why can't you leave mine alone?

MICIO: You're not being fair.

DEMEA: I'm not?

MICIO: You know that old saying—"Friends share and share alike."

DEMEA: Such wit!
          But your timing is off.

MICIO: Now Demea, listen—if that isn't asking
          too much. To start, if the money they spend is gnawing away
          at your soul, why not look at it this way?
                                        You tried to raise two sons
          on a limited income, thinking your budget would cover both.
          And of course, you thought I'd get married. Stick to what you
               planned
          initially: save and scrimp and sit on your nest egg. As much
          as you leave behind will be your glorious contribution,
          your legacy.
                         MY money comes as a windfall, so let them enjoy it
          NOW. Your savings won't be diminished; whatever else
          I chip in, consider profit.
                              Think it over, Demea.
          You'll save us all a lot of grief.

DEMEA: Forget the money.
          I'm talking about their morals—

MICIO: Hang on. I was getting to that.
          I tell you, Demea, human beings send out signals.
          All kinds of signals, from which we can infer behavior.
          Two different men can do the same thing: while in one case, you'll
               say,
          "No problem, won't hurt him the teeniest bit";
                                        in the other, you'll say,
          "No, sirree." It's not what you do, it's who does it.
                                        From what I see
          in these boys, I'm sure they'll turn out just fine. I see common
               sense,
          respect, and mutual affection. It's plain their hearts are big and their
               minds
          are broad. You can rein them in whenever you want. I know
          you're afraid they spend a tad too freely. But Demea, dear,
          although the passing years make us wiser in other regards,
          old age promotes a very bad habit: we worry too much about money.
          Relax. The compulsion for pinching pennies will come with time.

DEMEA: I'm afraid your pretty theories and happy-go-lucky heart
          will plunge us all in the gutter.

MICIO: Hogwash! Won't ever happen.
          Now why don't you drop the subject? Trust me. And wipe off that
               frown.

DEMEA: I guess I have no choice. But I take the boy home tomorrow.
Crack of dawn, and it's back to the country.

MICIO: Perfect. Smuggle
him out at midnight. But can't you look happy just for today?

DEMEA: And I'll drag that lute girl too.

MICIO: You'll harness his spirits with ease
if you yoke him to her. But make sure you keep HER tied down.

DEMEA: You bet I'll make sure. Out there she'll grind, and she'll bake to the
     point
she's so coated with flour and grit and soot that she looks like a
     cutlet.
And then I'll send her out to gather up twigs at high noon:
she'll come back toasted as black as a lump of charcoal.

MICIO: I like it.
Now you're talking. And then, if he were MY son, I'd twist
his arm and make him climb in bed with her.

DEMEA: Go on.
Make fun of me. You're so lucky, blessed with that sense of humor.

MICIO: You still have more?

DEMEA: All right, all right. I'll stop already.

MICIO: In that case, come on inside.

(He gestures for Demea to follow him into the house.)

                         Let's enjoy the rest of the day.

(Micio goes in. Demea follows but hesitates on the threshold, and then walks to
center stage.)

Act V, Scene 4 [855–881]

DEMEA: No matter how neatly you keep your accounts in life,
experience, age, and circumstance always show up
to toss something new on the books and teach you a lesson.
You find you don't know what you thought you did, and what
     seemed
so important in theory turns out to be pointless in practice.
That's what happened to me. I've run a hard race,
but now that I'm nearing the finish line, I give up.
And why? I've faced the facts. It's the easy-going,
tolerant types who win. And everyone knows it.
You need an example? Easy. Take me and my brother.

HE has always been a creature of leisure;

affable, unflappable, always the life of the party,
never an unkind word, forever a smile.
HE has devoted himself to self-indulgence,
and everyone loves him—they can't say enough about him.

But ME, the uncouth one, the mean one, the grim one, the cheap
    one,
the wild-eyed, pigheaded one—no, *I* got married.
At first it was utter misery, but then it got worse:
we had kids.
                What the hell? While *I*'ve been slogging away
and scraping together as much as I can for their sake,
I've lost the best years of my life. And now that I'm old
and worn, what's the fruit of my labor? They hate me. But HIM?
HE reaps the profits of dadhood without any effort.
HIM they love, they confide in—ME they avoid.
HIM they adore, they flock to—ME they ignore.
HIS health they pray for—but mine? They can't wait 'til I'm dead.
The boys I raised by my sweat—we're talking buckets—
HE buys off with a handful of obols. And ME?
I'm stuck with the grind while HE has all the fun.

(He smacks himself on the cheek.)

    —Get WITH it, Demea, GET WITH IT!
                                  TWO can play
at that game. Let's try and drip a little honey,
let's ply some winsome ways of our own. After all,
HE pushed me into this corner. I want their love
and approval too: if that means I lavish and coddle,
I'll give a first-rate performance. The money won't last,
but what does it matter? *I'll* be the first to go.

Act V, Scene 5 [882–888]

(Syrus enters, yawning, from Micio's house.)

SYRUS: Hey, Demea! Micio says don't wander off.

DEMEA: Who's that?
It's Syrus, old pal! Howya doing? How's everything going?

SYRUS:

(As he takes a step back and gives Demea a suspicious look.)

    Fine.

DEMEA: Fantastic!

(Aside.)

                  Hear that? I tossed in three nice ones: "old pal;

howya doing; how's everything going?" Not like me at all!

(Aloud.)

You're a pretty unselfish sort for a slave, and I'd like to help you.

SYRUS:

(Taking another step back.)

I'm grateful, I'm sure.

DEMEA: I mean it, Syrus. Just wait and see.

Act V, Scene 6 [889–898]

(Geta enters from Sostrata's house, still speaking to her within.)

GETA: I'm going next door, Ma'am. I'll ask when they're coming to get the
bride.
Oh look, here's Demea now.

(Aloud.)

Hello, sir. You're well, I hope.

DEMEA: Ah yes! Old whoozis—

GETA: It's Geta.

DEMEA: Of course! Well, *GETA,*
from what I've gathered today, I'd say you're a man of great value.
Someone who cares for his owners—the way I've seen YOU do,
GETA—
that's one hell of a slave, in my opinion. That's why
I'd like to give you a hand, if I get the chance.

(Aside.)

I'm trying
to be more folksy—and making terrific progress!

GETA: That's very
nice of you, Demea.

DEMEA:

(Aside.)

Man by man I'll sway the masses!

Act V, Scene 7 [899–923]

(Aeschinus enters from Micio's house, unaware of Demea.)

AESCHINUS: All this fuss over holy wedlock! The whole day's been shot!
I'll be dead by the time they decide on a caterer.

DEMEA: What's the matter,
       Aeschinus?

AESCHINUS: FATHER? That you? I didn't know you were here.

DEMEA: It's me, all right: your natural papa, heart and soul,
       who loves you more than anything else in the whole wide world.
       But why aren't you busy carrying your bride across the threshold?

AESCHINUS: I want to. But I can't. There's a holdup: the flute girl is late.
       And there's no one here to sing the wedding hymn.

DEMEA:

       (As he puts his arm around Aeschinus.)

                                                    Would you like
       some advice from dear old papa?

AESCHINUS: What's that?

DEMEA: Forget the hymn,
       the daisy chains, the party lights, the flute girls!
                                              Go knock
       a hole in the garden wall and bring her through right now!
       Remodel! Make it one big house! Invite her mom
       to move in! Even better—invite the whole family!

AESCHINUS: Great idea!
       YOU are one big sweetheart, Father.

DEMEA:

       (Aside.)

                                        Hear that? So now
       I'm a sweetheart. And my brother's house will be a regular
           roadway!
       Endless traffic! Endless expense! So what? I'm a sweetheart!
       Voted most popular! Loved by all!
                                        Two thousand here,
       a couple of thousand there—just send the bills to my brother,
       Croesus himself.

       (Aloud.)

                              Well, Syrus, why are you waiting? Go do it!

SYRUS: Do what?

DEMEA: Go tear down the wall.

       (To Geta.)

                              And YOU help the ladies come through.

GETA: God bless you, Demea! Such concern for our welfare—it comes from the heart, I can feel it!

(Geta exits into Sostrata's house. Syrus exits into Micio's house. He is seen carrying a large mallet behind the garden gate, which he swings wildly in the air; several loud thuds follow.)

DEMEA: I think they deserve it. Don't you?

AESCHINUS: I do.

DEMEA: The poor thing just gave birth. We can't just parade her through town now,
              can we? THIS is much nicer.

AESCHINUS: I've never seen better, Father.

DEMEA: Just MY little way of doing things. Look, here comes Micio.

Act V, Scene 8 [924–957]

(Micio enters from his house, still speaking to Syrus within.)

MICIO: My BROTHER told you to do it? Where is he?
                                        Demea, YOU told
              Syrus to tear down my wall?

DEMEA: Of course I told him to do it.
              Every detail counts when it comes to uniting these households.

(Geta struggles under the weight of Pamphila, as he carries her through Micio's garden. Demea clasps Aeschinus to his chest to distract Micio.)

              We must nurture these people. Support them. Clasp them hard to our bosom.

AESCHINUS:

(Muffled.)

              I have to agree with him, Daddy.

(Geta hobbles back through the garden to Sostrata's house.)

MICIO: I can't argue with that.

DEMEA: Dear god,
              I hope not! The least we can do is do our duty. First,
              the bride has a mother—

MICIO: She does. So what?

DEMEA: —a wonderful woman.
              Spotless reputation.

MICIO: So I've heard.

DEMEA: She's not young—

MICIO: So I've seen.

DEMEA: —too old to have more children. No one to care, she's all by herself alone.

MICIO: Is he trying to make a point?

DEMEA: The only decent thing you can do is marry her, Micio.

(He pushes Aeschinus forward.)

Aeschinus! Go for it! YOU persuade him.

MICIO: ME? GET MARRIED?

DEMEA: You.

MICIO: ME?

DEMEA: Yes, I said you.

MICIO: You jest.

DEMEA:

(To Aeschinus.)

                       Talk to him. Man to man. I bet he'll do it.

AESCHINUS: Oh Daddy, PLEASE?

MICIO:

(To Aeschinus.)

What are you listening to HIM for, you silly ass?

DEMEA: Don't fight it, Micio. There's no other option.

MICIO:

(To Demea.)

               You're out of your mind.

AESCHINUS: Oh, do it, Daddy! Please? For me!

MICIO:

(To Aeschinus.)

            You're nuts. Get lost.

DEMEA: Come on. Why not do your son a favor?

MICIO: Have you lost your senses entirely?

(Geta struggles under the weight of Sostrata, as he carries her across the garden.)

ME a bridegroom at sixty-five? Make that decrepit
old bag my wife? Is THAT what you're proposing?

AESCHINUS: Come on!
Besides, I already promised you'd do it.

MICIO: What do you mean,
YOU PROMISED? Charity starts in your own pocket, sonny.

DEMEA: Come now.
What if he asked you to sacrifice something REALLY BIG?

MICIO: As if it gets any bigger than this?

DEMEA: Oh, do him a favor!

AESCHINUS: Don't be a grouch.

DEMEA: Come on. Say yes.

MICIO: Would you please give UP?

AESCHINUS: If you give in.

MICIO: Look, this is coercion.

DEMEA: Then, Micio, why not
yield to the popular vote?

MICIO: In my opinion, it's sick.
It's tasteless, ridiculous, and utterly at odds with my lifestyle.

(He looks at Aeschinus.)

                                                        But—

if that's what you really want, I'll do it.

AESCHINUS: What a nice guy!
No wonder I love you!

(He gives Micio a big hug.)

DEMEA: But—

(Aside.)

                              And now what do I say?
I got what I wanted.

MICIO: Anything else?

DEMEA: Well, there's Hegio here,
their next-of-kin, our soon-to-be in-law. A very poor in-law.
We ought to do something nice for him.

MICIO: Like what?

DEMEA: You know

that little plot of land you have just outside of town?
The one you rent out? Let's give it to him.

MICIO: That LITTLE plot?

DEMEA: All right, that BIG plot. We still ought to do it. He cared for the girl
like a father. A damned good man, and now he's part of the family.
It has to be done.
                       Besides, I'm practicing what you preach.
Now didn't you say just a while ago—and you put it so well—
that the sin of old age is fussing too much about money? Yessir,
it's a nasty, embarrassing habit, one we should try to avoid.
Words truthfully spoken, Micio, and it's time to put them in action.

MICIO: I'm thrilled.
                     What's the use? If Aeschinus has his heart set on it,
Hegio gets the land.

AESCHINUS: Oh, Daddy!

(He gives Micio another hug and is joined by Demea.)

DEMEA: Real brothers at last!
Body and soul.

(Aside.)

              I'll give him enough rope to hang himself yet!

Act V, Scene 9 [958–997]

(Syrus enters from Micio's house.)

SYRUS: Mission accomplished, Demea.

DEMEA: What a fine helper! By golly,
in MY opinion, today is the day to set Syrus free.

MICIO: Free HIM? What for?

DEMEA: Uh, lots.

SYRUS: Dear Demea! A good man you are,
god knows. I've watched these boys ever since they were tots. I've
    done
my best to guide them,
                   to nurture their minds,
                         to give them PRINCIPLES!

DEMEA: You see? The products speak for themselves. But wait; there's more.
You can trust him to shop, then whip up dessert and bring home a
    whore
on a moment's notice—hardly a role for your average man.

SYRUS: You nice, sweet man!

(He gives Demea a hug.)

DEMEA: To top it off, he was such a help
in procuring the lute girl today. In fact, he took care of it all.
He deserves a reward. The example can't help but improve the other
slaves. Besides, that's what *Aeschinus* wants.

MICIO:

(To Aeschinus.)

                                        You really want this?

AESCHINUS: I do.

MICIO: . If you say so. Syrus, come here.

(Syrus approaches. Micio gives him a whack on the head, and then extends his hand
for Syrus to shake.)

                              Go free.

SYRUS:

(He rubs his head while still shaking Micio's hand.)

                                        You're too kind.
I can't thank you all enough—and Demea, that goes double for you.

(He extends his hand to Demea, who shakes it.)

DEMEA: Delighted to help.

AESCHINUS: Me too.

(He advances to shake Syrus's hand.)

SYRUS: Indeed, I'm sure you are.

(He sighs.)

But if only this moment of joy could be made to last an eternity!
If only my lovely wife Phrygia were standing here free by my side!

DEMEA: Now there's a remarkable woman.

SYRUS:

(To Micio.)

                                A top-notch wet nurse—the first
today to feed your grandson—you know, the son of your son?

DEMEA: By god, that's a serious point. If she really fed him first,
there's no question—she has to go free. It's only fair.

MICIO: Just for THAT?

DEMEA: Just for that. Don't argue. I'll pay you back later.

SYRUS: Oh, Demea!
Heaven grant your every wish and desire!

MICIO: Syrus,
you've done pretty well for yourself today.

DEMEA: He could still do better,
Micio. Why not advance him a little something to set up
house? He'll pay you back soon.

MICIO: A VERY little something.

(He forms a zero with his thumb and forefinger.)

DEMEA: He's worth his weight in gold.

SYRUS: I swear I'll pay it back—
but first hand it over.

AESCHINUS: Come on, Daddy!

MICIO: I'll give it some thought.

DEMEA: He'll do it.

(He winks and nudges both Syrus and Aeschinus.)

SYRUS: The best of men!

AESCHINUS: The finest of fathers! And mine!

(He gives Micio another hug.)

MICIO:

(To Demea.)

What happened? Why the sudden change of heart? The outpour
of generosity? The scatter of wild largess?

DEMEA: I'll tell you.
I wanted to show that all your lovable qualities, Micio,
what the boys consider good humor and tolerance—don't come
from sincere, upright, and honest living; they come from being
an indulgent, extravagant pushover who simply cannot say no.
Now, Aeschinus, if this is why you and your brother hate my way
of life, because right or wrong, I don't cater to all your whims,
I give up. Go spend, waste money, do whatever you want.
On the other hand, if you'd rather—given you're young and tend
to leap without looking, never giving a second thought—
if you'd rather have someone to hold you back, to set you straight,
and let you have your way when it's right, well, here I am,
the man for the job.

AESCHINUS: You take it, Father. It's yours. You know
what's best. But Ctesipho? What about him?

DEMEA: He's off the hook.
He keeps the girl. But she's the last.

MICIO: That's fair.

SYRUS:

     (To the audience.)

                        So clap!

Finis

Appendix 1: A Note on the PreAct of
The Wild, Wild Women

The text of *Bacchides* starts with a jerk. We are suddenly *in* the play, as Bacchis One and her sister, Bacchis Two—two upscale call girls—conclude what is evidently a tactical briefing. Standing apart from them is a rich and gormless young man who constitutes their objective: a "white horse" to underwrite and support the rescue of one of them from a contractual relationship with a soldier. All this, and much more, we are left to infer, without the help of deliberate exposition.

No other ancient play begins this way. The fact is, the oldest manuscript of *Bacchides* has *lost* the play's beginning, and no later ones have supplied the lack. It therefore falls on the translator-for-production to fill the gap. Helps do exist. Post-Plautine grammarians and others often cited Plautus as a source for, say, a rare word or an interesting grammatical form, and sometimes noted the play in which the anomaly occurred. Sifting by scholars has yielded a total of twenty-three fragments, coming to thirty-four lines or parts of lines, which occur nowhere else in the play, and so are presumed to come from the lost beginning. This is not much to reconstruct a sequence that may have been fairly substantial.

But enough, possibly, for an informed try at an approximation. The metrical form of a given fragment may show the *sort* of speech or lyric that it was taken from, and its content may clue its specific context—because we *do* have contexts. Certain things have to happen when Roman Comedies start: prologues explaining characters, set, and situation; one-sided dialogues stuffed with *stuff;* entrance monologues introducing new arrivals; first contacts between persons destined to be twined in love or hate by play's end. These necessities create a grid, as it were, on which the fragments may be scattered—though the fragments help determine the grid as well. The consequent backing and filling yield a structure to be filled in.

This is where the problem comes. Plautus is, let's say, an *extravagant* comedian. He hardly ever engages in the careful joining of plot-surge and character that is the peculiar glory of Menander and Terence. His approach is Aristophanic, in that anything or anyone onstage may be the excuse for a, well, a *party.* The audience must be informed, of course, but it must also be entertained—which is where the fun begins for the translator, who must build situations and yocks as well as language.

The result of my twisting and turning in this process is the preAct that I offer to start *Bacchides.* Let me emphasize that it is not a true reconstruction of what inevitably must have been. There are too many variables in the evidence for that. Rather, it is a demonstration of possibility, a *frinstance;* and it is a longish frinstance, whose implied text might have run to at least a fifth again of the text we have, making this one of Plautus's longer plays. This is possible and, I believe, necessary.

My principal hope is that this preAct will start the play adequately and work onstage.

N.B.: So that the interested may see where the preAct came from, I have indicated the occurrence of a fragment in the preAct by underlining and sidenote. The Roman numerals at the margins indicate the original ordering of the Latin fragments by Ritschl, as enshrined by Goetz. These are noticed, at least in parentheses, by modern editors. (I have passed over Fragments XXI and XXII, whose relation to *Bacchides* is extremely tenuous.) Bacchis One's first line, which kicks things off, began Menander's Greek source-play *Double Deceiver,* and is cited from Sandbach's *Fragmenta Aliunde Nota* to that play.

DOUGLASS PARKER

Appendix 2: A Supplementary Prologue to *The Wild, Wild Women*

The connection between Plautus's *Bacchides* and Euripides' *Bacchae* seems sure. Zeugma the tutor makes it quite clear in Act III, Scene 1:

> *Those sisters!*
> *Bacchis and Bacchis they call them, but what they are is BACCHAE!*
> *The wild, debauched devotees of the god of wine and lust!*
> *Get ye behind me, sisters, who suck the blood of men!*

Once established, it will not go away. The tragedy deals with the introduction of Bacchic worship into Athens; the comedy, if its dating at 190 B.C. or later is correct, issued in reaction to the same phenomenon in Italy. The student of both plays is inevitably led to shared analogies and recapitulated themes between the two plays. The prurient puritanism of Euripides' Pentheus is replayed in Zeugma and Curmudgeous, and his—and Thebes'—corruption in the fates of the young men *and* their fathers. The spying motif of the tragedy, moved from Pentheus's fir tree in the countryside to the cracked front door of a bordello, occurs over and over: Zeugma, Intensides, Curmudgeous, and Major Machismo all take their lickerish looks. And no one can contemplate Æsycome and Curmudgeous shambling to the slaughter in Act V without recalling the rush of the ancients Teiresias and Kadmos to join the Bacchic rout in the hills.

The following invention—a "divine prologue" delivered by the god Bacchus—is designed to point up the relationship, to attune the audience. It must be stressed that it has no basis in textual reality: no fragments tenuously support it as they do Æsygo's deferred prologue. It is not, like the preAct, a *frinstance,* but a *druther*—a whim supported by no hard evidence at all, an item that the perpetrator would *like* to be the case. The only real reason for its presence is the empty space at *Bacchides'* beginning.

Divine prologues are quite common in New Comedy, and this druther follows the standard structure: A god appears, gives some introduction to set and plot, establishes the reason for his or her concern, pronounces what he or she intends to do . . . and then disappears, never to return. So Bacchus here. His words are not to be performed, merely considered.

Should some director be so infected by the hubris of the passage as to include it in a production, let me point out that it is conceived as preceding the preAct, is designed to work with Æsygo's later prologue, and does not disclose the dramatic switch in Act V: the Corruption of the Old.

> (A blare, or a crash, or a puff of smoke, and suddenly, atop the house of Bacchis One, stage right, there appears the god Bacchus. He is dressed for his younger manifestation—dappled fawnskin, ivy crown. He starts with a tragic declamation, ripped bodily from Euripides' *Bacchae*.)

BACCHUS: *Behold me, Dionysus, son of Zeus,*
          at length arrived in this the land of Thebes,
          whom Sémelê bore, once brought to childbirth's bed
          by lightning's blaze and blast and . . .
                                        Damn, wrong play.
          Of *course.* It's not Euripides; it's Plautus.
          It's not the *Bacchae;* it's the *Bacchides.*
          This isn't Thebes; it's *Athens.*
                                        Accept my abject
          apologies, please. And now we'll begin again:
          Call me Bacchus.
                              Some years ago, I heard
          from afar that two of my diligent devotees,
          sisters who bring new verve to the oldest profession,
          were forced by circumstance to live apart.
          —I should say here that my concern for this
          delectable duo is hardly selfless. Their mother,
          unable to specify their respective fathers,
          turned her confusion into piety
          by giving them both the same exalted name —
          which is to say, *my* name. The firstborn girl
          received the name of *Bacchis.* When that worked out,
          dear addled Mom, who knew a good thing when she saw it,
          chose *Bacchis* to name her second daughter, too.
          Flattered, I took the role of tutelary god,
          and put the well-being of this toothsome twain
          high on my list of Things to Be Looked After.
          —I'd been away down East, and out of touch
          with business here in the West, and was shocked to find
          that Bacchis and Bacchis, who'd always worked as a pair,
          had been forced to break up the act and leave their native
          isle of Samos. One went to the East, as contract
          concubine of a consummate clod of a Major;
          the other hied her kit to this metro center.
          Well, ever the venturesome type, this Bacchis
          found the backing—I pulled a string or two—
          and set up shop in a very respectable section.
          Not the same as the snuggery over in Samos;
          but she's made quite a good start, as you can see:
          behold her house beneath me.

(He points directly down.)

                              Note the tiling,
          the cupids, the witty projections that stud the facade,
          the reliefs that make the doors a joy to behold.

(He points to his statue.)

Not least, of course, is the portrait bust that fronts
this house of Hedonism—good likeness, if
I do say so myself.

(Sincere and direct address to the audience.)

                           And may I observe
how nice to see so many of *you* here.
I don't get to these parts very much, these days.
I'm persona non grata . . . and all that that implies . . .

(He turns and indicates Curmudgeous's house, left.)

largely to types who inhabit houses like *that* one:
there on your right we have your typical yawner,
a dull-as-ditch-water, upper-middle abode.
The dwelling place of one Curmudgeous,
a community pillar with all the playful pizzazz
of the uptight uprights that keep his roof from collapsing.
The very house to incubate harrumphs
in stuffy seniors, aghast at the inroads made
on their soporific lifestyle by, well, Yours Truly.
I wouldn't be surprised if that were the very house
that produces all those pusillanimous rumors:
Young men corrupted, seduced into Sin by Bacchic
priestesses who possess no religion at all.
Conspiracies against the health of the state
cooked up in the stews, as it were.

(He points to the statue of Apollo in front of Curmudgeous's house.)

                           Fiction approved
by Apollo, whose likeness you see there, clogging
the thoroughfare in front of Monotonous Mansion.
So, stories go out of young men depraved over *here,*
deprived of huge endowments, and deconstructed.
By *me?* By sweet, beneficent Bacchus?
                           Slander!
I am, let us say, annoyed. And when I'm annoyed,
I am not nice to be with.
                           So, I've arranged it all:
today, I establish another Bacchic beachhead
in This Fair City, and restore the sisters
to one another, with floods of cash from one

(With a nod at Curmudgeous's house.)

who can afford it most, but like it least.
Corruption of the young?—I'll go beyond that
and leave this hole a happier hole than when
I found it.

And now I hide offstage, to move
in my mysterious ways and advance the careers
of Bacchis and Bacchis, bearers of Bacchus's bounty.
Though seen no more, I shall be *felt.*

Evoe . . .

(He disappears.)

Douglass Parker